S E O U L

WRITTEN BY **ROBERT KOEHLER**

Seoul Selection Guides: SEOUL

Written by Robert Koehler
Photographs by Ryu Seung-hoo & Robert Koehler

First edition published in Oct. 2009. Updated in Dec. 2009 and Jun. 2011.

Published by Seoul Selection
B1 Korean Publishers Association Bldg., 105-2 Sagan-dong,
Jongno-gu, Seoul 110-190, Korea
Tel: 82-2-734-9567
Fax: 82-2-734-9562
E-mail: publisher@seoulselection.com
Website: www.seoulselection.com

ISBN: 978-89-91913-58-5 13980

Printed in the Republic of Korea

Printed by Leeffect Prepress & Print
Effect Bldg., 459-13 Seogyo-dong
Mapo-gu, Seoul 121-841, Korea
Tel: 82-2-332-3584

Additional Photo credits
  Greg Curley: 244
  Joe McPherson: 385, 386, 387, 391
  David Mason: 329
  Top Table (Jinny Kang): 16, 387, 390
  The Institute of Traditional Korean Food (Yoon Sook-ja): 17, 383, 384, 385, 386, 389, 390, 393, 394, 460

TABLE OF CONTENTS

History & Culture

Maps

INTRODUCTION

Seoul—Korea's 600-Year-Old Capital

Admittedly, Seoul doesn't have quite the same kind of pull on the foreign imagination as cities in neighboring countries such as Beijing, Shanghai, Hong Kong and Tokyo. Ask a Westerner what they think of when they think of Seoul, and you're likely to get a blank stare at best...and mention of "M*A*S*H" or the North Korean nuclear program at worst. This is a real pity—few places in the world harmonize the ancient with the bleeding edge nearly as well as Seoul. You can be exploring venerable royal palaces and temples one moment and the next experiencing tomorrow's technology today. This is a city that, in just half a century, pulled itself up from post-war ruin and poverty to become one of Asia's most important financial and trading centers. The streets and markets pulsate with an energy unlike anywhere else in the world, and change is ever-present— Seoul could very well be the world's most dynamic city.

No city can be fairly reduced to a guidebook, no matter how many pages. Seoul, a bustling metropolis of over 10 million souls, is no different. One of the most energetic and dynamic capitals on the planet, Seoul must be experienced to be properly understood. All this humble guidebook seeks to do is to point the visitor in the proper direction.

How to Use This Book

For practical purposes, this guidebook is divided into two parts:

First Part

This section examines the city of Seoul—neighborhood by neighborhood— introducing the wealth of history, culture and entertainment to be found within. General tourist information is interspersed with helpful and informative tips about local culture and history in order to enrich your experience. Each chapter is concluded with information on recommended restaurants in the area.

Second Part

This part provides basic information that visitors must know, including customs procedures, visa information, hotel information and the like. For the convenience of the user, information has been arranged in a logical manner so that you can find what you want to know quickly. A small section on the Korean language has been included, too—it won't make you fluent, but it will help you get around.

Features

This guide contains a number of special features that aim to enrich your travel experience, including a section on history, maps, tips and notes on Korean culture.

Seoul's Best 7

Don't know where to begin? Too busy to fumble through the pages? Our opening "Seoul's Best 7" lists will put you on the right track.

History of Seoul

We've managed to pack several thousands of years of Korean history—including Seoul's 600 years as Korea's capital—into nine concise pages. While you'll learn a lot about the city's past while you're on the road, it helps to know a little bit before going in.

Maps

Most chapters have illustrated maps. Some are larger than others, however. The larger ones have letter-number coordinates that make it easier to locate sites mentioned in the text.

For example, the "C4, p38" next to "Seoul City Hall & Seoul Plaza" on p101 means "Look at coordinates C, 4 on the map on p38." If there are coordinates but no page number, it means use the map found in that chapter. If there's a page number and no coordinates, it means the map on said page is quite small and the destination easy to find.

Travel Tips

These notes give you helpful advice on tourist destinations and tour options. We'll tell you the best time to visit the Huwon Garden, give you info on free guided tours of Gyeongbokgung Palace, and more.

History and Culture

These notes provide detailed and helpful historical and cultural background information on places, individuals and stories related to the city. Wondering who King Sejong the Great was? Haven't a clue about the March 1 Uprising of 1919? Don't worry—we'll tell you all about them. You can read these while you're walking about or at your own leisure.

SEOUL MAP

Gilsangsa T

Suyeon Sanbang

Mt. Bugaksan

Gans
Mus

Cheong Wa Dae
(Blue House)

Seoul Selection
Bookshop
(Hank's Bookcafé)

Cha
Pala

Gyeongbokgung Palace

Gwanghwamun

Anguk
Stn.

Digital Media Street

Digital Media City

Gyeongbokgung Stn.
Jongno Tower

Insa-d

World Cup Park

Independence Gate

City Hall

Myeong
Cathedra

Yonsei Univ.

World Cup
Stadium Stn.

Euljiro 1-ga

Seoul World Cup Stadium

Nanji Hangang Park

Ewha Womans Univ.

Sungnyemun

Myeong-dong

Hongik Univ. Stn.

Hyundai
Dept. Store

Namdaemun Market

KT&G
Sangsang Madang

Mangwon
Hangang
Park

Hapjeong Stn.

Sinchon Stn.

Ewha Womans
Univ. Stn.

Hongik Univ.

Seoul Stn.

Namsan Cable Car

N Seoul

Playground
(Free Market)

Seoul Stn.

Millennium
Seoul Hilton

Seonyudo Park

Yanghwajin

Yanghwa Hangang Park

Samgakji Stn.

Yongsan Electronics Market

War Memorial of Korea

Seoul Marina

National Assembly

Yeouido
Hangang Park

Yongsan Stn.

Itaewon Marke

The National
Museum of Korea

63 Bldg.

Yeouido Stn.

Ichon Stn.

Ichon Hangang Park

Sindorim Stn.

Noryangjin Stn.

Hangang River

Noryangjin
Fish Market

Dongjak S

Guro Stn.

Guro Arts Valley

Dongjak S

Banp

National Cemetery

Boramae Park

Sillim-dong Sundae Alley
(Korean Sausage)

Seoul Nat'l Univ.

Isu St

Seoul Nat'l Univ. Stn.

Seongnagwon Garden

Dream Forest

Sangbong Bus Terminal

Choi Sunu's Old Home

Dongsoong Art Center

Daehangno

Marronnier Park

Gyeongdong Oriental Medicine Market

...gung

...okgung Palace

Heunginjimun

...gmyo ...al Shrine

Doota

Migliore

Dongdaemun Stn.

Chungmu Art Hall

Cheonggyecheon Stream

...un Stn.

Sindang-dong Tteokbokki Alley

Jangchung Jokbal Restaurants

Dongguk Univ. Stn.

Hanok Village/ ...se

W Seoul Walkerhill

...onal Theater of Korea

Children's Grand Park Stn.

Ttukseom Stn.

Gwangnaru Stn.

Gwangnaru Hangang Park

...g Museum of Art

Seoul Forest

Children's Grand Park

Cheonhodaegyo

...amilton Hotel

Seoul Waterworks Museum

Techno Mart

UN Village

Dong Seoul Bus Terminal

Seongsudaegyo

Donghodaegyo

...eoul Central Mosque

Hyundai Dept. Store

Galleria Dept. Store

Ttukseom Resort Stn.

Olympicdaegyo

Jamsilcheolgyo (Railroad Bridge)

...tn.

Yeongdongdaegyo

Cheongdamdaegyo

Ttukseom Resort

Jamsildaegyo

Olympic Park

Hannamdaegyo

Jaseng Hospital of Oriental Medicine

Jamwon Hangang Park

Gangnam-gil Street

Bongeunsa Temple

Cheongdam Stn.

Jamsil Sports Complex

Jamsil Hangang Park

BK Dong Yang Plastic Surgery Clinic

Sinsa Stn.

ASEM Tower

COEX

Samseong Stn.

Jamsil Stn.

Lotte World (Lotte World Folk Museum)

...g Park

Gangnam Kyobo Tower

Central City

The Ritz-Carlton, Seoul

LG Arts Center

Seolleung Stn.

Express Bus Terminal Stn.

Yeoksam Stn.

Gangnam Stn.

Seoul Nat'l Univ. of Education Stn.

Nambu Bus Terminal Stn.

...eoul Arts Center/ ...ational Gugak Center

Yangjae Citizen's Forest

3

4

1 Gyeongbokgung Palace p41
The oldest and grandest of Seoul's royal palaces, Gyeongbokgung Palace is a masterpiece of Korean traditional architecture and one of Seoul's most visited locations. It is also home to the National Palace Museum and National Folk Museum.

2 National Museum of Korea p209
The massive National Museum of Korea, located south of Mt. Namsan, is home to 150,000 artifacts, some of which date back to the paleolithic era.

3 Seoul Fortress p322
For most of its 600 years as a national capital, Seoul was a typically medieval walled city, ringed by 18 km of stone fortifications. Large stretches of those walls still exist, especially in the mountains surrounding the city, as do several of the old gates.

4 Jeong-dong p93
This quiet neighborhood of stately Western-style schools and churches next to Deoksugung Palace is Seoul's old legation quarter, where Westerners first established themselves after Korea opened up to Western trade in the late 19th century.

5 Seodaemun Prison Museum p189
Built in 1907, Seodaemun Prison—now a museum to the Korean independence struggle—was where many Korean freedom fighters were locked up during the dark years of Japanese imperial rule.

6 War Memorial of Korea p210
The War Memorial of Korea in Yongsan is a sprawling museum dedicated to Korean military history, particularly the Korean War.

7 Seoul Museum of History p105
This museum, located near the historic Gyeonghuigung Palace, details the long history of the city of Seoul, with particular emphasis on the Joseon era.

THE ARTS

1 Insa-dong p75
Seoul's most noted center for the Korean traditional arts and crafts, Insa-dong is an alley (actually, several alleys) full of small galleries, craft shops, art supply stores, Korean restaurants and traditional tea shops.

2 Buam-dong Galleries p148
Located north of the hectic downtown, the quiet Buam-dong and Pyeongchang-dong neighborhoods harbor a number of superb art galleries, including the Gana Art Center, Hwajeong Museum, Gaain Gallery, Kim Chong Yung Sculpture Museum, Gallery Sejul and Whanki Museum.

3 National Museum of Contemporary Art p263
The highlight of this massive complex in the Seoul suburb of Gwacheon is "The More the Better," a tower of 1,003 TVs erected by late video artist Nam-june Paik.

4 National Gugak Center p257
The National Gugak Center is Korea's preeminent center for Korean traditional music and dance. It hosts both regular and special performances throughout the year—admission is sinfully cheap, too.

5 Seoul Arts Center p255
This mammoth cultural center in southern Seoul includes a concert hall, opera hall, theater and art gallery. It plays host to many of Seoul's biggest performances.

6 Non-Verbal Performances p427
Korean non-verbal performances have been taking the world by storm. Some of the more popular shows include *Nanta, Jump, Sachoom* and *Battle B-boy.* You can include on this list Gwanghwamun Art Hall's *Pan,* a composite of Korean traditional folk performances.

7 Daehangno p167
The former site of Seoul National University, Daehangno is home to many small theaters as well as the Arko Art Center. Of particular interest is the non-verbal performance *Drawing Show,* which combines music, miming and magic.

1 N Seoul Tower p316
Located atop Seoul's landmark Mt. Namsan, the observation decks and restaurants of N Seoul Tower offer spectacular views of the city, both day and (especially) night. On a clear day, you can see all the way to Incheon and North Korea.

2 Rear Garden of Changdeokgung Palace p50
A UNESCO World Heritage Site, the Rear Garden of Changdeokgung Palace is breathtaking any season of the year. Seamlessly blending the natural and the man-made, it is the epitome of Korean traditional garden design.

3 Bukchon Hanok Village p69
A quaint residential neighborhood stretching from Gyeongbokgung Palace to Changdeokgung Palace, Bukchon is a maize of quaint alleyways that are home to Seoul's largest collection of Korean traditional homes, or *hanok*.

4 Hangang River p221
Perhaps Seoul's most defining topographical feature, the mighty Hangang River is a scenic spot all its own. Cruises provide wonderful views of the city, especially at night, while the riverbanks are lined with parks and other leisure facilities.

5 Mt. Bukhansan p335
If you're in a hiking mood, the rocky peaks of Mt. Bukhansan offer superb vistas of downtown Seoul. The granite face of Insubong Peak is one of Korea's most popular rock-climbing venues.

6 63 Building p224
Briefly the tallest building in Asia, the golden monolith of the 63 Building offers wonderful views of the city from its observation deck.

7 Banpo Bridge p241
At night, the Hangang River's Banpo Bridge becomes a massive rainbow fountain thanks to the 380 nozzles and 200 lights installed along its sides.

1 Korean Meat Dishes **p387**
Koreans enjoy meat, especially when they eat out. Dishes to try include *galbi* (barbecued ribs), *bulgogi* (marinated beef) and *samgyeopsal* (Korean style bacon).

2 Bibimbap **p389**
One of Korea's most representative dishes and increasingly popular overseas, *bibimbap* is a bowl of rice mixed with vegetables and seasoned with red pepper paste.

3 Street Food **p391**
Seoul's ubiquitous street stalls sell a wide range of cheap and tasty eats, including *gimbap* (rice rolls), *tteokbokki* (fried rice cakes), *twigim* (batter-fried goodies), *sundae* (Korean blood sausage), *odeng* (Japanese-style fish cakes) and more.

4 Royal Palace Cuisine **p384**
If it was good enough for the kings of the Joseon Dynasty, it's good enough for you. Diners are treated to a banquet table filled with a countless array of colorful dishes, along with the obligatory rice and soup.

5 Noryangjin Fish Market **p400**
A feast for the eyes and the taste buds, Noryangjin Fish Market is home to about 700 shops selling fresh seafood products—and by fresh, we mean "alive." Once you've selected your fish/crustacean of choice, market restaurants will be all too happy to cook it up for you. Open 24 hours a day.

6 Sindang-dong Tteokbokki **p164**
While *tteokkbokki* (rice cakes pan fried in a tangy red pepper sauce) may have originated in the royal palaces of the Joseon Dynasty, it is now a cheap comfort food of the masses.

7 Jangchung-dong Jokbal **p164**
Richly marinated pigs feet, sliced to order. The meat is usually topped with various condiments and eaten wrapped in a lettuce leaf. Best chased down with a shot of *soju* (Korean rice vodka). A Seoul specialty dish.

2

7

6

5

EWON SHOP

EWON SHOP

1
Korea's most famous traditional outdoor market, the sprawling Namdaemun Market is home to countless shops selling just about everything under the sun, including clothes, curios, ginseng, food and more.

2
Korea's fashion Mecca has over 20 malls and 30,000 shops, mostly dedicated to clothing. While it operates 18 hours a day, it really comes alive at night, when the massive crowds generate an energy found nowhere else.

3
Like Tokyo's Shinjuku district, Seoul's commercial heart of Myeong-dong is an area of bright lights, surging crowds, brand-name shopping and exciting nightlife. Seoul's best-known department stores, including the massive Lotte Department Store, are located here.

4
Home to Seoul's "Rodeo Drive," Apgujeong-dong is Seoul's most exclusive shopping neighborhood. Home to upscale department stores and designer boutiques, this is the place to go for your Gucci bag or Jimmy Choo shoes.

5
With its large number of foreign residents and denizens, the Itaewon neighborhood is famous for its foreigner-friendly shops with English and Japanese-speaking staff and (in the case of clothing) large sizes.

6
Responsible for some 70% of Korea's herbal medicine trade, Seoul Herbal Medicine Market (also known as Gyeongdong Market) is an intoxicating blend of exotic sites and aromas.

7
If you're looking for electronic gadgets, a new computer or the latest Xbox games, this is the place to go.

1 Mountain Hiking p311
Surrounded as it is by verdant mountains dotted with weathered fortresses and ancient temples, Seoul provides plenty of opportunities to stretch your legs and commune with nature.

2 Visit the DMZ p271
Korea is home to the world's last remaining Cold War frontiers, the Korean Demilitarized Zone (DMZ). This rare opportunity to peek into mysterious North Korea is just an hour's drive north of Seoul.

3 Temple Stay and Meditation p456
Many of Korea's ancient Buddhist temples, including several in the Seoul area, offer so-called "temple stay" programs where you can spend a weekend experiencing life at a monastery. Several temples also offer classes in English on Zen meditation.

4 Jjimjilbang (Steam Rooms) p448
Korean saunas, or *jjimjilbang*, are a great way to soak, steam and sweat your pains away. Sex-segregated, although usually equipped with a unisex common area, *jjimjilbang* not only have your obligatory baths and sauna, but also massage facilities, snack bars, PC cafes, entertainment facilities and more.

5 Hongdae Club Day p186
Get your dancing shoes on and head to the clubs of Hongik University —the heart of Korea's youth culture—to dance the night away. Every fourth Friday of the month is Hongdae Club Day, when you can get into 21 of the area's clubs for the price of one.

6 Oriental Medicine p458
Like neighboring China, Korea has an ancient medical tradition that includes herbal remedies, acupuncture, cupping and moxibustion. An alternative path to wellness.

7 PC Bang p450
Seoul is home to countless *PC Bang* (literally, "PC Room"), Internet cafés full of Koreans young and old engaged in Korea's unofficial national pastime—online gaming.

SEOUL: LAY OF THE LAND

Like any major city, Seoul can be a disorienting place for the uninitiated. Once you finally get your bearings, however, you'll find the city a fairly easy place to navigate. Seoul's spatial layout and topography also create a city of great scenic beauty.

Seoul is a fairly large city in terms of area—605.25 km^2 (233.7 sq mi) to be exact. The city straddles the Hangang River, which bisects the city into north and south, and is surrounded by a number of prominent mountains and mountain ranges, including the Bukhansan Mountains (with Seoul's highest peak at 836 m) to the north and Mt. Gwanaksan to the south. Several prominent peaks are located within the city itself, most notably Mt. Namsan (atop which sits N Seoul Tower, one of the city's most recognized landmarks) and Mt. Inwangsan, a mountain culturally important for its role in Korean shamanism.

Historically, the city of Seoul was a walled city roughly delineated by four mountain peaks—Mt. Bugaksan to the north, Mt. Namsan to the south, Mt. Naksan to the east and Mt. Inwangsan to the west. Development over the last century, however, has led the city to spill out way beyond its original container. The Hangang River contains a number of small islands, including Yeouido, the so-called "Manhattan of Korea."

Broadly speaking, Seoul today is divided into two zones. Gangbuk, literally "North of the River," encompasses those areas of Seoul north of the Hangang River, including the historic downtown area. The Gangnam area, literally "South of the River," encompasses those areas of Seoul south of the Hangang River. This is a much newer area of Seoul, developed since the economic boom beginning in the 1960s. It's an affluent region, home to wealthy residential districts, posh shops and impressive steel and glass business districts. Gangbuk and Gangnam are connected by over 20 bridges that cross the Hangang River.

Administratively, Seoul is divided into 25 *gu*, or districts. Many of Seoul's historic neighborhoods are located in Jongno-gu, for instance. Each *gu* is further divided into *dong*, or neighborhoods—see, for instance, Itaewon-dong, Yongsan-gu, Seoul. Houses and buildings have street numbers, too, but these often have little to do with geographic position and are rarely used for anything other than the mail. When giving or receiving directions, liberal use is made of local landmarks.

One legacy of the Korean War and the Cold War confrontation between the two Koreas is the presence of the sprawling US Army Garrison—Yongsan just south of Mt. Namsan. Although it is frequently not marked on maps, you can rest assured it's there, and access is limited for non-US military personnel. The base is scheduled to return to Korea in 2019; Seoul intends to use the property to build a grand downtown park.

CLIMATE

Seoul enjoys a continental climate with four distinct seasons—spring, summer, fall and winter. Summers can be quite hot and humid, with a brief rainy season between mid-June to July. Winters, on the other hand, follow a pattern of three days cold, four days mild (due to the influence of Siberian pressure systems). Heavy snow is not uncommon. Autumn is widely considered the most pleasant season, with high, cloudless skies and lovely scenery due to the changing fall foliage.

Average August temperatures are 22°C to 30°C, while average January temperatures are -7°C to 1°C.

SEOUL IN STATISTICS

- **Location** 126° 59' E and 37° 34' N
- **Size** 30.3 km from north to south and 36.78 km east to west
- **Area** 605.25 km² (233.7 sq mi)
- **Population (2007)** 10,421,782
- **Population Density** 17,219/km²
- **Male/Female Ratio** 5,174,655 men, 5,247,127 women
- **GDP per capita (2007)** US$16,629
- **Average Marrying Age (2009)** 31.72 (men), 29.30 (women)
- **Average Temperature** 22°C to 30°C (August), -7°C to 1°C (January)
- **Foreign Population (2007)** 229,072. 119,300 Chinese, 11,890 Americans, 6,864 Japanese
- **Consumer Price Indices (2005)** Food: 123.5, Housing: 121.3, Utilities: 126.1, Clothing: 111.6, Medical Care: 118.1, Education, Culture and Recreation: 129.9, Transportation and Communications: 108.7
- **Tourist Hotels (2007)** 126
- **Foreign Tourists (2008)** 5,133,676
- **Major Criminal Offenses (2008)** 16,609 cases
- **A Day in Seoul (2007)** Births: 274, Deaths: 106, Marriages: 209, Divorces: 67, Migrants: 7,845 people, Population Passing Through: 31,387, Subway Users: 6,215,000

Gwanghwamun Square

HISTORY OF SEOUL

With 600 years of history as Korea's capital, Seoul is an ancient city whose dramatic and at times tragic past is a microcosm of that of Korea as a whole. It's also a city that has remarkably transformed itself in the last half century or so from a medieval walled town to the bustling modern heart of one of the world's most vibrant economies. Evidence of the city's past can be found everywhere, from ancient royal palaces to grand colonial offices and shiny skyscrapers of glass and steel. Indeed, what makes Seoul such an interesting place is the sometimes breathtaking way in which the city blends past, present and future into a diverse urban space.

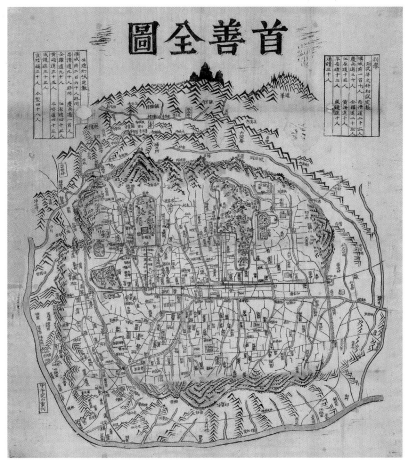

Map of Seoul produced by famed Joseon-era cartographer Kim Jeong-ho between 1824 and 1834

Ancient History

The area where the city of Seoul now stands—the fertile flood valley of the Hangang River—has been inhabited since the Stone Age. In the Amsa-dong region of what is now southern Seoul, archaeological evidence has been unearthed indicating that humans have lived here for some 3,000-7,000 years. As metalworking technology made its way to Korea, the size and social intricacy of the communities along the river developed rapidly.

Korea's first real "state," Gojoseon (Old Joseon), established itself in the northern part of the Korean Peninsula. When is a matter of some controversy—according to the 13th century Korean history book *Samguk Yusa* ("Memorabilia of the Three Kingdoms"), the kingdom was founded in 2333 BC by the king Dangun Wanggeom. It begins to appear in historical records from the seventh century BC. By the fourth century BC, it was a mighty state that

According to legend, the grandson of Heaven, the king Dangun Wanggeom is said to have founded the first Korean nation, Gojoseon, in 2333 BC. It is theorized by some that the term Dangun Wanggeom refers not necessarily to an individual, but to a title, a king who combined temporal and religious authority. In 1919, Korea's government-in-exile designated 2333 BC as year one in a new calendar system still in use today.

controlled much of northern Korea and Manchuria. From the third century BC, however, the kingdom began a decline. In 108 BC, the Chinese defeated Gojoseon in a war and set up four commanderies on the Korean Peninsula; the area that is now Seoul was placed under the Zhenfan commandery. These foreign invaders were not well received, however, and were eventually forced out of the Hangang River valley by native Korean tribal states.

Three Kingdoms Period

From 57 BC to AD 668, affairs on the Korean Peninsula were dominated by the epic struggle of three competing Korean kingdoms: Goguryeo, located in the northern half of the Korean Peninsula and parts of Manchuria; Baekje, which dominated the southwestern regions of Korea; and Silla, which commanded the southeastern regions of Korea. This period witnessed both endless strife and constantly changing alliances, as well as a flowering of Korean classical culture and great strides in social development. It was at this time that Buddhism, an important element in Korean traditional culture, entered the country from China.

During the Three Kingdoms Period, the strategic Seoul area was an object of inter-kingdom rivalry to control its fertile lands and important transportation routes. The kingdom of Baekje initially controlled the region, setting up its first capital in what is now northern Seoul. In AD 329, however, the kingdom of Goguryeo—led by the legendary conqueror King Gwanggaeto the Great—seized control of the Hangang River valley from Baekje. Baekje reasserted control before Goguryeo seized the valley again in 475. In 551, a resurgent Baekje formed an

Three Kingdoms Period (5th Century)

alliance with Silla to kick Goguryeo out of the Seoul area once and for all, but Silla took control of the region instead. Needless to say, Baekje was not pleased by this, but in the following war with Silla, the Baekje king fell in battle and Silla took final control over the Hangang River valley.

In 668, Silla brought an end to the Three Kingdoms Period when it finally conquered its rivals to unite most of the Korean Peninsula under its rule. Under Unified Silla, the Seoul area was named "Hanyang," a name that lives on in "Hanyang University," one of the city's top institutions of higher learning.

Goryeo

Silla's rule over the Korean Peninsula began to collapse in the late ninth century as the power of the royal court weakened and powerful families within and without the capital of Gyeongju (in southeastern Korea) asserted influence. Breakaway kingdoms formed, with one of these upstarts—the northern-based state of Later Goguryeo, led by King Wang Geon—conquering the Silla rump state in 918 and unifying the Korean Peninsula under the newly established Goryeo kingdom (from which the country takes its present English name of Korea).

The new state established its capital in the present-day city of Kaesong (in North Korea),

Goryeo celadon was a highly valued commodity in East Asia. © Yonhap

not far from Seoul. Under the early Goryeo kings, the city now called Seoul grew in influence. In 1067, the city was designated one of three sub-capitals and took on a new administrative importance. Palaces were built in the city, and as nearby subjects relocated to the growing town, the outline of Seoul's historic downtown area began taking shape. King Sukjong (r. 1095-1105) even prepared to move the royal capital to Seoul before his death cut the plan short.

In 1231, the Mongols invaded Korea. The Goryeo court moved to Ganghwa Island, where the notoriously water-shy invaders couldn't reach them, but the rest of the country was pillaged in good Mongol fashion. The Mongols launched six campaigns in Korea before the Goryeo king finally surrendered in 1259.

Under the influence of the Mongols, and later the Mongol-ruled Yuan Dynasty of China, the sub-capital system was done away with, and Seoul was temporarily demoted. The anti-Mongol King Gongmin (r. 1351-1374), however, attempted to bring back the regional sub-capital system. Under Gongmin's successor, King U (r. 1374-1388), the capital of the kingdom was briefly moved to Seoul in 1382.

Joseon

In 1392, General Yi Seong-gye seized power following a successful coup against the last Goryeo king and founded a new dynasty, the kingdom of Joseon. This new kingdom, founded on the ideology of neo-Confucianism, would bring some 500 years of stability to Korea and establish the basis of much of what is now regarded as Korean traditional culture.

Heeding the counsel of his friend and adviser, the Buddhist monk Muhak, Yi moved the capital of the new kingdom to Seoul, then called Hanyang (and later Hanseong). Royal palaces and shrines were built, and in 1394, the royal government officially took up residence in the new capital. Shortly thereafter, work began on an 18 km ring of walls to surround and protect the city—much of the walls still remains, as do several of their gates. In 1395, the grand Gyeongbokgung Palace—today one of Seoul's best known landmarks—was completed.

By 1405, most of the city planning was complete. Much attention went into planning the city, with palace, ministry, gate and road positions carefully determined by the demands of *feng shui*. In fact, Seoul's historic downtown area

King Sejong the Great, the most accomplished king of the Joseon Dynasty © Yonhap

Gyeongbokgung Palace

still holds true to this original plan.

The Renaissance of Joseon-era Seoul was the mid-18th century, when Korea was ruled by the energetic and reform-minded King Yeongjo. Trade along the Hangang River flourished, and commercial activity in the capital blossomed, as trade linkages were established with provincial areas of the country. For much of the city's history, the population hovered around 200,000.

Many of Seoul's most visited historical sites, including Gyeongbokgung Palace, Changdeokgung Palace, Deoksugung Palace, Namdaemun Gate, Dongdaemun Gate and Unhyeongung Villa, date from the Joseon era.

Daehan Empire

As the 19th century drew to a conclusion, Korea found itself subject to imperial pressures from the West and Japan. Raids by the French in 1866 (to avenge the death of French priests killed during a royal crackdown on Catholicism) and the Americans in 1871 (to avenge the burning of a US ship that had attempted to force open Korea for trade) failed to open up Korea, which—having witnessed the Western powers' pillaging of China—pursued a strict policy of isolation that earned it the moniker "the Hermit Kingdom." In 1876, however, the Japanese—employing gunboat tactics similar to those used by Commodore Perry on them just 20 years earlier—succeeded in forcing Korea to open up three ports for foreign trade. In 1882, Korea and the United States signed a trade and friendship treaty, which was soon followed by similar treaties with other Western powers.

King Gojong, the Korean monarch who ruled during much of this period, attempted to modernize his nation while fending off imperial threats, particularly from Japan and Russia. In 1895, Japan defeated China in the First Sino-Japanese War, and as a result, Korea's traditional relationship with China was severed. In 1897, Gojong renamed his kingdom the Daehan Empire to reflect the country's officially equal status with China.

The Daehan Empire period witnessed great changes in the city of Seoul. For the first time, foreigners were allowed to settle in the royal capital, with foreign legations setting up shop in the Jeong-dong neighborhood near Deoksugung Palace. Missionaries set up modern schools and hospitals (as well as, of course, churches), while an American company established the city's first electric company, tram system and water treatment facilities. Western architecture, such as the neoclassical Seokjojeon of Deoksugung Palace, was imported, and the city began to take on a decidedly modern appearance. Such was the transformation that British journalist and traveler Angus Hamilton remarked upon a visit, "The streets of Seoul are magnificent, spacious, clean, admirably made and well-drained. The narrow, dirty lanes have been widened, gutters have been covered, roadways broadened. Seoul is within measurable distance of becoming the highest, most interesting and cleanest city in the East."

The Seokjojeon Hall of Deoksugung Palace, Chungdong First Presbyterian Church and the magnificent Myeong-dong Cathedral are reminders of this period in time.

Emperor Gojong © Yonhap

Japanese Colonial Era

Unfortunately, King Gojong's attempt to modernize Korea proved too little, too late. In 1905, Japan defeated Russia in the Russo-Japanese War, ending Russian influence in Korea and giving Tokyo a free hand on the peninsula. In 1907, Japan forced Korea to become a Japanese protectorate, and in 1910, Japan officially annexed Korea, beginning a 35-year period of colonial rule.

The Japanese established their government-general in Seoul, which they renamed Keijo. Under Japanese rule, Seoul both expanded greatly and modernized. In 1905, Seoul's population was just 250,000. By 1936, it had grown to 730,000, including a large number of Japanese settlers. Many symbols of modern civilization like automobiles, trains, hotels, and movie theaters began appearing at this time. The old Seoul Station building and Seoul City Hall are two landmarks built by the Japanese.

Imperial rule proved harsh as well. The massive Gyeongbokgung Palace, a symbol of Korea's long history as an independent nation, was largely demolished, and in its place was built the imposing Japanese Government-General Building, designed in the shape of the Japanese character for "日" ("sun"). The colonial authorities showed little regard for Seoul's cultural and historical heritage, tearing down the city's ancient walls and several of its gates to build roads and trams. Well-to-do Japanese established residential areas along the slopes of Mt. Namsan,

Old Seoul Station

while in Yongsan, the Japanese military established a sprawling garrison. Resistance to Japanese rule, such as the massive protests of March 1, 1919, were put down with great brutality. As Korea entered the 1930s, the Japanese enforced policies of cultural Japanification, while Japan's wars in China, and eventually in the Pacific, took their toll in the colony as well in the form of military drafts, labor conscription and wartime deprivations.

Independence, Korean War and Reconstruction

With the defeat of Imperial Japan by the Allies in 1945, Korea at long last recovered its independence. This proved bittersweet, however—the victorious Allies placed Korea under their own administration, with Soviet troops occupying areas of the Korean Peninsula north of the 38th parallel and US troops occupying areas south of the 38th parallel. Initially intended as a temporary measure, this division—as in Germany—soon became permanent in the ideologically charged atmosphere of the Cold War. In 1948, the pro-Western Republic of Korea (i.e. South Korea) was declared in Seoul, soon to be followed by the declaration of the communist Democratic People's Republic of Korea (i.e. North Korea) in Pyongyang.

On June 25, 1950, tensions between the two hostile states came to a dramatic head when North Korea launched an armored blitzkrieg on the South. The Korean War did not start out well for the South—Seoul fell after just three days, and by August, South Korean forces, now joined by international (largely American) forces fighting under the UN flag, were pushed back to a small pocket around the southeastern port of Busan.

The defenders solidified, however, bringing the North Korean invasion to a halt, and on Sept 15, 1950, UN commander Gen. Douglas MacArthur pulled off a masterstoke, cutting the North Korean logistical lines with a daring amphibious landing at the West Sea port of Incheon. Unfortunately, this brilliant move was followed up by a poorly coordinated invasion of the North in a bid to reunify the Korean Peninsula, which in turn provoked a massive intervention by Chinese communist "volunteers." The Chinese pushed the South Koreans and their UN allies back past Seoul before the latter, regrouping and changing tactics, turned the tide again, pushing the front line back to the area around the 38th parallel by July of 1951. What followed was two years of brutal but, for the most part, territorially meaningless fighting while negotiators hammered out an armistice, which was finally reached on July 27, 1953.

As a result of the war, Seoul was devastated. The city had changed hands four times during the war, including three times in a six-month period. Much of the city's infrastructure was ruined, and much of its population—now swollen to 2.5 million due to an influx of refugees—reduced to living in makeshift camps. With resources tight, rebuilding the city proved a difficult task, even with the aid of Korea's wartime allies. Still, by the late 1950s, the capital was more or less back on its feet, although poverty and political instability would continue to plague the city.

The Miracle on the Han, the 1988 Olympics and the 2002 World Cup

Seoul, like the rest of Korea, began to undergo major changes following Gen. Park Chung-hee's bloodless coup on May 16, 1961. Park, who would officially be elected president in 1963, ruled Korea with an iron fist for 18 years until his assassination—by his own intelligence director—in 1979. While dictatorial, Park nevertheless brought about unprecedented economic growth: during his rule, GNP per capita increased twentyfold through a program of export-oriented

industrialization. The "Miracle on the Han," as this rapid industrialization was called, continued on through the 1980s and into the 1990s, transforming Korea from a poor, war-torn post-colonial state into one of the world's leading trade nations.

Needless to say, this dramatic economic growth greatly changed the face of Seoul. In 1974, the city's subway system—now one of the world's largest—began operation. Roads were built, housing projects constructed, offices and skyscrapers erected, and all the conveniences of a modern capital put in place. Nowhere was this more apparent than in Gangnam, the area of Seoul south of the Hangang River. Prior to the Miracle on the Han, this region was nothing but

World Cup 2002 © Yonhap

farmland. Today, it is the city's most affluent area, home to upscale shopping districts, high-end residential neighborhoods and major international business districts. On Yeouido, a previously flood-prone island that was home to little more than sand and a colonial-era airfield, Seoul's "Manhattan" was constructed, including the landmark 63 Building, briefly the tallest building in Asia.

Seoul's "coming out party" was the 1988 Summer Olympic Games, when the eyes of the world were focused on the city and its miraculous transformation into an East Asian economic, political and cultural center. Another sporting event, the 2002 FIFA World Cup Korea/Japan, again drew international attention to the city, which was widely praised for its successful hosting of the event and the enthusiastic outdoor celebrations that accompanied the matches.

In recent years, the city has been focusing attention away from "hard" issues like construction and towards "soft" issues like quality of life and the environment. In 2005, the Cheonggyecheon Stream—covered over in the 1950s and for decades the site of an unsightly covered highway—was restored in a much-lauded example of ecologically friendly urban renewal. In the same year, a massive park, Seoul Forest, was constructed in the formerly industrial zone of Ttukseom. In the western part of the city, the Nanjido Garbage Dump was transformed into one of the city's most beautiful green spaces, Haneul Park.

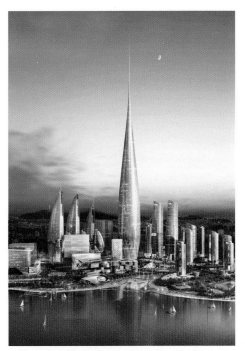

As Seoul rushes headlong into the future, environmental transformation and redevelopment are still at the forefront—a rejuvenation of the Hangang River is currently in the works, while massive redevelopment projects in Yongsan, Dongdaemun and elsewhere in the city will radically transform Seoul's skyline in the decades ahead. The city is also coping with increased globalization and multiculturalism, with ethnic neighborhoods sprouting up in several districts.

Illustration of future Yongsan international business zone
(Courtesy of Seoul Metro Government)

GWANGHWAMUN AREA

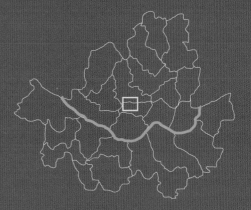

THINGS TO DO AND SEE

- Take in the history and beauty of
  Gyeongbokgung Palace, the largest of
  Seoul's historic royal palaces

- Relax in the lovely Biwon Garden of Changdeokgung
  Palace, Korea's most beautiful traditional garden
  and a UNESCO World Heritage Site

- Stroll around the enchanting alleyways of the quaint
  Bukchon neighborhood, a little piece of old Seoul

- Have a glass of wine in the chic Samcheong-dong area

- Sit in a traditional Korean café in Insa-dong, an alley known
  for its traditional atmosphere, culture and antique shops

- Learn about Korea's dramatic history in Jeong-dong, Seoul's
  old legation quarter with its exotic Western-style architecture

THE HEART OF OLD SEOUL

The Gwanghwamun area is the heart of old Seoul. In the Joseon era (1392—1910), this was the heart of power in Korea, with its mighty royal palaces, government ministries and official residences. A century later, little has changed — the presidential palace of Cheong Wa Dae looms behind Gyeongbokgung Palace, and many of Korea's most important government bodies are headquartered along Sejong-no Boulevard in front of Gwanghwamun Gate.

For visitors, the Gwanghwamun area is home to many of Seoul's top tourist attractions, including the historic royal palaces — full of grand halls, enchanting pleasure gardens and, most of all, centuries of history. In the quaint neighborhood of Bukchon, where Korean tile-roof homes are still the norm, you can lose yourself in the winding alleyways and wonderful traditional atmosphere of old Korea. When you're finished, stroll through the shops and galleries of Insa-dong, and perhaps have a cup of tea at a traditional Korean tea house. For more history, head to the old legation quarter of Jeong-dong, where you'll find beautiful old churches and other reminders of Korea's first interactions with the West.

Japsang on the roof of the Geunjeongjeon Hall of Gyeongbokgung Palace. *Japsang* are small animal statues that guard palace buildings against evil spirits and ghosts.

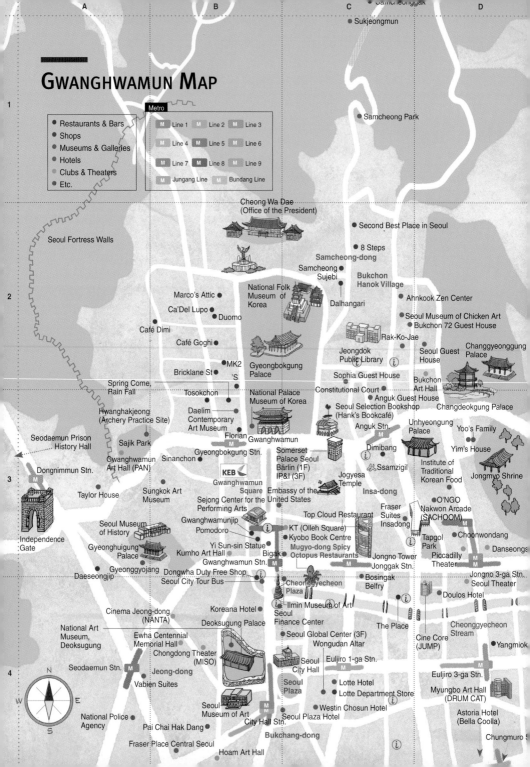

Gwanghwamun Map

Metro

- Restaurants & Bars
- Shops
- Museums & Galleries
- Hotels
- Clubs & Theaters
- Etc.

M Line 1 M Line 2 M Line 3
M Line 4 M Line 5 M Line 6
M Line 7 M Line 8 M Line 9
M Jungang Line M Bundang Line

Sukjeongmun

Samcheonggak

Samcheong Park

Cheong Wa Dae
(Office of the President)

Second Best Place in Seoul

8 Steps

Seoul Fortress Walls

Samcheong
Sujebi

Samcheong-dong

Bukchon
Hanok Village

Ahnkook Zen Center

Marco's Attic

Dalhangari

Seoul Museum of Chicken Art
Bukchon 72 Guest House

Ca'Del Lupo

Duomo

National Folk
Museum of
Korea

Rak-Ko-Jae

Seoul Guest
House

Changgyeonggung
Palace

Café Dimi

Café Goghi

Jeongdok
Public Library

Sophia Guest House

Bukchon
Art Hall

Changdeokgung Palace

MK2

'S

Gyeongbokgung
Palace

Bricklane St

Spring Come,
Rain Fall

Tosokchon

Constitutional Court

Anguk Guest House

Seoul Selection Bookshop
(Hank's Bookcafé)

Unhyeongung
Palace

Yoo's Family

Hwanghakjeong
(Archery Practice Site)

Daelim
Contemporary
Art Museum

National Palace
Museum of Korea

Anguk Stn.

Yim's House

Seodaemun Prison
History Hall

Sajik Park

Florian

Gwanghwamun

Dimibang

Institute of
Traditional
Korean Food

Jongmyo Shrine

Sinanchon

Gyeongbokgung Stn.

Somerset
Palace Seoul
Bärlin (1F)
IP&I (3F)

Ssamzigil

Dongnimmun Stn.

Gwanghwamun
Art Hall (PAN)

KEB

Gwanghwamun

Jogyesa
Temple

Insa-dong

Taylor House

Sungkok Art
Museum

Gwanghwamun
Square

Embassy of the
United States

Top Cloud Restaurant

Fraser
Suites
Insadong

O'NGO
Nakwon Arcade
(SACHOOM)

Seoul Museum
of History

Sejong Center for the
Performing Arts

Gwanghwamunjip

Pomodoro

KT (Olleh Square)

Kyobo Book Centre

Tapgol
Park

Choonwondang

Gyeonghuigung
Palace

Kumho Art Hall

Yi Sun-sin Statue

Bigak

Mugyo-dong Spicy
Octopus Restaurants

Jongno Tower

Piccadilly
Theater

Danseongsa

Gyeonggyojang

Gwanghwamun Stn.

Jonggak Stn.

Daeseongjip

Dongwha Duty Free Shop

Seoul City Tour Bus

Cheonggyecheon
Plaza

Bosingak
Belfry

Jongno 3-ga Stn.
Seoul Theater

Doulos Hotel

Koreana Hotel

Ilmin Museum of Art

Cinema Jeong-dong
(NANTA)

Deoksugung Palace

Seoul
Finance Center

The Place

Cine Core
(JUMP)

Cheonggyecheon
Stream

National Art
Museum,
Deoksugung

Ewha Centennial
Memorial Hall

Seoul Global Center (3F)

Wongudan Altar

Yangmiok

Chongdong Theater
(MISO)

Jeong-dong

Seoul
City Hall

Euljiro 1-ga Stn.

Seodaemun Stn.

Vabien Suites

Seoul
Plaza

Lotte Hotel

Lotte Department Store

Euljiro 3-ga Stn.

Myungbo Art Hall
(DRUM CAT)

National Police
Agency

Pai Chai Hak Dang

Seoul
Museum of Art

City Hall Stn.

Seoul Plaza Hotel

Westin Chosun Hotel

Astoria Hotel
(Bella Coolla)

Fraser Place Central Seoul

Bukchang-dong

Chungmuro

Hoam Art Hall

Heungnyemun Gate, built in 1867

GYEONGBOKGUNG PALACE B2

History

Gyeongbokgung Palace is the most prominent of Seoul's royal palaces thanks to its commanding location in the downtown Gwanghwamun neighborhood. The palace has a tumultuous past. It was first built in 1394 by King Taejo, the founder of the Joseon Dynasty, as the nerve center of the new royal capital of Hanseong (now known as Seoul). It was, along with the Jongmyo Shrine and several other major altars, one of the first structures built in the new capital, and its location at the southern foot of Mt. Bugaksan was carefully determined by the principles of *feng shui*.

Like the Forbidden City in Beijing, Gyeongbokgung Palace was a city unto itself, full of residences, offices and shrines attended to by an army of servants and officials. The complex was ringed by stone walls, passage through which was controlled by a series of imposing gates. In front of the palace, along what is now the broad boulevard of Sejongno, the royal government created "Yukjo Geori" ("Six Ministries Street"), where the ministries of the royal government were located.

During the Japanese invasions of 1592-1598, the palace was burnt to the ground—by the city's slave population, it would turn out, who took advantage of the wartime confusion and flight of the king to destroy the slave registers. When the war ended, the royal family took up residence at another palace, and Gyeongbokgung languished in ruin until 1867, when a major rebuilding project restored it to its former grandeur. This period of glory would not last long, however—in 1895, the strong-willed Empress Myeongseong was assassinated by Japanese agents, and King Gojong fled the palace, never to return. After Japan's annexation of Korea, much of the palace was pulled down—only 10 buildings were left standing.

Since Liberation, Gyeongbokgung has been the focus of much restoration effort—work continues to this day. In 2010, restoration work was completed on Gwanghwamun, the palace's iconic front gate.

Experiencing Gyeongbokgung Palace

Visiting a Korean palace can be a bittersweet experience. There is no doubting the ascetic beauty of the architecture, with its emphasis on harmony with the natural surroundings. Unfortunately, however, most of the buildings are empty, the palaces having been stripped of their artworks and furnishings during the Japanese colonial era.

Most tours of Gyeongbokgung Palace begin at Gwanghwamun Gate, a major downtown landmark. The gate, guarded by two stone *haetae* (mythical creatures that protected the palace from misfortune), has been moved several times over the last century, and was recently restored to both its original position and form.

Once you're past the gate, the palace is composed of several smaller complexes, the most imposing of which is the courtyard surrounding the massive main throne hall, or Geunjeongjeon. The stone courtyard, surrounded by handsome cloisters, has stone markers where court officials used to stand during royal processions. To the west of the Geunjeongjeon courtyard is the equally impressive Gyeonghoeru, a two-story banquet pavilion surrounded by a large, picturesque pond. To the rear of the palace are the extraordinary Hyangwonji Pond and Hyangwonjeong Pavilion—the pavilion, sitting on a small island connected to land by a pretty wooden bridge, blends in perfectly with the mountains that form its backdrop. This is one of the most photographed site in Korea.

Other points of interest include the newly restored Geoncheonggung (behind Hyangwonji Pond), where Empress Myeongseong* (see p45) was assassinated in 1895; the Jibokjae (next to Geoncheonggung), a mixture of Korean and Chinese architectural styles; and the lovely terraced garden of Amisan (behind the Queen's Residence), with its beautiful ornamental chimneys.

TIPS

FREE GUIDED TOURS

Free guided tours for the palace in English are given at 11 am, 1:30 pm and 3:30 pm. Tours begin outside the information office inside Heungnyemun Gate and take about an hour. Tours are also given in Japanese and Chinese—inquire at the information office for times.

CHANGING OF THE GUARD

Changing of the Guard ceremonies take place every hour on the hour from 10 am to 3 pm in front of Heungnyemun Gate, which is located between Gwanghwamun Gate and the main courtyard.

HOLIDAY EVENTS

While just about any time of year is good for visiting Gyeongbokgung Palace, visiting on the Korean holidays of Chuseok (Thanksgiving) in the autumn and Seollal (Lunar New Year) in the winter is especially rewarding—the palace hosts traditional folk games, which are popular with local and foreign tourists alike.

GENERAL INFORMATION

Hours: 9 am to 6 pm (Mar to Oct), 9 am to 5 pm (Nov to Feb). Ticket sales stop one hour to closing. Closed Tuesdays
Admission: 3,000 won
Getting There: Gyeongbokgung Station, Line 3, Exit 5; Gwanghwamun Station, Line 5, Exit 1

[1] Magnificent Gyeonghoeru Pavilion [2] Reenactors guard Heungnyemun [3] *Haetae* statue in front of Gwanghwamun Gate [4] The beautiful Hyangwonjeong Pavilion and Hyangwonji Pond

Museums in the Palace

• National Palace Museum of Korea B3

Established in 1992 as the Royal Museum at Deoksugung Palace, this museum was relocated to Gyeongbokgung with a new name. The National Palace Museum includes over 40,000 artifacts from the royal court of the Joseon kingdom. The permanent collection includes a wide range of artifacts, including royal seals and records, imperial clothing, architecture, court paintings and musical instruments, royal palanquins and a Joseon water clock. On the first floor of the museum is Gogung Tteurak, a museum shop/cafe where you can purchase distinctly Korean souvenirs as well as enjoy a cup of Korean traditional tea.

• **Hours** 9 am to 6 pm (weekdays), 9 am to 7 pm (weekends) Ticket sales stop one hour to closing. Closed Mondays • **Admission** Free • **Getting There** Gyeongbokgung Station, Line 3, Exit 5; Gwanghwamun Station, Line 5, Exit 1 • **Tel** 3701-7500 • **Website** www.gogung.go.kr

• National Folk Museum of Korea C2

Located inside Gyeongbokgung Palace, the National Folk Museum of Korea is devoted to preserving traditional Korean folk culture. Housing over 2,240 artifacts, the museum's exhibition educates visitors on how Koreans lived from traditional times to the present day. The museum is divided into three separate sections: the first section displays the material artifacts of the Korean

people from prehistoric times to the modern age, including bronze culture, pottery, and printing culture; the second exhibit presents artifacts from Korean lifestyle, including agrarian tools and weaving implements; and finally, the third exhibition hall traces the major life events of a member of Joseon's elite, such as coming-of-age ceremonies, wedding ceremonies, and memorial services.

• **Hours** 9 am to 6 pm (Mar to Oct), 9 am to 5 pm (Nov to Feb), 9 am to 7 pm (Sat, holidays). Ticket sales stop one hour to closing. Closed Tuesdays • **Admission** Free • **Getting There** Gyeongbokgung Station, Line 3, Exit 5; Anguk Station, Line 3, Exit 1 • **Tel** 3704-3114 • **Website** www.nfm.go.kr

EMPRESS MYEONGSEONG

The Empress Myeongseong (1851-1895), also known as Queen Min, is one of the most fascinating—and most tragic—figures of the late Joseon era. Born into the Min family, a once powerful clan that had grown impoverished over the ages, she was orphaned by age 9. Still, she drew the attention of the wife of the powerful prince regent, Heungseon Daewongun (see p147), who was tasked with finding a wife for his son, the young King Gojong (see p91). The future queen, born of a noble family but with no close relatives who might compete for influence, was the perfect choice. In 1866, she and King Gojong—two years her junior—were married.

Korean court politics had long been dominated by factionalism, and the young queen became a master of it. Before long, she headed a faction to rival that of the Heungseon Daewongun himself, with the enmity between the two quite public. When she finally succeeded in forcing the prince regent to retire from the palace in 1872, she gained complete control over the court, placing her relatives in high positions.

The queen oversaw a dramatic time in Korean history—internally, the country was beset by divisions between conservatives and reformers, while beyond Korea's shores, the Great Powers looked on with imperial ambitions. Her inclinations were generally with reformers and the West—much of Korea's modernization of the late 19th century took place under her patronage. This put her at odds with conservatives (led by the still influential Heungseon Daewongun) and, perhaps more importantly, Imperial Japan. On Oct 8, 1895, a gang of ruffians—widely believed to have been organized by Japanese resident minister Miura Goro—broke into Gyeongbokung Palace and assassinated the powerful queen. Although 65 men, including Miura, were charged in Japan for complicity in the killing, none were convicted.

Queen Min, posthumously made empress in 1902, has today become a symbol of the tragedy of Korea's history, a heroic figure who stood up to foreign aggressors and paid the ultimate price.

The Last Empress, a musical about Empress Myeongseong, debuted in 1995 as Korea's first original musical. © Yonhap

The Huwon Garden's Aeryeonji Pond in autumn

CHANGDEOKGUNG PALACE

Gyeongbokgung Palace might be Seoul's largest palace, but for many, Changdeokgung Palace is its most beautiful. A UNESCO World Heritage Site, Changdeokgung is the epitome of Korean traditional architecture, its structures striking a fine balance with the natural landscape. The most beautiful part of the palace, however, is its rear garden, or Huwon, widely regarded as the finest example of Korean traditional gardening. If you are able to visit only one palace in Seoul, make it this one.

You can tour the palace grounds freely (after paying admission, of course), but to enter the Huwon, you need to join a guided tour. See the TIPS on p50 for more details.

History

Construction of Changdeokgung began in 1405 and was completed in 1412. Like Gyeongbokgung, it was burnt to the ground during the Japanese invasions of 1592-1598, but unlike Gyeongbokgung, it was rebuilt after the war for use as the royal residence. Fire proved a persistent problem—a blaze in 1623 destroyed almost everything except the main throne hall, and another in 1917 caused a great deal of damage. In order to "restore" the palace following the 1917 blaze, the Japanese took down and moved several buildings from Gyeongbokgung Palace to Changdeokgung Palace.

Built by King Sunjo in 1828, the Yeongyeongdang was designed in the style of a country gentry home in order to give the crown prince a taste of rural gentry life.

For 254 years from 1618 to 1872, Changdeokgung was the royal seat of government. In 1907, it briefly became the royal seat of government again, when Korea's last reigning monarch, Emperor Sunjong, ruled from the palace following the forced abdication of his father, Emperor Gojong. Furthermore, following their return from Japan in 1963, the Korean royal family used a small portion of the palace as a residence until the death of the crown princess—herself Japanese—in 1989.

The palace complex—including its spectacular gardens—was registered with UNESCO in 1997. In registering the palace, the UNESCO committee called it "an outstanding example of Far Eastern palace architecture and garden design, exceptional for the way in which the buildings are integrated into and harmonized with the natural setting, adapting to the topography and retaining indigenous tree cover."

GENERAL INFORMATION

Hours: See TIPS on p50. Closed Mondays **Admission:** 3,000 won (general tour), 5,000 won (Ongnyucheon and Nakseonjae tour), 15,000 won (open tour) **Getting There:** Exit 3 of Anguk Station, Line 3. Walk past the Hyundai Building **Tel:** 762-8261 **Website:** www.cdg.go.kr

Experiencing Changdeokgung Palace D2

The Palace Complex

Tours of Changdeokgung Palace begin at the imposing Donhwamun Gate. The original gate was built in 1412, while the current gate dates from 1609, making it the oldest of Seoul's palace gates.

Just past the gate is a small stone bridge that crosses a stream—this is a common feature at all of Seoul's palaces. Carved in the lower part of the south side of the bridge is a turtle, and on the north a *haetae*—these are the protecting gods of the palace. Constructed in 1411, it is the oldest stone bridge in Seoul.

The main courtyard of the palace is dominated by the Injeongjeon, the main throne hall; the current structure dates from 1804. Things to notice in the throne hall are the beautiful folding screen behind the throne, the intricate carvings on the ceiling, and the somewhat out-of-place Western-style parquet floor, lights and curtains, installed in 1908.

Just to the northwest are a number of other attractive palace structures as well, including the Huijeongjeon, which was moved to Changdeokgung from Gyeongbokgung in 1920 and is adorned with Western furniture.

1 Visitors before the Injeongjeon thone hall 2 Nakseonjae, where Korea's last crown princess passed away in 1989 3 Details on palace building 4 Buyongji Pond in its autumn splendor

Nakseonjae

Nakseonjae is a small collection of buildings in the southeastern corner of the palace complex. This complex, built in 1847, has a distinctly feminine feel, built as it was as a residence for a royal concubine and the royal mother and grandmother. Be sure to check out the rear garden, too, with its fantastic circular stone gate and the lovely Sangnyangjeong Pavilion.

From 1963 to 1989, Nakseonjae was the place of residence of the last descendants of the Korean royal family—most notably, Crown Princess Yi Bang-ja (born Princess Masako of Nashimoto), the wife of Crown Prince Euimin.

Nakseonjae is only open for viewing on Friday, Saturday and Sunday.

Huwon Garden

The most beautiful spot in Changdeokgung Palace is the Huwon Garden, the epitome of Korean traditional gardening. Like English gardens, the Korean gardens seek to utilize the surroundings in as natural a way as possible—hillsides, streams, and rocks become integral parts of the garden. Nothing is forced. Pavilions, ponds and other man-made elements are added to complement the landscape, not dominate it.

The Huwon Garden is broken into three sections. The most visited section is the area surrounding Buyongji Pond, a square-shaped artificial pond with a small, circular island in the middle—the shape of the pond and island is an expression of Korea's traditional view of the cosmos. The pond is surrounded by several beautiful pavilions, the most outstanding of which is the Buyongjeong Pavilion, built in 1792.

TIPS

Admission, Guided Tours and an All-Palace Tour

Admission to the Changdeokgung Palace itself is 3,000 won. This will allow you to walk freely around the palace itself and the Nakseonjae complex. It will NOT get you access to the Huwon Garden, however.

To enter the Huwon Garden, you need to join a separate guided tour. Tickets to this tour are 5,000 won, and can be purchased from the gate at the entrance of the garden. English tours are conducted twice daily—at 11:30 am and 2:30 pm. If you're a Korean speaker, or don't care about the guides' explanations, you could join a Korean tour, which are held almost hourly from 10 am to 4:30 pm. Tours in Japanese and Chinese are available, too.

In addition, you can also purchase a 10,000 won ticket that will get you into Changdeokgung Palace (including the Huwon Garden), Changgyeonggung Palace, Gyeongbokgung Palace, Deoksugung Palace and the Jongmyo Shrine. Good for up to a month, these tickets can be purchased at each palace.

Main throne hall of Injeongjeon, built in 1804

Past the Buyongji Pond area, just through the stone Bullomun Gate ("No Aging Gate"), is another pond, the Aeryeonji Pond, which is particularly spectacular in autumn when the surrounding trees turn bright red. Also nearby is the spectacular Yeongyeongdang, a villa built in the style of a Joseon-era gentry residence. Built by the crown prince in the early 19th century, it has a wonderful rustic beauty about it.

Past the Aeryeonji area is the inner parts of the garden. These sections were, until recently, closed to the general public. One of the highlights of the inner garden is the Gwallamjeong Pavilion, a uniquely designed gazebo shaped like an open fan. Nearby is the Jondeokjeong Pavilion, a hexagonal gazebo dating from 1644. Further inward is the scenic Ongnyucheon Stream, with an artificial waterway where the king and his court would play royal drinking games amidst the natural beauty.

History and Culture

SECRET GARDEN?

The Huwon Garden has undergone a series of name changes over its history: previous names include the Bugwon (North Garden) and Geumwon (Forbidden Garden). It took its current name during the time of King Gojong (r. 1863-1907). During the Japanese colonial period, it was renamed the Biwon (Secret Garden) — this name is still frequently heard, but officially frowned upon.

Descendants of the Joseon kings perform the Jongmyo Daeje rite

JONGMYO SHRINE D3

The Jongmyo Shrine houses the memorial shrines of the kings and queens of Korea's ancient Joseon kingdom. One of the oldest Confucian shrines in Korea, its simple design is considered the epitome of Joseon-era Confucian architecture (see Korean Confucianism on p308). Its long, unadorned halls, built to harmonize with the surrounding woods, display the modesty and love of nature so typical of Korean Confucianism, while its structure and layout encapsulate Confucianism's social hierarchy.

The shrine is also, along with Changdeokgung Palace, one of Seoul's two UNESCO World Heritage Sites. And it is the site of the annual Jongmyo Daeje rite, accompanied by the Jongmyo Jeryeak, a piece of Korean traditional court music designated by UNESCO a "Masterpiece of the Oral and Intangible Heritage of Humanity."

History

As the memorial shrine of the kingdom, Jongmyo Shrine was one of the first structures built in Seoul when Yi Seong-gye—King Taejo—moved the capital of his new kingdom here in 1394. Like many other important structures, it was burned down in the Japanese invasions of 1592-1598, but rebuilt in 1601. Since then, the shrine complex has remained miraculously untouched in its original condition.

Today, the shrine—or at least its main hall—holds the memorial tablets of 19 kings

Performing the Jongmyo Daeje rite

and 30 queens. The rooms holding the memorial tablets are themselves simple and unadorned. The two-building complex itself, however, is appropriately stately—when it was first constructed, the shrine's main hall may very well have been the longest building in Asia. The complex is located to the east of Gyeongbokgung Palace; to the west of the palace was built another shrine, Sajik Shrine (a form of urban planning derived from Imperial China).

Jongmyo Daeje Rite

The time to go to Jongmyo Shrine is the first Sunday in May, when it plays host to the Jongmyo Daeje, a spectacular performance of Korean traditional court music and dance. In the Joseon era, the ceremony—a memorial rite to monarchs past—was held five times a year,

History and Culture

CUTTING THE SPIRIT OF THE KINGDOM

Jongmyo Shrine used to be connected to Changgyeonggung Palace (see p57). In the Japanese colonial era, however, a road was built between the palace and shrine to symbolically sever the spiritual link between the royal family and its ancestors. Palace and shrine have now been reconnected via an overpass—if you are visiting Changgyeonggung Palace, it's worth visiting Jongmyo, too, although the closing time of the overpass entrance is a half hour earlier than the main entrance.

led by the king and queen. Temporarily suspended during the Japanese colonial era, it was brought back after Korea's liberation in 1945 and is now held just once a year. During the highly ritual-conscious Joseon era, the ritual was considered absolutely vital to the nation's survival and prosperity.

The dance and music for the rite is particularly elaborate and features rarely seen Korean traditional musical instruments. The music itself was composed in the 15th century by King Sejong the Great (see p409), replacing the Chinese music previously used in the rite. The dance, meanwhile, features 84 female dancers dressed in purple court attire.

TIPS

ENGLISH TOURS

English-language guided tours are given twice daily at 10 am and 3:30 pm. Chinese, Japanese and Korean language tours are given as well. You should call ahead to reserve a spot, however—give them a ring at 765-0195.

GENERAL INFORMATION

Hours: 9 am to 6 pm (weekdays), 9 am to 7 pm (weekends, public holidays) Mar to Oct; 9 am to 5:30 pm (weekdays, weekends) Nov to Feb. Ticket sales stop one hour to closing. Closed Tuesdays **Admission:** 1,000 won **Getting There:** Five minute walk from Jongno 3-ga Station (Exit 11 of Line 1, Exit 8 of Line 3, Exit 8 of Line 5) **Tel:** 765-0195 **Website:** http://jm.cha.go.kr

Housing the memorial tablets of 19 kings and 30 queens, the main hall of Jongmyo Shrine was the longest building in Asia when it was built.

Tile roofs of Changgyeonggung Palace

CHANGGYEONGGUNG PALACE D2

Changgyeonggung Palace has a rather odd history. It was originally built in 1484 as a retirement home for a former king. The place was torched during the Japanese invasions of 1592-1598, and rebuilt in 1616. In 1907, when Emperor Sunjong moved from Deoksugung Palace to Changdeokgung, Changgyeonggung was turned into a park, complete with a zoo and botanical garden. This "parkification" was completed by the Japanese in 1910, when they renamed the place from Changgyeonggung ("Changgyeong Palace") to Changgyeongwon ("Changgyeong Garden") and opened it to the general public. In 1983, the zoo was removed and the compound restored to "palace" status. But it still feels like a park, and the botanical garden is still there.

Carvings of phoenixes, a symbol of royal authority, on the stone steps leading to Myeongjeongjeon Hall

Experiencing Changgyeonggung Palace

Honghwamun Gate and Okcheon-gyo Bridge

You enter the palace through the Honghwamun Gate, built in 1616. With its lovely curved roof, it is one of the most picturesque of Seoul's palace gates. After the gate, there is a beautiful stone bridge that crosses a small stream. If you look at the side of the bridge, a goblin face is carved into the side. This goblin was carved to ward off evil spirits. The carvings on the railings, meanwhile, are meant to prevent fire.

Main Courtyard, Myeongjeongjeon Hall

Like Korea's other palaces, there is a broad courtyard just in front of the main throne hall, the Myeongjeongjeon. The Myeongjeongjeon is smaller than the throne halls of Gyeongbokgung or Changdeokgung, but it's beautifully designed with some particularly intricate cloisters behind it. Built in 1616, it is the oldest throne hall of Seoul's palaces The carvings on the stone steps are also worth looking at. To the left of the main hall is the Munjeongjeon, the site of one the most tragic stories of the Joseon Dynasty (see below).

THE KING WHO KILLED HIS OWN SON

History and Culture

King Yeongjo (r. 1724-76) is widely regarded as one of the Joseon Dynasty's most capable kings, a deeply Confucian and erudite leader who did his best to rule Korea according to Confucian ideals. Under his administration, Korea recovered economically from the destructive Japanese and Manchu invasions of the 16th and 17th centuries. He reorganized the kingdom's tax system to lessen the burden on his subjects and encouraged the wealthy—himself included—to live modestly.

If Yeongjo had a failing, however, it was his two sons—his eldest died early, which left his youngest—Prince Sado—as successor to the throne. Unfortunately, Crown Prince Sado was mentally ill. Deeply fearful of his stern and demanding father, he would erupt in murderous rages, wantonly killing palace servants and raping court ladies. Yeongjo realized he could not let his son take over the kingdom. He had a sturdy rice chest placed before the Changgyeonggung's Munjeongjeon Hall. He ordered Sado to climb in the chest, which was then closed and left in the sweltering summer heat. It took eight days for Sado to starve to death.

Unlike his father, however, Sado had better luck with offspring. He left behind a young son who would succeed his grandfather as King Jeongjo, a brilliant reformer who promoted science and technology. The spectacular Hwaseong Fortress of Suwon (see p293) is one of his most notable legacies.

1 | 2 | 3 | 4 — [1] Chinese pagoda near Chundangji Pond [2] Victorian-style glasshouse of Changgyeonggung Botanical Garden, built in 1907 [3] Throne of Changgyeonggung Palace [4] Weathered tree and pavilions in rear garden of Changyeonggung Palace

Myeongjeongmun Gate in front of Myeongjeongjeon Hall

Goblin carving, Okcheon-gyo Bridge

Chundangji Pond

The site of Chundangji Pond was originally a royal farm plot, but in 1909, a Japanese-style pond was dug, complete with a Japanese-style pavilion and boats. The pavilion and boats are now gone, but the pond—lined by beautiful trees—still remains.

Chinese Seven-Story Pagoda

On the shores of the pond is a rather odd seven-story pagoda. Exhibiting definite Lamanist influence, it was built in 1470 in China. In 1911, the Japanese purchased the pagoda from an antique dealer and placed it on the side of Chundangji Pond—basically, it's a really nice garden ornament.

Botanical Garden

The Victorian-style glasshouse of the Changgyeonggung Botanical Garden was built in 1907 as Korea's first such glasshouse. The building was designed by Hayato Fukuba, who was in charge of the Shinjuku Imperial Garden in Tokyo, and constructed by a French company. The glasshouse houses rare flora, including tropical plants.

GENERAL INFORMATION

Hours: 9 am to 6:30 pm (Apr to Oct), 9 am to 5:30 pm (Nov to Mar) 9 am to 5 pm (Dec to Feb). Closed Mondays **Admission:** 1,000 won **Getting There:** Exit 4, Hyehwa Station, Line 4. Walk 15 minute **Tel:** 762-4868~9 **Website:** http://cgg.cha.go.kr

TIPS

WIND AND PLACENTAS

On a hill towards the west side of the palace's rear garden are a Joseon-era wind-measuring instrument and a stone monument containing the placenta of King Seongjong (r. 1457-1494). In the eastern part of the rear garden, there's also a Joseon-era astronomical stand. These artifacts were originally kept elsewhere, but were moved to the palace when the Japanese turned it into a park.

ENGLISH TOURS

English language tours are given 11 am and 4 pm. Korean, Japanese and Chinese language tours are given as well.

Changgyeonggung Botanical Garden

Small shoe shop in Samcheong-dong neighborhood.
The area is home to many small boutiques.

SAMCHEONG-DONG

To the east of Gyeongbukgung Palace is a trendy area of cafés, restaurants and boutiques known as Samcheong-dong. It's a great area to escape the urban jungle and relax amidst a pleasing harmony of charmingly traditional and fashionably modern.

Dongsipjagak Guard Tower A4

The Dongsipjagak stands at the entrance of Samcheong-dong Road. While it was once the southeast guard tower of Gyeongbokgung Palace, road development in the colonial era has turned it into a traffic island. The tower was built in 1880.

Samcheong-dong Road A3, B2, C1

Samcheong-dong Road follows along the eastern wall of Gyeongbokgung Palace. To the left is the beautiful stone wall of the palace—lined by a row of impressive ginkgo trees, this makes for one of the best walks in Seoul in autumn, when the trees turn bright yellow. To the right is a series of art galleries, including Gallery Hyundai, Geumho Gallery, Growrich Gallery, Artsonje Center, Gallery Hak Go Jae, Geum San Gallery, Kukje Gallery and Gallery Ihn.

Where Tradition and Modernity Meet

Follow Samcheong-dong Road up, and you'll eventually reach a fork—one fork heads to Cheong Wa Dae (the presidential mansion), while the other takes you to a road of cafés, restaurants and the Prime Minister's Residence. For now, choose the latter.

Samcheong-dong is known throughout Seoul for its blend of tradition and modernity. Located in the area of Seoul known as Bukchon (see p69), this laid-back area is known for its relatively high number of Korean traditional homes, or *hanok*. Many of the *hanok* have been turned into cafés, restaurants and wine bars. Joining them are newer cafés and bars built in trendy modern styles. It's a popular place to walk around and, should the mood strike, enjoy a glass of wine in a charming setting. For window shoppers, there are a good number of small boutiques, including shops for shoes, handbags, accessories and ties.

Samcheong-dong has seen a good deal of development in recent years—now, it's one of the "in" places to set up shop. This has been both a blessing and a curse—the concentration of trendy cafés and restaurants has proven beneficial to the local economy, and the local establishments are undoubtedly pleasant. If you're a fan of gentrification, you'll love it. If not, well, you'll find things to dislike, too.

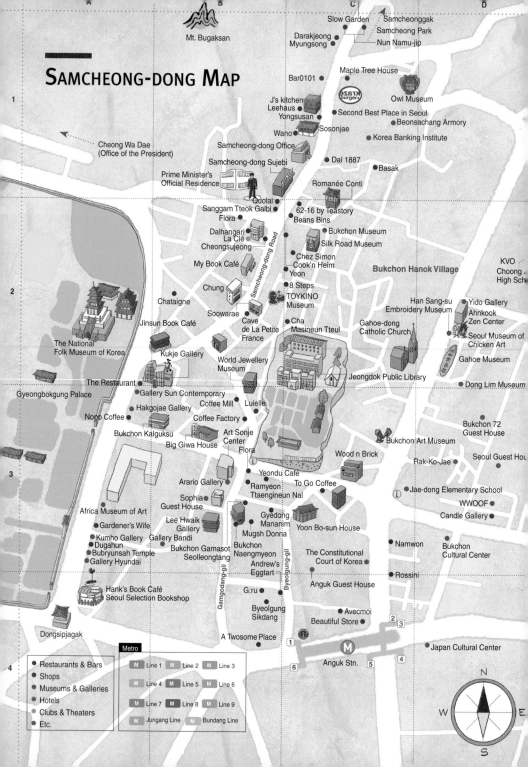

SAMCHEONG-DONG MAP

Mt. Bugaksan

Slow Garden
Samcheonggak
Darakjeong
Myungsong
Samcheong Park
Nun Namu-jip

Maple Tree House

Bar0101
Owl Museum

J's kitchen
Leehaus
Yongsusan
Second Best Place in Seoul
Beonsachang Armory

Wano
Sosonjae
Korea Banking Institute

Cheong Wa Dae
(Office of the President)
Samcheong-dong Office
Dal 1887

Samcheong-dong Sujebi
Basak

Prime Minister's
Official Residence
Romanée Conti

Qdolai

Sanggam Tteok Galbi
62-16 by Teastory
Flora
Beans Bins

Dalhangari
Bukchon Museum
La Clé
Silk Road Museum
Cheongsujeong

Chez Simon
My Book Café
Cook'n Heim
Yeon
Bukchon Hanok Village
KVO
Choong
High Sch

Chung
8 Steps

TOYKINO
Museum
Han Sang-su
Embroidery Museum
Yido Gallery
Chataigne
Ahnkook
Zen Center

Soowarae
Cave
de La Petite
France
Cha
Masineun Tteul
Gahoe-dong
Catholic Church
Seoul Museum of
Chicken Art

Jinsun Book Café
Gahoe Museum

Kukje Gallery
World Jewellery
Museum
Jeongdok Public Library
Dong Lim Museum

The National
Folk Museum of Korea

The Restaurant
Gallery Sun Contemporary
Coffee Mill
Luielle

Gyeongbokgung Palace
Hakgojae Gallery
Coffee Factory
Bukchon 72
Guest House

Nono Coffee
Bukchon Kalguksu
Art Sonje
Center
Wood n Brick
Bukchon Art Museum
Seoul Guest Hou

Big Giwa House
Flora
Rak-Ko-Jae

Yeondu Café
To Go Coffee
Jae-dong Elementary School

Arario Gallery
Ramyeon
Ttaengineun Nal
WWOOF

Sophia
Guest House
Gyedong
Mananim
Yoon Bo-sun House
Candle Gallery

Africa Museum of Art
Lee Hwaik
Gallery
Mugsh Donna
Namwon
Bukchon
Cultural Center

Gardener's Wife
Gallery Bandi
Bukchon Gamasot
Seolleongtang
Bukchon
Naengmyeon
The Constitutional
Court of Korea
Rossini

Kumho Gallery
Dugahun
Bubryunsah Temple
Gallery Hyundai
Andrew's
Eggtart
Anguk Guest House

Hank's Book Café
Seoul Selection Bookshop
G:ru
Avecmoi
Japan Cultural Center

Byeolgung
Sikdang
Beautiful Store

Dongsipjagak
A Twosome Place
Anguk Stn.

Samcheong-dong Restaurants & Cafés

Samcheong-dong is filled with restaurants, cafés and wine bars. Many of them make use of Korean *hanok* home that have been renovated or newly built for the purpose. This provides diners with a refined and tranquil ambiance quite distinct from other neighborhoods of Seoul. A number of places have rooftop seating with nice views of the historic surroundings.

You'll have a variety of eateries from which to choose, including upscale Korean cuisine to French wine and fondue. Just stroll around and choose the one that catches your fancy. Page 110 has a list of some establishments you might wish to try.

Chic Boutiques

In addition to restaurants and cafés, Samcheong-dong has tons of small boutiques and shops that are popular with young Seoulites. In particularly high supply are accessory shops, but don't miss the bag and shoe shops, either. Goods sold here tend to be on the upper end of the price range, but the quality is quite good.

TIPS

BEONSACHANG ARMORY C1

An interesting little piece of Korea's early modern history can be found on the grounds of the Korea Banking Institute. This building, the Beonsachang, was Korea's first modern armory, built by Chinese laborers in 1884. Designed (presumably) by a Chinese architect, the building reveals both Chinese and Western architectural styles. It is now empty, and unfortunately, rarely open, although visitors are welcome to appreciate its exterior.

CHEONG WA DAE TOUR A1

The impressive presidential mansion of Cheong Wa Dae, also known as the Blue House (from the color of the roof tiles), is the center of power in Korea. Security around here is tight— take note of the plain-clothes security personnel as you walk along the road leading to the complex. Tours are conducted four times a day (10, 11 am, 2, 3 pm) from Tuesday to Saturday, but you need to apply at least 10 days in advance to go through the proper security screening. Visit the Cheong Wa Dae website (http://english.president.go.kr) for more information.

KOREAN POLITICS

For several decades following independence, the Republic of Korea was ruled by military dictators who took power through military coups. In 1987, however, protests forced democratic elections, a tradition that has held ever since.

Fundamentally, Korea is a presidential republic, led by a strong executive. Legislation, meanwhile, is handled by the National Assembly, Korea's parliament. Korea has an independent judiciary as well, with both a Supreme Court and a Constitutional Court.

The Constitution of the Republic of Korea—promulgated in 1948 and last revised in 1987—is the basic law of the land.

Korea's president is elected by direct vote every five years. He or she is assisted by a cabinet and an appointed prime minister. Korean presidents are limited to just one term. The presidential residence is Cheong Wa Dae, located just behind Gyeongbokgung Palace.

The unicameral National Assembly, meanwhile, consists of 299 representatives—243 directly elected from single-seat constituencies and 56 by proportional representation. Lawmakers are elected to four-year terms. Like the US Congress, the National Assembly is divided into a number of issue-based committees. Unlike the president, lawmakers are not subject to term limits. The National Assembly gathers at the domed National Assembly Building (see p224) in Yeouido.

The names of Korean political parties have changed a good deal over the history of the republic. Currently, the largest party in the Korean National Assembly is the Grand National Party (Hannara-dang), a pro-business and pro-US conservative party. The main opposition party is the Democratic Party (Minjudang), a more centrist party that favors more active engagement with North Korea. The current President, Lee Myung-bak, is a member of the Grand National Party.

An interesting feature of the Korean government is an independent commission for human rights, the National Human Rights Commission. The presence of this body is in large part a reaction to human rights abuses committed by Korea's past military dictators. It has been doing some very interesting work in unlocking Korea's recent past, much of which has until recently been taboo for political reasons.

Regional governments are led by directly elected governors/mayors and legislatures. Seoul Metropolitan Government is, legally speaking, its own province, and is led by a mayor (elected to a four year term) and a city council.

KOREAN GOVERNMENT WEBSITES

Cheong Wa Dae	www.president.go.kr
National Assembly	www.assembly.go.kr
Supreme Court of Korea	eng.scourt.go.kr
Constitutional Court	english.ccourt.go.kr
National Human Rights Commission	www.humanrights.go.kr

Museums and Galleries

The Samcheong-dong area has a number of interesting museums and galleries, including:

• Gallery Hyundai A3

This gallery of modern art includes both the Gallery Hyundai proper and the nearby Gallery Dugahun. • **Hours** 10 am to 6 pm. Closed Mondays • **Admission** Free • **Tel** 734-6111~3 • **Website** www.galleryhyundai.com

• Kumho Museum of Art A3

This museum opened in 1989 with the goal of discovering and supporting local artists throughout Korea. • **Hours** 10 am to 6:30 pm. Closed Mondays • **Admission** 2,000 won • **Tel** 720-5114 • **Website:** www.kumhomuseum.com

• Kukje Gallery B2

Recognized by Jonathan Borofsky's statue of a woman walking along its roof, the Kukje Gallery holds regular exhibits of local and overseas modern artists. • **Hours** 10 am to 6 pm (Mon—Sat), 10 am to 5 pm (Sun) • **Admission** Free • **Tel** 735-8449 • **Website** www.kukjegallery.com

• Hakgojae Gallery A3

Housed in a lovely Korean traditional house, the Hakgojae Gallery holds exhibits of Korean and overseas modern artists. • **Hours** 10 am to 7 pm (Tue—Sat), 10 am to 6 pm (Sun). Closed Monday • **Admission** Free • **Tel** 720-1524~6 • **Website** www.hakgojae.com

---

GETTING TO SAMCHEONG-DONG

Samcheong-dong Road is approached via Exit 1, Anguk Station, Line 3 (walk towards Gwanghwamun Gate), or Exit 4, Gyeongbokgung Station, Line 3 (walk past Gyeongbokgung Palace). Once you see Dongsipjagak, head up that road.

TIPS

SEOUL SELECTION BOOKSHOP A4

Also on Samcheong-dong Road, near Dongsipjagak is Seoul Selection Bookshop, one of Seoul's best places to score English-language books on Korea or DVDs of Korean films with English subtitles. It also has a café with helpful staff happy to provide tourist information.
(Hours: 9:30 am to 6:30 pm. Closed Sundays, T. 734-9565, www.seoulselection.com)

History and Culture

WHY "SAMCHEONG-DONG"?

The name Samcheong-dong can be translated as "District of Three Clean (or Pure) Things." This is sometimes translated as meaning, "good mountains, good water and good people." Another interpretation has it that the name comes from the Samcheongjeon, a shrine that enshrined the Godhead of Taoism, the "Three Pure Ones" — Taecheong (Grand Pure One), Sangcheong (Supreme Pure One) and Okcheong (Jade Purity). Regardless of which version you prefer to believe, there's no denying the neighborhood's abundant charms.

Snow-covered roofs of 31 Gahoe-dong, Bukchon's most famous alleyway of Korean *hanok* homes.

BUKCHON

To get a feel for what Seoul was like prior to its late 20th century modernization, head to the Bukchon area between the palaces of Gyeongbokgung and Changdeokgung. This neighborhood, composed of winding alleys and Korean tile-roof homes, is the perfect place to get lost in. Few places in the city are as charming.

History

Owing to its politically strategic location between the palaces, Bukchon—or "North Village"—was long the preserve of Seoul's high-official elite. In the early 20th century, its large estates were broken up into smaller units to accommodate the city's growing population. It's at this time that the neighborhood took its current form of winding alleys with Korean *hanok** (see next page) homes packed so closely together that, when seen from above, it appears to be a sea of black tile.

In recent years, Bukchon has received a good deal of attention from city authorities who view the area as a tourism resource. This has been a mixed blessing. The city has been pumping money into the neighborhood to protect and restore the *hanok* homes. At the same time, the growing tourist trade has led some *hanok* owners to turn their properties into commercial establishments such as guest houses, cafés and wine bars. This has proven controversial, with some critics decrying its harm to the residential neighborhood's traditional character.

Experiencing Bukchon

Given the lay of the neighborhood, it would be difficult to give a precise A-to-B style walking course. Broadly speaking, there are two main *hanok* clusters—31 Gahoe-dong to the west, and 11 Gahoe-dong (where many of the galleries are located) to the east. You can use the map as a general guideline, but you're best off just wandering from spot to spot, discovering as you go. Points of interest include:

• 31 Gahoe-dong C2
This is Bukchon's most famous cluster of *hanok* homes. Located on a gently sloping hill, the road provides outstanding views both at the bottom and at the top, where you can view modern downtown Seoul beyond the traditional tile roofs of Bukchon.

Hanok

Literally meaning "Korean home," the term *hanok* came into being after Korea's opening to the West in order to differentiate Korea's traditional architecture from the newer Western-style buildings. The major characteristics of a *hanok* are a) the use of flues to heat the floor (a system called *ondol*) and b) large unheated wooden floors, or *maru*, to keep the home cool in summer. Wealthier homes, such as those found in Bukchon, have black-tile roofs (commoner homes were traditionally roofed with straw), are multi-structured, and have central courtyards called *madang*.

Hanok are built solely from wood, stone and earth—the yellow earth used in the walls, called *hwangto* in Korean, is said to have physical benefits for the occupants. Windows and sliding doors are usually made from Korean paper, or *hanji*, although more modernized *hanok* use glass. Like other Korean traditional structures, *hanok* are deliberately modest—they are rarely if ever painted, and they emphasize "human" scale. Bukchon *hanok* often have elegant front gates.

One never wears shoes in a *hanok*. You sleep on the floor, using a brightly-colored cushioned comforter called a *yo*.

• Bukchon Cultural Center D3

This lovely *hanok* home was built in 1921 and is modeled on the Yeongyeongdang villa of Changdeokgung Palace. It is now owned by Seoul Metropolitan City and used as an information and cultural center, providing tours of the neighborhood and hosting classes and workshops. • **Hours** 9 am to 6 pm • **Admission** Free • **Tel** 3707-8388 • **Website** http://bukchon.seoul.go.kr

• Gahoe Museum D2

This *hanok* gallery is home to one of Seoul's best collections of traditional folk paintings and amulets. Craft programs available. Visitors are treated to green tea, too! • **Hours** 10 am to 6 pm Closed Mondays • **Admission** 3,000 won • **Tel** 741-0466 • **Website** www.gahoemuseum.org

• Seoul Museum of Chicken Art D2

You read that right—chicken art. Take in all the international chicken art you could ever wish to see. You'd be shocked to learn how many times this writer has been asked for its location. • **Hours** 10 am to 6 pm. Closed Mondays & public holidays • **Admission** 3,000 won • **Tel** 763-9995 • **Website** www.kokodac.com

1	
2	3
	4

1 Spring blossoms and *hanok* in Bukchon 2 Mats at Han Sang-su Embroidery Museum 3 Seoul Museum of Chicken Art 4 Choong Ang High School

• Han Sang-su Embroidery Museum D2

Features the work of master embroiderer Han Sang-su. Hands-on programs available, too. • **Hours** 10 am to 5 pm. Closed Mondays • **Admission** 3,000 won • **Tel** 744-1545 • **Website** www.hansangsoo.com

• Dong-Lim Knot Museum D2

This museum is dedicated to *maedeup*, Korean traditional decorative knots. Like many other Bukchon museums, hands-on programs are conducted. • **Hours** 10 am to 6 pm. Closed Mondays • **Admission** 2,000 won • **Tel** 3673-2778 • **Website** www.shimyoungmi.com

• Dugahun A3

Formerly the residence of a relative of the royal family, this 100-year-old *hanok* has been renovated as a café/wine bar/French-Italian restaurant. A tad pricey, but it's a great place to spend the evening. Even has a Cuban cigar menu. • **Hours** Tea Time: 2:30 to 4 pm. Closed Mondays; Wine Time: 10 pm to 12 am. Closed Sundays • **Tel** 3210-2100 • **Website** www.dugahun.com

• Choong Ang High School D2

Bukchon isn't all *hanok*. The main hall of Choong Ang High School, one of Seoul's most historic secondary schools, was built in Tudor Gothic-style in the 1930s, while the two red brick buildings behind it are even older.

31 Gahoe-dong

• Jeongdok Public Library C2

Formerly Kyunggi High School, one of the country's most elite high schools, the wooded campus is a great place to stroll around, especially in spring (when the cherry blossoms bloom) and fall. The library building itself dates from 1937.

• Yoon Bo-sun House C3

Located not far from the Jeongdok Public Library, this lovely home of a former president is one of the grandest *hanok* in the neighborhood, with lovely gardens. Unfortunately, it's not usually open to the public, although small concerts are sometimes held there.

• Hakgojae Gallery A3

Hakgojae, the term after which the gallery is named, means "a place where the old is studied." Following this theme, the gallery's motto is "Creation of the new by understanding the old." The edifice of the gallery embodies this theme—the exterior and front building are a traditional *hanok*, while a back building and the interior of the gallery are modern constructions. Hakgojae exhibits both traditional pieces and contemporary art.

- **Hours** 10 am to 7 pm, Tue to Sat; 10 am to 6 pm, Sun (Mar to Oct); Tue to Sun 10 am to 6 pm (Nov to Feb).
- **Admission** Free • **Getting There** Anguk Station, Line 3, Exit 1 • **Tel** 720-1524
- **Website** www.hakgojae.com

GETTING TO BUKCHON
Bukchon is best approached via Exit 1, 2 or 3 of Anguk Station, Line 3. From there, you're best off looking at the map on p64.

TIPS

BUKCHON GUEST HOUSES
A number of the *hanok* homes in Bukchon have been renovated for use as guest houses. These places give visitors a chance to experience a Korean traditional home and are popular with foreign visitors. Most provide Korean meals, and some even host cultural events and programs. For a list, see Accommodation section on p370.

Rak-Ko-Jae

CULTURAL SENSITIVITY
Bukchon is an area so beautiful that you sometimes forget that people actually live there. Bukchon is, first and foremost, a residential area, and a quiet one at that. In the past, residents have complained about foreigners knocking on the gates of random *hanok* homes asking, "Is this a guest house?" There have also been complaints about loud, drunk foreigners, too. When you visit Bukchon—and especially if you're staying there—please keep the neighbors in mind.

Korean craft shop in Insa-dong.

INSA-DONG

Insa-dong is one of Seoul's most well-known destinations for foreign visitors. The neighborhood, which in the old days was called (for reasons unknown) "Mary's Alley," is lined with antique shops, small galleries, traditional craft shops, cafés and restaurants. So popular is it with tourists that in recent years it has become, well, "touristy," but it's still a fascinating area...with a little history to it as well.

Layout

Insa-dong has a "main drag," so to speak, that runs from its entrance near Anguk Station to opposite Tapgol (Pagoda) Park. From this main street radiate many smaller alleyways that are well worth exploring. Also in the Insa-dong area are several areas of historical and cultural interest, including Unhyeongung Palace, Minga Daheon, Cheondogyo Central Temple, Jogyesa Temple and Seung Dong Presbyterian Church. On Sundays, cars are forbidden from entering the main street, turning it into a (very crowded) pedestrian road.

History

A number of sites in and around Insa-dong, including Tapgol Park, Cheondogyo Central Temple and Seung Dong Presbyterian Church, are closely tied with the March 1 Independence Movement* (see p78) of 1919. Ironically enough, given both this history and the neighborhood's role today as a center of Korean traditional arts, antique shops and art sellers began congregating in the area in the 1930s, when Insa-dong became 'ground zero' for the plundering of Korean cultural treasures by Imperial Japan.

Sites of Interest

Unhyeongung Palace C1

Unhyeongung Palace was not really a "palace" per se, although King Gojong did live there until the age of 12 (1863), after which he ascended to the throne and moved to Changdeokgung Palace. The residence is more notable as the home of Heungseon Daewongun (see p147), the conservative prince regent who was the effective ruler of Korea during Gojong's minority and for a good time afterwards. The palace, built between 1863 and 1873, is a typical upper-class Korean home, characterized by the rustic Confucian modesty so characteristic of the period. • **Hours** 9 am to 6 pm (Nov to Mar), 9 am to 7 pm (Apr to Oct). Closed Mondays • **Admission** 700 won. Free for lunch hours (noon to 1 pm, Tue to Fri) • **Tel** 766-9090 • **Website** www.unhyeongung.or.kr

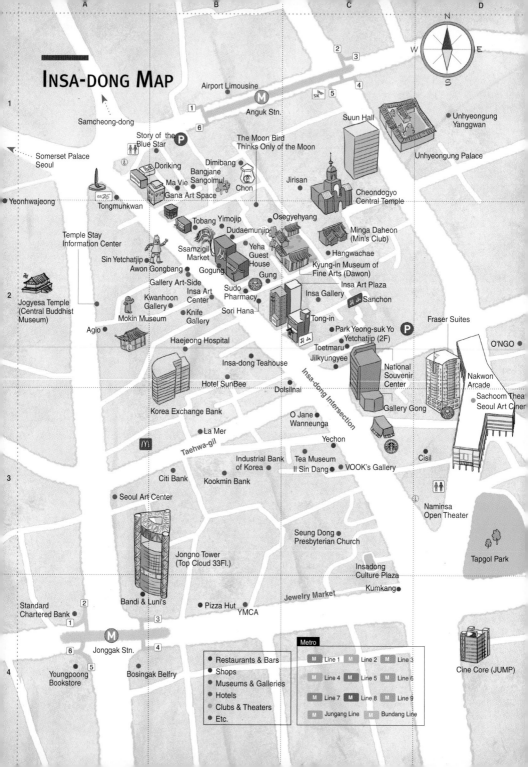

INSA-DONG MAP

N / **E** / **S** / **W**

A / B / C / D

1 / 2 / 3 / 4

Samcheong-dong

Somerset Palace Seoul

Yeonhwajeong

Jogyesa Temple (Central Buddhist Museum)

Temple Stay Information Center

Agio

Story of the Blue Star

Doriking

Ma Vie

Tongmunkwan

Gana Art Space

Dimibang

Bangjane Sangolmul

Chon

Jirisan

Airport Limousine

Anguk Stn.

sk 5

Suun Hall

Cheondogyo Central Temple

Unhyeongung Yanggwan

Unhyeongung Palace

Tobang Yimojip

Dudaemunjip

Osegyehyang

Yeha Guest House

Sin Yetchatjip

Awon Gongbang

Gallery Art-Side

Kwanhoon Gallery

Mokin Museum

Samzigil Market

Gogung

Insa Art Center

Knife Gallery

Gung

Sudo Pharmacy

Sori Hana

Minga Daheon (Min's Club)

Hangwachae

Kyung-in Museum of Fine Arts (Dawon)

Insa Art Plaza

Insa Gallery

Tong-in

Sanchon

Haejeong Hospital

Insa-dong Teahouse

Hotel SunBee

Korea Exchange Bank

La Mer

Taehwa-gil

Citi Bank

Kookmin Bank

Seoul Art Center

Jongno Tower (Top Cloud 33Fl.)

Standard Chartered Bank

Bandi & Luni's

Pizza Hut

YMCA

Jongno Tower

Dolsilnai

Insa-dong Intersection

Park Yeong-suk Yo Yetchatjip (2F)

Toetmaru

Jilkyungyee

National Souvenir Center

Fraser Suites

O'NGO

Nakwon Arcade

Sachoom Thea

Seoul Art Ciner

Gallery Gong

O Jane Wanneunga

Yechon

Tea Museum

Il Sin Dang

VOOK's Gallery

Cisil

Naminsa Open Theater

Seung Dong Presbyterian Church

Insadong Culture Plaza

Kumkang

Jewelry Market

Tapgol Park

Cine Core (JUMP)

Jongga Stn.

Youngpoong Bookstore

Bosingak Belfry

Metro

M	Line 1	M	Line 2	M	Line 3
M	Line 4	M	Line 5	M	Line 6
M	Line 7	M	Line 8	M	Line 9
M	Jungang Line	M	Bundang Line	

- Restaurants & Bars
- Shops
- Museums & Galleries
- Hotels
- Clubs & Theaters
- Etc.

The Moon Bird Thinks Only of the Moon

Unhyeongung Yanggwan D1
This white neo-Baroque home, located just behind the Unhyeongung Palace, was built in 1912 as the home of Heungseon Daewongun's grandson. When he died, the home was given to Prince Yi Wu, who died in the atomic bombing of Hiroshima. It has a beautiful garden as well. • **Hours** Closed Sundays.

Seung Dong Presbyterian Church C3
Founded in 1902, this red-brick Romanesque church is one of Korea's oldest Protestant churches. It played a major role in the Korean Independence Movement of March 1, 1919.

Cheondogyo Central Temple C1
This massive red brick Art Nouveau building, located just across from Unhyeongung Palace, is the central place of worship of Cheondogyo, a strongly nationalist religious group that mixes Korea's traditional faiths with elements of Christianity. The cathedral-like temple, designed by a Japanese architect, was completed in 1921. During the colonial era, the Cheondogyo faith produced many independence activists, including a large number of the leaders of the March 1 Independence Movement.

Minga Daheon (Min's Club) C2
This "modernized" *hanok*, built in the 1930s by one of Korea's first modern architects, is now a fusion restaurant and wine bar with an interior that mixes traditional and Victorian. • **Hours** Lunch: noon to 2:30 pm (3 pm on weekends), Dinner: 6 to 11:30 pm (Order should be made by 9:30 pm) • **Tel** 733-2966 • **Website** www.minsclub.co.kr

Unhyeongung Palace, former villa of the 19th century regent Heungseong Daewongun

March 1 Independence Movement

History and Culture

Japan's annexation of Korea in 1910 marked the start of a dark period of at times brutal colonial rule. Opposition to Japanese rule reached a peak in 1919, when President Woodrow Wilson's proclamation of the right of self-determination at the Paris Peace Conference sparked a nationalist uprising in Korea. On March 1, 1919, 33 Korean nationalists met at a restaurant in Insa-dong to read a declaration of independence. In Tapgol Park, a Korean student read a copy of the declaration before a massive crowd, while copies of the declaration were read throughout the country. The crowds evolved into processions and demonstrations that were put down with great brutality by the Japanese, who killed and arrested thousands of Koreans. The March 1 Independence Movement is considered a catalyst of the Korean nationalist movement. To commemorate the movement, March 1 has been declared a public holiday in Korea.

Tapgol Park D3

Also known as Pagoda Park, so named for the massive Wongaksa Pagoda, an intricately carved 10-story marble structure now protected from the elements in a case of glass. Tapgol Park has the distinction of being Seoul's first modern park, designed in 1897 by John McLeavy Brown, a British advisor to King Gojong. On March 1, 1919, crowds of Koreans gathered here to listen to a reading of the Declaration of Independence, provoking protests and marches that were ultimately put down by the Japanese with considerable brutality.

Jogyesa Temple A2

Jogyesa Temple is the headquarters of the Jogye Order of Korean Buddhism* (see p81), Korea's largest Buddhist sect. This is one of Seoul's most active Buddhist temples—be sure to visit during the Buddha's Birthday festivities, usually held in late April or early May. Compared to some of Korea's most famous Buddhist monasteries located in the countryside, the complex is not terribly big or especially old (it was founded only in 1910), but its Korean-style halls are nevertheless beautiful, especially its massive Main Hall. If you want to take in the chanting, visit just before sunrise or in the late afternoon. There's a Buddhist history museum located on the complex, too. • **Tel** 732-2183 • **Website** www.jogyesa.kr

Temple Stay Information Center A2

Just across from Jogyesa Temple is a massive new Temple Stay Information Center, which as the name would suggest provides information on stays at one of

1	2
	3
4	

[1] Korean masks in an Insa-dong shop [2] Ssamziegil Market [3] Reflection, Unhyeongung Yanggwan [4] Traditional tea house "Insa-dong"

Korea's beautiful Buddhist monasteries. The center also has a restaurant (serving vegetarian Buddhist cuisine) and a cafe.
• **Hours** 9 am to 6 pm. Open all year round
• **Tel** 2031-2000 • **Website** eng.templestay.com

Galleries & Museums

Kyung-in Museum of Fine Arts C2
This fine gallery blends modern and traditional. It includes a Korean traditional home, Korean garden and traditional tea house. • **Hours** 10 am to 6 pm • **Admission** Free
• **Tel** 733-4448~9 • **Website** www.kyunginart.co.kr

Gallery Art-Side B2
Founded in 1999, this gallery focuses on Asian contemporary art. • **Hours** 10 am to 6 pm. Closed Mondays & public holidays • **Tel** 725-1020

Insa Art Center B2
The Insa Art Center is a new landmark in Insa-dong that combines traditional Korean arts and modern art. This impressive six-floor art complex boasts four exhibition halls that presents a diverse range of styles and pieces for visitors to enjoy. • **Hours** 10 am to 7 pm
• **Admission** Free • **Tel** 736-1020 • **Website** www. insaartcenter.com

Kwanhoon Gallery B2
Opened in 1979, this is one of the neighborhood's oldest display spaces for modern art—accordingly, it has helped to launch the career of many a young artist.
• **Hours** 10:30 am to 6:30 pm • **Admission** • **Tel** 733-6469 • **Website** www.Kwanhoongallery.com

Mokin Museum A2
This intriguing museum contains some 8,000 wooden figures of people and animals. The

TIPS

TEMPLE STAYS
Many of Korea's Buddhist temples conduct so-called "temple stay" programs, where for relatively little money you can live the life of a Buddhist monk for a weekend, meditation sessions and all. These have proven quite popular with foreign visitors looking to experience a bit of Korea's traditional culture. For more information, contact the Temple Stay Information Center (T. 2031-2000, eng.templestay.com A2) located just across from Jogyesa Temple A2.

ZEN MEDITATION
Interested in Zen? The International Zen Center of Hwagyesa Temple (T. 900-4326), located in the mountains of northern Seoul, hosts Zen meditation sessions and dharma talks in English every Sunday at 1 pm (instructions for first-time beginners begins at 12:30). Ahnkook Zen Center (T. 732-0772 D2, p64) in Bukchon also holds Zen classes for foreigners every Saturday 2:30 to 4 pm.

LOTUS LANTERN FESTIVAL
One of Seoul's biggest celebrations is the Lotus Lantern Festival, a Buddhist festivity held in May highlighted by a spectacular evening parade through the heart of downtown Seoul. For more information, see p436.

KOREAN BUDDHISM

One of Korea's traditional faiths, Buddhism still enjoys a healthy following—as of 2005, 22.5% of the population professed to be Buddhists, making it the country's second largest religion behind Christianity (29.2%). Korea's endless mountains are dotted with Buddhist temples and monasteries, and Buddhism has had a great impact on Korean philosophy, literature and arts. Many of Korea's most famous treasures, including the Seokguram Grotto and Tripitaka Koreana, are Buddhist works.

HISTORY OF KOREAN BUDDHISM

Buddhism originated in India some 2,400 years ago, and came to the Korean peninsula via China in the fourth century. It first came to the Korean kingdoms of Goguryeo and Baekje (see p26) in 372 and 384, respectively. The new faith was warmly received in both kingdoms. It got a considerably colder reception in Silla, where the religion first entered in the fifth century. According to legend, the turning point took place in 527, when a Buddhist court official by the name of Ichadon was martyred—when he was beheaded, it's said milk poured from his neck rather than blood. Under King Chinhung (r. 540-576), Buddhism was made the state religion in Silla.

When Silla unified Korea in 668, the peninsula experienced a Golden Age of peace and stability. Enjoying state patronage, Buddhism flourished in this environment. Countless Buddhist temples, such as Gyeongju's grand Bulguksa Temple, were built throughout the country. Several of Korea's greatest Buddhist theologians—including the great Korean monks Wonhyo and Uisang—were active in this era, too. Towards the end of Silla, the practice of *seon*—better known in the West as Zen—began to take roots.

Buddhism continued to flourish under the Goryeo kingdom (918-1392), where

Burning incense on Buddha's Birthday   Main Hall, Jogyesa Temple

Buddhism was the state religion. During this period, there was a movement toward reconciling scholastic Buddhism—with its emphasis on learning the Buddhist sutras—and Zen, which emphasized enlightenment through mediation. The Tripitaka Koreana, a priceless woodblock print edition of the Buddhist canon still in existence at Haeinsa Temple near Daegu, was produced in the 13th century to protect the country against Mongol invasion.

Unfortunately, however, state patronage also led to corruption, and by the end of the Goryeo era, Confucian scholars were attacking the vice and greed of Buddhist temples, which often controlled considerable land and wealth. When the Confucians took control of the country and established the Joseon kingdom (1392-1910), they placed difficult new conditions on Buddhism. They limited the number of temples, restricted who could join the monkhood, and most notably, drove the temples into the mountains. Buddhist monks were barred from the cities. The situation improved somewhat from the 16th century, however, thanks to the active participation of Buddhist monks as warriors in the Imjin War (1592-1598) against the Japanese.

During the Japanese colonial era (1910-1945), Japanese Buddhist orders set up temples in Korea and interfered in Korean Buddhist traditions. Most notoriously, they allowed Buddhist monks to marry; traditionally, Korean Buddhist monks were celibate. This proved a lasting controversy—even after independence, arguments between married and celibate monks would plague Korean Buddhism. In modern times, Buddhism has had to hold its own against the rising popularity of Christianity and a general trend towards secularism and materialism resulting from Korea's industrialization and modernization. Overall, it hasn't done too poorly—nearly half of Koreans who consider themselves religious are Buddhists. Moreover, even non-Buddhists generally recognize the rich heritage the religion has left Korea.

BUDDHIST ORDERS

Like Christianity, Korean Buddhism is broken into several sects:

- **Jogye Order:** The Jogye Order is by far Korea's largest Buddhist order. Officially established in 1962 but with a history that goes back over 1,000 years, the Jogye Order merges *gyo* (scholastic Buddhist) and *seon* (Zen). In keeping with Korean tradition, its monks are celibate. The order controls most of Korea's major Buddhist temples, including its headquarters of Jogyesa in downtown Seoul.
- **Taego Order:** The Taego Order separated from the Jogye Order over the question of married monks, a legacy of Japanese colonial rule. In Seoul, the Taego Order controls Bongwonsa Temple near Yonsei University—the village in front of the temple houses the monks' families.
- **Cheontae Order:** Emphasizing the Lotus Sutra, this order is perhaps best known for the massive Buddhist temple of Guinsa in Danyang, Chungcheongbuk-do.

Korean collection includes figures carved from the Joseon era to the present day. If you're into totemism, you'll enjoy this gallery immensely. The wooden gallery itself, built in 1955, is pleasant enough, as is the cafe on the roof.
• **Hours** 10 am to 7 pm, closed Mondays
• **Admission** 5,000 won • **Tel** 722-5066
• **Website** www.mokinmuseum.com

• Insa Gallery C2

Opened in 1994, this modern art gallery has introduced to the public many works by both veteran and up-and-coming arts. Its special exhibits are always noteworthy.
• **Hours** 10 am to 6:30 pm (Mon to Sat); 10:30 am to 6 pm (Sun) • **Admission** Free • **Tel** 735-2655

Insa Art Center

• VOOK's Gallery C3

This gallery takes its name from "Visual Book"—basically, it's a gallery of art, photography, design, architecture and fashion books. Oh, and comics, too.
• **Hours** 10:30 am to 6 pm • **Admission** Free • **Tel** 737-3283

• Knife Gallery B2

It's a gallery. Full of knives. 6,000 knives, in fact, from all over the world. And by knives, we also include swords and other potentially deadly cutting tools. If this sort of thing appeals to you, this is your place. They sell knives, too. • **Hours** 10 am to 7 pm (weekdays); 11 am to 6 pm (weekends) • **Admission** 1,000 won • **Tel** 735-4431

Performing Arts

• Sachoom Theater D3

Sachoom Theater is a new theater dedicated to the dance musical *Sachoom*, a Korean abbreviation for "Dance if you are in love." Like other Korean non-verbal performances, one of the advantages here is that you can still enjoy it even if you can't understand Korean. The show was a big hit at the 2008 Edinburgh Fringe Festival. • **Admission** 50,000 won • **Showtimes** Mon to Fri 8 pm / Sat 4 pm, 7:30 pm / Sun 4 pm • **Tel** 070-8249-3023 • **Website** www.sachoom.com

• IBK Jump Theater D4

A dazzling comic martial arts show, *Jump* combines traditional Korean taekwondo with *taekkyeon* and other modern Asian martial arts for a spectacular nonverbal performance. The cast of champion gymnasts and martial arts athletes has performed over 1,500 times all over the world. A masterful display of martial arts, this performance combines slapstick comedy and an entertaining plotline for a thoroughly enjoyable show.

• **Hours** Mon 8 pm / Tue to Sat 4, 8 pm / Sundays & Public holidays 3, 6 pm • **Admission** 40,000 to 50,000 won • **Getting There** Jonggak Station, Line 1, Exit 4 • **Tel** 722-3995
• **Website** www.hijump.co.kr

Shops

There are tons of shops in Insa-dong. The neighborhood is mostly known as a place to pick up art, antiques, craft supplies and traditional clothing—indeed, Insa-dong's history as a center of arts and antiques goes back over a century. If you're looking for distinctly Korean souvenirs, this would be a good place to look. Be warned, however—Insa-dong is overflowing with tourists, so some of the shops can be a tad on the touristy side.

• Ssamzigil Market B2

This trendy, four-floor complex is a market within a market. Contains 70 shops including handicraft stores, souvenir shops, art galleries and restaurants.

• **Hours** 10 am to 8:30 pm • **Tel** 736-0088
• **Website** www.ssamzigil.co.kr

• Tong-in C2

Founded in 1924, this is one of Insa-dong's best-known antique shops. 1st Floor: Contemporary crafts. 2nd Floor: Traditional Korean crafts. 3rd Floor: Revival furniture. 4th Floor: Korean antiques. • **Hours** 10 am to 7 pm (Apr to Sep); 10 am to 6 pm (Oct to Mar) • **Tel** 733-4867

Tong-in

• National Souvenir Center C2

Popular with foreign tourists. Get your traditional crafts for friends and family back home here. • **Hours** 10 am to 8 pm •
Tel 739-8587

• Awon Gongbang B2

This cute little Insa-dong shop—run by four siblings—specializes in metal crafts made by the owners themselves over some 20 years. Most of the goods are reasonably priced. • **Hours** 10:30 am to 7:30 pm • **Tel** 734-3482

• Jilkyungyee C2

This designer specializes in "modernized" *hanbok*, or Korean traditional clothing. The designs here are both comfortable, practical and beautiful—the writer of this guidebook wears them himself. • **Hours** 9 am to 9 pm • **Tel** 734-5934 • **Website** www.jilkyungyee.co.kr

• Tongmunkwan A1

Opening in 1934 and run by the same family for three generations, this shop bills itself as the nation's oldest bookshop. Specializing in valuable old books and documents, many of its wares are absolutely priceless. • **Hours** 10:30 am to 5:30 pm. Closed Sundays. • **Tel** 734-4092 • **Website** www.tongmunkwan.co.kr

TIPS

CAR-FREE SUNDAYS

On Sundays, cars are prohibited from driving along Insa-dong. This makes Sunday a particularly nice day to visit—you can stroll unmolested by traffic, and locals set up various stalls on the street to sell crafts and other items.

• Park Yeong-suk Yo C2

If this ceramics shop was good enough for Queen Elizabeth II, who visited in 1999, it's probably good enough for you. In fact, some of their wares are sitting in the British Museum. • **Hours** 10 am to 6 pm • **Tel** 730-7837

• Sori Hana B2

One of the most popular traditional craft shops in Insa-dong, some 30% of the crafts sold here are done by famous designers (the other 70% are originals done by the shop itself). Pick yourself up traditional knots or cushions, or perhaps a nice necktie with the Korean alphabet printed on it.
• **Hours** 9:30 am to 8 pm • **Tel** 738-8335

• Il Sin Dang C3

If you'd like to take up the arts of calligraphy or papercraft, Il Sin Dang has been selling, for 20 years, calligraphy brushes, traditional paper, ink and other things you'll need. It's fun just to walk around this place.
• **Hours** 9 am to 8 pm • **Tel** 733-8100

GETTING TO INSA-DONG

The north end of Insa-dong is approached via Exit 6 of Anguk Station, Line 3. The south end, meanwhile, is reached via Exit 1 of Jongno 3-ga Station, Line 1, 3 or 5.

Junghwajeon Hall, the main throne hall of Deoksugung Palace, dates from a 1906 reconstruction

DEOKSUGUNG PALACE B4, p38

Deoksugung Palace is the most "urban" of Seoul's palaces, located in the heart of the city just across from Seoul City Hall. In fact, it's two palaces in one—one a Korean traditional palace, complete with brightly colored tile-roofed structures, and the other a Western-style palace highlighted by the grand neoclassical Seokjojeon Hall.

Built as a villa in the 15th century, the palace was greatly expanded at the end of the 19th century as a residence for Emperor Gojong (see p91), who moved here in 1897 following a year's residency at the nearby Russian legation. In 1907, he was forced to abdicate under Japanese pressure, but he continued to live at the palace until his death in 1919.

Experiencing Deoksugung Palace

Daehanmun Gate

Ordinarily, the main entrance to a palace faces south, in accordance with *feng shui*. Daehanmun Gate, however, was moved to the east some time after its initial construction. The current gate dates from a 1906 reconstruction. It is here that changing of the guard ceremonies (see TIPS on p90) are held three times a day (11 am, 2 and 3:30 pm).

> **TIPS**
>
> **ENGLISH LANGUAGE TOURS**
>
> English language tours of the palace are given at 10:30 am on Tuesday to Friday, and 1:40 pm on Saturday and Sunday. Japanese, Chinese and Korean language tours are also available.

Junghwajeon Hall

The main throne hall of the palace, this splendid building burnt down in 1901 and was rebuilt in 1906. Be sure to check out its colorful ceiling, with its two carved dragons.

> **GENERAL INFORMATION**
>
> **Hours:** 9 am to 9 pm (Ticketing closes at 8 pm.) Closed Mondays
> **Admission:** 1,000 won **Getting There:** City Hall Station, Line 1, Exit 2; Line 2, Exit 12 **Tel:** 771-9951

Seokjojeon Hall

This massive neoclassical hall, designed by a Briton and completed in 1910, was built as Gojong's royal residence. It is now a museum.

National Museum of Contemporary Art, Deoksugung Annex

Another massive neoclassical building, this one was completed in 1939 as the so-called Yi Royal Family Museum. Today it is the Deoksugung Annex of the National Museum of Contemporary Art, one of the finest museums in the country. Some of the city's biggest-name exhibitions are held here. • **Hours** 9 am to 6 pm. (Tue to Thu); 9 am to 8:30 pm (Fri to Sun). Closed Mondays • **Admission** Free to 5,000 won (depends on exhibition) • **Tel** 368-1414

Jeonggwanheon Pavilion

One of Seoul's quirkier pieces of older architecture, this part-Korean, part-Romanesque pavilion was built by a Russian architect as a coffee house for Emperor Gojong.

A Cup of Coffee for the Emperor

History and Culture

During his stay at the Russian legation (see p89), King Gojong developed a taste for coffee, prepared for him by Antoinette Sontag, the sister-in-law of the Russian minister and the founder of Seoul's first Western hotel. He took his newfound love of java with him when he left the Russian legation for his new home at Deoksugung Palace. He commissioned Russian architect Aleksey Seredin-Sabatin to build him a pavilion in which the king could sit and enjoy a cup of coffee.

The result was an amusingly eclectic building mixing Western Romanesque designs with Korean motifs—check out the deer and flower patterns in the railings and frieze. It is irregularly used for coffee and tea events even today, and is open to the public every Saturday.

Jeonggwanheon Pavilion

1 Window, Deoksugung Palace 2 Stone markers where high officials used to stand in front of Junghwajeon Hall 3 Junghwajeon Hall 4 Deoksugung Palace from above

TIPS

Changing of the Royal Guard Ceremony

Now the capital of a presidential republic, Seoul might no longer have a resident monarch, but it still has a changing of the royal guard ceremony.

In the days of the Joseon kings, the palace gates were guarded by an elite military unit called the Sumungun. The unit was tasked with opening and closing the gates and patrolling the area around the palace. This tradition fell out of practice with the end of the monarchy, but was revived in 1996 to give both residents and visitors a taste of the lost culture of the royal palaces.

Changing of the guard ceremonies take place in front of the Daehanmun Gate of Deoksugung Palace three times a day at 11 am, 2 and 3:30 pm (no ceremonies on Monday). In addition to the period attire—various colors represent different ranks and position—the affair is accompanied by the beating of drums, the barking out of orders and Korean traditional martial music. The pageantry of it all tends to be quite popular with visitors, as evidenced by the crowds of camera and camcorder-toting tourists that gather for the ceremonies.

KING GOJONG AND THE RISE AND FALL OF THE DAEHAN EMPIRE

At the close of the 19th century, Korea was in trouble. Centuries of stability under the kings of the Joseon Dynasty had disintegrated in a perfect storm of internal conflict and external pressure from the imperial powers.

In 1895, a modernized Japan handily defeated the Qing Dynasty of China, making it the most powerful country in East Asia. Competing for influence in the region was Russia, with strong interests in northeast China. In the Korean court, already long plagued by factional strife, pro-Russian and pro-Japanese politicians struggled for dominance.

In 1884, pro-Japanese reformers staged a coup, taking control of the royal court. In 1895, the powerful pro-Russian queen of King Gojong, Queen Min, was assassinated at Gyeongbokgung Palace by ruffians (widely believed to have taken place at the behest of the Japanese legation), forcing the king and the crown prince to seek refuge at the Russian legation in Jeong-dong. During the king's yearlong stay at the legation, the Russians used their influence to replace the pro-Japanese court with pro-Russian figures.

This culminated with King Gojong leaving the Russian legation in 1897 and taking up residence at Deoksugung Palace. There he declared the Daehan Empire, placing himself on equal footing as the Chinese emperor. The empire proved a dramatic time. Feeling the need to modernize or perish, Emperor Gojong worked to bring his country into the modern world. Diplomats, businessmen, missionaries and teachers flocked to the country. Modern schools and hospitals were built, railroads and streetcar systems opened, churches established, and electricity and water facilities developed. Treaties were signed with various countries, and foreign businessmen obtained concessions in mining, transportation and other industries throughout the country.

Unfortunately for the kingdom, the foreigners also brought imperial ambitions. In 1904, the competition between Japan and Russia for dominance in the region came to a head with the Russo-Japanese War, won by Japan in 1905. With the Russians out of the way and the Americans, British and French doing little to stop them, the Japanese strong-armed the Korean court into signing the Protectorate Treaty of 1905, giving control of Korea's foreign relations to Japan. When Emperor Gojong tried to fight this by sending a delegation to the Hague Convention of 1907, the Japanese forced him to abdicate in favor of the crown prince. Finally, on Aug 22, 1910, the Japanese made their rule over Korea complete with the Japan-Korea Annexation Treaty, so starting 35 years of colonial rule.

With its harmonization of Korean traditional and "modern" Western elements, Deoksugung Palace is a symbol of the Daehan Empire.

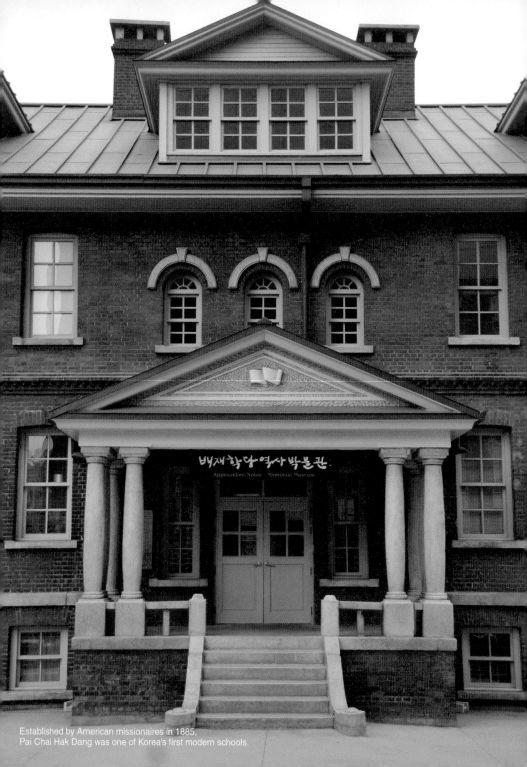

Established by American missionaires in 1885,
Pai Chai Hak Dang was one of Korea's first modern schools.

JEONG-DONG

A pleasant tree-lined neighborhood to the west of the Deoksugung Palace, Jeong-dong is where many of Seoul's first foreign legations, schools and churches were built in the late 19th and early 20th century. As such, the area was a major entry point for the introduction of foreign culture into Korea—Seoul's first Protestant churches, first modern schools and first modern hotel were all built there. Today, the area retains a somewhat exotic foreign charm, and a good number of historical buildings— many designed by Americans, Britons and Russians—still remain.
• **Getting There** Exit 2 of City Hall Station, Line 1, or Exit 12 of Line 2.

Experiencing Jeong-dong
Deoksugung Palace Wall
The stone wall running along the south side of the palace is one of Seoul's most favored strolling spots, particularly in fall.

Seoul Museum of Art
Formerly the home of the Supreme Court, this museum is one of Korea's leading museums of contemporary art. The façade of the building dates from 1928. The museum is home to a collection of 1,432 works of art in such genres as Western painting, oriental painting, sculpture, crafts, photography and calligraphy. Highlights include 93 paintings donated by renowned Korean female painter Cheon Kyung-Ja. • **Hours** 10 am to 8 pm. Closed Mondays • **Admission** Free • **Tel** 723-2491 • **Website** http://seoulmoa.seoul.go.kr

Pai Chai Hak Dang
Korea's first modern intermediate school, the school was founded in 1885 by American Methodist missionary Henry Gerhard Appenzeller, who also founded Chungdong First Methodist Church just down the street. All that remains of the original school is the old East Hall.

DANGEROUS FOR YOUR RELATIONSHIP?   *History and Culture*

According to a popular saying, if you stroll along the Deoksugung Palace Wall with a loved one, you'll split up by the time you reach the end. As for the origins of this saying, there are two popular theories. The first notes that the family court used to be located nearby, so couples seeking a divorce would, by necessity, pass by the stone wall. The second theory is that the spirits of female palace servants—who forwent marriage to serve the court, often doing the difficult work court ladies refused to do— still reside in the neighborhood.

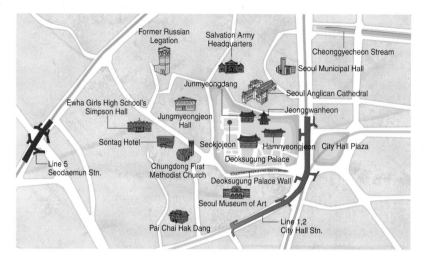

Chungdong First Methodist Church

This stately American-style Gothic church of red-brick was built in 1897 and is Korea's oldest existing Protestant church. The church played a major role in opening Korea to the West and social modernization.

Salvation Army Headquarters

Completed in 1928, this massive neoclassical structure is hidden away on the road that passes in front of the US ambassador's residence, so it doesn't see a lot of visitors, which is unfortunate because it's quite pretty.

Seoul Municipal Hall

This modernist structure was built in 1935 as a cultural hall. After Liberation, it was home to Korea's first parliament. It is now used as the meeting place of Seoul Municipal Council.

Seoul Anglican Cathedral

This beautiful Romanesque-style granite church, built in 1926, is the mother church of Korea's Anglican faithful. The design also incorporates Korean motifs, especially along the roof. English services are held at 9:30 Sunday morning in the cathedral crypt chapel and at 5:00 Sunday evening in the main cathedral. • **Tel** 739-0785

1 Old Russian Legation 2 Stone wall of Deoksugung Palace 3 Historic Chungdong First Methodist Church

of Seoul Anglican Cathedral

Jungmyeongjeon

Built in 1900, this Russian-designed building was originally part of Deoksugung Palace. Historically, it's quite important as the site for the signing of the Protectorate Treaty in 1905, under which Korea signed away its foreign policy decision-making to Japan. In modern times, it was used as a social club, and it is now being restored for use as a museum.

Ewha Hak Dang

Founded in 1886 by American Methodist Episcopal missionary Mary F. Scranton, Ewha Hak Dang eventually grew into Ewha Middle and High Schools and Ewha Womans University, the world's largest women's university. All that is left of the old school is Simpson Hall (built in 1915), a museum on the campus of Ewha Girls' High School.

Former Russian Legation

As Russia was one of the two imperial powers with the most at stake in Korea (the other being Japan), its legation was a busy place in the years prior to the Russo-Japanese War. Following the assassination of his queen, Empress Myeongseong, Emperor Gojong fled along with the crown prince to the Russian Legation, where they stayed for a full year. Most of the old embassy was burnt down during the Korean War; all that remains is its central tower.

Beautiful Romanesque exterior of Seoul Anglican Cathedral

Non-verbal performance 'Nanta' (Photo courtesy of Nanta)

Performing Arts

• Chongdong Theater B4, p38

Located in Jeong-dong area, the Chongdong Theater is the only theater in Seoul devoted solely to live traditional stage performances. Chongdong Theater has presented a 90-minute traditional performance every day of the year since 1997 in an effort to keep the spirit of Korean traditional performing arts alive in the modern day. The theater's performances focus on the four core genres of Korean traditional music—traditional dance, *pungmul*, *pansori* and musical instruments. These shows are primarily geared towards foreign visitors; all performances are accompanied by English subtitles, and performers are available for pictures in their traditional garments after each performance. Tickets run between 20,000 and 40,000 won. • **Tel** 751-1500 • **Website** www.mct.or.kr

• Nanta Theater B4, p38 / E3, p119 / D3, p248

A unique performance that draws around 300,000 visitors each year, Nanta is a nonverbal performance that combines traditional Korean *samulnori** rhythms with modern music, comedy, martial arts and dance, all in the setting of a kitchen. This high-energy production includes audience participation, for an unpredictable and delightful musical show that can be enjoyed by an international audience. Tickets range from 50,000 won to 60,000 won, with three performances daily. There is another Nanta theater in Gangnam, too • **Tel** 739-8288 • **Website** http://nanta.i-pmc.co.kr

Samulnori

History and Culture

Literally "music of four objects," *samulnori* is a form of percussion music with its roots in the peasants' music of Korea's rural villages. Rice farming was—and, to some extent, still is—a communal activity. To build community spirit and make the drudgery more enjoyable, farmers would form bands to perform a mixture of percussion music, acrobatic dancing and singing called *nongak* (farming music). This music, also frequently called *pungmul*, also served to drive away evil spirits and ensure a bountiful harvest.

In 1978, Kim Duk-soo—a musical prodigy and former member of the famous Korean traveling performance troupe Namsadang—and three other former Namsadang colleagues formed the group SamulNori, which took *nongak*, modified it a bit and put it on stage. The resulting performance sparked a dramatic rebirth of interest in Korean traditional music, both in Korea and overseas. Today, *samulnori* groups exist all over Korea and in countries with large Korean populations. A tireless showman and promoter, Kim himself has worked ceaselessly to promote the Korean traditional performing arts to new audiences.

The instruments used in *samulnori* are the *kkwaenggwari* (a small, hand-held gong), *janggu* (hourglass drum), *buk* (a larger, barrel-shaped drum) and *jing* (a large gong)—the instruments are said to represent the thunder, earth, clouds and wind, respectively. Initially performed as a quartet, *samulnori* bands can now contain up to 30 or more performers.

Kim Duk-soo now runs a regular Korean traditional performing arts program at Gwanghwamun Art Hall (A3, p38) near Sajik Park. The performance, "PAN," (see p426) features a number of Korean performing and dramatic arts, including *samulnori*. For more information, call 722-3416 or visit www.ghmarthall.co.kr.

Kim Duk-soo (second from left) performing *samulnori* with troupe

Stepping stones across Cheonggyecheon Stream, a favorite downtown leisure spot

CITY HALL AREA

The City Hall area, with its mixture of old Korean charm and modern-day energy, is a microcosm of the dynamic contrast between old and new that is Korea. Beautiful and intriguing at any time day or night, this wonderful district is a place where you could spend an entire day wandering around, soaking in history while getting a glimpse of the future.

• **Getting There** City Hall Station, Line 1 or 2

Seoul City Hall & Seoul Plaza C4, p38

The nerve center of one of the world's most dynamic cities, Seoul City Hall is also one of Seoul's most significant pieces of early Western-style architecture. Built in 1926 by the Japanese colonial government, Seoul City Hall is an imposing, almost menacing gray faux-stone building. At the time of the writing of this book, City Hall was undergoing a major renovation, with the old building being included in a massive, new, state-of-the-art City Hall complex (to be completed in 2012).

Seoul Plaza, the large oval-shaped grass park in front of City Hall, has been a favorite leisure spot for Seoul residents since it opened in 2004. In winter, a large outdoor ice rink is set up on the plaza—it's very popular with Korean families and teens. Unfortunately for tourists, but perhaps good for democracy, the plaza is also a favorite location for political demonstrations, most of which are harmless but can be quite noisy.

Bukchang-dong C4, p38

Behind the Seoul Plaza Hotel and across from Seoul Plaza is the neighborhood of Bukchang-dong, known for its vibrant nightlife. If you're looking for a bite to eat, there are tons of places to choose from in the alleys behind the Seoul Plaza Hotel.

Seoul Finance Center & Mugyo-dong C4, p38

As you head towards Gwanghwamun from Seoul City Hall, you'll pass two grand skyscrapers: the Seoul Press Center (home of The Seoul Shinmun newspaper) and the Seoul Finance Center. The Seoul Finance Center, a new 30-story building, is a good place to go for international dining. The first and second floor basements are full of eateries serving up food

WONGUDAN ALTAR C4, p38

Also near Seoul Plaza is the Wongudan Altar, one of Seoul's truly hidden gems. Tucked away in the Westin Chosun Hotel garden, the three-story octagonal shrine, built in 1899, brings to mind the Temple of Heaven in Beijing. Following the proclamation of the Daehan Empire in 1897, Emperor Gwangmu (formerly King Gojong) would visit the altar to pray for a bountiful harvest. The Wongudan cuts a dramatic figure against a backdrop of skyscrapers and electronic signboards.

from all corners of the globe, including Thailand, Vietnam, India, Japan and China. There's also a deli. The restaurants here are very popular with the many diplomats and foreign financial workers who work in the neighborhood.

But for something truly Korean, try Mugyo-dong Octopus Alley. This is home to one of Seoul's most famous dishes, Mugyo-dong pan-fried octopus (*nakji bokkeum*). If you like really spicy food, this is a very good place to start. A two-person serving will run you about 14,000 won. For a bit more, you can enjoy live octopus (*san nakji*)—consuming a still-squirming octopus is a dining experience you're unlikely to forget.

Cheonggyecheon Plaza C4, p38

Cheonggyecheon Plaza marks the head of the Cheonggyecheon Stream, one of Seoul's newest and most talked-about leisure spots. For decades an unsightly elevated highway, the urban waterway was restored and opened to the public in September 2005. The stream runs some 5.8 km and is a popular walking course, with its distinctive bridges and diversity of neighborhoods.

A ROYAL GRUDGE
History and Culture

A short walk from Cheonggyecheon Plaza brings you to the Gwangtonggyo Bridge, the first of the bridges over the Cheonggyecheon Stream. The stone bridge was first built in 1410 by King Taejong (r. 1400-1418). Taejong, who was instrumental in his father's overthrow of the Goryeo Dynasty to found the new dynasty of Joseon in 1392, was an exceptionally energetic and capable ruler who centralized power in the monarchy. He was also one of the most ruthless monarchs in Korean history—to get power, he killed his half-brother (who had been named crown prince), forced one elder brother into exile and intimidated the other into abdicating the throne. One person who was especially deep in Taejong's doghouse was his stepmother, Queen Sindeok, who had promoted the elevation of her own son, Taejo's half-brother, to crown prince. Although the queen died in 1397 and Taejong killed her two sons the following year, Taejong was a man who could hold a grudge. When his father died, Taejong had Queen Sindeok posthumously demoted to royal concubine and raided her tomb for stones to built Gwangtonggyo Bridge so, it is said, people could walk on her tomb stones every day.

Gwangtonggyo was torn down when Cheonggyecheon Stream was covered over, but rebuilt (using some of the original stones) when the stream was restored in 2006.

The plaza is dominated by "Spring," a 20-meter-high blue-and-red sculpture in the shape of a marsh snail by American pop artists Claes Oldenburg and Coosje van Bruggen. Admittedly, it's not for everyone.

There are several ways to get around the Cheonggyecheon. One, of course, is to walk it. Another is to take one of the special double-decker buses (see p367)—there are five tours a day, departing from in front of the Dongwha Duty Free Shop in Gwanghwamun.

Ilmin Museum of Art C4, p38

The Ilmin Museum of Art served as the headquarters of The Dong-A Ilbo newspaper from 1926 to 1992. It is now a contemporary art museum, although it also houses a considerable collection of Korean ceramics, paintings and calligraphy from the Joseon and Goryeo eras. There's a documentary film archive, too. • **Hours** 11 am to 7 pm. Closed Mondays • **Admission** Free • **Tel** 2020-2055

Kyobo Book Centre C3, p38

Korea's largest book store, this monster shop in the basement of the Kyobo Insurance Building has Seoul's largest collection of foreign language books, making it very popular with resident foreigners. It also houses a large stationery store with a wide selection of goods.
• **Hours** 9:30 am to 10 pm • **Tel** 1544-1900

Bigak C3, p38

This monument housed in a Korean-style pavilion, located just in front of the landmark Kyobo Buidling, was built in 1902 to celebrate the 40th anniversary of King Gojong taking the throne.

Bigak

Gwanghwamun Square B3, p38

In August 2009, work was completed on a new square in the heart of the old downtown. Stretching from Gwanghwamun Gate to the Kyobo Building,

TIPS

BOSINGAK

A short walk from Kyobo Book Store in the direction of Jonggak Station (Line 1) brings you to a large, Korean-style belfry. In Joseon times, its bell was rung to announce the daily opening and closing of Seoul's city gates. The evening and morning bells also marked the beginning and end to the nighttime curfew enforced in the royal capital. So central was this bell to city life that the street on which it is located—which was, as it is today, one of Seoul's most important roads—was named "Jongno," or "Bell Street." The current pavilion dates from a post-Korean War reconstruction. In today's Korea, it is most famous for the bell-chiming ceremony held here at midnight of New Year's Eve, when crowds gather here to watch Seoul's mayor and other city notables ring in the new year.

THE RIOT POLICE

History and Culture

Due to Korea's, ahem, vibrant history of student and labor activism, the riot police—or *jeongyeong* ("Battle Police")—can often be found around Gwanghwamun. With their battle gear and Darth Vader-like helmets, they leave a ferocious impression. Riot police frequently face off against student and labor groups in violent but oddly ritualized battles, especially in May, the so-called "protest season."

The ironic thing about the riot police is that unlike other police officers, most are not volunteer professionals—they are young draftees doing their mandatory military service. Accordingly, it's not uncommon for riot officers to face off against their university juniors.

While Korea's protest culture lives on, one thing you won't find any more is tear gas, which used to be a defining feature of Seoul life in the 1980s. This is the result of a deal struck between the police and protesters—the cops would stop using tear gas, and the protesters would stop using Molotov cocktails.

To the riot police's credit, while clashes are frequent, actual deaths are rare.

Gwanghwamun Square is a pedestrian-friendly public space highlighted by two imposing statues of war hero Admiral Yi Sun-sin* (see p107) and King Sejong the Great* (see p409). In summer, the square's water fountain—lit up at night—is a popular retreat, particularly for families.

The square also provides good views of Gwanghwamun Gate, Gyeongbokgung Palace and Mt. Bugaksan.

Sejong Center for the Performing Arts B3, p38

Established in 1978, the Sejong Center has a long history of serving as a hub of performing arts in Seoul. The Center features a wide range of performing arts, including drama, various musical genres and art. The Grand Theater is the cornerstone of the performing arts center—a state-of-the-art performance facility with three tiers, accommodating a maximum of 3,022 patrons. Other facilities include three art galleries, an arts academy, and an art garden.

For up-to-date information on current performances in English, check out the Sejong Center homepage at www.sejongpac.or.kr/english • **Tel** 399-1111

Seoul Museum of History B3, p38

Opened in 2002, this museum presents the history and culture of Seoul from prehistoric times to the modern age. This establishment is considered a museum of the people, as over 70% of the museum's holdings were public donations. Exhibits explore the history of the city, the life of Seoulites throughout history, and the city's cultural heritage. A recently created highlight is a 1:1,500 scale model of the entire city. • **Hours** Weekdays 9 am to 9 pm; Weekends & holidays 9 am to 7 pm (Mar to Oct), 9 am to 6 pm (Nov to Feb) • **Admission** Free • **Tel** 724-0274 • **Website** http://museum.seoul.kr

Gyeonghuigung Palace B3, p38

Built as a secondary palace in 1616, Gyeonghuigung became a royal residence in 1624, when Changdeokgung Palace was set alight as rebels occupied Seoul. Just prior to Japan's annexation of Korea in 1910, however, the palace was completely dismantled to make room for a school.

In 1988, Seoul began to rebuild the old

Passageway, Gyeonghuigung Palace

palace. Many of the major structures have been restored, including the old throne hall and surrounding cloisters. The front gate of the palace, Heunghwamun Gate, is original. • **Admission** Free • **Hours** 9 am to 6 pm (weekdays), 10 am to 6 pm (weekends, holidays). Closed Mondays • **Getting There** Gyeonghuigung Palace is just behind Seoul History Museum, and is a 5 minute walk from exits 1 or 8 of Gwanghwamun Station, Line 5. • **Tel** 724-0274~6

Gyeonggyojang A3, p38

Located on the grounds of Samsung Gangbuk Hospital, this old Western-style home, built in the 1930s for a Korean gold mining magnate, served as the office of Kim Ku, one of Korea's most beloved independence activists who served as the president of Korea's government in exile in China during World War II. He was assassinated on the second floor in 1949 (the bullet holes can still be seen in the window). The second floor has now been turned into a museum.

• **Getting There** See "Taylor House" below.

Taylor House (Dilkusha House) A3, p38

A walk up the hill from the Gyeonggyojang will eventually bring you to a handsome if somewhat rundown red-brick mansion that is now being used by several families as a residence. This house was originally the residence of Albert Taylor, an American correspondent whose father owned a gold mine in what is now North Korea. On its cornerstone is written the word "Dilkusha," the name of an Indian palace Albert's actress wife had visited on tour. Next to the home is a 420-year-old ginkgo tree.

• **Getting There** First walk past Seoul History Museum and Gyeonghuigung Palace (see above) until you reach Gangbuk Samsung Hospital. The Gyeonggyojang is located on the hospital campus. From the hospital, walk to the Hong Nanpa House (there's a street sign marking its direction). From the Hong Nanpa House, follow the road until it reaches its end, where you'll find the Taylor House.

YI SUN-SIN AND THE IMJIN WAR

In Korea's long history, there are few heroes as beloved as Yi Sun-sin (1545-1598), the 16th century admiral lauded as the Lord Nelson of Korea. Showing promise in the military arts from a young age, Yi earned his first battlefield victories with a successful campaign against Manchurian Jurchen raiders in 1580s. It was during the brutal Imjin War of 1592-1598, however, that Yi's brilliance was put on full display.

By the 1590s, the Japanese warlord Hideyoshi Toyotomi had unified Japan and had set his sights on something far grander—the conquest of China. To do this, of course, he first needed passage through Korea. A Japanese request to allow Japanese troops passage through Korea was rejected by the Korean court, who were allies of Ming China. So Japan decided to invade Korea instead.

When Japan's army landed on the Korean shore near today's Busan in May 1592, the differences between the two clashing armies could not be more stark. The massive Japanese invasion force was a competently led professional force containing many battle-hardened veterans of Japan's century of civil war. They were armed with the arquebus, early guns introduced to Japan by the Portuguese and mass-produced by Japanese gunsmiths. The Koreans, on the other hand, had let their undersized, poorly led, poorly trained and poorly armed army languish, ignoring advice by wiser scholars and officials. The result was predictable, but still spectacular—the Japanese invaders made short work of resistance as they rushed up the peninsula. By early June, the royal capital of Seoul had fallen; by July, the Japanese had taken Pyongyang. Things looked bleak for the Koreans.

If the Japanese had a weakness, though, it was that their army was dependent on bases in Japan for supplies and troops. Admiral Yi exploited this weakness to brilliant effect. In a series of naval battles against the Japanese in the waters off Korea's southern coast, Yi shattered several larger Japanese fleets with few losses of his own. In one battle, the Battle of Sachon on May 29, 1592, 26 Korean ships sunk an entire Japanese fleet of 70 ships to the bottom of the sea with no friendly losses. In another battle, the Battle of Hansan Island of Aug 14, 1592, a Japanese fleet of 73 ships—sent from Busan to resupply the Japanese army in northwestern Korea—met Yi's fleet of 56 ships.

Some 47 Japanese ships were destroyed, and 12 captured. Again, Yi lost no ships of his own. Unable to supply his troops by sea, Hideyoshi was forced to give up his ultimate goal of invading China.

TURTLE SHIP

Adding to Yi's brilliance was an innovative new piece of naval technology, the turtle ship, or *geobukseon*. These large, heavily armored ships—designed by Yi himself—may not have been "ironclad," as was until recently claimed, but it did have a fully covered deck designed to deflect enemy fire. The deck was also covered with iron spikes to deter would-be boarding parties—a crucial defense, since boarding enemy ships to engage in hand-to-hand combat was a popular naval tactic of the age. It was armed with 11 cannon—Japanese ships, by contrast, rarely carried cannons—and smoke emitted from the ship's bow helped hide its movements. While it's open to question just how important the ships were in Yi's victories—the fact is, there were never more than a handful of such ships involved in any of his battles—they nevertheless have come to symbolize the admiral's ingenuity.

Geobukseon replica, War Memorial of Korea (See p210)

While the Japanese proved no match for Yi, the Korean royal court was another matter. A clever plot instigated by a Japanese double agent resulted in Yi being arrested for treason in 1597. Relieved of command, he was brutally tortured and would have been executed if not for pleas from his supporters in the royal court. Demoted to the rank of common infantryman, he was placed under the command of another famous military leader, Gen. Kwon Yul, where he carried out his duties faithfully without complaint.

13 vs 333

Between 1594 and 1596, the Koreans, Japanese and Ming Chinese (who had sent an expeditionary force to Korea to battle the Japanese) engaged in negotiations to end the war. For a time, it appeared as if the negotiations might succeed, and the Japanese and Chinese withdrew the bulk of their forces. Unsatisfied, however, Hideyoshi launched a second invasion in 1597, this one limited to conquering Korea only. Outnumbered by the Chinese and Koreans, the Japanese force was bottled up in Korea's southeast, but at sea, the invaders took advantage of Admiral Yi's absence to trounce his successor, the ineffective Admiral Won Gyun. In the Battle of Chilcheollyang, a Japanese armada overwhelmed Won's fleet and destroyed it, effectively leaving Korea without a navy.

Following the disaster, the Korean king pardoned Yi and placed him back in command. The admiral had a tough road ahead of him—the defeat at Chilcheollyang left him with a mere 13 ships. For him, though, 13 ships was enough—in the ensuing Battle of Myeongnyang, Yi's tiny fleet met a Japanese force of 333 ships off the southwestern tip of Korea and absolutely annihilated it, using the local terrain and currents to great effect. Deprived of their supply lines, the Japanese were once again forced to halt their offensive.

In September 1598, a dying Hideyoshi ordered the withdrawal of his army from Korea. In December, Yi fought his final battle against the Japanese, leading an allied Korean-Chinese fleet against a Japanese fleet preparing to withdraw Japanese troops back to Japan. Again, the Japanese were soundly defeated, but this time, Korean victory came at a terrible price—as the Koreans were pursuing the fleeing Japanese, a Japanese arquebusier shot Admiral Yi in the chest. He died a few minutes later, but not before ordering his death be kept a secret from his men. His death in battle has further enhanced his reputation as the "Nelson of the East."

Perhaps the greatest compliment ever paid Yi was, ironically enough, by a Japanese naval hero, Admiral Togo Heihachiro. After shattering the Russian fleet at the Battle of Tsushima (1905) of the Russo-Japanese War, a well-wisher praised him as a "god of war," likening him to Lord Nelson. Togo replied, "I appreciate your compliment. But,... if there ever were an Admiral worthy of the name of 'god of war,' that one is Yi Sun-sin. Next to him, I am little more than a petty officer."

Battle reenactment at Battle of Myeongnyang Festival, held every October in Haenam, Jeollanam-do
(Photo courtesy of South Jeolla Provincial Office)

PLACES TO EAT: GWANGHWAMUN AREA

Near Gwanghwamun & Gyeongbokgung Palace p38

Bärlin The best German restaurant not just in Seoul, but in all of Korea. A very classy place with a distinctively German feel. (T. 722-5622) C3

Top Cloud Located at the top of the distinctive Jongno Tower, this Western restaurant is better known for its outstanding views. (T. 2230-3001) C3

Samcheong-dong & Bukchon p64

There are countless little cafés and eateries in this neighborhood. Some favorites include:

Samcheong-dong Sujebi Great potato noodle soup shop. And always crowded. (T. 735-2965) C1

Nun Namu-jip Famous for its kimchimari guksu noodles and tteokgalbi (minced meat and rice cake). (T. 739-6742) C1

Second Best Place in Seoul An old-style teahouse that is legendary for its patjuk (red bean porridge). (T. 734-5302) C1

Leehaus Some 200 kinds of wine in a relaxing and very-well designed setting. Particularly nice in summer. (T. 730-3009) C1

Slow Garden This airy cafe serves coffee, wine and beer, but is most famous for its waffles. (T. 737-7187) C1

Maple Tree House Delicious meats in a relaxed, wine-bar like atmosphere. (T. 730-7461) C1

Yongsusan Does Kaesong-style Goryeo royal cuisine in a luxurious setting. Highly recommended. (T. 732-3019) C1

Sosonjae Decently priced Korean traditional cuisine made from seasonal berries, fruits and vegetables. (T. 730-7002) C1

Wano Don't let the hanok fool you—this place does stylishly presented Japanese cuisine. (T. 725-7881) C1

Yeon This hanok cafe welcomes travelers, and is a great place for a cup of tea or after-work drink. (T. 734-3009) C2

8 Steps European cuisine in a charming old Korean hanok setting. (T. 738-5838) C2

Cook'n Heim Brings together hamburgers, art and a Korean garden. (T. 733-1109) C2

Romanée Conti A wonderful French restaurant/wine bar in a gorgeous restored *hanok*. Great views over the neighborhood. (T. 722-1633) C2

Chung A bit pricier than your average Chinese restaurant, but in a much classier setting. (T. 720-3396) B2

Cave de La Petite France Good French cuisine and French wine in a cozy, exotic atmosphere. (T. 739-1788) B2

Hwangsaengga Kalguksu Handmade Korean noodles and dumplings. Extremely popular, especially at lunch time. (T. 739-6334) B3

Bukchon Naengmyeon Located in the lovely Bukchon neighborhood, Bukchon does some of the best Pyongyang-style *naengmyeon* (cold wheat noodles) in Seoul. (T. 720-7110) B3

Bukchon Gamasot Seolleongtang Not far from Bukchon's Jeongdok Public Library, this place specializes in *seolleongtang*, a cloudy soup made from ox bone. (T. 725-7355) B3

Ramyeon Ttaengineun Nal Wildly popular, this cheap ramyeon noodle restaurant is near Jeongdok Public Library. (T. 733-3330) B3

Gyedong Mananim MSG-free Korean cuisine with assorted vegetables and herbs marinated in soy sauce. (T. 722-2337) B3

Coffee Factory Terrific coffee house with a great atmosphere, very good cakes and waffles, and excellent coffee. (T. 722-6169) B3

Dalhangari While the interior might seem rather café-esque, this Samcheong-dong restaurant does organic Korean course cuisine (*jeongsik*) that is both tasty and good for you. (T. 733-7902) B2

Big Giwa House Also near Jeongdok Library, this place specializes in raw crab preserved in soy sauce. (T. 722-9024) B3

Insa-dong p76

You could get lost in the vast number of restaurants in the alleys here. Vegetarians will be pleased to know there are a couple of vegetarian restaurants (not especially common in Korea) in the area. This is also a good place to sample Korean traditional alcohol, particularly the rice beer of *makkeolli*.

Min's Club Located in a beautiful hanok near Cheondogyo Central Temple, this place does fusion cuisine in an early 20th century setting. (T. 733-2966) C2

Jirisan An attractive Korean restaurant serving Korean table d'hote cuisine. (T. 723-4696) C1

Sanchon Run by a former Buddhist monk, Sanchon is one of Seoul's best-known restaurants and specializes in vegetarian Buddhist temple cuisine. Music and dance performances take place in the evenings. Lunch: 22,000 won. Dinner: 39,600 won. Folk performances—8 to 8:40 pm. Hours: 11:30 am to 10 pm. (T. 735-0312) C2

Osegyehyang Specializing in vegetarian cuisine, this restaurant serves a variety of tasty Korean and Chinese dishes sans meat. Quite yummy, but no booze—the place is run by followers of the Quan Yin Method. Hours: noon to 9 pm. (T. 735-7171) B2

Toetmaru Most famous for its barley-rice *bibimbap*, a mixture of barley and rice covered with soybean paste stew, and crab marinated in soy sauce. Reasonably priced, too. (T. 739-5683) C2

MYEONG-DONG AREA

THINGS TO DO AND SEE

- Do some serious shopping in Myeong-dong's department stores and brand-name shops.

- Wander around the massive Namdaemun Market, Seoul's most famous traditional market, where you can find just about anything under the sun. Try the spicy hairtail stew, a market specialty.

- Appreciate the beauty of Myeong-dong's colonial era architecture.

Myeong-dong is often compared to Tokyo's Shinjuku district, and for good reason. It's a neighborhood of bright lights, surging crowds, exciting nightlife and infinite energy. The central commercial district of Seoul, Myeong-dong is primarily known as a shopping district—it is home to a number of department stores, brand-name outlets and mid-range shops. If entertainment is what you're after, you can find that in abundance, too, in the district's restaurants and bars. It's not without its history, though—some of Seoul's best examples of historic architecture, such as the Bank of Korea Museum and Myeong-dong Cathedral, can be found along its streets. It's even got the closest thing Seoul can claim to a Chinatown.

Near Myeong-dong is the bustling Namdaemun Market, Seoul's most famous outdoor market and one of the city's most popular tourist destinations. Here, you'll find almost everything under the sun, including clothing, ginseng, eyeglasses and curios. Also nearby is Seoul Station, one of the world's busiest train stations and the main point of transit to the rest of Korea.

Fountain lit up in its holiday best
at Myeong-dong Intersection

Neon signs aplenty in Myeong-dong

MYEONG-DONG

Myeong-dong is, above all else, a shopping district, and most of the people who visit do so either to drop money or watch other people drop money.

As one of the city's chief fashion centers and a popular nightlife spot, Myeong-dong tends to attract a younger crowd (and a significant number of Japanese tourists). Stores are in the mid- to high price range, with a large number of major international brand outlets as well. And then there are the department stores, including the landmark Migliore, Lotte and Shinsegae.

General Layout

Myeong-dong has a single "main drag," so to speak, where you'll find many of your high-end brand-name shops. The alleyways, meanwhile, are where you'll find mid-range and cheaper brands. Several of the department stores are located just outside the main area.

Shopping Highlights

Myeong-dong Migliore F4

This department store at the entrance of Myeong-dong's main street contains about 1,000 shops specializing in clothing and accessories. • Hours 11 am to 11:30 pm. Closed Mondays • Tel 2124-0001

Lotte Department Store D2

The Myeong-dong branch of the Korean-Japanese shopping giant. If you're going really upscale, check out Lotte Avenue L next door. • Hours 10:30 am to 8 pm • Tel 771-2500

Lotte Young Plaza D3

This department store, which specializes in ladies apparel, caters to younger women. • Hours 11:30 am to 9:30 pm • Tel 771-2500

> **GETTING THERE**
> The Myeong-dong area can be reached via Myeong-dong Station, Line 4 or Euljiro 1(il)-ga Station, Line 2.

Shinsegae Department Store C4

Seoul's oldest department store comprises a historic "old store" and a large, newly built "new store" next door. • Hours 10:30 am to 8 pm • Tel 1588-1234

Noon Square D3

Formerly the Avatar mall, Noon Square is full of fashion distributors like Mango, Steve Madden, H&M, UGG, Level 5, Foot Locker and Zara. • Hours 10 am to 11 pm • Tel 3783-5005

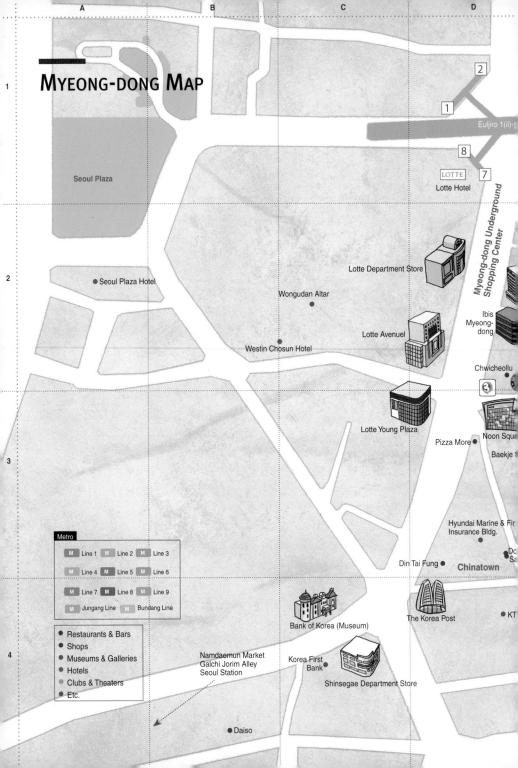

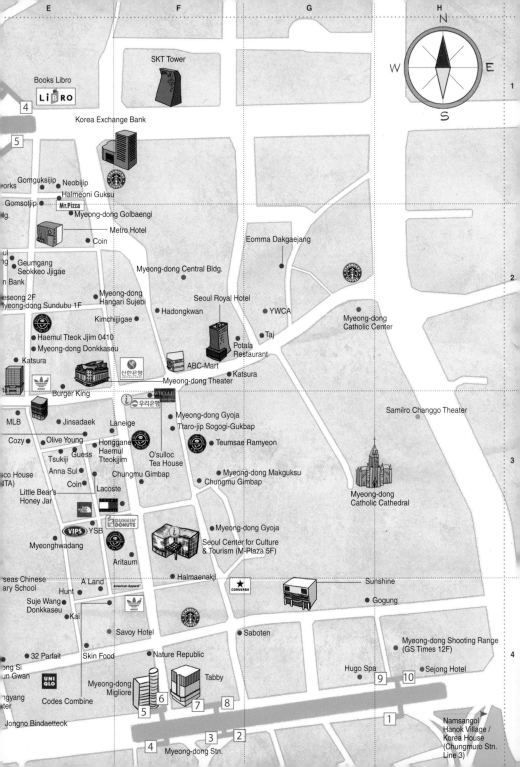

Colonial Architecture of Myeong-dong

While it may not rival the Bund of Shanghai, Myeong-dong is one of Seoul's treasure troves of colonial-era architecture. Myeong-dong began its life as a commercial hub in the 1930s, when Japanese colonists turned it into their primary shopping and business district. Much of the neighborhood's older architecture was lost due to war and breakneck economic development and construction, but beneath the glitter and lights, there are a few stately monuments to the district's history.

Bank of Korea Museum C4

Located at Myeong-dong Intersection, this castle-like neo-Renaissance building, completed in 1912, first served as the headquarters of the Bank of Choson, the central bank of Japan's Korean colony. The building was designed by pioneering Japanese architect Tatsuno Kinko, who also designed Tokyo Station and the Bank of Japan. Today, it serves as a museum to Korea's banking history. • **Hours** 10 am to 5 pm. Closed Mondays • **Tel** 759-4881

Korea First Bank C4

Originally the Choson Savings Bank, this imposing neoclassical office across from the Bank of Korea Building was completed in 1933. Now used as a branch of Standard Chartered First Bank Korea.

Shinsegae Department Store C4

Formerly the Mitsukoshi Department Store and completed in 1930, the recently restored Shinsegae Department Store next to Korea First Bank is the last of Seoul's colonial era department stores.

KEPCO Building D2

A little way up the road from Myeong-dong Intersection and across from the Lotte Department Store is the KEPCO Building, an office of the Korean power company. Built for the Japanese-owned Keijo Electric Company in 1928, it was the first building in Korea that incorporated earthquake-proof and fire-proof designs.

Former National Theater of Korea E2

The Baroque-style former National Theater of Korea was built in 1934 as a movie theater. After Liberation, it was used as the National Theater of Korea

1 Decorative ironwork on the door of the old Korea First Bank 2 Renaissance-style Bank of Korea, completed in 1912 3 Myeong-dong Lotte Department Store 4 Grand Gothic interior of Myeong-dong Cathedral

Myeong-dong Intersection at night

until the 1970s. It has now been renovated as Myeong-dong Theater, a state-of-the-art performing arts and culture center.

Myeong-dong Cathedral G3

Arguably Korea's most beautiful piece of non-Buddhist religious architecture, Myeong-dong Cathedral is the spiritual center of Korea's Catholic community and a fortress in Korea's democratization movement.

Designed by French missionary priests and built by Chinese masons, the cathedral was completed in 1898. It is a Gothic masterpiece, built of locally produced red and black brick and featuring a high vaulted ceiling. There's a crypt chapel, too, containing the relics of several martyrs. A number of the auxiliary buildings are nearing or over 100 years of age, too.

In addition to being a house of worship, the cathedral has played a major role in Korea's political and social history. In the 1980s, when Korea was ruled by a military dictatorship, pro-democracy demonstrators took refuge in the church, which the police were reluctant to storm. Even today, social activists, including labor activists and migrant laborers, can often be seen in front of the church, demonstrating in support of their various causes.

• **Hours** English masses are held at 9 am on Sundays. • **Tel** 774-1784

Myeong-dong Chinatown D3

The closest thing Seoul has to a true Chinatown is located just behind the massive Seoul Post Tower, near the old Chinese Embassy and the century-old Hansung Chinese Elementary School. Basically, it consists of two alleys of Chinese restaurants and bookshops. If you're in the mood for a Chinese mooncake, there's a bakery here selling them, so enjoy.

MYEONG-DONG HISTORY

History and Culture

Myeong-dong began its life as a quiet residential village in the Joseon era. With the coming of the Japanese in the early 20th century, however, the neighborhood was transformed into the colonialists' primary commercial district. It was at this time that much of the neighborhood's historic architecture was constructed.

The Korean War left much of Myeong-dong in ruins. When it was rebuilt in the late 1950s, many bookshops and tea houses opened up in the area, in large part thanks to the presence of the National Theater, which attracted Seoul's artistic and cultural elite. The National Theater would eventually move, and Myeong-dong's reign as Seoul's cultural heart passed, but soon enough, upper-end shops began moving into the area, and with them Seoul's fashion mecca was born.

Today, Myeong-dong is Seoul's commercial and financial hub, home to many large banks and brokerage companies, business headquarters and, of course, shops, eateries and drinking establishments.

Gate to sprawling Namdaemun Market

NAMDAEMUN AREA

The Namdaemun area, so named for the Namdaemun Gate, is the home of Seoul's most famous outdoor market, Namdaemun Market. This colorful market, spread out over several blocks, attracts visitors from far and wide with its energy, great deals and exotic charm. Traders flock to it to buy goods wholesale for resale in their home cities and nations.

Also in the Namdaemun area are several sites of historic interest, including Sungnyemun Gate (now under reconstruction after a 2008 fire), Seoul Station and Yakhyeon Catholic Church.

Namdaemun Market

Namdaemun Market has a history that goes back 500 years to the start of the Joseon era, when merchants set up shop just outside the city walls near the current location of the market. The current market dates from 1922 and is, along with Dongdaemun Market, one of Seoul's two largest markets.

The market has over 10,000 shops, both large and small. It's most known for clothing, agricultural goods, everyday goods, foodstuffs and medical supplies, although these are but a few of the things that can be found. Foreign tourists find the ginseng products, seaweed and curios to be of particular interest, but even if you're not buying anything, it's great just to stroll around and take in the market atmosphere, with vendors hawking their wares and customers engaging in serious haggling. You might also want to check out the so-called *dokkaebi* market* (see p128) while you're here, too.

Layout and Hours

Namdaemun Market is a pretty sprawling place ringed by eight entry gates. As in many Korean shopping districts, shops tend to congregate by kind, so clothing shops will be gathered in one spot, eyeglass shops in another, fabric shops in another, and so on. Be sure to consult the map on p126.

The market is open both day and night. Shop hours differ from place to place, but the thing to remember is that the wholesalers operate primarily at night. Sunday is probably not the best day to go, but many shops are open nonetheless.

Shopping Highlights

Sungnyemun Imported Goods Arcade

Located near Gate 1, this underground shopping arcade is chock-full of imported goods like clothing, food and electronics. If you're looking for imported booze, this isn't a bad place to visit.

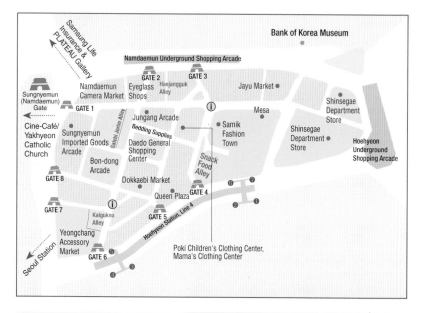

Bank of Korea Museum

Namdaemun Underground Shopping Arcade

GATE 2   GATE 3

Samsung Life Insurance & PLATEAU Gallery

Namdaemun   Eyeglass   Haejangguk   Jayu Market
Camera Market   Shops   Alley

Sungnyemun (Namdaemun) Gate   GATE 1   Mesa   Shinsegae Department Store

Cine-Café/   Jungang Arcade
Yakhyeon   Sungnyemun   Samik   Shinsegae
Catholic   Imported Goods   Bedding Supplies Fashion   Department   Hoehyeon
Church   Arcade   Daedo General   Town   Store   Underground
                              Shopping   Shopping Arcade
             Bon-dong   Center   Snack
             Arcade   Food
                                                Alley
GATE 8   Dokkaebi Market

                              Queen Plaza   GATE 4

GATE 7
             Kalguksu
             Alley   GATE 5

Yeongchang
Accessory
Market   GATE 6   Poki Children's Clothing Center,
                             Mama's Clothing Center

Seoul Station

Galbol Jorim Alley

Hoehyeon Station, Line 4

Bon-dong Arcade

Lots of discount women's clothing stores, along with shops selling foodstuffs like ginseng and seaweed.

Jungang Arcade

Clothing, cosmetics, electronics, dry goods, folk crafts and handicrafts, mostly sold wholesale. This is also a great place to pick up kitchenware and Korean traditional clothing.

Daedo General Shopping Center

Kitchenware, decorative goods, men's accessories like Zippo lighters, and more.

Jayu Market

More bag shops than you can shake a stick at.

Clothing shop / Namdaemun Camera Market

Yeongchang Accessory Market

If you're looking for an accessory—any accessory—you can find it here.

Queen Plaza

Women's clothing, women's clothing and more women's clothing.

Poki Children's Clothing Center, Mama's Clothing Center

If you've got kids, this is the place to get them clothed.

Samik Fashion Town

A combination market/department store for fashion

Mesa

A shopping mall for men's and women's fashions. • **Tel** 2128-5000

Dokkaebi Market

Underneath the Namdaemun market is another shopping area with a ton of goods, including imported foods and liquors. The entrance is near the Namdaemun Gate.

Namdaemun Camera Market

Along the edge of the market nearest Sungnyemun Gate is a collection of camera shops. This is the best place in Seoul to pick up camera equipment, including used supplies.

GETTING TO NAMDAEMUN AREA

Namdaemun Market is best approached via Hoehyeon Station, Line 4. Seoul Station and Yakhyeon Catholic Church, meanwhile, are reached via City Hall Station, Line 1 and 2.

TIPS

HAGGLING

Unlike in the big department stores and brand-name shops of Myeong-dong, haggling and bargaining is a perfectly accepted means of doing business in Namdaemun. In fact, it's encouraged. You'll also want to check the quality of the goods you purchase to ensure you're getting your money's worth.

CHECK THE QUALITY!

Namdaemun sells a lot of low-cost stuff, which is nice, but you need to check the quality first, lest you spend your hard-earned won on complete garbage.

EYEGLASSES

The Namdaemun area is famous for its large number of eyeglass shops that produce high-quality and fashionable eyewear for much less than you'd probably pay at home. If you've been looking to buy new glasses or contacts, this is the place to do it. See the map for location.

GALCHI JORIM

In the bowels of Namdaemun Market is an alley of restaurants specializing in *galchi jorim*, a cheap, spicy stew of boiled hairtail fish and radish. It's a local specialty, and particularly nice with a bowl of milky Korean rice wine, or *makgeolli*. The most popular restaurant for this dish is Hee-rak (T. 755-3449).

Sites of Interest

Sungnyemun Gate

Prior to a fire in February 2008, the Sungnyemun Gate—or Namdaemun (Great South Gate)—was the oldest building in Seoul and one of the city's most recognizable landmarks. The fire—an incomprehensible act of arson—destroyed the gate's wooden superstructure and left a nation in tears. Now undergoing reconstruction, the gate will be restored to its previous glory by 2013.

PLATEAU

Just across the street from the Sungnyemun Gate and in front of the landmark Samsung Life Insurance Building is the gallery PLATEAU, the permanent home to two of Rodin sculptures, the Gates of Hell and the Burghers of Calais. It also hosts regular exhibits of Korean and international modern art. • **Hours** 10 am to 6 pm. Closed Mondays • **Entry** 3,000 won • **Tel** 1577-7595

Seoul Station

Seoul Station is one of the world's busiest train stations, and one of Seoul's primary transportation links with the rest of the country. This is where you'd catch trains—including the high-speed KTX—to Daejeon, Daegu, Busan and other destinations in southeast Korea. The station also comes equipped with a

DOKKAEBI? DOKKAEBI MARKET?

History and Culture

The *dokkaebi* is one of the most popular of Korean cultural motifs, found in countless myths, folk paintings and temple murals. A Korean goblin or troll, the *dokkaebi* is the transformed spirit of inanimate objects—often discarded home objects like brooms and fireplace pokers. Something of a lovable if mischievous rogue, the *dokkaebi* enjoys playing tricks on the wicked and rewarding the virtuous. They're also keen to challenge wayward travelers to roadside matches of Korean wrestling, or *ssireum*, for right of passage. They tend to live in caves, abandoned homes, old trees and deep valleys, and come out at night. Interestingly enough, *dokkaebi* traditionally have only one leg.

In lore, the *dokkaebi* usually carries a large club—he can use this club to grant you any object you wish. Be warned, however: whatever you receive has been stolen from someone else, as the club can summon only objects that currently exist.

Dokkaebi Markets, on the other hand, are open air flea markets—they usually specialize in used goods, although smuggled goods (often from US military bases) can frequently be found, too. People will offer varying explanations of the market's name, but in fact, it's a mispronunciation of the correct name for such markets—*dottegi* market, which means "market where you can get anything."

shopping center.

Prior to the completion of the new steel-and-glass station, the city was served by the old Seoul Station, the pretty, Renaissance-style brick building with the Byzantine dome next to the new station. Now a protected landmark, the old station was completed in 1925 and designed by Tokyo Imperial University professor Tsukamoto Yasushi. He

Renaissance-style Seoul Station, one of the most impressive colonial-era buildings in Seoul

modeled his design on Tokyo Station, which is said to be modeled on Amsterdam Centraal station. The interior of the building is now being renovated for use as a cultural center.

Yakhyeon Catholic Church

Yakhyeon Catholic Church, located on a hill overlooking the Namdaemun area, was Korea's first Western-style Catholic Church, completed in 1892. The church, built of red and black brick, was designed by French missionary Father Eugene-Jean Georges Coste in Gothic and Romanesque styles. This style would, in turn, become the model for many of Korea's early churches. It's a beautiful little spot with a terrific view.

French-built Yakhyeon Catholic Church, Korea's oldest Western-style church

PLACES TO EAT: MYEONG-DONG AREA

Myeong-dong is one of Korea's biggest entertainment areas, full of restaurants, bars and clubs. Some highlights include: p118

Gogung The Myeong-dong branch of the legendary Jeonju *bibimbap* restaurant. If you want to try this typically Korean dish, try it here. (T. 776-3211) G4

Yeongyang Center Myeong-dong's oldest restaurant keeps it simple—roasted chicken and *samgyetang*, or chicken ginseng soup. (T. 776-2015) E4

Myeong-dong Donkkaseu A well-known specialist in the fine art of Japanese-style pork cutlets. (T. 776-5300) E2

Ttaro-jip Sogogi-Gukbap *Gukbap*, literally "soup rice," is a bowl of rice served with a beef-broth soup, usually served with clots of beef blood (actually, quite yummy). In winter, this is a perfect tummy-warmer. (T. 776-2455) F3

Potala Restaurant Run by a 10-year Tibetan resident of Korea, this restaurant near Myeong-dong Cathedral does wonderful Tibetan and Nepali food and drink, including a variety of Tibetan dumplings, Tibetan butter tea and Tibetan booze. (T. 070-8112-8848) F2

Halmeoni Guksu Another ancient Myeong-dong restaurant, dating back to 1958. They specialize in Korean noodles. (T. 778-2705) E1

Chungmu Gimbap Cheap-but-filling Chungmu *gimbap* (small rice and seaweed rolls served with sliced spicy squid) and *tteokbokki* (spicy ricecakes). (T. 755-8488) F3

Myeong-dong Gyoja A Myeong-dong institution that has been serving up great food since 1969. Specializes in *guksu*, noodles and *mandu*, Korean-style dumplings. (T. 776-5348) F3

Din Tai Fung The Myeong-dong branch of the famous Taiwanese dumpling chain. (T. 771-2778) D3

Woo Rae Oak This 50-year-old establishment near Euljiro 4-ga (not far from Myeong-dong) has a reputation for two things: being pricey and serving very, very good food. It's most famous for its Pyongyang-style *naengmyeon* (cold wheat noodles), which are said to rival those of Pyongyang itself, but its meat dishes are absolutely heavenly. If you're willing to part with a bit of cash, you won't be disappointed. (T. 2265-0151) A3, p158

Dohyangchon Located in Myeong-dong's Chinatown, this small bakery is famous for its mooncakes and other Chinese cakes and cookies. (T. 776-5671) D3

Baekje Samgyetang This Myeong-dong eatery has been around for about 40 years, and specializes in *samgyetang* (Korean ginseng chicken soup), a summertime favorite. (T. 776-2851) E3

Myeonghwadang: A 30-year-old Myeong-dong institution, this little place is famous for its cheap *mandu* (dumplings), *tteokbokki* (spicy rice cakes), *gimbap* (rice rolls) and *kalguksu* noodles, served in a tin pot. (T. 777-7317) E3

Jinsadaek: This eatery blends its classic Korean interior with good southwestern Korean cooking. Most of the dishes are foreigner friendly, but if you were hoping to try the notorious *hongeohoe* (see p389), this is a good place to do it. (T. 774-9605) E3

Saemaeul Sikdang: A franchise, this meat restaurant specializes in briquette-cooked *bulgogi*—thin slices of pork bathed in a tangy red pepper sauce. They also do a good *kimchi* and pork stew. (T. 777-7008) E2

Honggane Haemul Tteokjjim: Seafood, noodles and rice cakes, cooked in a spicy pepper sauce. Yum, yum, yum. (T. 318-0131) E3

Hadongkwan: This place has been doing *gomtang*, a rich beef soup, for some 60 years. Dump your rice into the soup for added taste. (T. 776-6565) F2

Bella Coolla 63: The New York-style Italian restaurant of Chungmuro's Astoria Hotel is a pleasant place with a classic atmosphere (the building dates from 1959) and terrific food. Give the prawn ravioli a try. Brunch served, too. (T. 2275-7473) D4, p38

Korea House: Located on the foot of Mt. Namsan near Chungmuro Station, this beautiful complex of Korean traditional halls—formerly used as a state guest house—not only serves Korean palace cuisine, but also puts on cultural performances. See p319. (T. 2266-9101) p316

O'sulloc Tea House: With a design as clean and fresh as the green tea it serves, this modern teahouse serves tea, cake and ice cream made from green tea cultivated on Korea's southern island of Jeju-do. (T. 774-5460) F3

Chwicheollu: A small, simple, restaurant, this place serves only dumplings—and only three kinds at that—but it has been doing so for over 60 years. (T. 776-9358) D2

Katsura: This very popular Japanese restaurant serves up fried Japanese goodies in the afternoon and sashimi and sake at night. Pretty cheap for a Japanese restaurant, too. (T. 779-3690) E2, F2

Myeong-dong Golbaengi: Another old, Myeong-dong institution, this pub serves *golbaengi muchim* (a seafood salad made of sea snails and shredded vegetables with a spicy red pepper sauce), which makes a perfect accompaniment for beer or *soju*. (T. 778-1659) E2

Sandong Gyoja: Cozy and charmingly humble, this Chinatown restaurant does all the Chinese standards (see p391), but it is truly famous for its dumplings and, above all, its *ohyang jangyuk*, marinated slices of steamed pork with five flavors. Enjoy it with a bottle of *goryangju* (Chinese: *kaoliang*), a strong Chinese spirit made from sorghum. (T. 778-4150) D3

SEONGBUK-DONG AREA

THINGS TO DO AND SEE

- Visit the Seongnagwon, one of Seoul's best Korean traditional gardens

- Check out the priceless pieces of art at Gansong Art Museum

- Walk along some of Seoul's old fortress walls

- Enjoy a cup of coffee in Pyeongchang-dong, one of Seoul's most relaxing neighborhoods

- Have dinner at Seokparang, one of the city's best Korean restaurants and a wonderful piece of Joseon-era architecture

Pleasure Gardens in the Hillsides

Located to the north of the main downtown area, Seongbuk-dong and the surrounding areas are a world away from the pulsating streets of Gwanghwamun and Myeong-dong. Instead, here in the hills at the foot of Mt. Bukhansan, you find peaceful, affluent communities that blend with the greenery and mountainsides. It is, in fact, a favored residential location among Seoul's diplomatic community. The area is so tranquil, in fact, that it's almost as if you're not even in Seoul.

It is also an area full of culture, with art galleries, museums, Buddhist temples and Korean gardens. One of Seoul's finest collections of art, the Gansong Art Museum, is located here—it's definitely worth the visit when it's open in March and October. Compared with other areas of the city, it is blissfully devoid of tourists, so if you like to take in your sites in peace, this is probably your place.

Art For Life →

Beautiful Korean traditional halls of Samcheonggak

Spring blossoms at Samcheonggak

SEONGBUK-DONG

Seongbuk-dong is a relaxing neighborhood of Korean gardens and historic Korean homes. As an added bonus, if you're visiting in May or October, it's also home to one of Korea's best museums, the Gansong Museum of Art. Most of the primary sites are within easy walking distance of one another, although Samcheonggak and Gilsangsa Temple (see p139) are a bit out of the way and may require a cab ride.

Seongnagwon Garden C3

While almost every visitor to Seoul goes to Changdeokgung Palace's Huwon Garden (and with good reason), few if any come to the Seongnagwon, which, like its more famous palace cousin, is an outstanding example of Korean traditional gardening. In fact, even many locals are unaware of its existence. This is a great pity, since Seongnagwon is one of the city's most beautiful, most tranquil locations.

Seongnagwon Garden was originally a villa used by Sim Sang-eung, a high-ranking official under King Cheoljong (r. 1849-1863). Later, it was used as a detached palace by Yi Gang, or Prince Imperial Ui, the fifth son of King Gojong. In fact, it was here that Yi Gang died in 1955.

The garden is divided into three sections—an entrance, an inner garden (where the main villa buildings are located) and a rear garden. All three areas are distinct and equally enjoyable. The rear garden, in particular, has a wonderful pond overlooked by a grand wooden pavilion. Here, there is nothing to disturb your peace of mind other than the chirping of the birds and the sounds of running water.

Note: The garden is currently closed while it undergoes a major restoration (completion date unknown).

• **Hours** Closed Sundays • **Getting There** Getting to Seongnagwon Garden is a bit tricky. The easiest way is to take a taxi from Exit 6 of Hansung University Station, Line 4. • **Tel** 920-3412

Choi Sunu's Old Home C3

Not far from Seongnagwon is the former home of the late Choi Sunu, a renowned Korean art historian and director general of the National Museum of Korea. His wonderful *hanok* home has now been opened to the public as part of the National

Inner garden, Choi Sunu's Old House

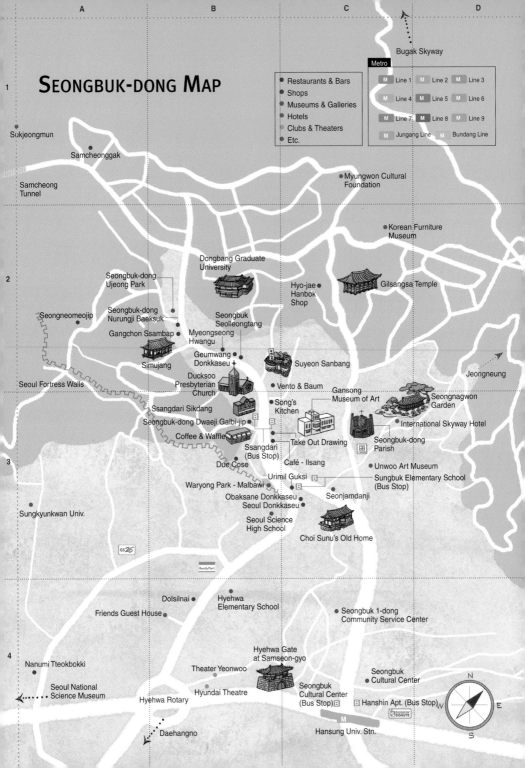

SEONGBUK-DONG MAP

Bugak Skyway

Metro

M Line 1	M Line 2	M Line 3
M Line 4	M Line 5	M Line 6
M Line 7	M Line 8	M Line 9
M Jungang Line	M Bundang Line

- Restaurants & Bars
- Shops
- Museums & Galleries
- Hotels
- Clubs & Theaters
- Etc.

Sukjeongmun

Samcheonggak

Samcheong Tunnel

Myungwon Cultural Foundation

Korean Furniture Museum

Dongbang Graduate University

Seongbuk-dong Ujeong Park

Hyo-jae Hanbok Shop

Gilsangsa Temple

Seongbuk-dong Nurungji Baeksuk

Seongbuk Seolleongtang

Seongneomeojip

Gangchon Ssambap

Myeongseong Hwangu

Simujang

Geumwang Donkkaseu

Suyeon Sanbang

Jeongneung

Seoul Fortress Walls

Ducksoo Presbyterian Church

Vento & Baum

Gansong Museum of Art

Seongnagwon Garden

Song's Kitchen

International Skyway Hotel

Ssangdari Sikdang

Seongbuk-dong Dwaeji Galbi-jip

Coffee & Waffle

Take Out Drawing

Seongbuk-dong Parish

Ssangdari (Bus Stop)

Café - Ilsang

Due Cose

Unwoo Art Museum

Urimil Guksi

Sungbuk Elementary School (Bus Stop)

Sungkyunkwan Univ.

Waryong Park - Malbawi

Obaksane Donkkaseu
Seoul Donkkaseu

Seonjamdanji

Seoul Science High School

Choi Sunu's Old Home

GS25

FamilyMart

Dolsilnai

Hyehwa Elementary School

Friends Guest House

Seongbuk 1-dong Community Service Center

Nanumi Tteokbokki

Hyehwa Gate at Samseon-gyo

Theater Yeonwoo

Seongbuk Cultural Center

Seoul National Science Museum

Hyundai Theatre

Seongbuk Cultural Center (Bus Stop)

Hanshin Apt. (Bus Stop)

Hyehwa Rotary

Hansung Univ. Stn.

Daehangno

Trust of Korea (www.nationaltrust.or.kr), a civic group modeled on its English counterpart and dedicated to preserving Korea's historical and natural heritage. The home, which was built in the 1930s, has a lovely inner courtyard that is especially nice in spring and fall. It is a perfect example of the adaptation of *hanok* architecture to 20th century living.

> • **Hours** 10 am to 4 pm (Apr to Nov), closed from Dec to Mar. Ticketing closes at 3:30 pm. Closed Mondays & Sundays • **Admission** Free • **Getting There** Just a short walk from Seongnagwon Garden (see above) • **Tel** 3675-3401

Samcheonggak A1

Hidden in the hills overlooking Samcheong-dong is Samcheonggak, a beautiful Korean garden/cultural center built initially as a venue for the inter-Korean Red Cross talks of 1972. Throughout the 70s, it was one of Seoul's three most famous restaurants, and served as an exclusive entertainment venue for high-ranking officials and politicians, who came to wine, dine

> **TEA ON THE TERRACE**
> When you're at Samcheonggak, sit on the outdoor terrace and order a cup of coffee or tea—the views of the city and mountainsides are worth it.

and be merry with comely female entertainers or *gisaeng** (similar to Japanese geisha, see p141).

In the 1980s and 1990s, its star began to wane, and it eventually closed down. In 2000, however, it was purchased by Seoul Metropolitan Government and completely restored. It is now operated by the Sejong Center for the Performing Arts and open to the public.

The site now contains a pricey Korean restaurant and a tea house. For visitors, it offers beautiful views of the surrounding mountains, and the gardens and Korean traditional halls make for a relaxing stroll far from the hustle and bustle of downtown Seoul. Spring is a particularly nice time to visit, when the flowers—and the cherry blossoms, especially—are in full bloom.

> • **Hours** Open 24 hours • **Admission** Free • **Getting There** The easiest way to get to Samcheonggak is to take a 10-minute taxi ride from Gwanghwamun Station, Line 5 or Gyeongbokgung Station, Line 3. • **Tel** 765-3700 • **Website** www.samcheonggak.or.kr

Gilsangsa Temple C2

Gilsangsa Temple is an oasis of Zen tranquility in the heart of the city. It likes to think of itself as surrounded by, but not a part of, the secular world, and visitors are likely to agree.

As far as temples go, Gilsangsa has a very short history, having been founded only in 1997. That said, the background to its founding is rather interesting. The site where the temple now sits was originally one of Seoul's three greatest Korean restaurants, the Daewongak. Like Samcheonggak, the Daewongak was an elite restaurant and *gisaeng* house remotely located in the hills overlooking Seoul, far from prying eyes. In 1987, however, the owner of the restaurant—a former *gisaeng* herself then residing in Los Angeles—donated it and its considerable real estate to a famous Buddhist monk so that it might be converted into a Buddhist temple, which it duly was.

Much of the temple is spread throughout a densely forested mountain valley that is beautiful every season of the year. Its remote location makes it an ideal place for the practice of Zen—the temple's meditation hall, the House of Silence, is open every day from 10 am to 5 pm. The temple also has a tea house and benches where you can take a break from the weary world. If you'd like to engage in some serious meditation, however, the temple has a temple stay program on the fourth Saturday and Sunday of the month—call them up for more details. • **Admission** Free

TIPS

LOOKING FOR GIFT IDEAS?
Just across from Gilsangsa is Hyojae C2, a shop run by Lee Hyojae, *hanbok* (Korean clothing) and Korean fabric designer. In addition to clothing, you'll find *bojagi* (Korean wrapping cloths), tea mats, cushions, table clothes and a wide variety of other goods designed by Lee herself. Give it a look. (T. 720-5393)

• **Getting There** Buses for Gilsangsa depart from the Dongwon Mart some 30 meters past the bus No. 1111 stop near Exit 6 of Hansung University Station, Line 4. Buses leave at 8:30, 9:20, 9:40, 10 am, noon, 1, 3 and 4:30 pm. • **Tel** 3672-5945~6
• **Website** www.kilsangsa.or.kr

Simujang B2

This simple *hanok* home was the residence of Buddhist monk, poet and independence activist "Manhae" Han Yong-un. Built in 1933, it is quite unique in that unlike most *hanok* homes, which face south, this one faces north. The reason for this is simple, actually—Han did not want his house to face the Government-General building, the nerve center of the Japanese colonial administration.

Han, who dedicated his entire life to Korean independence, unfortunately didn't live long enough to see it: he died at Simujang in 1944. After his death, his daughter, the famous Korean dancer Han Yeong-suk, lived here until the Japanese ambassador moved in across the street, after which she moved to a different part of the city. The building is now used as a memorial.

Suyeon Sanbang C2

A wonderfully atmospheric teahouse, Suyeon Sanbang is truly a hidden gem. Built in the 1930s, this *hanok* was the home of Korean novelist Lee Tae-jun. His granddaughter converted his home into a Korean traditional teahouse, and so it

GISAENG: SPEAKING FLOWERS

Perhaps no figure from Korea's past has been so romanticized as the *gisaeng*, the female courtesans of the Joseon era. Somewhat similar to the more famous *geisha* tradition of Japan, these remarkable women entertained wealthy and powerful men—in order to do this, they were trained in such arts as dance, music and poetry. Among the most educated and cultured women of their age, some even became noted poets and artists in their own right. They were also called *hae'eohwa*, which means "flowers that can understand words."

Usually coming from humble families, aristocratic families fallen on hard times or born to *gisaeng* themselves, *gisaeng* often began their training at special schools—called *gyobang*—before the age of 10. Their careers tended to be short—few *gisaeng* managed to continue their careers past their early 20s, and all were required by law to retire by age 50. If a *gisaeng* was lucky, she could become the concubine of a wealthy man; if not, she often found herself at work or even owning a drinking establishment of her own. Not all *gisaeng* entertained, per se—some were dressmakers, while others specialized in medicine.

The *gisaeng* system continued throughout the Joseon era and into the Japanese colonial era, with training centers in Seoul and Pyongyang growing particularly famous. During Korea's post-independence development and modernization drive, however, many aspects of Korean traditional culture disappeared as social customs and norms changed. The *gisaeng*, her role now supplanted by much more economical bar hostesses with little of the former's artistic or conversational training, faded into history. Today, the *gisaeng* exists only in TV dramas and silver screen historical epics, a romantic symbol of Korea's past.

FAMOUS GISAENG

• **Hwang Jini:** The most famous of Korea's *gisaeng*, this early 16th entertainer was the perfect combination of beauty and brains. Her beautiful poems reflect both the beauty of nature, especially of her hometown of Kaesong, and the sadness of love lost.

• **Non Gae:** Following the capture of the fortress city of Jinju in the Imjin War, the invading Japanese decided to celebrate their victory with a grand banquet at a pavilion overlooking the Namgang River. During the banquet, the *gisaeng* Non Gae managed to lure a high-ranking Japanese general, Keyamura Rokusuke, to the edge of the pavilion. Embracing the general, she leaped from the pavilion into the waters below, killing both herself and the enemy general.

remains.

If you're going to enjoy a cup of tea anywhere in Seoul, this should be near the top of your list of venues. The beautiful modernized *hanok*, which incorporates Korean and Japanese architectural styles, is a peaceful and charming place to sit and relax. The teahouse has a large garden where, season and weather permitting, you can sit and enjoy your tea amidst natural splendor.

• **Hours** 11:30 am to 10 pm • **Tel** 764-1736

Gansong Museum of Art C3

Gansong Museum of Art is probably the best museum in Korea you've never heard of. Korea's first private art museum, it was created in 1938 from the personal collection of Jeon Hyeong-pil, a wealthy Korean art collector who worked tirelessly to protect Korea's artistic heritage at a time when countless works of art were being virtually plundered by Japanese collectors. His efforts resulted in a collection of art that rivals even the National Museum of Korea.

The collection, housed in a stately building from the late 1930s, includes 12 national treasures and 10 other national cultural properties. Highlights of the collection include "Cheongja Sanggam Unhak Munmaebyong" (National Treasure No. 68), an inlaid Goryo celadon porcelain piece; "Geumdong Samjon Bulham" (National Treasure No. 73), a gilt bronze Buddhist canister; and an original copy of the "Hunmin Jeongeum" (National Treasure No. 70), an outline of the Korean writing system of *hangeul** (see p409) as proclaimed by King Sejong the Great. The museum also contains many works of art by some of Korea's best-known painters, including Joseon-era greats like "Hyewon" Sin Yun-bok and calligrapher "Chusa" Kim Jeong-hui.

The only drawback to the museum is that it holds exhibits just twice a year, once in May and once in October. • **Hours** 10 am to 6 pm (Open only May and October)

• **Admission** Free • **Tel** 762-0442

GETTING TO SEONGBUK-DONG

The nearest subway access to the Seongbuk-dong sites is Exit 6 of Hansung University Station, Line 4. From there, you can either start walking (takes about 15 minutes), catch a cab or take bus 1111 or 2112 to Hongik Middle and High School, which is near the Choi Sunu's Old Home.

1	
2	3
	4

[1] Celebrating baby's first birthday, Samcheonggak [2] Pavilions of Seongnagwon Garden, a beautiful example of Korean landscaping [3] Front gate of Gilsangsa, a former gisaeng house-turned-Buddhist temple [4] Suyeon Sanbang, an enchanting Korean traditional teahouse

Korean traditional rubber shoes in front of San Motungi Café in Buam-dong

BUAM-DONG

If Seongbuk-dong is tranquil, nearby Buam-dong is even more so. Relatively untouched by developers, this lovely piece of urban undevelopment is regarded as a little piece of the countryside in the big city. This is no joke—if you didn't know better, you'd have no idea you were in Seoul.

The peaceful, rural atmosphere of the neighborhood lends itself to cafés and galleries, and these you will find in abundance. Sections of Seoul's old city walls can be found intact—these offer fine views of the surrounding mountains.

Changuimun Gate

At the entrance to Buam-dong is Changuimun Gate, also known today as Jahamun Gate (the "Violet Mist Gate"), one of several lesser gates that controlled access to the royal capital. The gate, and the fortress walls of which it was an integral part, still stand today in almost perfect condition. The current structure dates from 1740, although restoration work was done in 1958.

Fortress Walls

Snaking up and down Seoul's surrounding mountains is a series of ancient fortress walls, which had for centuries protected the capital from enemies both foreign and domestic. Construction on them began in 1396; the walls were built by some 200,000 laborers in just a year, an impressive piece of engineering considering the ruggedness of the terrain. See p322 for more information.

TIPS

BUGAKSAN HIKE
You can hike along much of the fortress, although due to ecological and security concerns, there are limits. See Mountains chapter (p311) for more details.

Whanki Museum

The Whanki Art Museum is dedicated to the works of world-renowned modern abstract painter, Kim Whanki. The museum contains over 1,000 works by the late artist, housed in a stunning museum that incorporates the natural elements found in Kim's work. In addition to Kim's work, the museum has taken it upon itself to hold regular exhibits of works by young, promising Korean artists. • **Hours** 10 am to 6 pm. Closed Mondays • **Admission** 7,000 won • **Getting There** Take green bus 7022, 1020 or 0212 from Exit 3 of Gyeongbokgung Station, Exit 3. • **Tel** 391-7701~2

GETTING THERE
Take Bus 1020, 7022 or 7018 from Exit 3 of Gyeongbokgung Station, Line 3 and get off at Buam-dong Office.

Seokparang

In addition to being one of Seoul's most luxurious Korean restaurants, Seokparang is also a cultural property in and of itself. Parts of the 150-year-old Korean mansion originally belonged to a villa owned by Heungseon Daewongun* (see next page), the prince regent of Korea who was a major figure in the late Joseon era. Set amidst beautiful gardens, the villa harmonizes Korean architectural forms with Chinese influences, such as the use of brick and circular windows. All in all, it's an astoundingly lovely place.

To create the perfect dining atmosphere, Seokparang made use of some of Korea's leading artisans. The collection includes ceramic ware by Yi Eun-gu, a renowned artisan who's devoted more than 30 years of life to producing traditional ceramic art; a traditional brassware dinner set forged by Yi Bong-ju (Important Intangible Cultural Asset Property No. 77); and elegant white porcelain tableware created by Professor Kim Ik-Yeong.

The restaurant specializes in Korean palace cuisine—meals come with rice, soup and a dizzying array of side dishes. Fine dining doesn't come cheap, however—set-menu prices vary between 45,000 to 100,000 won per person.

• **Hours** noon to 3 pm (lunch); 6 to 10 pm (dinner) • **Getting There** Leave Exit 3 of Gyeongbokgung Station, Line 3 and take green bus 0212, 1020, 1711, 7018, 7022 to Sangmyung University. • **Tel** 395-2500 • **Website** www.seokparang.co.kr

Courtyard of Seokparang, a princely villa that has been converted into one of Seoul's best restaurants

HEUNGSEON DAEWONGUN

The most powerful political figure of the late Joseon era, the prince regent Heungseon Daewongun (1821-1898), born Lee Ha-eung, was a key player in some of the most important events of Korea's early modern history. The father of King Gojong, Heungseon Daewongun was an arch conservative who was the primary architect of Korea's policies of isolation that earned the nation the nickname, "the Hermit Kingdom."

In 1864, the unlettered King Cheoljong—a figurehead of the powerful Andong Kim family—died, and it was left to the Andong Kims to choose the next king. Pretending to be a powerless, unambitious man, Lee—the future regent—tricked the Kims into placing his young son—the 14-year-old King Gojong—on the throne, with Lee himself named royal regent. Until 1873, when Gojong reached majority, Lee—who as regent took the name Heungseon Daewongun (Regent Heungseon)—ruled Korea with an iron will. Even after Gojong's assumption of direct royal rule, the Daewongun continued to wield considerable influence.

Portrait of Heungseon Daewongun at Seoul History Museum © Yonhap

Under the Daewongun, the dominance of the Andong Kim clan was finally brought to an end. He also closed Korea's system of *seowon*, countryside Confucian academies that had become breeding grounds of the factional rivalry that had plagued court politics. Deeply Confucian and well-aware of China's less-than-pleasant interaction with the West, he was deeply suspicious of both foreigners and foreign ideas, particularly Catholicism, which had entered Korea in the 18th century. In 1866, he launched a brutal crackdown on Catholicism, executing thousands of Korean Catholics and nine French missionaries, provoking a retaliatory raid that same year by a French naval squadron on the west coast island of Ganghwa. Also in 1866, a US schooner sent to Korea to demand a trade treaty was burned and its crew killed, leading to a raid on Ganghwa Island by US marines in 1871 (see p276). All this confirmed to Daewongun that foreigners were bad news, solidifying his policy of isolation.

The Daewongun's grip on power could not last, however. In 1873, his son took direct control, with real power wielded by the king's strong-willed and reform-oriented consort, Queen Min (see p45). In 1882, the Daewongun seized power once again by supporting a mutiny by the Korean army against its Japanese military advisors (in which the Japanese legation was attacked), but the mutiny was crushed by Chinese troops commanded by future Chinese president Yuan Shikai, who had the elderly Korean statesman abducted back to China, where he was held for four years. The last years of his life was marked by one last return to power to lead Japanese-backed modernization reforms in 1895, but he soon retired for the last time following the assassination of Queen Min that year. He died at Unhyeongung Palace (see p75) in 1898.

Gana Art Center

With the largest floor space in the country, this beautiful gallery—designed by noted architect Jean-Michel Wilmotte—is not only a great place to take in modern art, but also a wonderful place to relax, with an especially pleasant outdoor sculpture garden.

• **Hours** 10 am to 7 pm • **Admission** 3,000 won • **Getting There** Take green bus 1020 or 1711 from Exit 3, Gyeongbokgung Station, Line 3 • **Tel** 720-1020 • **Website** www.ganaart.com

Gana Art Center

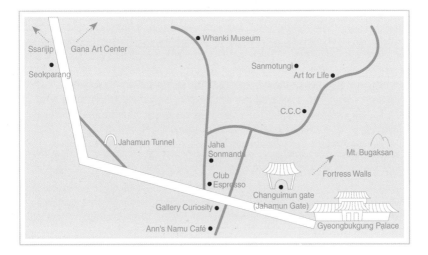

[1] San Motungi Café, one of Buam-dong's many chic coffeehouses [2] Coffee and scone, Club Espresso [3] Changuimun (Jahamun) Gate, one of the old gates of Seoul's old fortress walls, built in 1740. [4] Art for Life, an Italian restaurant/theater in a renovated Korean-style *hanok*

PLACES TO EAT: SEONGBUK-DONG & BUAM-DONG

Seongbuk-dong p138

The Seongbuk-dong area is famous for two things—the so-called *gisa sikdang* (driver's restaurants), frequented by Seoul's legion of taxi drivers, and *donkkaseu* (tonkatsu) restaurants. The former serve generous portions of reasonably priced food in a setting conducive to those eating alone (actually something of a rarity in Seoul), while the latter are, of course, Japanese-style breaded pork cutlets.

Gisa Sikdang

Ssangdari Sikdang Rice, grilled pork, side dishes—what more do you need? They also do a good *budaejjigae* ("Army Base Stew," a stew of *kimchi*, ramyeon noodles, sausages, baked beans and rice cake). Incredibly popular. (T. 743-0325) B3

Seongbuk-dong Dwaeji Galbi-jip One of the oldest restaurants in the area, this place specializes in grilled pork, served with rice and consumed in leaves of cabbage. (T. 764-2420) B3

Donkkaseu

Geumwang Donkkaseu This place does a roaring trade in breaded pork cutlets served Korean-style, which is to say, big and fat. Hours: 9:30 am to 10 pm. (T. 763-9366) B2

Obaksane Donkkaseu This is another famous Seongbuk-dong pork cutlet place that's been around forever. Hours: 9 am to midnight. (T. 3673-5730) C3

Seoul Donkkaseu Nice and clean. Oh yeah, and they serve good pork cutlets. Hours: 9 am to midnight. (T. 766-9370) C3

Other

Kitchen Run by food stylist and an interior designer, this quaint restaurant is nothing if not picturesque. The "vintage" atmosphere is helped by all the antiques on display. Menu highlights include seafood and cheese *tteokbokki* (spicy pan-fried rice cakes) and good pizza. (T. 747-1713) B3

Seongbuk-dong Nurungji Baeksuk This place does a fine baeksuk, or chicken stew. Afterwards, scorched rice is mixed into the remaining soup. One chicken will run you about 37,000 won, which'll feed four. (T. 764-0707) B2

Seongbuk Seolleongtang As the name would suggest, this place does *seolleongtang*, a hearty soup made from the leg bones of an ox. Particularly nice in winter. (T. 762-3342) B2

Buam-dong p148

Jaha Sonmandu With great views of the surrounding mountains, this restaurant specializes in handmade *mandu*, or dumplings. *Manduguk* (dumpling soup) and *tteok manduguk* (dumpling soup with rice cakes) are popular, but if you're looking for something even more filling, try the *kimchi mandu jeongol*, a stew of *kimchi* and dumplings. (T. 379-2648)

Art for Life Part gallery, part concert hall, part restaurant, this Italian restaurant—run by a couple who just happen to be former musicians with the Seoul Philharmonic Orchestra—is located in a beautifully renovated Korean *hanok* home. Hours: 11:30 am to 10 pm, (breaktime: 3 to 5 pm weekdays, 3 to 4 pm weekends). Closed Mondays. (T. 3217-9364)

Ssarijip Located not in Buam-dong, but in nearby Gugi-dong, this is one of Seoul's best places to try *bosintang*, or dogmeat soup. Located in a Korean-style *hanok* home with a wonderful courtyard, the restaurant is packed in the summer, but is still a relaxing place to have a meal. A bowl of *bosintang* will cost you 15,000 won, but a heavier stew, or *jeongol*, is worth the money at 28,000 won. Hours: 11:30 am to 9:30 pm. (T. 379-9911)

Sanmotungi With wonderful views of the surrounding mountains, this beautiful coffee house, housed in a castle-like stone home, is known among locals as the filming locale of a popular TV series. Hours: 11 am to 10 pm. (T. 391-4737)

Club Espresso Outstanding fresh-brewed coffee in a pleasant atmosphere. This is where Seoul Selection bookshop gets its coffee beans from. Hours: 9 am to 11 pm. (T. 764-8719)

Ann's Namu Café Another pretty Buam-dong café, this place is much more directed at female customers—in fact, it's done up like a woman's room. Has pancakes and waffles, too. Hours: 10:30 am to 8 pm. (T. 379-5939)

DONGDAEMUN AREA

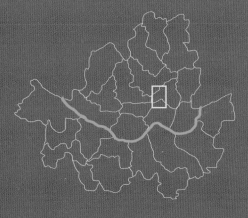

THINGS TO DO AND SEE

- Shop for clothing at Dongdaemun Market
- Enjoy some spicy *tteokbokki* in Sindang-dong Tteokbokki Alley
- Sample Mongolian and Uzbek cuisine in Central Asia Village
- Take in the young culture scene in Daehangno

VIBRANT ENERGY OF SEOUL'S FASHION MECCA

Dongdaemun — or Great East Gate — is most known as the home of the bustling Dongdaemun Market, Seoul's fashion mecca. At night, this place sizzles with energy, with shoppers from all over descending on its countless malls, shops and markets in search of bargain buys on quality clothing. All the shopping gives rise to a vibrant, if somewhat grittier, nightlife.
At the same time, the Dongdaemun area is about more than just fashion shopping. Near the market is Central Asian Village, the center of Seoul's thriving Mongolian and Central Asian communities. Also nearby are Sindang-dong Tteokbokki Alley, famous for its *tteokbokki* (spicy pan-fried rice cakes) and Jangchung-dong, a neighborhood synonymous with *jokbal* (pork shanks). Also in the area is Daehangno, Seoul's theater district, where you can take in a show and soak in the youthful enthusiasm of the local denizens.

Heunginjimun Gate, Dongdaemun

Dongdaemun History & Culture Park and Doosan Tower

DONGDAEMUN MARKET

Twenty-six shopping malls, 30,000 specialty shops and 50,000 manufacturers. All within a 10-block radius. Welcome to Dongdaemun Market.

Dongdaemun Market is the place to go for fashion. Period. Apgujeong-dong, south of the Hangang River, might have the luxury brands, and Myeong-dong the international brand outlets, but for fashion junkies looking for unique designs at decent prices, Dongdaemun is the place to go. Heck, even if you're not into clothing, it's a great place to go, particularly at night, when all its lights, action and crowds make for an impressive show of human energy.

Hours

Dongdaemun is open pretty much all day and all night, but retailers and wholesalers keep different hours. Retailers are usually open from 10 am to 5 am the next morning, while wholesalers are open from 8 pm to 8 am the next morning. Many shops close on Mondays.

Layout

Dongdaemun Market sprawls over several city blocks south of the Cheonggyecheon Stream, split in two by a main north-south street. Major landmarks include the 34-floor Doosan Tower, Migliore Department Store and Dongdaemun Stadium (now demolished to make way for Dongdaemun Design Plaza & Park). Broadly speaking, the newer, glitzier Dongdaemun of bright lights and towering malls is to the west of the main road, while the older, grittier Dongdaemun of smaller shops is to the east around what was Dongdaemun Stadium.

GETTING THERE

Two subway stations service the sprawling Dongdaemun Market, Dongdaemun Station (Lines 1 & 4) and Dongdaemun History & Culture Park Station (Lines 2 & 4). See the map on the next page.

TIPS

LOOKING FOR BARGAINS

You'll often find the item you're looking for at several stores—look around and see if you can find it at a bargain price. You can usually haggle the price down (usually some 10 to 20%), too, especially if you're paying in cash.

CROWDS!

If you're looking to shop in relative peace, go on weekdays during daylight hours. But if you really want the Dongdaemun experience, go at night, especially on a Friday or Saturday—the crowds are simply electric.

DONGDAEMUN DESIGN PLAZA AND PARK C3

A landmark redevelopment project by famed British architect Zaha Hadid, this eye-catching complex—which organically blends landscaping and architecture—is scheduled for completion in 2011, and will contain outdoor green space, exhibition halls, shops, restaurants and more. Part of it—Dongdaemun History & Culture Park—is already open to the public and is well-worth the visit.

DONGDAEMUN MAP

Hyehwa Rotary

A **B** **C** **D**

1

Filipino Market
Caterina
Platters
Dongsoong Art Center
Chunnyun Jazz Bar
Drawing Show Theater
Sungkyunkwan Univ.
Hakrim Dabang
Arko Arts Theater
Hyehwa Stn.
Beer Cabin
Marronnier Theater
Naksan Park
Hansung Univ.
Platters
Seoul Nat'l Univ. Hospital
Daehangno
Arko Art Center
Marronnier Park
Korea National Open Univ.
(Former National Industry Institute)
Former Daehan Hospital
Daehangno Theater

Changsin Stn.

Naksan Myogaksa

2

Gyeongdong Oriental Medicine Market

Mt. Namsan

Ewha Womans Univ.
Dongdaemun Hospital
Everest
Doosan Art Center
Two Hotel
Heunginjimun
(Dongdaemun Gate)
Dongmyo Stn.
Dongmu Shrine
Pharmacy Area
Dongdaemun Stn.
Somunnan Dak
Wonjo Hanmari
Dongdaemun General Market
Jongno 5-ga Stn.
Broiled Fish Alley
Wedding Goods Market
Used Books Alley
Best Western Hotel
Gwangjang Market
Pyeonghwa Market
Cerestar
Doota
New Pyeonghwa Market
Dong Pyeonghwa Market
Cheong Pyeonghwa Market
Cheonggyecheon Stream
Jungang Market
Migliore
3
Bangsan Market
Woo Rae Oak
Dongdaemun Design Plaza and Park—under construction
Designer Club
Chungmu Art Hall
Hwanghak-dong Flea Market
Park of Seoul Hunlyunwon
National Medical Center
Hello apM
U US
U US
Nuzzon
Jungbu Market
Western Co-op Residence Hotel
Good Morning City
Dongdaemun History & Culture Park
Darkhan
Samarkand Café
Ala-Too Café
Central Asia Village
Dongdaemun Stadium Stn.
Hanyang Technical High School
Sindang Stn.
Ojang-dong Naengmyeon Alley
Hyundai Residence
Gwanghuimun Gate
Chungmuro
Kyungdong Presbyterian Church
Sindang-dong Tteokbokki Alley
I Love Tteobokki
Mabongnim Halmeoni Tteokbokki
Jongjeom
Pyeongyang Myeonok
Jangchung Jokbal Restaurants
Grand Ambassador Seoul
Fat Grandma's Place
Pyeongan-do Jokbaljip
4
Dongguk Univ. Stn.
Original Jangchungdong Grandmother's Place
Dongguk Univ.
Cheonggu Stn.
National Theater of Korea
Shilla Seoul
5F
Noblian Branch Clinic of Jaseng Hospital of Oriental Medicine

DONGDAEMUN GATE C2

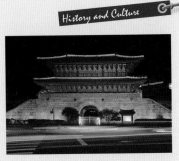

History and Culture

Since a disastrous 2008 fire destroyed the Sungnyemun (Namdaemun) Gate, the Dongdaemun Gate is—along with Sukjeongmun Gate on Mt. Bugaksan—one of only two of Seoul's old main city gates still standing. More properly called Heunginjimun, the gate has a history going back to 1396, when Seoul's old city walls were first constructed, although the current structure dates from 1869.

The gate consists of a solid stone base with a two-story wooden superstructure. A unique feature is the half-moon wall built in front of the main gate, which was used for additional defense. Unfortunately, the gate is not usually open to the public.

Shopping Highlights

Doosan Tower B3

This 34-floor landmark, known colloquially as Doota, gets about 100,000 customers a day, which should probably tell you something. Clothing, accessories, beauty supplies—it's all in there. • **Hours** 7 pm to 5 am next day (Mon to Tue), 10:30 am to 5 am next day (Tue to Sat), 10:30 am to 11 pm (Sun) • **Tel** 3398-3114

Migliore B3

The Dongdaemun branch of the Korean department store. Nine total floors of fashion. • **Hours** 10:30 am to 5 am next day. Closed Mondays • **Tel** 3393-0001

Cerestar B3

Yet another Dongdaemun shopping mall. • **Hours** 10:30 am to 5:30 am next day. Closed Mondays • **Tel** 2048-0047

Hello apM B3

Yep, it's a massive Dongdaemun clothing mall. • **Hours** 10:20 pm to 5 pm next day. Closed Tuesdays • **Tel** 6388-1114

Pyeonghwa Market A3

This is one of the oldest wholesale markets in the country. Customers tend to be a bit older, but it does have the largest hat market in Korea. The market has also played an important role in the Korean labor movement—in 1970, a young worker by the name of Chun Tae-il set himself alight to protest the working conditions at the market, inspiring fellow workers and activists to take action. The market was formed some 56 years ago, mainly by North Korean refugees who settled in the neighborhood after the Korean War. Working with just one or two sewing machines, they would make clothes or dye US military uniforms and resell them.

Dongdaemun General Market B3

The shops here specialize in reasonably priced fabrics, providing the Dongdaemun fashion machine with much of its fuel. • **Hours** 8 am to 7 pm.

Other Shopping Opportunities Around Dongdaemun Market

Gwangjang Market A3

One of Seoul's oldest markets, Gwangjang Market is most famous for its silks and *hanbok* (Korean traditional clothing) market. Also noted for its alley of cheap food stalls, with *bindaetteok* (mung bean pancake) something of a specialty.

Gwangjang Market has a very special history. In 1905, the Japanese forced Korea to sign a protectorate treaty, after which Japanese merchants gained control over the spawling Namdaemun Market. In response, nationalist-minded merchants, gathered the funds and property needed to start a Korean-owned market. This was the Gwangjang Market—when it opened in 1905, it became Korea's first regular market.

Korean *hanbok* clothing, Gwangjang Market

• **Hours** 7 am to 7 pm • **Getting There** Exit 8, Jongno 5-ga Station, Line 1

Used Books Alley B3

Once *the* place to buy books in Seoul. The glory days of this alley of about 50 booksellers are long gone, but it's still interesting to snoop around—you can come across the unexpected treasure.

TIPS

GINSENG, THE MAGIC ROOT

Korean ginseng—Panax ginseng C.A. Meyer—has been a prized commodity for centuries. In East Asia, ginseng root is used as a tonic: its rejuvenating properties are widely lauded (even if scientific studies of its effects have proven inconclusive).

Korean ginseng (or in Korean, *insam*) is usually called Goryeo ginseng, named for the medieval Korean kingdom that oversaw great developments in Korea's ginseng cultivation. The ginseng root is sold in three forms:

UNDRIED GINSENG (*SUSAM*) This is fresh ginseng, straight from the ground. It spoils easily, however, making it difficult to transport.

WHITE GINSENG (*BAEKSAM*) Grown for four to six years and then peeled and sun-dried, white ginseng tends to be cheaper, but supposedly has less of a therapeutic effect.

RED GINSENG (*HONGSAM*) Grown for six years and then steamed unpeeled, red ginseng is considered of highest medical value among commonly available ginseng.

If you're lucky, you might happen upon some mountain ginseng, or *sansam*. Its restorative properties are the stuff of legend—it's said wild ginseng roots can be several hundreds of years old, and one such root recently sold for US$54,400. Ten-year-old wild ginseng roots will usually run you about 100,000 won.

Ginseng also finds itself in a variety of foods and teas. Chicken ginseng soup, or *samgyetang*, is a popular dish in summer time—it's a whole young chicken, stuffed with rice and cooked in a broth ginseng, dried jujube, garlic and ginger. Ginseng tea is also easy enough to find—served with honey, it's a great pick-me-up.

Gyeongdong Oriental Medicine Market D2

Not too far from Dongdaemun is Seoul's largest Oriental medicine market, Gyeongdong Oriental Medicine Market (also called Seoul *Yangnyoungsi*). It's a fascinating place to walk around, just to take in the incredible selection of exotic herbs and medications, including the ever-popular (with foreign tourists, anyway) bottles of snake liquor— snake cured in alcohol. Ginseng, of course, is the most popular product.

• **Hours** 9 am to 7 pm. Closed Sundays
• **Getting There** Exit 2 of Jegi Station, Line 1

Medicinal herbs, Gyeongdong Oriental Medicine

Bottles of liquor with ginseng and centipedes preserved inside

Hwanghak-dong Flea Market D3

At this streetside market, you can find just about anything if you look hard enough. Home to about 500 shops, this used to be the place to go for antiques, but nowadays, the goods on display have greatly diversified. If you live in Korea and are looking for used appliances, this is your spot. It's got tons of old books and videos, too, if that's your thing. • **Hours** 9 am to 7 pm.

MULTICULTURAL SEOUL

History and Culture

Korea has long prided itself on its ethnic homogeneity. In recent years, however, the claim to homogeneity has weakened greatly in the face of globalization and stark demographic trends. Some one million foreign-born individuals now live in Korea, many of whom are migrant workers from China, Southeast Asia and Central Asia. Another recent trend is foreign women—mostly from China, Vietnam and the Philippines—coming to Korea to marry Korean men, particularly in the countryside, where there is a lack of marriageable women. These new arrivals have injected new elements into the Korean cultural landscape, bringing with them their foods, languages and customs. In Seoul and its surrounding suburbs, this has even led to the creation of ethnic neighborhoods like Central Asia Village in Dongdaemun and Little Nigeria in Itaewon.

The most noticeable side effect of this has been the sprouting up of ethnic restaurants throughout Seoul. Not so long ago, it was difficult to find anything other than Korean, Chinese, Japanese and (bad) Western cuisine. Now, you can find restaurants serving food from all over the world, be it Indian, Uzbek, Mongolian, Nepali, French, Italian or Mexican.

Other Sites Around Dongdaemun Market

Central Asia Village B3

In recent years, Seoul has witnessed an influx of foreign residents as the Korean economy grows and globalizes. One of the best places to witness this is the so-called Central Asia Village near the former Dongdaemun Stadium. The village is a small collection of shops, businesses and restaurants near Dongdaemun Stadium run and frequented by Korea's increasingly large population of Central Asian immigrants. Although this is not a residential district like the ethnic communities that have formed in many North American and European cities, the Cyrillic signboards, exotic cuisine and distinctly Central Asian faces and dress that visitors find when they visit give the neighborhood its distinct character—Korea meets the Silk Road.

On a weekend, the village is jam-packed with Mongolians, Uzbeks, Russians and other folks from Central Asia, many of whom are involved in the import-export trade or work in the small factories of Seoul's industrial suburbs. For the Western visitor, the neighborhood's draw is the exotic Central Asian restaurants, especially Mongolian and Uzbek. There are a good many Mongolian and Central Asian shops as well, although most of these cater to an exclusively Central Asian clientèle.

Other Sites Around Dongdaemun

Donggwan Wangmyo Shrine D2

This shrine to the east of Dongdaemun Gate, in the middle of Hwanghak-dong Flea Market, is quite unique in that it was built to honor the Chinese general Guan Yu (AD 162-219), famed for his exploits during China's Three Kingdoms Period. Mind you, Korea never had a tradition of honoring Guan Yu, but in the 16th century, Ming Chinese generals dispatched to Korea to help defeat the Japanese in the Imjin War (the Japanese invasions of 1592-1598) demanded the shrine be built, and the Korean court—dependent on Chinese military aid—was not in a position to refuse.

The shrine incorporates Chinese elements into its design, including the brilliant brick masonry and radiant decoration. Completed in 1601, it is one of the oldest wood buildings in Seoul. Oddly enough, for such a pleasant place, it doesn't get as many foreign visitors as you might think, perhaps due to its distance from the downtown palace cluster. • **Admission** Free • **Getting There** Dongmyo Station, Line 1 and 6

Gwanghuimun Gate C3

Built in 1717 and restored in 1975, Gwanghuimun Gate—not far from Dongdaemun Market—was one of Seoul's old minor gates. It was used to remove dead bodies from the capital during the Joseon era.

Gwanghuimun Gate

Kyungdong Presbyterian Church B4

Completed in 1981, this funky-shaped red brick church near the Jangchung Gymnasium is a masterpiece of modern architecture, designed by one of Korea's all-time greatest architects, the late Kim Swoo-geun. Its stark interior is designed to resemble an old Roman catacomb.

• **Hours** Open for services at 7:30 pm on Wednesday and 9:30 and 11:30 am on Sunday • **Tel** 2274-0161

Jangchung Jokbal Restaurants B4

The area around the church is famous for its restaurants specializing in *jokbal*, or boiled pig's feet, usually served in slices and eaten wrapped in lettuce leaves with *kimchi*. Great stuff.

Sindang-dong *Tteokbokki* Alley C4

Not far from Dongdaemun, around Sindang Station, is an alley specializing in the Korean dish *tteokbokki*, pan-fried rice cakes served in red pepper sauce with ramyeon noodles, fried dumplings and an assortment of other ingredients. Great in wintertime, and best enjoyed with a shot of *soju* (see on p393 Korean Food section).

National Theater of Korea A4

The National Theater of Korea is a unique performing space designed to accommodate a wide range of performance styles. It is home to the national drama, Korean opera, national orchestra and national dance companies of Korea. Besides the main performance hall, the National Theater includes an outdoor stage where free concerts and movies are offered during the summer season.

• **Getting There** Dongguk University Station, Line 3, Exit 6 • **Tel** 2280-4115~6 • **Website** www.ntok.go.kr

[1] National Theater of Korea [2] *Jokbal*—Korean cured pork shanks—in Jangchung-dong [3] Cyrillic signs of Little Mongolia in Central Asia Village [4] Beautiful red-brick Kyungdong Presbyterian Church, a masterpiece of Korean architect Kim Swoo-geun

INFORMATION

10F	MIAT MONGOLIAN AIRLINES SALES AGENCY OF KOREA	02-777-9292 10Давхар 1001тоот	G GLOB International Gro
9F	АНГОРА ОПТӨМ И ВРОЗНИЧУ 9ЭТАЖ 901 тоот	GUEN DODO.cosmetics КЛИНИК УСЧИН ГОО САЙХАН 8ДАВХАР 902	
8F	몽골전문결혼정보사 ТАНИЛЦАХ АЛБА 803	ГОО САЙХНЫБАРАА БӨӨН НИЖИГЛЭН 804 Т.2269-2328~9	"NOMA" Ka
	ГАР УТАС БА КАРТ (B1)		
7F	НАХИА Усчин 707	706	"БОДЬ ИНТЕРН (705) Т.2
	ФИРМА "ДВОЕ" ЮБКИ, БРЮКИ, БЛУЗКИ И ДР. 8ТЭЖ 80TK ТЕЛ-02/2272-3422	УНЭРЧ КОРЕЙ ХХК 702 тоот Утас:02-2269-8203, 010-2369-7013	НОС TEL.960-310
6F	КАРТЫН ТӨВ 604 тоот VTAC 02-2275-3309 800-2475	MARAL International 601 ТООТ	607 T2-2274-
	ЗООС KOPEA 405 тоот	605 ТООТ OS Telecom КАРТЫН ТӨВ www.ostelecom.co.kr	ДЭЭЖИН КОРИА Т.2275-0779 603 ТООТ Ц
		ӨРНӨЛТ 505 тоот ХХК	НАЙМАН ШАРГА TEL: 02)2263-3307 NO.505 СИ
AMA TREND	06	KHAMAG Mongol ТЕЛ.02-2273-3750, 011-9826-0001	501 тоот MONKOREA
		АPU KOREA CO.,Ltd	407 тоот VI
	중앙디지털포트 B1	화신문구	ӨНГӨТ КАНОН НЭРИЙН ХУУДАС АНГ ОПТӨМ и

"Art Makes Life More Interesting than Art," Arko Art Gallery

DAEHANGNO

Daehangno, or "University Street," gets its name as the former location of Korea's most prestigious university, Seoul National University, which moved south of the Hangang River in the 1970s (the College of Medicine still remains, however). Today, the neighborhood has become Seoul's "theater district," with over 300 small theaters that put on regular performances. The area is virtually synonymous with "youth culture," as university students from all over gather in places such as Marronnier Park to take in outdoor performances and frequent the many cafés and restaurants. Daehangno also has a bit of history, with a number of impressive pieces of colonial architecture.

Arko Art Center A1
Part of Marronnier Park, the red-brick Arko Art Center has played an important role in the development of Korean modern art by providing a relatively inexpensive place to hold exhibits. The museum is also a popular date destination, with a café on the second floor. • **Hours** 11 am to 8 pm (Mar to Oct), 11 am to 7 pm (Nov to Feb). Closed Mondays • **Admission** 2,000 won • **Tel** 760-4850~2

Dongsoong Art Center A1
One of Daehangno's major performing arts venues, Dongsoong Art Center hosts a wide variety of shows. Perhaps its most unique facility is the Hypertheque NADA, a cinema dedicated to non-mainstream and art-house films. • **Hours** Depends on programs • **Tel** 766-3390

Small Theaters
With over 300 small theaters in the neighborhood, including the noted Saemtoh Parangsae Theater, Jeongbo Small Theater and Hakjeon Theater, Daehangno is Seoul's theater district, even if the city's larger theaters (like the Sejong Center and National Theater) can be found elsewhere. Most of the area's theaters are tiny places with no more than a few dozen seats (some, however, are larger, with 100 seats or more), giving performances a truly intimate feel.

LANGUAGE BARRIER
Most of the performances are in Korean, but they're still worth attending, especially if you are familiar with the work or have someone who can translate for you.

SEOUL PERFORMING ARTS FESTIVAL
In autumn, the Daehangno area hosts the Seoul Performing Arts Festival (see p438), Korea's largest festival for the performing arts. A month-long celebration, it features performances by artistic troupes from all over the world. See www.spaf.or.kr for more information.

Marronnier Park A2

This small urban space often plays host to outdoor theatrical and musical performances, especially on the weekends, and as such is packed with young people. Even when nothing's going on, it's a pleasant place to relax.

Sungkyunkwan University A3, p138

One of Seoul's top universities, Sungkyunkwan University traces its illustrious history back some 600 years to 1398, when it was founded as the country's top Confucian academy. The university museum (Hours: 10 am to 4 pm, closed weekends) is well worth visiting, as is the campus's Joseon-era Confucian shrine.

TIPS

LIVE JAZZ
If jazz is your thing, Daehangno is home to one of Seoul's best jazz clubs, Chunnyun Jazz Bar. Admissions are 8,000 won (Mon to Thur) & 10,000 won (Fri to Sun), although if you order a meal or cocktail, this is waived. (T. 743-5555) A1

Former Daehan Hospital A2

The former Daehan Hospital, located just in front of Seoul National University Medical Center, was created in 1907 as Korea's top medical facility. Designed by a Japanese architect, the massive red-brick building is recognizable by its grand neo-Baroque clock tower.

Former Main Hall of Seoul National University A2

A little piece of the "old" Daehangno, this historic structure—covered in scratch tile—was built in 1931 and designed by Park Gil-ryong, one of Korea's first Western-style architects.

Former National Industry Institute A2

Another symbol of Korea's pre-colonial attempts at modernization, this German-style wooden edifice on the campus of Korea Open University was built in 1908 as an educational facility to teach students about modern industries.

Filipino Market A1

Head to Hyehwa Catholic Church (near Hyehwa Rotary) on a Sunday to check out the Filipino Market, a makeshift bazaar of Filipino food, Filipino groceries, Filipino CDs and DVDs, phone cards and other goods from the sunny archipelago. See p407. • **Hours** 9 am to 5 pm, Sunday

1 Posters for Daehangno's many shows 2 Puck-up basketball game, Marronnier Park 3 Chunnyun Jazz Club, one of Seoul's best live jazz venues 4 Former Daehan Hospital, a beautiful neo-Baroque building completed in 1907

PLACES TO EAT: DONGDAEMUN AREA

Like most of the rest of Seoul, you'll be tripping over restaurants large and small.

Jangchung-dong Jokbal

The Jangchung-dong *Jokbal* (pig's feet) street specializes in, well, boiled pig's trotters, one of Seoul's best regarded cuisines. The meat is served in slices, which are consumed typically wrapped in lettuce. It is usually consumed with a bottle of Korean vodka, or *soju*. Some restaurants to try include: p158

Original Jangchungdong Grandmother's Place The grandmother is no longer around, but her son is. Unlike the other *jokbal* restaurants, which are charmingly gritty establishments, this one has been rebuilt and is relatively clean. (T. 2279-9979) B4

Pyeongando Jokbaljip Serving great *jokbal* for half a century. (T. 2279-9759) B4

Fat Grandma's Place Originally unnamed, it earned its current moniker from customers because it's run by a grandmother. Who is fat. Oh, and she does very good food. (T. 2273-5320) B4

Central Asia Village

The restaurants in Central Asia Village specialize in foods from Mongolia, Uzbekistan and elsewhere. Highlights include: p158

Samarkand Café Samarkand Café does fine Uzbek cuisine in a friendly atmosphere. Quite popular and pretty cheap, too. (T. 2277-4261) B3

Darkhan A Mongolian restaurant popular with Korea's large Mongolian worker population. (T. 2278-4633) B3

Ala-Too Café Another friendly Uzbek place, this one on the second floor above an Uzbek/Russian bakery that is similarly recommended. (T. 2277-9212) B3

Everest Located on the second floor of a nondescript building in an equally nondescript neighborhood not far from Dongdaemun Station is one of the best (and most popular!) Nepali restaurants in Seoul—get here at the wrong time, and you're going to wait on line. If you need your curry fix, this is a highly recommended place to go. The food is awesome and the prices are surprisingly reasonable. (T. 766-8850) C2

Daehangno

Tons of little cafés and restaurants, mostly aimed at a younger crowd.

Platters Near Marronnier Park, Platters is a 1950s-style American diner complete with good burgers, milkshakes and Philly cheesesteaks. (T. 744-7651) A1, p158

Nanumi Tteokbokki A cheap hole-in-the-wall that has attained legendary status with students at nearby Sungkyunkwan University. (T. 747-0881) A4, p138

Caterina A popular area wine bar and Italian restaurant with a charming atmosphere. (T. 764-3201) A1, p158

Sindang Tteokbokki Town

This alley near Sindang Station is famous throughout the country for its *tteokbokki*, or spicy pan-fried Korean rice cakes, served with fried dumplings and *ramyeon* noodles. Probably not good for your cholesterol, but quite delicious. Some of the better-known eateries are: p158

Mabongnim Halmeoni Tteokbokki One of the oldest places in the alley, they've been doing this dish for over 50 years. (T. 2232-8930) D4

I Love Sindang-dong They mix it up a bit with a variety of unique *tteokbokki* dishes. If you're looking to spook your cardiologist, try the cheese *tteokbokki*, rice cakes stuffed with mozzarella. (T. 2232-7872) C4

Jongjeom Serving *tteokbokki* for 25 years, so they know how to do it. (T. 2234-3649) D4

SEODAEMUN AREA

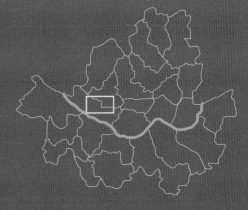

THINGS TO DO AND SEE

- Eat, drink and be merry with the college crowd around Sinchon

- Buy some crafts at Hongdae's Free Market

- Sample Korea's indie music and dance culture at one of the many clubs in front of Hongik University

- Stroll among the ivy-covered campuses of Yonsei and Ewha universities

- Learn about the sacrifices of Korea's independence movement at Seodaemun Independence Park

Seodaemun refers to the district to the west of the Gwanghwamun area, outside where the Seodaemun Gate (Great West Gate) used to stand. This area—particularly the area around Sinchon Station—is Seoul's college town, home to several of Korea's top universities and some of Seoul's best nightlife and entertainment. The club area in front of Hongik University is particularly well-regarded by locals and foreigners alike. If you're looking to taste the vibrant energy of Korea's youth culture, this is the place to find it.

Mind you, however, this region of Seoul is more than just drinking, eating and partying. The university campuses of Yonsei and Ewha, both a century old, are quite beautiful with their ivy-covered Gothic halls. Seodaemun Independence Park, home of Seodaemun Prison Museum, is a stark reminder of Koreans' struggles under brutal Japanese colonial rule.

Ewha Campus Complex, designed by French architect Dominique Perrault

Yonsei University

SINCHON

When you mention Sinchon to the average Seoulite, they immediately think of colleges. In the Sinchon area are some of Korea's most prestigious universities, including Yonsei University, Ewha Womans University, Hongik University and Sogang University. The streets in front of these institutes of higher learning are packed with young people shopping, eating and drinking, especially on a Friday or Saturday evening, when the area becomes one big party.

• **Getting There** Sinchon Station, Line 2

Nightlife

When we're talking about Sinchon, we're talking about drinking and having a good time. Many of the bars in the area are popular with foreigners, although unlike Itaewon with its large (but decreasing) US military contingent, most of the foreigners you find in Sinchon are local English teachers and exchange students. Popular bars include:

• **Norae Haneun Saramdeul:** Somewhat cramped, this bar gets a good mix of Westerners and Koreans and lots of dancing on the weekend. (T. 325-7808) B3, p178

• **Woodstock:** As the name would suggest, this local institution specializes in classic rock, with décor to match. (T. 334-1310) C3, p178

• **Watts on Tap:** This Canadian-owned pub, popular with the expat crowd, mixes a good beer selection with decent pub food. (T. 010-5552-5568) C2, p178

• **BlueBird:** One of Sinchon's better-known jazz bars. Wonderful atmosphere. (T. 332-3831) C2, p178

• **Mike's Cabin:** Run by a Korean-American, this cozy bar is also popular with the expat crowd. Tends to be quieter than Norae Haneun Saramdeul. C2, p178

• **Bar Tei:** Armed with an exotic Bohemian atmosphere, a good music selection of classic rock, alternative rock, Brit pop and modern rock, and cheap beer, this bar is quite popular. (T. 365-3824) C2, p178

• **Gopchang Jeongol** Located not far from the Sanwoolim Theater, this Hongdae bar is famous for its large collection of Korean classic rock LPs. There's a decent choice of Western and Korean beverages and if you're hungry, the food is pretty good, too. (T. 3143-2284) B2, p184

Of course, this list is not meant to be exhaustive—you're best advised to just walk around until you find something you like.

SINCHON/HONGDAE MAP

Restaurants & Bars
Shops
Museums & Galleries
Hotels
Clubs & Theaters
Etc.

Metro

M Line 1	M Line 2	M Line 3
M Line 4	M Line 5	M Line 6
M Line 7	M Line 8	M Line 9
M Jungang Line	M Bundang Line
M Gyeongui Line	M A'REX Line

Bongwonsa Temple

Seodaemun Prison
Independence Gate

Yangpuni Jumak

Watts on Tap
Norae Haneun
Saramdeul

Tess
Rough 2

Hongik Univ. Stn.

BlueBird

Mike's Cabin

Yonsei Univ.

Sinchon
Severance
Hospital

Manokamana
Mussel & Muggle

Bokseonggak   Wan Chai
Wood Stock   Chois' Tacos
Tiffany Hotel

Migliore

Ewha Womans Univ.

Sinchon Railway Stn.

Judy's

Eunha Hair & Make

Zen Hair   Shopping
District

Badasok
Hoetjip

Sinchon Sinuiju
Chapssal
Sundae

Sanwoollim Theater

Cheolgil Wang
Galbisal

Plum   Crux Hotel
Reem Hotel   Artreon

On The Border
Mexican Grill &
Sinchon Stn. Cantina

Nylon
Indonara   Yes apM

Ewha Womans Univ. Str

Hotel Seokyo

KT&G
Sangsang
Madang

Hongik Univ.

Playground
(Free Market)
Club Area

Wausan

Hyundai Department Store
Palsaek
Samgyeopsal
Cheongdam-dong
Pojangmacha

Sogang Univ.

N
W   E
S

Sangsu Stn.

See p184

Gwangheungchang Stn.

Daeheung Stn.

Historic Universities

Yonsei University and Ewha Womans University are two of Korea's most prestigious universities. Yonsei, in fact, is Korea's oldest university, having been founded in 1885 by US missionaries. Ewha Womans University, meanwhile, is the world's largest women's university, with a storied history that goes back to 1886. Both universities were modeled on American universities of the time; accordingly, both campuses are full of romantic, ivy-covered Gothic stone buildings. The campuses also offer a chance to learn about the contributions Christian missionaries made in Korea's educational and social history.

Yonsei University C2

One of Korea's top three universities, Yonsei possesses a storied history dating back to 1885. Yonsei University Medical School and Severance Hospital trace their lineage back to Korea's first modern hospital, the Gwanghyewon, founded by American Presbyterian missionary, doctor and diplomat Horace Allen. The rest of the school traces its

Statue of an eagle, the symbol of Yonsei University

lineage to Chosun Christian College, founded in 1915 by Allen's fellow missionary, Horace Grant Underwood.

Several generations later, the Underwoods are still in Korea and involved with the university, which is now—along with Seoul National University and Korea University—generally regarded as one of Korea's top three universities.

Most of the campus's historic structures can be found in the "old campus" a short walk from the main gate—you'll know it from the courtyard surrounded by three handsome ivy-colored buildings. The H.G. Underwood Statue, which stands in the center of the courtyard, is Seoul's oldest statue, having been first erected in 1928 (and pulled down twice, first by the Japanese and then by the communists). The old stone buildings were designed by Henry Killiam Murphy, an American architect more famous as an advisor to Chinese Nationalist leader Chiang Kai-shek, who hired him to design a modern capital for China in Nanjing.

Also of interest, located to the west of the main campus, is the Underwood Memorial Hall. Built in 1927, this was the very American-style home of the Underwood family. • **Getting There** 10-15 minute walk from exits 2 or 3 of Sinchon Station, Line 2

Ewha Womans University D2

Founded in 1886 by American Methodist Episcopal missionary Mary F. Scranton, Ewha Womans University began as Ewha Hak Dang, now the site of Ewha Girls High School in Jeong-dong. The name, incidentally, means "Pear Blossom Academy" and was bestowed upon the school by none other than King Gojong.

College courses were added to Ewha Hak Dang's curriculum in 1910, and professional courses in 1925. In 1935, the school moved to its current campus in Sinchon, not far from Yonsei University. Finally, in 1946, it was promoted to a full-fledged university.

MISSIONARIES AND KOREAN CHRISTIANITY

History and Culture

Christianity first came to Korea in the 18th century, when Catholicism entered the country from China. At the end of the 19th century, Protestant missionaries from the United States, Great Britain, Canada and Australia began missions in Korea following its opening to the West. In addition to their religion, these missionaries brought social and political change as well—Christians were at the forefront of improving the lot of women in Korean society, for instance, and many Christians were active in the independence struggle against the Japanese.

Today, Christianity is Korea's largest religion, and Korea now produces the world's second largest number of Christian missionaries behind the United States.

One of the most enduring contributions of the Western missionaries was the creation of modern schools and universities. Many of the first missionaries were educators in addition to being preachers, setting up many of Korea's first high schools and universities. Yonsei and Ewha universities are just two examples.

Needless to say, Ewha produced many of Korea's female "firsts," including Korea's first female PhD, its first female lawyer, its first female Constitutional Court justice and its first female prime minister.

Of the historic buildings, the most impressive is the grand Pfeiffer Hall, the administrative main hall of the university. Built in 1935, the Gothic structure was designed by W.M. Vories & Company Architects Ichiryusha, a Japan-based architectural firm founded by William Merrell Vories, an American missionary/English teacher who married into Japanese royalty and became one of Japan's first modern architects. The Ada Prayer Chamber, a small Gothic chapel on the third floor, is a hidden gem.

On a much more modern note is the artificial steel and glass valley connecting the main entrance with the Pfeiffer Hall. Designed by world-famous French architect Dominique Perrault, it was completed in 2008. • **Getting There** Five minute walk from exits 2 or 3 of Ewha Womans University Station, Line 2.

Ewha Shopping Area D3

The area in front of Ewha Womans University is a noted shopping area for women's clothing, accessories, beauty supplies, and other things feminine. Many renowned—or at least well-costumed—hair and nail salons can be found in the area as well.

1 Old ivy-covered hall, Yonsei University 2 Student boxing club, Yonsei University 3 Ewha Campus Complex, designed by French architect Dominique Perrault 4 Ada Prayer Chamber, Pfeiffer Hall, Ewha Womans University

"Hongdae," the heart of Seoul's indie culture

Hongik University Area

Hongik University E2 has one of Korea's top art and design schools, and accordingly, the area around campus has a distinctively artsy feel, with tons of small galleries, art schools and art supply stores in the surrounding neighborhood. On the weekends, you can purchase arts and crafts—many created by local students—at the Hope and Free markets held in front of the university.

For visitors, however, the area around Hongik University is best known as an entertainment district, especially renowned for its many music and dance clubs. Indeed, Hongdae is the beating heart of Korea's "indie" culture, where young people challenge the conservative cultural mores that dominate much of the rest of Korean social life. The highlight of the Hongdae schedule is the monthly "Club Day," (see p186) when a fixed price will get you into about a dozen area clubs.

• **Getting There** Hongik University Station, Line 2

Hope and Free Markets E3

The Hope and Free markets, held in a playground in front of Hongik University every Saturday and Sunday, respectively, give you the chance to purchase crafts handmade by local students and other artistic types around town. Similar to a flea market—the primary difference is that the goods sold are not used, but rather original creations. It's a great place to pick up reasonably priced art by young, up-and-coming talent.

KT&G Sangsang Madang F3

This newly opened cultural complex, easily recognizable by its black floral design, gives local indie artists a venue to show off their stuff, and holds a cinema, gallery, performance hall, café, classrooms and more. • **Hours** 10 am to midnight (1am on the weekends), but each floor keeps its own hours • **Tel** 330-6200

MULTINATIONAL GROWING PAINS
History and Culture

Increasingly, Hongdae has taken on a cosmopolitan vibe as more and more foreigners—English teachers and GIs in particular—discover its dynamic charms. In fact, Hongdae has become the second most popular entertainment district for foreigners after Itaewon. Truth be told, this hasn't been universally welcomed by all of the neighborhood's denizens—US military personnel, in fact, have been ordered by their commanders to keep away from the area, while the local press will on occasion run the odd salacious article concerning the alleged misdeeds of supposedly oversexed foreign English teachers who frequent the clubs. Regardless, most Hongdae clubs and patrons are very welcoming of foreign clientèle, provided they behave properly.

HONGDAE MAP

Legend:
- Restaurants & Bars
- Shops
- Museums & Galleries
- Hotels
- Clubs & Theaters
- Etc.

Rolling Stones

Cheolgil Wang Galbisal

Sanwoolim Korean-style Bar

Lydian

Sky High

All of Rock

Modern Design Museum

The Post Theater

Train Tracks (Meat Restaurant Alley)

Moonji Cultural Institute

Music City

Geek Live House

Flower Shop

산울림 KOFIC 한국영화진흥위원회

Sanwoolim Theater

Sukara Café (1F)

Coffee Prince

Gopchang Jeongol

Live Club Bbang

Kryolan

Café Suda

Jangarang

Jenny's Bread

Jammers

Club Badabie

Coffee Lab

Alternative Space LOOP

Samjin Pharmacy
B-Boy Theater (B1)

Ppullalla Gallery

75015

Taehwa Pla:
Bowling Cer

Café Kkum (B1)
Cellar15 (1F)
Ullim (2F)
IAN Café (3F)
Louis Vins (4F)

Pomponnette

Zorba the Greek

Stereo

Café Undo

Sha

Shim's Tapas

Ding Dong

Market M

Bar Daq

Cup n Plate

Prug

I-Gong

Come Sta?

Anseong Mart

OFFºC

Sinchon Stn.

Mapo Lifelong
Learning Center

Tora-b

Hongik Galbi

Banjiha
Lounge

Café Danchu

6

물 한방울 어린이공원

Witjandari
Children's Park

7

Jongno Bindaetteok

FamilyMart

Tourist Information

Pedestrian-Friendly Street

P.A.C.E

5

Hair & Joy

Richemont Baker

4

Lotte Cinema

KFC

9

PARIS BAGUETTE

M

8

3

Live and Loud

2

1

Hongik Univ. Stn.

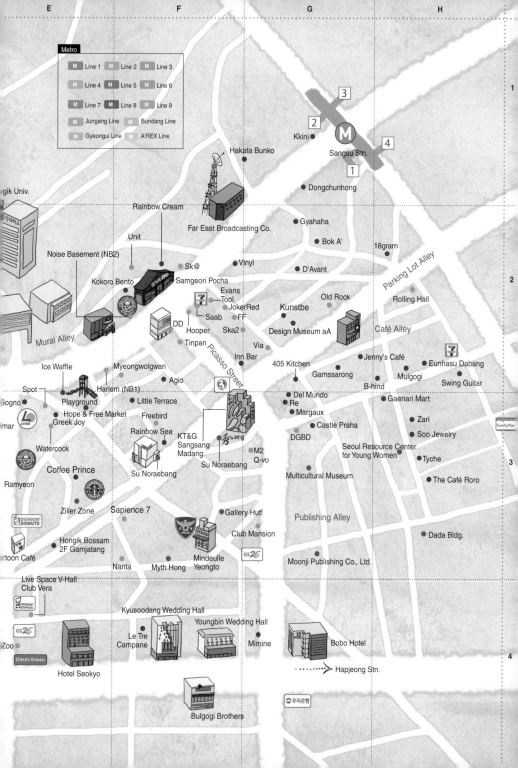

E   F   G   H

Metro

M Line 1   M Line 2   M Line 3
M Line 4   M Line 5   M Line 6
M Line 7   M Line 8   M Line 9
M Jungang Line   M Bundang Line
M Gyeongui Line   M A'REX Line

3

2

4

Kkini

Sangsu Stn.

1

Hakata Bunko

Dongchunhong

ongik Univ.

Gyahaha

Rainbow Cream

Bok A'

18gram

Unit

Far East Broadcasting Co.

Noise Basement (NB2)

Sk@

Vinyl

D'Avant

Parking Lot Alley

Kokoro Bento

Samgeori Pocha

Evans

Old Rock

Rolling Hall

Tool

JokerRed

Kunstbe

DD

Saab

FF

Design Museum aA

Café Alley

Hooper

Ska2

Mural Alley

Tinpan

Via

405 Kitchen

Jenny's Café

Eunhasu Dabang

Inn Bar

Gamssarong

Mulgogi

Swing Guitar

Ice Waffle

Myeongwolgwan

B-hind

Spot

Harlem (NB1)

Agio

Del Mundo

Gaenari Mart

Sogno

Playground

Re

Zari

Hope & Free Market

Little Terrace

Margaux

Soo Jewelry

mar

Greek Joy

Freebird

Castle Praha

DGBD

Watercock

Rainbow Sea

KT&G
Sangsang
Madang

M2
Q-vo

Seoul Resource Center
for Young Women

Tyche

Coffee Prince

Su Noraebang

Su Noraebang

Multicultural Museum

The Café Roro

Ramyeon

Ziller Zone

Sapience 7

Gallery Hut!

Publishing Alley

Dada Bldg.

Club Mansion

Hongik Bossam
2F Gamjatang

GS25

Cartoon Café

Nanta

Myth Hong

Mindeulle
Yeongto

Moonji Publishing Co., Ltd.

Live Space V-Hall
Club Vera

GS25

Kyusoodang Wedding Hall

Youngbin Wedding Hall

Zoo

Le Tre
Campane

Mimine

Bobo Hotel

Omuto Tomato

Hotel Seokyo

Hapjeong Stn.

우리은행

Bulgogi Brothers

FamilyMart

1

2

3

4

B-Boy Theater C2

The B-Boy Theater presents an open run of the wildly popular nonverbal performance, "Battle B-boy." This unique performance combines street B-boy dancing with Korean traditional dance and East Asian music for an engaging nonverbal performance that appeals to audiences of all ages. This performance's transport of street dancing to the stage has been an enormous success, in large part because of its open, audience-engaging style that energizes all who watch it. NOTE: Closed till September 2011. • **Admission** 50,000 won • **Getting There** Hongik University Station, Line 2, Exit 9 • **Tel** 323-5233 • **Website** www.sjbboys.com

Hongdae Club Scene

The clubs in front of Hongik University have something of an interesting history. Unlike the clubs of Itaewon, Hongdae's music and dance clubs often started out as artists' studios that were later transformed into clubs. Beginning in the 1990s, these clubs provided a much-needed space for Korea's developing punk and indie music scene.

It's a neighborhood that basks in its alternative chic, and the clubs here have not been without controversy. The performances, relatively tame compared to those in the West, have occasionally sparked outrage from more conservative elements of the Korean public. In 2005, for instance, a local punk group flashed viewers during a popular TV program, leading city authorities to threaten a crackdown on clubs. This never came to pass, as most appreciate the utility of a space to allow independent musicians a place to do their thing. All visitors are likely to find lots of people having fun. • **Getting There** The "Hongdae" club area is reached from Exit 9 of Hongik University Station, Line 2

TIPS

CLUB DAY & SOUND ROAD

"Club Day"—held every last Friday—used to be the highlight of the Korean club scene, when a 20,000 won ticket got you into 21 local clubs. In February 2011, however, the event was suspended amidst talk that it had become over-commercialized. In May of that year, a local association of clubs announced Club Day would restart from June, focused on nine dance clubs and 10 cafés. Live music clubs, meanwhile, would put together a "Sound Road" every last Sunday from July.

As of the writing of this book, details were still scant.

ELECTRONIC
M2: T. 3143-7573 G3
Via: T. 3141-2046 G2
Tool: T. 010-3112-0338 F2
JokerRed: T. 019-345-7122 F2
HIPHOP
Harlem (NB1): T. 326-1716 E2
Q-Vo: T. 3143-7574 G3
DD Club: T. 011-783-4024 F2
Hooper: T. 336-3445 F2
Saab: T. 324-6929 F2
MIXED
Ska 2: T. 010-8004-4635 G2
Myoungwolgwan: T. 3142-1357 F2
ROCK
Freebird: T. 335-4576 F3
DGBD: T. 322-3792 G3
Soundholic: T. 3412-4203 D3
FF: T. 011-9025-3407 F2
Spot: T. 322-5956 E3
JAZZ
Evans: T. 337-8361 F2
Watercock: T. 324-2422 E3

1 2 3 4 [1] Even foreigners can participate in Hongdae's Free Market [2] Underpass artwork, near Hongik University [3] Crafts for sale, Hongdae Free Market [4] A very colorfully decorated public bathroom, Hondae Free Market

독립문

Independence Gate, erected in 1896

SEODAEMUN PRISON MUSEUM & INDEPENDENCE PARK

Independence Park, the focal point of which is the imposing Seodaemun Prison Museum, pays tribute to the sacrifices of those who fought for Korea's independence throughout the 35 years of Japanese colonial rule (1910 to 1945).

Independence Gate A3, p38

The entrance to Independence Park is Independence Gate, a massive stone gate modeled on the Arch of Triumph in Paris. Designed by a Swiss engineer with funds collected by Korean independence activists, the monument was erected in 1896.

Its history is a bit complex, with a twist of irony. The gate was placed in the location of an older gate, the Yeongeunmun Gate, where during the Joseon era (1392-1910) Korean kings would welcome Chinese envoys—at the time, China and Korea shared an "elder brother–younger brother" relationship in accordance with the traditional Confucian view of international relations. When Japan defeated China in the first Sino-Japanese War in 1895, this relationship between Korea and China was severed, and Korea became "independent." The old gate was razed and the new Independence Gate built in its place. By removing Chinese influence in Seoul, Korea's "independence" simply gave the Japanese a free hand to do as they liked in Korea. Ironically, Korea's "independence" turned out to be the first step on the road to colonization. • **Getting There** Exit 4 of Dongnimmun Station, Line 3.

Seodaemun Prison History Hall A3, p38

For a most sobering look at Korea's colonial past, the place to go is Seodaemun Prison, now a museum and the former "place of residence," so to speak, of many a Korean independence activist during the dark ages of Japanese colonial rule.

The prison complex has a rather surreal atmosphere. In a way, it's actually a very beautiful place. Surrounded by granite mountain peaks, the prison is located in a particularly pretty neighborhood of Seoul. The complex itself consists of well-landscaped lawns and handsome red-brick buildings dating from the final days of the Daehan Empire (see p91). All in all, for a former penitentiary, it's a surprisingly pleasant place to stroll around.

Ultimately, however, Seodaemun Prison is an example of "dark tourism." The front entrance of the prison, with its imposing gate and ominous guard tower, bring to mind Auschwitz. It's a monument preserved so that future generations of Koreans never forget their painful history of oppression and victimization at the hands of foreign aggressors.

Korean flag hangs proudly on wall of Seodaemun Prison, where many Korean independence activists were imprisoned during the Japanese colonial era

Prison cells, Seodaemun Prison Museum

Some of the prison buildings are open to the public. The engineering wing, in fact, has been set up complete with graphic displays of the torture inflicted on prisoners and an educational video. Not for the weak of heart or those allergic to over-the-top acting. One of the cell blocks has been opened to allow visitors to stroll up and down and enter some of the cells. This is probably the most impressive part of the prison—the cells have been left just as they were, and their cold walls say more than 1,000 propaganda videos.

In one corner of the complex, removed from the brick buildings, is a wooden Japanese-style building. This is where female prisoners were held. It was here that Ewha High School student and independence activist Ryu Gwansun was tortured to death in 1920.

If there's one aspect of the prison museum that is lacking, however, it's the almost complete lack of mention that the complex was used as a prison in the post-independence era, too—all the way until 1987, in fact. Under Korea's post-war military dictators, many democracy activists and dissidents were made "guests" of the facility.

Near the prison complex are a number of other statues and monuments to Korea's independence movement.

- **Hours** 9:30 am to 6 pm (Mar to Oct), 9:30 am to 5 pm (Nov to Feb). Closed Mondays
- **Admission** 1,500 won • **Getting There** Exit 5 of Dongnimmun Station, Line 3
- **Tel** 360-8590 • **Website** www.sscmc.or.kr

Other Sites of Interest

Sajik Park A3, p38

Sajik Park is home to Sajikdan shrine, where the kings of Joseon used to perform the Sajikdaeje, a religious service to two gods: Sasin (the god of earth) and Jiksin (the god of the harvest). The rite was a prayer for peace and a bountiful harvest, and featured processions, sacrificial offerings, special attire, and music and dance. In 1908, however, the rite was discontinued under Japanese pressure, and the shrine was turned into a park. In 1988, the rite was restarted, and is held once a year on National Foundation Day (Oct 3).

While most of the Sajikdan was destroyed by the Japanese, two stone altars still remain. Also remaining is its stately front gate, which dates from 1720. Just behind the park is another shrine to Dangun (see p281), Korea's mythical founder, and a short walk from there will bring you to the Hwanghakjeong, a Joseon-era archery ground that is still in use. • **Getting There** Walk 10 minutes from Exit 1 of Gyeongbokgung Station, Line 1.

INDEPENDENCE DAY AND THE KOREAN FLAG   *History and Culture*

Korea celebrates its Independence Day, or *Gwangbokjeol* ("Restoring the Light Day"), on August 15. This was the day Japan surrendered to the Allies in 1945, bringing the Pacific War—and the Japanese Empire in Korea—to an end. Of course, Japan's surrender didn't bring true independence, per se—Korea was then divided and occupied by the United States in the south and the Soviet Union in the north, and an independent Republic of Korea wasn't declared until three years later.

Independence Day is usually marked with flying flags and presidential speeches. Seoul City Hall is usually decorated in some patriotic way, too.

The flag of the Republic of Korea—the Taegeukgi—is perhaps the world's most philosophical flag. In its center is a large red and blue Taoist *yin-yang*, which represents the harmony of opposites that is the origin of all things. The four trigrams that surround the *yin-yang* come from the *I Ching*, and symbolize justice, wisdom, vitality and fertility. They are also references to the classical elements. The white background, meanwhile, symbolizes the purity of the Korean people.

King Gojong proclaimed the Taegeukgi as Korea's national flag in 1883. After Korea's colonization by Japan, the flag continued to be used by the Provisional Government of the Republic of Korea in China, and was brought back once the Republic of Korea was established in 1948.

PLACES TO EAT: SEODAEMUN AREA

The Hongdae and Sinchon areas are young areas catering to a young crowd, and the restaurants reflect this. There are a few international options here, too.

Wan Chai A Chinese restaurant frequented by students. (T. 392-7744) C2, p178

Bokseonggak Another well-known Chinese restaurant. (T. 392-1560) C2, p178

Palsaek Samgyeopsal Specializes in Korean-style bacon, or *samgyeopsal*. (T. 719-4848) C3, p178

Choi's Tacos A taco place. Run by a man named Choi. Does a really good trade. (T. 362-2113) C2, p178

On The Border Mexican Grill & Cantina The largest Mexican restaurant chain in the United States has a shop near Sinchon Station. Good place to go for a margarita. (T. 324-0682) C3, p178

Cheolgil Wang Galbisal A particular favorite of this writer, they do wonderful Korean *galbi* served with outstanding bean-paste soup, or *doenjang jjigae*. Reasonably priced, too. (T. 332-9543) B1, p184

Greek Joy Near Hongik, this is one of the best (and one of the few!) Greek eateries in Korea. (T. 338-2100) E3, p185

Manokamana Indian and Nepali cuisine not far from the front gate of Yonsei University. (T. 338-4343) C2, p178

Sinchon Sinuiju Chapssal Sundae A short walk from Sinchon Rotary, this restaurant specializes in *sundae* (Korean blood sausage). Give the rich, spicy *sundae jeongol* (sundae stew) a try. (T. 715-1772) B3, p178

Mussel & Muggle With a French-trained chef in the kitchen, this place near Sinchon's Hyundai Department Store does Belgian-style mussels, mussel pasta and even a mussel pizza. (T. 324-5919) C2, p178

Shanti Nepali and Indian chefs serve authentic dishes from their home countries. Not far from Hongik University. (T. 325-1779) D3, p184

106 Ramyeon This Hongdae place does instant noodles—and only three kinds at that—but what they do is good. Try the spicy *budae jjigae ramyeon*, which comes with sausage. (T. 3142-1241) D3, p184

Cheongdam-dong Pojangmacha A good place to have a bottle of *soju* over a *gyeran mari* (egg roll), fried chicken's feet or spicy bean sprout soup. (T. 363-4377) C3, p178

Yangpuni Jumak A Korean-style pub, the house specialty is its *gyeran mari* (egg roll) and *pajeon* (Korean pancake), which goes well with a bowl of *dongdongju* (Korean rice beer). (T. 338-3285) C2, p178

Tyche Near Hongdae's KT&G Sangsang Madang, this wine bar has a pleasantly unpretentious atmosphere and does decent steak and Italian food, too. (T. 333-9577) H3, p185

Little Terrace Or more precisely, "This Little Terrace Has Mesmerized Me," this fifth-floor wine bar serves affordable wines in a romantic atmosphere. Oh yeah, and it's got a terrace with nice views. (T. 333-3310) F3, p185

Castle Praha A taste of the Czech Republic in Korea, this Czech-style beer hall houses a microbrewery (run by a Czech brew master) that produces dark and wheat beers in addition to your standard pilsener. (T. 334-2121) G3, p185

Re Possibly the only venue in Seoul where you can sit in a tent, pitched indoors, while drinking wine while listening to reggae. The bar is also associated with efforts to help Tibet - as if that wasn't obvious. (T. 322-5743) G3, p185

Le Tre Campane A great place to go for genuine thin-crust, oven baked pizza and other Italian dishes. (T. 336-3378) F4, p185

Kokoro Bento This popular eatery does Japanese-style box lunches, or bento, and does them well. Take-out available, too. (T. 338-3822). F2, p185

Mimine Loved by the Hondae crowd, this youthful "Korean snack bar" does quick Korean eats like pan-fried rice cakes (*tteokbokki*) and tempura (*twigim*). It's particularly noted for its gungmul tteokbokki, pan-fried rice cakes in a very spicy soup. (T. 070-4042-8011) G4, p185

Gam Salon So named because the place is made from the wood of the persimmon (gam) tree, Gam Salon is best known for its delicious hand-made burgers. (T. 337-9373) G2, p185

YONGSAN AREA

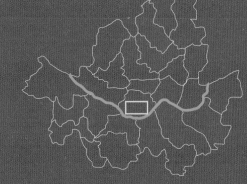

THINGS TO DO AND SEE

- Sample the international cuisine and atmosphere of Itaewon, one of Seoul's most popular entertainment and shopping districts, particularly for foreigners

- Appreciate Korea's illustrious history and culture at the mammoth National Museum of Korea

- Play on captured North Korean tanks and learn about the Korean War and Korea's military history at the War Memorial of Korea

- Buy some computer equipment or new software at Yongsan Electronics Market

- Enjoy some peaceful contemplation at Wonhyo Catholic Church

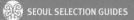

WHERE THE WORLD MEETS SEOUL

Wedged in between Mt. Namsan and the Hangang River, Seoul's gritty Yongsan district is Seoul's multicultural center, with the city's largest concentration of foreigners. Many of these foreigners have traditionally been US military personnel based at the sprawling US Yongsan Garrison, but in recent years, they've been joined by a growing number of English teachers, businessmen and traders from other Western countries, Japan, Africa and the Middle East. There are also a large number of tourists and visitors from other Asian nations, especially China. Increasingly, Koreans from other parts of Seoul are descending on the district's multicultural neighborhoods—especially Itaewon—to sample the exotic cuisines and cultures.

Yongsan has more to see than just foreigners, however. The recently completed new National Museum of Korea is one of the largest museum facilities in the world, and a mandatory stop for any visitor to Seoul. Near the US military base is the imposing War Memorial of Korea, where you can learn about Korea's turbulent history. The bustling Yongsan Electronics Market, meanwhile, is Korea's best place to stock up on gadgets and software. Near the electronics market are Yongsan Seminary and Wonhyoro Catholic Church, one of Seoul's oldest churches and an oasis of calm in the urban jungle.

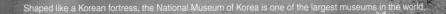

Shaped like a Korean fortress, the National Museum of Korea is one of the largest museums in the world.

Multicultural streets of Itaewon

ITAEWON

Now the heart of Seoul's expatriate community, Itaewon got its start in the early 20th century, when it was a residential district for Japanese colonialists. The Japanese left in 1945 following their defeat in the Pacific War, but they were replaced by the Americans, who set up shop in the massive Japanese military compound in Yongsan (now the US Army Garrison—Yongsan). Itaewon, located next to the base, became a GI playground, and over the ensuing decades it would acquire a well-deserved reputation for rowdiness and seediness.

Times, however, have changed dramatically. Over the last decade, Itaewon's streets have grown increasingly diverse—today, you are just as likely to meet a Pakistani laborer or a Chinese tourist as you are a US soldier. High atop a hill in the heart of the neighborhood, Seoul's largest Islamic mosque looms majestically, while below, shoppers and fun-seekers of all colors and nationalities flock to the area's famous shops and foreign eateries. Koreans—who used to avoid Itaewon like the plague—now flock here in droves; on a weekend, you can find countless Korean couples and families strolling about its streets, taking in its exotic sights, tastes, smells and sounds.

As part of the transformation process, Itaewon has been gentrifying. If seedy dives filled with questionable characters and women of easy virtue are what you're looking for, you'll still find them aplenty, but they've taken a back seat to much more upscale establishments catering to Seoul's cultured class. Where country-western clubs and pickup joints once held sway, classy European bistros, elegant wine bars and quaint cafés now reign. Depending on who you ask, this is either the tragic loss of Itaewon's "traditional" identity or a long and badly needed improvement in the neighborhood's culture.

• **Getting There** Itaewon Station, Line 6 drops you off right in the heart of Itaewon. The Haebangchon area, however, is easiest reached via Noksapyeong Station, Line 6.

Layout

The heart of Itaewon is the "main drag" which runs east-west starting from Noksapyeong Station in the west. It's along here that you'll find many of the neighborhood's landmark shops, eateries and bars. You'll find quite a bit in the alleyways off the main drag, too, particularly south of Itaewon Station—it's here that you'll find the infamous "Hooker Hill," as well as Seoul's largest concentration of gay bars and clubs—and behind the Hamilton Hotel, where you'll find more upscale establishments.

For a list of Itaewon bars and restaurants, check out the Restaurants section of this chapter.

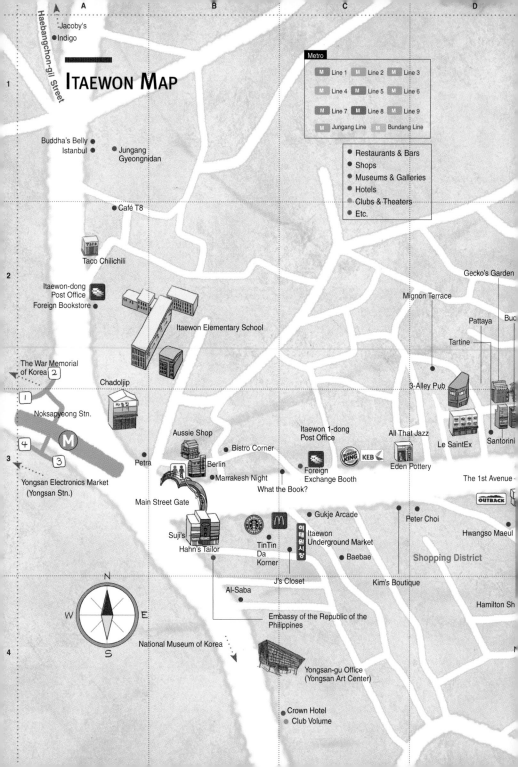

ITAEWON MAP

Haebangchon-gil Street

Jacoby's
Indigo

Metro

M	Line 1	M	Line 2	M	Line 3
M	Line 4	M	Line 5	M	Line 6
M	Line 7	M	Line 8	M	Line 9
M	Jungang Line	M	Bundang Line

● Restaurants & Bars
● Shops
● Museums & Galleries
● Hotels
● Clubs & Theaters
● Etc.

Buddha's Belly
Istanbul
● Jungang
Gyeongnidan

● Café T8

Taco Chilichili

Itaewon-dong
Post Office
Foreign Bookstore ●

Itaewon Elementary School

The War Memorial
of Korea ⌐2⌐

Chadoljip

Noksapyeong Stn.

M

Yongsan Electronics Market
(Yongsan Stn.)

Main Street Gate

Aussie Shop
● Bistro Corner
Petra
Berlin
● Marrakesh Night

What the Book?

Suji's
Hahn's Tailor
TinTin
Da
Korner

Al-Saba

J's Closet

Embassy of the Republic of the
Philippines

National Museum of Korea

Gecko's Garden

Mignon Terrace

Pattaya
Buc
Tartine

3-Alley Pub

Itaewon 1-dong
Post Office

All That Jazz
Le SaintEx
Santorini

BURGER KING   KEB

Foreign
Exchange Booth

Eden Pottery

The 1st Avenue

OUTBACK

● Gukje Arcade
Peter Choi
Hwangso Maeul

Itaewon
Underground Market
● Baebae
Shopping District

Kim's Boutique

Hamilton Sh

Yongsan-gu Office
(Yongsan Art Center)

Crown Hotel
● Club Volume

N
W   E
S

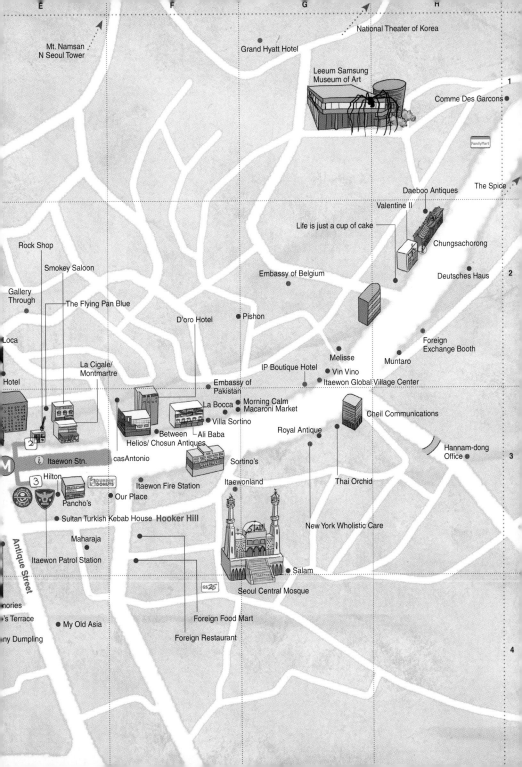

National Theater of Korea

Grand Hyatt Hotel

Mt. Namsan
N Seoul Tower

Leeum Samsung
Museum of Art

Comme Des Garcons

1

FamilyMart

The Spice

Daeboo Antiques

Valentine II

Life is just a cup of cake

Chungsachorong

Rock Shop

Smokey Saloon

Deutsches Haus

2

Gallery
Through

The Flying Pan Blue

Embassy of Belgium

Loca

D'oro Hotel

Pishon

Foreign
Exchange Booth

La Cigale/
Montmartre

Melisse

Muntaro

Hotel

IP Boutique Hotel

Embassy of
Pakistan

Vin Vino

Itaewon Global Village Center

La Bocca

Morning Calm

Macaroni Market

Cheil Communications

Villa Sortino

2

Royal Antique

Between
Helios/ Chosun Antiques

Ali Baba

Hannam-dong
Office

3

casAntonio

Sortino's

i Itaewon Stn.

Hilton

3

Itaewon Fire Station

Itaewonland

Thai Orchid

Pancho's

Our Place

New York Wholistic Care

Sultan Turkish Kebab House Hooker Hill

Maharaja

Itaewon Patrol Station

Salam

GS25

nories

Seoul Central Mosque

's Terrace

ny Dumpling

My Old Asia

Foreign Food Mart

Foreign Restaurant

Antique Street

4

الله أكبر

Built in 1976, Seoul Central Mosque is the center of Seoul's Muslim community.

Sites of Interest

Seoul Central Mosque G3

Sitting atop Hooker Hill, Seoul Central Mosque—a beautiful white beacon of human decency looking down upon the decadence of Itaewon—is Korea's largest Islamic house of worship, built in 1976. The area around the mosque has a number of good Middle Eastern restaurants and shops specializing in religious items and goods imported from the Middle East. • **Tel** 793-6908

Leeum Samsung Museum of Art G1

One of Seoul's finest art museums can be found in Itaewon on the lower slopes of Mt. Namsan north of the "main drag." The architecturally stunning Leeum Samsung Museum of Art, which opened in 2004, was designed by renowned designers Mario Botta, Jean Nouvel and Rem Koolhaas and is home to beautiful pieces of Korean traditional and Western art, including several national treasures. The museum got its start with the personal art collection of Samsung founder Lee Byung-chul. • **Hours** 10:30 am to 6 pm. Closed Mondays • **Admission** 10,000 won • **Tel** 2014-6900

'Hooker Hill' F3

While much of the rest of Itaewon is in the process of gentrification, you can still find some of the old-time sleaze on the appropriately named "Hooker Hill," an alley of seedy bars and clubs to the south of Itaewon's main drag. One feature of the alley is the so-called "juicy bar," where male clients buy overpriced drinks for hostesses in return for a bit of conversation, and the "*soju* kettle," a local firewater of *soju* and fruit juice, usually served in soft drink bottles.

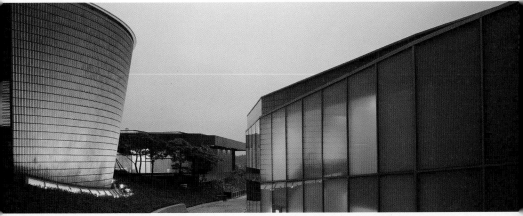

Leeum Samsung Museum of Art

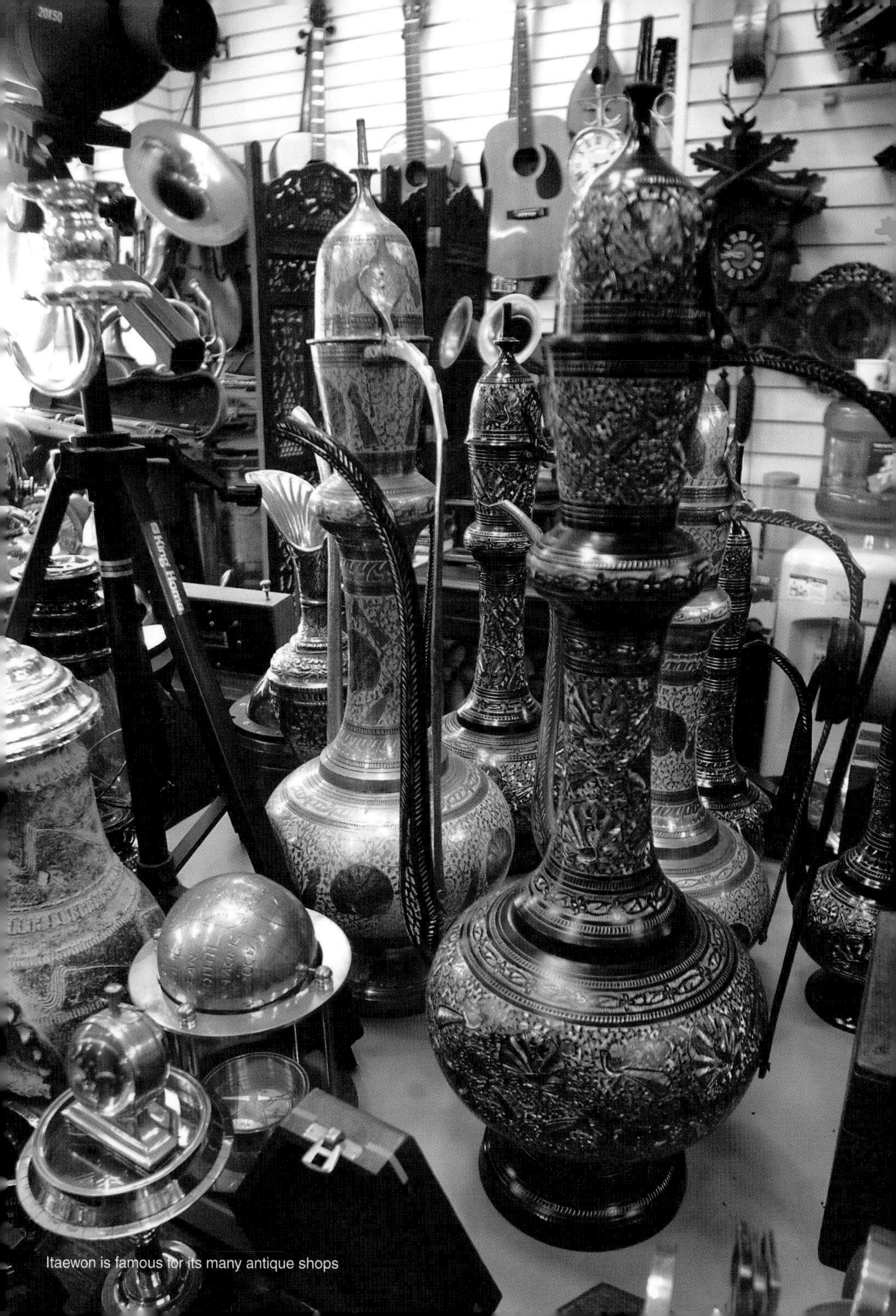

Itaewon is famous for its many antique shops

Shopping

Itaewon is a popular shopping center with foreigners thanks to its English-friendly environment and the availability of larger sizes. Of particular shopping note are:

Tailor-Made Suits D3

Tailor shops—many of them around for decades—line Itaewon's main drag, and you're likely to be asked more than once if you'd like to have a suit made. (see TIPS)

Antiques E3

Itaewon, along with Insa-dong, is Seoul's best place to purchase antiques. Unlike Insa-dong, however, most of the shopkeepers here speak English and Japanese. In shops like Chosun Antique (T. 793-3726, F3) and Kim's Antique Gallery (T. 796-8841, F3), you can find handsome old Korean dressers and tables, Korean doors, brasswork and much, much more. Of course, expect to pay antique prices.

Hamilton Shopping Center E3

Located next to the Hamilton Hotel, the Hamilton Shopping Center is four stories of shops specializing in clothing, souvenirs and traditional goods.

Leather Goods D3

You'll find leather goods in abundance—selling bags, shoes, jackets and other items made from, well, leather.

TIPS

TAILOR-MADE SUITS

Itaewon's main drag is home to many tailors who specialize in tailor-made suits. In fact, as you're walking along, you'll likely be approached by at least one tailor. Suits can run anywhere from 300,000 won to over a million, depending on the materials. Hahn's Tailor (T. 793-0830, B3) gets good reviews from customers. Also good for tailored shirts is Hamilton Shirts (T. 798-5693, D3), which will deliver shirts to your hotel room.

LANGUAGE BARRIER NO MORE

Most of the establishments in Itaewon have staff that speak English and Japanese, so don't worry about communication difficulties.

HOMO HILL F3

While times are changing, Korean society is still rather conservative, and it cannot be said Seoul has a thriving gay nightlife scene. Itaewon is a rare exception to this. On a hill not far from Hooker Hill is a collection of gay and lesbian bars and nightclubs. Some clubs cater to the transvestites, too.

HAEBANGCHON A1

A short walk from Itaewon, past Noksapyeong Station and up towards Namsan Third Tunnel is Haebangchon, a residential neighborhood originally founded after the Korean War by refugees from North Korea (hence the name, which literally means, "Liberation Village"). Today, it is inhabited by a large number of foreigners, particularly English teachers from the West, Nigerians and Filipinos. Accordingly, it is home to a number of decent foreign restaurants. Give it a look.

Goryeo-era
Gyeongcheonsa Temple Pagoda
(National Treasure No. 86), main hall of
National Museum of Korea

MORE YONGSAN SITES

National Museum of Korea

The National Museum of Korea—previously located in the Gwanghwamun area—opened in its new home in Yongsan in October 2005. And an impressive home it is—almost half a kilometer in length and six stories in height, it's the largest museum in Asia and the sixth largest museum in the world in terms of floor

space, covering 28,542.3 m². Its massive design is said to resemble a Korean traditional fortress, and the museum grounds are decked out with ponds, Korean traditional gardens and other facilities that make it a pleasant enough place to visit even before you walk through the door. The museum makes use of the cutting edge in museum technology to ensure that its precious collection of artifacts could survive anything short of a direct nuclear hit.

The museum's regular exhibits are divided up as follows:

- **Floor 1:** Archaeological Gallery, Historical Gallery
- **Floor 2:** Fine Arts Gallery I, Donation Gallery
- **Floor 3:** Fine Arts Gallery II, Asian Arts Gallery

All in all, the museum has a collection of 150,000 artifacts and works of art, although only a fraction of these are on display at any given time. The collection includes many of Korea's most treasured pieces of art, including Silla-era Buddhist art, Goryeo-era celadon ceramics and Joseon-era paintings. In the awe-inspiring main lobby is the giant Gyeongcheonsa Temple Pagoda, a beautifully carved 13-meter marble structure dating from the Goryeo era.

The museum also hosts regular special exhibits that are well worth the price of admission. Guided tours of the museum are also given—English language tours are available daily at 2:30 to 3:30 pm.

- **Hours** 9 am to 6 pm (Tue, Thur, Fri), 9 am to 9 pm (Wed, Sat), 9 am to 7 pm (Sun, holidays)
- **Admission** You can see the permanent exhibit for free, but there's an entry charge for special exhibits (entry depends on the exhibit) • In addition to the exhibits, the museum has a good deal of other facilities as well, including performance halls and a theater. • **Getting There** Ichon Station, Line 4 or Joongang Line, Exit 2 • **Tel** 2077-9045~7 • **Website** www.museum.go.kr

Artillery piece and Two Brothers Statue, War Memorial of Korea

The War Memorial of Korea

The War Memorial of Korea is a massive space that includes both indoor and outdoor exhibition halls. The most moving aspect of the entire complex is the Memorial Hall: upon the walls running along the entire front perimeter of the building are inscribed the names of all the soldiers whose lives were lost during the Korean War. The list of names go on forever—Korean casualties are listed by unit, while UN casualties are listed by nation, with the exception of the United States, whose war dead are listed by state. Visually jarring, Memorial Hall is a powerful reminder of the devastation of war. The indoor exhibition hall details the war history of Korea from the Three Kingdoms Era to the present, with the vast majority of the complex dedicated to the events of the Korean War (see p273). The section on the Korean War is meticulously detailed and well organized, using a fine balance of artifacts, text and audiovisual materials to give visitors a comprehensive understanding of the war. The outside exhibition showcases the actual equipment used during the Korean War, as well as the Korean War Monument and Two Brothers Statue.

• **Hours** 9 am to 6 pm. Ticket sales stop one hour to closing. Closed Mondays • **Admission** Free • **Getting There** Samgakji Station, Line 4 or 6, Exit 12 • **Tel** 709-3139 • **Website** www.warmemo.or.kr

Yongsan Electronics Market

Compared with other places in Asia, Korea is, by and large, not a cheap place to pick up electronic goods, despite the fact that Korean companies like Samsung and LG produce some of the world's finest cell phones, computers, LEDs and other digital products. This is particularly the case with imported electronics—you'll find what you're looking for, but don't expect big bargains.

To buy gadgets on the relatively cheap, head to Yongsan Electronics Market, a collection of several markets and malls located behind Yongsan Station. You'll find stereo equipment, computers and computer supplies, software, office equipment and other electronic goodies for prices 20% less than where you'd find them elsewhere—and in the case of imported goods, up to 50% less.

Gamers will love the underground computer game market, where you can find all the latest computer game titles. After all, Korea—where StarCraft and World of Warcraft have virtually become national pastimes—is one of the world's biggest markets for computer games.

PC users have found the Promised Land—you'll find many small shops where you can have top-of-the-line desktops built for under US$1,000. Mac users, on the other hand, will find fewer shops catering to their needs, but the growing popularity of Apple products in Korea has made life much easier for Mac users than it used to be. You'll find a Mac store on the first floor of the ETLAND mall.

Most of the shops are open from 10 am to 8 pm, and are closed on the first and third Sundays of the month. • **Getting There** The market is located near Yongsan Station, Line 1 or Sinyongsan Station, Line 4

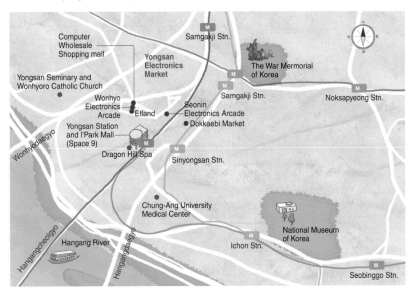

Yongsan Station and I'Park Mall

Attached by a skyway to the electronics market are Yongsan Station and I'Park Mall, one of Seoul's newest shopping malls, with everything you'd expect in a shopping mall, including restaurants and one of Seoul's best movie theaters. Yongsan Station is Seoul's second largest train station and the primary point of departure for destinations in Korea's southwest, such as Jeonju, Gwangju and Mokpo.

Yongsan Seminary and Wonhyoro Catholic Church

Just a 10-minute walk from the Yongsan Electronics Market, on the campus of Sacred Heart Girls High School, is one of Seoul's hidden treasures, the Yongsan Seminary and Wonhyoro Catholic Church. The red-brick church itself isn't big— it's little more than a chapel built for the former seminary next door. It is, however, pretty, and sits on a slope overlooking Yongsan. Designed by Father Eugène Coste of the Paris Foreign Missions Society, it was completed in 1902, making it one of the oldest churches in the country. The Georgian-style former seminary (now museum) is even older, dating from 1892.

US ARMY GARRISON—YONGSAN
History and Culture

Sprawling over 2.5 km² of prime Seoul real estate just south of Mt. Namsan, the US Army Garrison—Yongsan is both a symbol of the "alliance forged in blood" between Korea and the United States and a historical reminder of Korea's painful past.

In the late 19th century, the Qing Dynasty occupied a strategic location on the Hangang River before they were kicked out by the Japanese, who established a massive military compound and headquarters. When the Japanese were defeated in World War II, out went the Japanese troops, and in came the Americans. In fact, a number of historic buildings in the garrison, including the headquarters of the 8th US Army, were built by the Japanese.

Needless to say, hosting a massive foreign military complex in the heart of their capital has proven controversial among Koreans. In 2003, Korea and the US agreed to transfer Yongsan back to Korea; the US side would move its headquarters to the city of Pyeongtaek, some 90 km to the south, by 2012. Seoul Metropolitan City announced it would use the land to build a massive park, something akin to New York City's Central Park. In 2008, however, the new presidential administration of Lee Myung-bak, fearing a weakening of US resolve to defend Korea, pushed the transfer date back to 2016.

US Army Garrison—Yongsan is off-limits to all but US military personnel and US military civilians, although on-base friends can sign you in for a visit (depending on your nationality).

1
2 3
4

[1] Viewing the priceless artifacts at the National Museum of Korea [2] Please don't climb on the captured communist tank. War Memorial of Korea [3] Yongsan Station is not only a major transportation hub, but also home to the I'Park Mall [4] Charming Wonhyoro Catholic Church, built in 1902

PLACES TO EAT: YONGSAN

Yongsan—or at least Itaewon—is THE place to come in Seoul for international eats. You'll find eateries from all over the world—standard Western fare, Middle Eastern cuisine, Thai food, Indian curries, Korean barbecue and more. In recent years, the restaurants have grown increasingly upscale—or at least less grungy. p202

Sortino's One of the best Italian restaurants in Seoul, run by an expatriate Italian-Canadian. A tad pricey, but worth it. (T. 797-0488) F3

La Cigale Famous for its Belgian-style mussels, this classy place is particularly popular in summer, when its outdoor seating is a blessing. (T. 796-1244) E3

Le Saint Ex The oldest French restaurant in Seoul, this cozy bistro is run by a long-time French expatriate. (T. 795-2465) D3

Gecko's Terrace Overlooking Itaewon Station, this European-style pub has good pub food and a cozy atmosphere, although it does get crowded on a weekend. (T. 749-9425) E3

Gecko's Garden Owned by the same person as Gecko's Terrace, this tapas bar behind the Hamilton Hotel is a favorite spot in summer with its wonderful outdoor garden. (T. 790-0540) D2

Buddha's Belly A Thai-themed wine bar that serves Thai cuisine in a classy setting. (T. 796-9330) A1

casAntonio Along with Sortino's, one of the best Italian restaurants in Seoul. Perfect combo of fine cuisine and class atmosphere. (T. 794-8803) F3

Taco Chilichili A short walk up from Noksapyeong Station, this very popular Mexican restaurant has burritos to die for. (T. 797-7219) A2

Moghul One of Seoul's oldest Indian restaurants, this eatery is a bit pricey, but its tranquil atmosphere is such that you wouldn't know you were in Itaewon. (T. 796-5501) D3

Jacoby's In this writer's opinion, the best burgers in Korea can be found here. Just be sure to go on an empty stomach: these monsters aren't light eating. (T. 3785-0433) A1

Salam A good Turkish restaurant near Seoul Central Mosque. (T. 793-4323) G3

The Spice Fine European dining: the head chef studied under Gordon Ramsay. Pricey, but not terribly so. Trendy atmosphere. (T. 749-2596) H1

Petra Good Middle Eastern cuisine, with a view overlooking Noksapyeong Station. (T. 790-4433) A3

La Bocca This outstanding Italian cafe, deli and wine bar mixes good food with a relaxing atmosphere. Good for brunch, too. (T. 790-5907) F3

Indigo A pleasant little Haebangchon café with good food and a warm atmosphere. (T. 749-0508) A1

HANGANG RIVER AREA

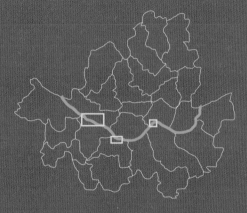

THINGS TO DO AND SEE

- Take a cruise on the mighty river

- Check out the 63 Building on Yeouido, the Manhattan of Seoul

- Feed the deer at Seoul Forest

- Learn about Korea's early modern history at Yanghwajin Foreigners' Cemetery and Jeoldusan Catholic Martyrs Shrine

- Take in the views at Haneul Park near World Cup Stadium

- Head to the Banpo Bridge to watch the beautiful Moonlight Rainbow Fountain

A River Runs Through It

If Seoul were to have a defining topographical characteristic, it would be the Hangang River. Flowing down from its headwaters high in the mountains to the east, the Hangang River has for centuries brought life to the plains of central Korea, allowing cities and civilizations to flourish. It has irrigated the soils, brought trade and commerce, served as a defensive barrier against attack, and in recent years, provided the residents of Seoul with a much beloved place of rest and relaxation.

The Hangang River more or less bisects the city of Seoul along an east-west line, and in so doing forms a very important socio-economic border. To the north is the old city of Seoul, with its historic sites, commercial centers and many working-class neighborhoods. To the south is the new city of Seoul, home to glass skyscrapers, wide avenues, upscale shops and posh apartments. The divide between Gangbuk (north of the river) and Gangnam (south of the river) is as wide as the river is broad, and no discussion of Seoul's pending social and political issues would be complete without it. While the Hangang River has always been one of Seoul's biggest scenic attractions, recent years have witnessed great efforts on the part of the city to really make the fullest use of the waterway. Parks have been built, bridges lit, historical sites restored and more. One of the nicest achievements of this was the opening in 2005 of Seoul Forest, which bills itself as the "Central Park of Seoul." Another major park opened recently is Haneul Park near the massive World Cup Stadium—the park, amazingly enough, was built on a landfill. Of course, the old standbys still work just as well, such as taking in the views from the observatory of the 63 Building—briefly the tallest building in Asia—located at the tip of Yeouido, the so-called "Manhattan of Seoul."

Hangang River and Banpo Bridge

Wedding hall in Ttukseom area, Hangang River

Hangang River Cruise Boat Docks

Sangam Pier
Jamdubong Pier
Seoul Forest Pier
Ttukseom Pier
Yangwha Pier
Seoul Marina
Yeouido Pier
Yeongdong Bridge
Jamsil Bridge
Hangang Bridge
Hannam Bridge
Dongjak Bridge
Jamsil Pier

RIVER CRUISES

The best way to see the river is via one of the city's popular river cruises. These cruises run from about midday to late at night, although the evening cruises—especially around sunset—tend to be the most popular. This is an extremely pleasant way to spend an hour or so, and a great way to take in riverside landmarks such as the Hangang bridges and the golden 63 Building.

You can board ferries at one of three piers—Yeouido, Jamsil and Ttukseom. One-way and round-trip courses are available—see the time tables below.

TIPS

HANGANG RIVER BRIDGES
There are a total of 27 bridges that cross the Hangang River in the Seoul area. Some of these bridges are lit up at night to provide spectacular night views. The futuristic Olympic Bridge in the eastern part of the city is particularly stunning.

Some of the bridges are quite historic as well. Hangang Railway Bridge A, for instance, was completed in 1900, and several others were built in the Japanese colonial era.

Courses

Type	Pier	Travel Time	Fee
Ordinary Cruise	Yeouido, Jamsil, Ttukseom	1 hour	11,000 won
Live Music Cruise	Yeouido, Jamsil, Ttukseom	70 min	15,000 won
BBQ Cruise	Yeouido	90 min	60,000 won
Buffet Cruise	Yeouido	90 min	60,000 won

*Reservations necessary for the BBQ and Buffet ferries.

- **Yeouido:** Yeouido ⟶ Banpo Bridge ⟶ Yeouido
- **Jamsil:** Jamsil ⟶ Banpo Bridge ⟶ Jamsil
- **Ttukseom:** Ttukseom ⟶ Banpo Bridge ⟶ Ttukseom

• **Yeouido Pier** Exit 3 of Yeouinaru Station, Line 5 • **Jamsil Pier** Exit 7 of Sincheon Station, Line 2. Walk about 20 minutes (or take a cab) • **Ttukseom Pier** Exit 8 of Ttukseom Station, Line 2. Walk about 10 minutes • **Website** www.hcruise.co.kr (C&Hangangland)

Saetgang Bridge over Yeouido Saetgang Ecological Park

YEOUIDO

Koreans often refer to Yeouido as the "Manhattan of Seoul," and while this is no doubt an exaggeration, the comparison is not completely without basis. Like its cousin in New York, Yeouido is a river island, and it's Seoul's political, financial, commercial and media heart. The 63 Building, Seoul's landmark skyscraper, is located here.

Yeouido is very much a product of Korea's post-war economic miracle. Prior to industrialization starting in the 1960s, Yeouido was a flood-plagued sandy island with a name meaning, in fact, "Useless Island." During the Japanese colonial period, the imperial authorities built Korea's first international airport on the island. In the 1970s, Korea's development-minded dictator Park Chung-hee pushed an ambitious program to turn the erstwhile "useless island" into a new commercial and political center. In 1975, the green dome of the National Assembly Building was completed, providing a new home to the Korean parliament. Korea's major political parties, media companies, banks and investment houses and other major companies soon followed.

If you're expecting towering, Art Deco skyscrapers à la New York, you'll be disappointed—Yeouido is, in fact, not an especially exciting place. Still, there are a number of things to see.

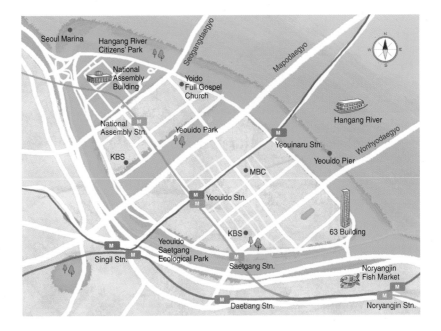

63 Building

249-meters high, this golden monolith was an architectural wonder when it was completed in 1985. Until the completion of the OUB Centre in Singapore one year later, it was the tallest building in Asia, and it remained the tallest building in Korea until 2002. The name refers to the number of floors, although this is somewhat misleading—only 60 floors are above ground.

The building houses a shopping center, an IMAX Theater and a popular aquarium, in addition to restaurants, conference centers and, of course, offices. The most popular destination, however, is the observation deck, which offers some of the best views of the city. • **Hours** 10 am to 10 pm • **Observation deck** 12,000 won • **Aquarium** 17,000 won • **IMAX Theater,** 12,000 won • **Total package** 33,000 won (10% discount prices available if you bring passport/foreigner ID card) • **Tel** 789-5663

View from 63 Art Hall, 63 Building

National Assembly Building

Home of the Korean parliament, this landmark green-domed building with pleasant gardens was completed in 1975. Also nearby is the National Assembly Library. If you'd like to see Korean democracy in action, you can take a tour of the hall—just apply at the visitor's center. • **Hours** 9 am to 6 pm (weekdays), 9 am to 5 pm (weekends). Admission closes one hour before closing • **Tel** 788-2885

TIPS

SPRINGTIME IN YEOUIDO

The time to go to Yeouido is spring, when the island's countless cherry blossoms bloom. Yeouido Park hosts the Yeouido Cherry Blossom Festival at this time—it's Seoul's most popular cherry blossom event, and is accompanied by music and other cultural events.

HALLELUJAH!

Yoido Full Gospel Church, located near the National Assembly, is the mother of all megachurches—with 830,000 members as of 2007, it is the largest Christian congregation in the world. Not bad considering that when it was founded by Rev. David Yonggi Cho in 1958, the Pentecostal church was little more than a tent church.

Services take place almost all day Sunday—these truly are impressive events of faith and devotion. Foreign language services in English, Chinese, Japanese, Spanish, Bahasa and Russian are also provided. See http://english. fgtv.com for more information.

1		
2	3	
	4	

[1] Enjoying the spring blossoms of Yeouido [2] With 830,000 members, Yoido Full Gospel Church is the largest Christian church in the world [3] Golden tower of the 63 Building, one of Seoul's most recognized landmarks [4] National Assembly Building, home of the Korean parliament

Yeouido Park

Formerly an asphalt plaza that doubled as a parade ground and emergency airstrip, Yeouido Park was transformed into a beautiful stretch of green in 1999. The park consists of three separate zones, including a lovely Korean traditional garden. There's also a bicycle road popular with both bikers and rollerbladers—bike rentals are available. Behind the National Assembly Building is Yunjungno Street, famous throughout Korea for its beautiful cherry blossoms in spring. • **Tel** 3780-0562 • **Getting There** Yeouido Subway Station or Yeouinaru Subway Station, Line 5

TIPS

YEOUIDO SAETGANG ECOLOGICAL PARK

The wetlands on the south side of Yeouido island have been turned into an aquatic park, complete with wooden walking paths. If you're in the neighborhood, it might make for a nice stroll. See the map on p223.

Noryangjin Fish Market

Seoul's largest fish market, Noryangjin Fish Market is a 24-hour affair, although the fish auctioning takes place in the early morning hours before 6 am. Here you can find the bounty of the sea in its countless manifestations. Much of the produce is sold while alive, while nearby restaurants will be happy to cook up your fish (or slice it up raw) for you. See p400 for more details. • **Hours** 24 hours • **Getting There** Noryangjin Station, Line 1

Beautiful cherry blossoms of Yeouido Park

Sunrise over the Hangang Railway Bridge

TRAGEDY OF THE HANGANG BRIDGE

When the Korean War started on June 25, 1950, South Korea was caught off-guard. Within three days, North Korean troops had entered Seoul. South Korea hastily moved its capital to Daejeon and, in a panic, prepared the bridges over the Hangang River for demolition to slow the enemy advance.

On the morning of June 28, the order came to blow the bridges. Unfortunately, in the case of the Hangang River Bridge, it was clogged with refugees and retreating soldiers, and no effort was made to clear them. There wasn't even a warning given. In a great explosion, several bridge spans were dropped into the river, sending an estimated 300-800 people to their deaths.

If this wasn't bad enough, the bridge was destroyed with three divisions of the South Korean Army still on the northern side of the river, along with much of the army's heavy equipment. Many of these troops were captured and killed by the North Koreans, and it was a long time before the South Korean army could recover from the losses.

In September of that year, the colonel who ordered the demolition—perhaps on orders from above—was court-martialed and shot, although a posthumous trial 16 years later cleared him of wrong-doing.

Bicycle built for two, Seoul Forest

SEOUL FOREST

Seoul Forest B1, p254

Seoul Forest, completed in 2005, likes to think of itself as Seoul's answer to New York's Central Park or London's Hyde Park. Like the Cheonggyecheon, it was one of then Seoul mayor Lee Myung-bak's controversial high-profile projects. Also like the Cheonggyecheon, it was a bit of a rush job (built in just three years) that nevertheless represented a substantial improvement over what was there before. Central Park it's not, but it's a very pleasant place indeed.

Prior to the construction of the park, the Ttukseom area was a gritty industrial area in need of redevelopment. Now, it is a 1,156,498 m² oasis of green in a city trying to rediscover its ecological roots. The park is divided into several zones, including a Culture and Arts Park, Eco Forest, Environmental Education Park, Wetland Park and Hangang Riverside Park. Linking all these areas is a series of walking paths and bridges, some of them architecturally pleasing.

One of the star attractions of the park is its large population of Sika deer—you can't pet them, as they're supposedly "wild," but you can still feed them. There's more wildlife, too, including chipmunks and a variety of birds.

• **Hours** 24 hours • **Admission** Free • **Getting There** Walk 5 minutes from Exit 8 of Ttukseom Station, Line 2. By boat, cruises from Yeouido stop by Seoul Forest on the way to Jamsil. • **Tel** 460-2901~2926

Seoul Waterworks Museum B1, p254

Located right next to Seoul Forest, Seoul Waterworks (now Seoul Waterworks Museum) was founded in 1903 by two American businessmen, Henry Collbran and Harry R. Bostwick. Although Collbran and Bostwick were railwaymen by profession, they still managed to win a number of concessions from the Korean royal government, including the rights to build Seoul's tram system, Seoul's first electric system and the Seoul-Incheon railroad. The pretty red-brick building is home to several displays teaching visitors the history of Seoul's water system. You can enter the massive sand filters, too.

• **Hours** 10 am to 8 pm (weekdays), 10 am to 7 pm (weekends), March to Oct; 10 am to 7 pm (weekdays), 10 am to 6 pm (weekends), Nov to Feb. Closed Mondays
• **Admission** Free • **Tel** 3146-5936

Grave of Brig. Gen. Charles Le Gendre, a French-born US Army officer and Civil War veteran who served as a military adviser to King Gojong

YANGHWAJIN

Yanghwajin Foreigners' Cemetery

A short walk from Hapjeong Station (Line 2 and 6) on a little plot of land overlooking the Hangang River is Yanghwajin Foreigners' Cemetery. The cemetery dates back to 1890, when the untimely death at the age of 33 of American Presbyterian missionary and doctor J. W. Heron prompted the royal government to purchase the land as a burial spot for Westerners. Currently, 551 individuals are buried at Yanghwajin, including 279 Americans, 31 Britons, 19 Canadians and 18 Russians. Although the spot is technically named "Yanghwajin Foreign Missionaries' Cemetery," only 167 of the occupants are missionaries; also buried here are soldiers, diplomats, journalists and others.

It's the final resting place of many of the first Westerners who came to Korea, and the names on the headstones are a virtual who's who of East-West cultural exchange. If you know the history of the individuals buried here, so much the better (if you don't, but can read Korean, there are information posts in front of many of the more notable graves). Even if you haven't the slightest clue about Korean history, the graveyard is a very pleasant place to walk about, especially in summer, when the shade of the cemetery's trees provides much welcomed relief. Because of the international character of the occupants, the headstones come in an assortment of sizes and styles, from simple blocks of stone to Celtic crosses and elaborately decorated obelisks. Epitaphs can be found in English, French, German, Italian, Russian, Chinese and Japanese. The epitaphs themselves are quite interesting to read. Homer B. Hulbert's gravestone, for instance, reads, "I would rather be buried in Korea than in Westminster Abbey." • **Hours** 10 am to 5 pm. Closed Sundays • **Getting There** Exit 7 of Hapjeong Station, Line 2 • **Tel** 332-9174

Roses near the grave of British newspaperman and Korean independence activist Ernest Bethell

Jeoldusan Catholic Martyrs' Shrine

A short walk from Yanghwajin Foreigners' Cemetery brings you to Jeoldusan Catholic Martyrs' Shrine, one of the holiest spots in the country for Korean Catholics.

After its introduction in the 19th century, Catholicism in Korea experienced a period of great hardship. In 1866, the last and ultimately most severe of a series of persecutions of Catholics was launched. The royal government, then led by the xenophobic prince regent Heungseon Daewongun (see p147), executed nine French missionaries who had illegally smuggled themselves into Korea. In response, the French sent warships up the Hangang River, eventually landing at the cliffs of Yanghwajin. The ships were forced to withdraw, and in his fury Heungseon Daewongun declared that Yanghwajin, now soiled by the Westerners, had to be washed clean with the blood of those responsible for the foreign presence—the Catholic faithful. Over the next six years, thousands of Catholics were dragged to the top of cliff and beheaded, their bodies cast off onto the rocks below. Afterwards, the cliff became known as Jeoldusan, or "Decapitation Hill."

Much later, in 1966, Catholics built a church and memorial hall atop the cliffs, which offer a fine view of the Hangang River. The area below the hill was turned

Jeoldusan Catholic Martyrs' Shrine, built where thousands of Korean Catholics were executed in the late 19th century

into a park graced with many moving pieces of religious art, including a prominent statue of Korea's first Catholic priest, Macao-educated Father Andrew Kim Tae-gon, who was martyred in 1846. The memorial hall and church do a respectable job of teaching visitors about the early history of the Catholic Church in Korea and contain a number of relics from the martyrs, 103 of whom were deified in 1925 and 1968 (giving Korea the fourth largest number of Catholic saints in the word).

Pope John Paul II visited Jeoldusan in 1984; his visit has been commemorated with a bust of the late pontiff in the shrine's garden.

Statue of Father Andrew Kim Tae-gon, Korea's first Catholic priest

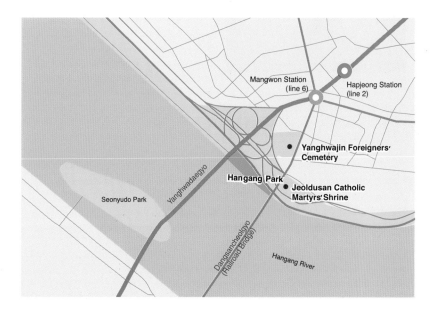

KOREAN CHRISTIANITY

Spend any amount of time in Korea, and you'll soon discover the country's vibrant Christian community. The Seoul skyline is dotted by neon crosses fixed atop the city's countless churches. Several of the world's largest churches, including the 830,000-man Yoido Full Gospel Church (see p224), are located here. It's estimated that about 28% of Korea's population is Christian (18% Protestant, 10% Catholic), the second highest percentage in Asia (behind the Philippines). In terms of enthusiasm, however, Korean Christians are second to none. In fact, according to recent news reports, Korean

Stained glass, Myeong-dong Cathedral

churches dispatch the second largest number of Christian missionaries abroad (behind only the United States), a stunning accomplishment given Korea's small population.

Korean Christianity wasn't always so flourishing, however. In the late 17th century, works by the Italian Jesuit missionary Matteo Ricci were first brought to Korea via royal tribute missions. By the latter half of the next century, reformist scholars had established a church led by a system of lay clergy. It was an experience almost unparalleled in Catholic history—a church establishing itself without the help of foreign missionaries.

The new faith was viewed with abject horror by Korea's Confucian establishment, however, and Catholicism underwent several bloody persecutions throughout the 19th century. Many Catholics were killed, and those who survived often fled to remote mountain villages, where they established small communities of believers far from the persecution in the cities. Not even Western missionaries were immune—in the great persecution of 1866, for example, nine French priests were executed, sparking an armed conflict with France.

By comparison, Protestantism came later, and as a result had a much easier time of it. Unlike the Catholics, who were forced for over a century to pray and proselytize illegally, often at great risk to life and limb, Protestant missionaries from the United States, Canada, UK and Australia entered Korea in the late 19th century as diplomats, doctors and educators, often with the support of the royal authorities, who viewed them as agents of modernization. Indeed, Protestant missionaries played an important role in Korea's modernization, setting up many of the country's first modern hospitals, schools and universities (as well as, of course, churches).

Korean Christianity went through a rough patch under Japanese imperial rule. The

Japanese distrusted the Western missionaries (most of whom were expelled at the start of the Pacific War) and viewed the churches—many of which had become centers of anti-Japanese nationalist activities—with suspicion. Still, at least until the 1930s, the religion continued to flourish. Christian activity in northern Korea was so vibrant, in fact, that the city of Pyongyang (ironically enough, now the capital of atheist North Korea) was called the "Jerusalem of the East."

Liberation from colonial rule, post-war economic development and Korea's close relationship with the United States provided the environment for a second boom in Korean Christianity. The number of Korean Protestants jumped from just over 623,000 in 1960 to over 8 million in 2005. Their influence on society grew, too—of Korea's post-Liberation presidents, three (Syngman Rhee, Kim Young-sam and Lee Myung-bak) were Protestants and two (Kim Dae-jung and Roh Moo-hyun) were Catholic. In particular, Christians played a major role in Korea's democratization movement of the 1970s and 1980s.

While Korean Christianity is certainly more vibrant than many of their coreligionists in the West, the country's newfound affluence has not been without its effect—in recent years, there's been a drop in the growth rate of Korean churches. This has been accompanied with a resurgence in interest of Korea's more traditional faiths, particularly Buddhism. Not that you'd be able to tell this from the enthusiasm of Korean churchgoers, though.

Relief of martyrs, Jeoldusan Catholic Martyrs' Shrine

Taking a relaxing stroll in Haneul Park, World Cup Park

RIVERSIDE PARKS

Hangang River Citizens' Park

Much of the Hangang River's banks has been transformed into park space in the form of Hangang River Citizens' Park. This is really 12 separate parks rather than one large one, with separate areas in (from west to east) the Gangseo, Nanji, Yanghwa, Seonyudo, Mangwon, Yeouido, Ichon, Banpo, Jamwon, Ttukseom, Jamsil and Gwangnaru districts. Each section is unique and equipped with sports and leisure facilities like tennis courts, swimming pools and picnic grounds.

Seonyudo Park p233

Of the 12 districts, Seonyudo Park is probably the best known. The park, originally the site of an old water treatment plant, makes use of its industrial past to create a wonderful ecological zone. Linking the park, which is actually on an island in the middle of the river, is the beautiful arched Seonyugyo Bridge, a pedestrian walkway that is lit up in the evening to make one of Seoul's most beautiful night views. • **Hours** 6 am to midnight • **Getting There** Seonyudo Park is best reached via taxi from Exit 1 of Dangsan Station, Line 2. See the map on p233. • **Tel** 3780-0590

World Cup Park

There was a time not so long ago when the Nanji district of Seoul was something of a national shame. For over a decade Seoul's primary landfill, the area amounted to little more than a big, noxious-smelling mountain of garbage. Due to the strong odors emitted by the eyesore, the entire area was covered with a meter of topsoil after the landfill was closed in 1993.

Then something amazing happened—plants and animals began returning to the Nanji area, which had since been deserted by humanity. Encouraged, city authorities spent six years stabilizing the waste and another year building the 3,471,090 m² park known today as World Cup Park. The park opened in May of 2002, just in time to celebrate its namesake, the 17th FIFA World Cup co-hosted in Korea and Japan.

The park is huge—it actually consists of five smaller parks, including the area in front of the imposing World Cup Stadium and two massive ziggurats of green—formerly mountains of garbage—that have been transformed into Haneul (Sky) and Noeul (Sunset) parks.

- **Pyeonghwa Park:** This area in front of World Cup Stadium includes a pond, picnic grounds and some beautiful marshland.

- **Nanjicheon Park:** This riverine environment follows the Nanjicheon Stream.

- **Nanji Hangang Park:** This park area, which runs alongside the Hangang River, has a number of sporting facilities and a pier where you can catch boats for a river cruise.

- **Haneul Park:** Once a mountain of garbage, this hill now provides some of the best views of Seoul in the city. Wind turbines at the top generate power for the park. The park is especially known for its scenic steps and beautiful reeds.

- **Noeul Park:** So named because this lesser of the two former trash heaps offers some of Seoul's best sunsets. Golf nuts might also wish to make use of its nine-hole golf course.

> • **Hours** 24 hours, but Haneul Park closes at sunset. • **Getting There** Exit 1 of World Cup Stadium Station, Line 6. There's a free shuttle to the park from the nearby Mapo Agriculture-Fisheries Market. • **Tel** 300-5500, 3780-0612 (Nanji Hangang Park)

Seoul Yacht Club enjoys an afternoon on the river, Nanji Hangang Park

1 Sebit Dungdungseom (Floating Island) 2 Spring blossoms of Seonyudo Park 3 Wind turbine, Haneul Park, World Cup Park 4 Enjoying the summer near World Cup Stadium

Banpo Bridge Moonlight Rainbow Fountain

Banpo Bridge Moonlight Rainbow Fountain & Floating Island

If you'd like to see a real riverine spectacle, head to the Banpo Bridge in the evening to see the Moonlight Rainbow Fountain. Five times a day (six on Friday, Saturday and Sunday) some 10,000 LED nozzles installed along the side of the bridge let loose with a 20-minute-long, multicolored barrage of water (sucked up from the river below with pumps) in time with musical selections from Beethoven, Vivaldi and others.

Just next to the bridge, Sebit Dungdungseom—"Floating Island" in English—is Seoul's newest architectural gem. Floating on the Hangang River, the complex (to be completed by September 2011) is designed to be a combined culture, convention and leisure facility. It is best seen at night, when it is lit up.

• **Hours** noon, 5 pm, 8 pm (weekdays); extra 9 pm show on weekends (Apr to Jun); noon, 6 pm, 8 pm, 9 pm (weekdays), extra 10 pm show on weekends (July to Aug) • **Getting There** The best place to witness the fountain is Banpo Hangang Park, which can be reached via Exits 8-1 or 8-2 of the underground arcade of Express Bus Terminal, Lines 3, 7 or 9.

TIPS

RIVER FUN

Biking: Hangang Bicycle Trail runs almost 41.13 km along the southern bank of the Hangang River, and 28.81 km along the north bank. Non-stop, it should take about two hours to complete the course, but there are plenty of bike racks and rest stops along the way should you decide to take a break and take in the scenery. Bike rental shops can be found at several places along the way—for more information about rentals, call the Dasan Call Center at 120.

Swimming: While swimming in the river itself is probably not recommended, the Ttukseom, Mangwon, Gwangnaru, Jamsil, Jamwon and Yeouido districts of Hangang River Citizens' Park have swimming pools— admission is 5,000 won. Be warned, however—the pools can get quite crowded.

Rollerblading: Rollerblading is allowed at Ichon Hangang Park's skating rink—rentals available for 2,000 won. 9 am to 7 pm.

Windsurfing: In the summer months, you can find many Seoulites windsurfing on the waves of the Hangang River. To learn how to windsurf, call Seoul Windsurfing Association at 457-3773. Tuition is 100,000 won per day, including gear rental, or 200,000 won for three days.

Yachting: The newly opened Seoul Marina offers sailing lessons and reaonably priced boat rentals. Renting a single-person dinghy will cost you 4,000 won an hour (if you've got a sailing license). T. 423-7888. If you've got the money, you can join the 700 Yacht Club for a deposit of 10,000,000 won? This will give you much discounted rates for boat rentals. If you don't have that kind of money just yet, you can rent a 35-foot cruiser for an hour and a half for about 250,000 won. You can enjoy the clubhouse, too. Call them at 376-5616.

Water Skiing: If water skiing is more your thing, give the Korea Waterski and Wakeboard Association in Ttukseom a call at 2203-0488 or Seoul Water Skiing Association at 498-9026.

GANGNAM AREA

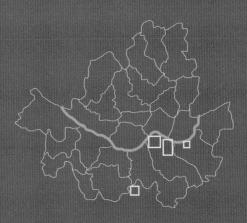

THINGS TO DO AND SEE

- Shop 'til you drop—or your creditors call
- People-watch at a café in Apgujeong, Sinsa-dong or Garosugil
- Get lost at Lotte World, the world's largest indoor amusement park
- Relive Olympic glory at Olympic Park
- Watch the ponies at Seoul Race Track in Gwacheon

PARTYING WITH KOREA'S NOUVEAU RICHE

The Hangang River divides the city of Seoul roughly in half, with the "old city" to the north and the "new city" to the south. The southern half, referred to in Korean as Gangnam ("South of the River"), is the home and playground of Seoul's nouveau riche. Prior to Korea's "Economic Miracle" beginning in the 1960s, Gangnam was nothing but rice paddies. From the 1970s, however, the government and developers moved into the area with a vengeance, building it up into a residential and commercial district to flaunt the country's growing wealth.

It goes without saying that Gangnam differs from the neighborhoods north of the river in significant ways. If the dominant image of the old city is one of history, grit and winding back alleys, that of Gangnam is one of planned neighborhoods, skyscrapers of glass, posh shops and astronomically high real estate prices. The well-heeled and well-groomed residents of this fair neighborhood evoke feelings of both hatred and envy from residents of less tony areas. Even if you hate the rich, the cafés and clubs of Gangnam are the place to see and be seen in Seoul. A note on the terminology, however—in general use, Gangnam has two meanings. The first refers to all areas south of the Hangang River. The second collectively refers to the three districts of Gangnam-gu, Seocho-gu and Songpa-gu, Seoul's three toniest residential and commercial districts.

Giorgio Armani shop in the posh Cheongdam-dong neighborhood

Bag shop MCM in Cheongdam-dong

APGUJEONG-DONG & CHEONGDAM-DONG

In a land of posh, the neighborhoods of Apgujeong-dong and Cheongdam-dong are the poshest of all. Very mention of the neighborhoods evokes visions of chic boutiques, designer labels, trendy bars and cafés and imported luxury cars. This is pretty much what you'll find, so what you think of the place depends on what you think of the aforementioned chic boutiques and luxury driving. That said, many of the denizens here are not actually residents—attempts to appear so notwithstanding—so backpackers shouldn't feel completely out of place, and the cafés and sizzling nightlife should not be missed.

Apgujeong-dong

There was a time—not that long ago as far as Korean history goes—that the area that is now one of the ritziest shopping areas on the planet was little more than a picturesque riverside of hills and trees. In the 15th century, a high-ranking official built a pleasure pavilion overlooking the Hangang River—it's from the pavilion that the neighborhood takes its name. The gazebo has long since disappeared, and in its place has grown the world's 10th most expensive shopping district in terms of rent. This is Seoul's Beverly Hills, with its very own "Rodeo Drive" where you can max out your credit card. Apgujeong-dong is filled with smaller clothing shops, expensive cafés and young shoppers. One landmark is the eclectic Galleria Department Store.

Cheongdam-dong

Named for a particularly nice pond that existed here at some time in the distant past, Cheongdam-dong is now the wealthiest district in all of Seoul. Like Apgujeong-dong, it is known for its upscale boutiques, designers and clubs—only more so. Cheongdam-dong also attracts a slightly older crowd than Apgujeong-dong, with local shoppers and patrons generally in their 30s and 40s.

Shopping Areas to Note

Rodeo Street C1, C2

This winding road linking Apgujeong-dong and Cheongdam-dong is everything its famous namesake in Los Angeles is, minus the palm trees. This is really Korea's fashion mecca—design trends begin here and move to Dongdaemun afterwards. If you're looking for big-name foreign brands like Prada, Gucci, Dolce & Gabbana, Brooks Brothers, Hugo Boss, Jil Sander, Armani and Louis Vuitton, you've come to the right spot. In addition to shops, the street also has beauty salons, high-end restaurants and movie theaters.

APGUJEONG/CHEONGDAM MAP

A   B   C   D

1

S-OIL

신한은행 SHINHAN BANK

Hanyang Apt.

Gal

KB

하나은행

Apgujeong Stn. Line 3

All Day Brunch

Bonjuk

Little Saigon

Sotdae
Saju Café

H Cube Gallery

Rodeo Street

Jeongdong Arcade

UNIQLO

Yeongyar
Center

678

Ye-Hall

Andrew's Eggtart

Gallery Hyundai
Gangnam

Hohwabanjeom

Adellia

Princess Hotel

GS25

Tasty Boulevard

Beans Bins

Chadoljip

Monkey Beach

Mafia

CONVERSE

Chicken Place

Jaseng Hospital of
Oriental Medicine

Ari

Schadheli

Mado

Seoseogalbi

Boat Whistle

Hwajeonmin

Badaro
Ganeun Gisa

De Chocolate
Coffee

Wonjo Chogajip

Papa Bubble

Can

2

In the Box

Codes
Combine

General Idea

Dies

Saemaeul Sikdang

Zen Hideaway

Design Café

MINI STOP

Toni & Guy

Peppermint Dream

Gangseomyeonok

GS25

Sanbong Hwaro Gui

Sakkayana

Kloo

SK

Samgyeopsal &
Kimchijjigae

Byugdoljib

Milk Bar

Jaeminan Jogakka
Saju Café

Macos Adamas

Dashing Diva
Han Style

MINI STOP

Ed Hardy

Take Urban

3

Oriental Spoon

Mandarina Duck

Terry Gallery

Samwon Garden

Rock & Roll

Il Mare

Dosan Park
Dosan Ahn Chang-Ho
Memorial Hall

MuiMui

Ske

Homestead Coffee

MINI STOP

The Queen

Space*C, Coreana Art &
Culture Complex

Café Mou

Café Papergarden

Jeonjasinbal

staSera

Caffèra

Gorilla in the Kitchen

Paris Croissant Kitchen

Gulbi Maeul

Woolim Cheong
Theater

RALPH LAUREN

Walking Slowly

Kraze
burgers

Sony

Kim Yeon Ju Boutique

IMART Gallery

Jahayun Clinic

Platinum
Microbrewery

Hak-dong Intersection

JuJu

Atelier Hermès

Cheongdam
Sundubu

T.G.I. FRIDAYS

4

Triple O

Cine City

BENNIGAN'S
GRILL & PASTA

Gangnam-gu
Office Stn. Line 7

Daily F

Horim Art Center

Hwassi 167 Degrees

Mercado

BMW

Dosan Intersection

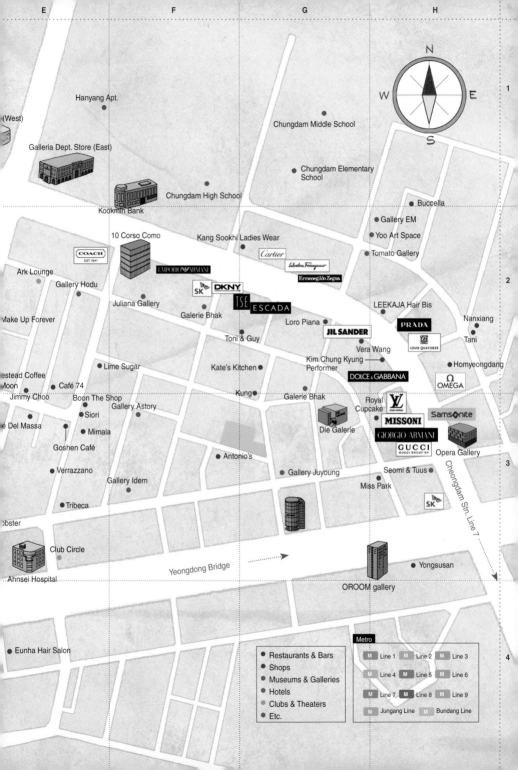

Galleria Department Store E1

The most easily recognizable Apgujeong-dong landmark, the west wing of this luxury department store is covered with 4,330 glass disks that reflect light in the day and are lit up at night. The department store comes in two flavors— expensive and very expensive. The West Wing carries all sorts of high-end items, while the East Wing carries almost exclusively luxury brands and caters to older shoppers of financial means. • **Hours** 10:30 am to 8 pm (Mon to Sat), 8:30 pm (Fri to Sun) • **Tel** 3449-4114

Boon The Shop E3

A large multi-brand boutique that is both architecturally interesting and financially debilitating. • **Hours** 11 am to 8 pm • **Tel** 542-8006

Jimmy Choo E2

If this shoe brand was good enough for *Sex and the City*, it's good enough for you. • **Hours** 11 am to 8 pm. Closed Sundays • **Tel** 3443-4570

Cheongdam-dong's UNC Gallery, home to work by Korean contemporary artists.

GAROSU-GIL A2, P254

Garosu-gil—which basically translates as "Tree-Lined Street"—is perhaps as close to Paris as you'll find in Seoul. This pleasant little road is indeed lined with trees (ginkgo trees, to be precise), and is chock-full of European-style streetside cafés and wine bars, with some cozy boutiques and shops thrown in for good measure. Sure, the prices are a bit pretentiously high, but it does make for a nice breather from some of Seoul's more, ahem, energetic neighborhoods. In part due to the influence of the popular US cable TV series "Sex and the City," American-style brunch has also become something of a neighborhood fad.

Interestingly enough, the neighborhood started as an artists' enclave. Many of the establishments still have a decidedly artsy feel to them, even if the artists themselves have since moved on to other neighborhoods.

CHEONGDAM-DONG GALLERY STREET

Cheongdam-dong is more than just posh shops and cafés, mind you. In recent years, it has also become home to a number of hot new art galleries that cater to young and financially endowed collectors. About 50 galleries have gathered in the area, many specializing in cutting-edge and experimental work by up-and-coming artists. Most of the galleries can be found on the stretch of road between Galleria Department Store and Cheongdam-dong Catholic Church.

Used Luxury Goods

While Cheongdam-dong plays host to the city's largest concentration of luxury brand names, Apgujeong-dong has a number of places that sell used luxury goods for up to 60% off what you'd spend for them new.

Eating and Drinking

When you're done shopping, Apgujeong-dong and Cheongdam-dong are overflowing with chic (and pricey!) cafés, bars and restaurants. As with shopping, places in Cheongdam-dong tend to be more expensive. The area around Dosan Park B3 in Cheongdam-dong, in particular, is famous for its well-designed cafés. See the Places to Eat section (p264) for a listing of establishments.

Something of an Apgujeong tradition are the so-called "*saju* cafés," where you can have your fortune—as determined by your time and date of birth—read to you as you sip a cup of coffee. Of course, it helps if you speak Korean or have someone on hand who does.

While not Apgujeong-dong or Cheongdam-dong, the nearby tree-lined street of Garosu-gil (see TIPS) also has a large number of trendy bars, cafés and restaurants.

GETTING THERE

The main shopping area is actually a bit of a walk from Apgujeong Station, Line 3. You're probably best off taking a cab from the station. Garosu-gil, meanwhile, is best approached via Exit 8 of Sinsa Station, Line 3.

COEX Mall (Samseong-dong) c2

Located in the landmark World Trade Center Seoul complex of Samseong-dong, the COEX Mall is the largest underground mall in Asia. With over 260 shops, it's a great place to go on a rainy day. It's a very popular destination for foreign visitors and has everything you'd expect in a mammoth shopping mall—stores, restaurants, cafés, a very popular movie theater, Korea's best aquarium, and even a museum dedicated to Korea's gift to global culinary cuisine—kimchi.

Also part of the complex are two luxury hotels and one of Seoul's best casinos. Just across from the mall is Bongeunsa Temple, one of Seoul's biggest Buddhist temples (See TIPS on p255).

Shopping

As one of the biggest malls in Asia, COEX is a place where you can find just about anything under the sun. The best place to score luxury goods is the Hyundai Department Store, which is attached to the mall. For clothes shoppers, global casual brands like Nike and Levi's are represented, as are many Korean designers.

The COEX branch of Korean bookseller Bandi & Luni's is one of the best places in Korea to get English-language books. Nearby is Evan Music, one of Korea's largest shops for music and movies.

Movie Theater

The COEX Megabox Cineplex has 16 screens and is always running popular titles from Korea, the United States and elsewhere. Thanks to its size and awesome décor, it's one of the most popular movie theaters in the country.

COEX Aquarium

The COEX Aquarium is the only themed aquarium in Korea and a great place to walk around even if you don't particularly enjoy watching fish be fish. Especially cool is the "undersea tunnel," where you can get a bottom's up view of a wide variety of sea life, including sharks. • **Hours** 10 am to 8 pm • **Admission** 17,500 won • **Tel** 6002-6200

Kimchi Field Museum

Yep, it's a museum that's all about kimchi. Kimchi relics, kimchi displays, kimchi tasting rooms, kimchi in art, a kimchi store—more kimchi than you can shake a stick at. • **Hours** 10 am to 6 pm (Tue to Sun). Closed Mondays • **Admission** 3,000 won • **Tel** 6002-6456

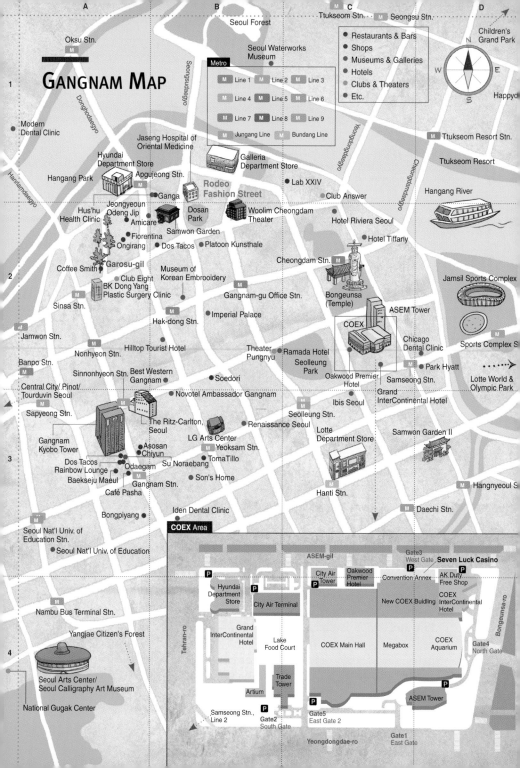

GANGNAM MAP

Oksu Stn.

Seoul Forest

Ttukseom Stn.   Seongsu Stn.

Children's
Grand Park

Happyo

Seoul Waterworks
Museum

Metro

M Line 1	M Line 2	M Line 3
M Line 4	M Line 5	M Line 6
M Line 7	M Line 8	M Line 9
M Jungang Line	Bundang Line

- Restaurants & Bars
- Shops
- Museums & Galleries
- Hotels
- Clubs & Theaters
- Etc.

Modern
Dental Clinic

Hangang Park

Hyundai
Department Store

Jaseng Hospital of
Oriental Medicine

Apgujeong Stn.

Galleria
Department Store

Ttukseom Resort Stn.

Ttukseom Resort

Rodeo
Fashion Street

Lab XXIV

Hangang River

Ganga

Jeongyeoun
Odeng Jip

Hus'hu
Health Clinic

Amicare

Dosan
Park

Woolim Cheongdam
Theater

Club Answer

Hotel Riviera Seoul

Hotel Tiffany

Samwon Garden

Fiorentina

Ongirang

Dos Tacos

Platoon Kunsthale

Cheongdam Stn.

Coffee Smith

Garosu-gil

Club Eight

Museum of
Korean Embroidery

Bongeunsa
(Temple)

Jamsil Sports Complex

BK Dong Yang
Plastic Surgery Clinic

Gangnam-gu Office Stn.

ASEM Tower

COEX

Sinsa Stn.

Hak-dong Stn.

Imperial Palace

Chicago
Dental Clinic

Sports Complex S

Jamwon Stn.

Banpo Stn.

Nonhyeon Stn.

Hilltop Tourist Hotel

Theater
Pungnyu

Ramada Hotel
Seolleung
Park

Samseong Stn.

Park Hyatt

Lotte World &
Olympic Park

Sinnonhyeon Stn.

Best Western
Gangnam

Soedori

Oakwood Premier
Hotel

Grand
InterContinental Hotel

Central City/ Pinot/
Tourduvin Seoul

Novotel Ambassador Gangnam

Ibis Seoul

Sapyeong Stn.

Gangnam
Kyobo Tower

The Ritz-Carlton,
Seoul

LG Arts Center

Seolleung Stn.

Renaissance Seoul

Lotte
Department Store

Samwon Garden II

Asosan
Chiyun

Yeoksam Stn.

Dos Tacos

Rainbow Lounge

Odaegam

Su Noraebang

TomaTillo

Hangnyeoul S

Baekseju Maeul

Café Pasha

Gangnam Stn.

Son's Home

Hanti Stn.

Daechi Stn.

Bongpiyang

Iden Dental Clinic

Seoul Nat'l Univ. of
Education Stn.

Seoul Nat'l Univ. of Education

Nambu Bus Terminal Stn.

Yangjae Citizen's Forest

Seoul Arts Center/
Seoul Calligraphy Art Museum

National Gugak Center

COEX Area

ASEM-gil

Gate3
West Gate   Seven Luck Casino

City Air
Tower

Oakwood
Premier
Hotel

Convention Annex

AK Duty
Free Shop

Hyundai
Department
Store

City Air Terminal

New COEX Buidling

COEX
InterContinental
Hotel

Tehran-ro

Grand
InterContinental
Hotel

Lake
Food Court

COEX Main Hall

Megabox

COEX
Aquarium

Gate4
North Gate

Bongeunsa-ro

Trade
Tower

ASEM Tower

Artium

Samseong Stn.,
Line 2

Gate2
South Gate

Gate5
East Gate 2

Gate1
East Gate

Yeongdongdae-ro

PERFORMING ARTS IN GANGNAM

The Gangnam area is home to several major performing arts venues, including the massive Seoul Arts Center complex and the National Gugak Center, Korea's leading center for Korean traditional music and dance.

Seoul Arts Center A4

The Seoul Arts Center showcases the diversity of Korea's cultural traditions including five arts buildings all in a single complex, each devoted to a different genre of art. The Opera House, designed with a roof resembling a traditional Korean aristocrat's hat, is a seven-story building that includes the 2,300-seat Opera Center for operas, the 700-seat Towol Theater for plays, and the Jayu Theater for experimental productions. Korea's national ballet and opera companies are based at the Arts Center. The Music Hall is Korea's first exclusively music-focused performance hall, with a 2,523-seat Concert Hall and a more intimate Recital Hall. It's also the home base of Korea's national choir, the Korea and Seoul symphony orchestras, and the Seoul Performing Arts company.

Also included on the Seoul Arts Center complex are the Hangaram Art Museum, Seoul Calligraphy Art Museum and Hangaram Design Museum. • **Getting There** Take green bus No. 4429 from Exit 5 of Nambu Bus Terminal Station, Line 3 • **Tel** 580-1300 • **Website** www.sac.or.kr

Seoul Calligraphy Art Museum A4

The first and only exclusively calligraphy-focused museum in the world, the Seoul Calligraphy Art Museum is comprised of ten small exhibition halls that showcase both traditional and innovative modern works of calligraphy. Additionally, the Calligraphy Art

TIPS

SEVEN LUCK CASINO C2

Seven Luck Casino's Gangnam branch is located at the Convention Annex Building of COEX Center in Samseong-dong. Like most of Korea's other casinos, it's strictly for foreigners, but if you like to gamble, it's a fun place with an interesting East-meets-West atmosphere. All your favorite games—blackjack, baccarat, Tai-Sai, roulette, Caribbean poker and slot machines—are represented. Hours: 24 hours, 365 days a year. (T. 3466-6100)

BONGEUNSA TEMPLE C2

Just across from the World Trade Center Seoul complex is the Buddhist temple of Bongeunsa, one of Seoul's largest. It was founded in 794, and although the temple was heavily damaged during the Korean War, a few old buildings survived, along with some precious examples of Buddhist art. Temple stay programs are available. The 23 meter tall statue of the Maitreya Buddha cuts an impressive figure as it looks out upon World Trade Center Seoul skyscraper.
Getting There: Exits 5 and 6 of Samseong Station, Line 2. (T. 545-1448, www.bongeun. org)

Seoul Arts Center

Museum offers many educational programs on *hangeul* calligraphy and traditional painting. • **Hours** 11 am to 8 pm (Mar to Oct), 11 am to 7 pm (Nov to Feb) • **Admission** Free • **Tel** 580-1651

National Gugak Center A4

Located adjacent to the Seoul Arts Center, the center is comprised of two theaters, an outdoor performance area and a traditional performing arts museum. Every Saturday at 5 pm from May through December, the Yeakdang theater presents a 90-minute show of traditional Korean folk songs, drumming, *pansori* and court dances for only 10,000 won per seat. From early May to early December, the Umyeondang theater presents a show of similar content at the same price performed by younger artists. • **Getting There** Take green bus No. 4429 after getting off at Nambu Bus Terminal Station, Line 3, Exit 5 • **Tel** 580-3300 • **Website** www.gugak.go.kr

Classical Korean music at National Gugak Center

LG Arts Center B3

Opened in 2000, the LG Arts Center is an exceptional performing arts venue in the heart of Seoul's business district. Designed to accommodate a diverse range of performing arts genres, the Arts Center was built with a revolutionary system that completely isolates the street noise from the acoustics of the performance hall. The arts center also aims to include a selection of innovative performances in each season's program to introduce new forms of performance to Seoul audiences.
• **Getting There** Exit 7 of Yeoksam Station, Line 2 • **Tel** 2005-0114 • **Website** www.lgart.com

Merry-go-round, Lotte World

LOTTE WORLD (JAMSIL)

Lotte World is not just an amusement park—it's its own city. According to one 2002 survey, it was the seventh most popular amusement park in the world. This sprawling complex in Seoul's Jamsil neighborhood includes the world's largest indoor amusement park, an outdoor amusement park, a folk museum, a department store, a major luxury hotel and Korea's best ice skating rink. If you have kids, they'll love it. Big kids will find plenty of things to do, too.

Also nearby is the beautiful Seokchon Lake, which makes for fine walks.

• **Hours** 9:30 am to 10 pm (Mon to Thu) 9:30 am to 11 pm (Fri to Sun) • **Admission** 38,000 won (day pass), 26,000 won (day admission); 31,000 won (night pass, after 4 pm), 22,000 won (night admission, after 4 pm) 15,500 won (night admission, after 7 pm) • **Getting There** Exit 4 of Jamsil Station, Line 2 and 8 • **Tel** 411-2000 • **Website** www.lotteworld.com

Indoor Park

"Adventure," Lotte World's indoor amusement park, is truly a sight to behold: four floors of fun, covered by a Victorian-style glass dome. Its scale is such that it's almost surreal. In the center is a fine indoor ice skating rink that's popular with young couples. You've got your full assortment of games and rides, with festivals, parades, light shows and other spectacles thrown in for good measure. You can get a good view of the complex from the monorail that takes you around both the indoor and outdoor parks.

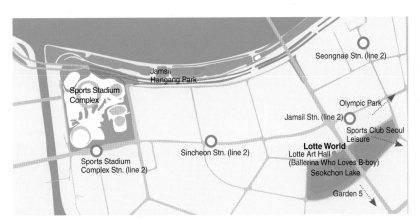

Christmas show at Lotte World

Outdoor Park

The outdoor park known as "Magic Island," is so called because it's built on an island in Seokchon Lake. Like Disneyland, it's got a big magic castle. Here you have another wide range of rides and games, including the ever-popular Gyro Drop, which drops you 70 meters in 2 seconds. There are also boat excursions on the lake.

Folk Museum

The popular Folk Museum is Lotte's contribution to Korea's cultural heritage. Here you'll find an exhibit hall with Korean cultural relics, miniature palaces and villages, a performance hall and more.

Seokchon Lake

Originally a tributary of the Hangang River, this body of water was turned into an artificial lake in 1971. Later road construction split the lake in two. The 2.5-km-wide lake makes for one of Seoul's best walking and jogging areas and is particularly nice at night when Lotte World's Magic Island is lit up.

Other Parks in the Area

Olympic Park

Dedicated to one of Seoul's watershed moments, its hosting of the 1988 Summer Olympic Games, Olympic Park is one of the city's nicest pieces of greenery. This

World Peace Gate, Olympic Park

massive park is home to several large stadiums and arenas left over from the Olympic Games, a plethora of monuments and sculptures (including the impressive World Peace Gate), grass fields, sports facilities and even a velodrome. Ponds and pleasure pavilions add to the experience.

Of more historical interest is Mongchon Toseong Fortress, an ancient earthen fortress constructed by the ancient kingdom of Baekje (18BC-660AD), which established its first capital in the area. The area was excavated during the construction of the Olympic stadiums, providing a valuable glimpse of life in that early era. The fortress is contained within the confines of the park.

Olympic Park's stadiums are now frequently used as concert venues, particularly when popular overseas groups come to town. • **Getting There** Jamsil Station and Jamsillaru Station, Line 2; Olympic Park Station, Line 5; Mongchontoseong Station, Line 8

Yangjae Citizen's Forest A4, p254

This pleasant piece of urban greenery was completed in 1986, just in time for the Asian Games of that year and the 1988 Olympics. It's got trees, sports facilities, walking paths, and everything else you'd want in a park. There's also a memorial to Yun Bong-gil, a Korean freedom fighter best known for tossing a bomb at Japanese leaders in Shanghai in 1932, an act for which he was arrested and executed by the Japanese. • **Getting There** Exit 7 of Yangjae Station, Line 3. Walk for 20 minutes. • **Tel** 575-3895

Starting gate of Seoul Race Park

GWACHEON

The pleasant Seoul suburb of Gwacheon is mostly a residential neighborhood, but it is also home to a number of sites of tourism interest.

Seoul Grand Park

Seoul Grand Park boasts beautiful indoor and outdoor botanical gardens and Korea's largest zoo featuring over 3,000 animals of over 300 species. Particularly impressive are the indoor botanical garden and rose garden. The dolphin show is also quite popular. • **Hours** 9 am to 7 pm (Mar to Oct), 9 am to 6 pm (Nov to Feb), 9 am to 10 pm (Jul to Aug) • **Admission** 3,000 won (zoo), 2,000 won (dolphin show) • **Tel** 500-7335

Seoul Land

Seoul Land was Korea's first theme park. It has since been surpassed by places like Everland and Lotte World, but it's still not a bad place for the kiddies.
• **Hours** 9:30 am to 8 pm • **Admission** 17,000 won, 31,000 won (free pass), 28,000 won (night pass) • **Tel** 504-0011~6

National Museum of Contemporary Art

This architecturally splendid museum on the slope of Mt. Cheonggyesan houses many outstanding works of modern art by Korean and international artists. The collection focuses on 20th century Korean painting, sculpture and crafts. Its centerpiece is the Ramp Core, a spiral staircase that winds around late video artist Nam June Paik's "The More, the Better," an 18.5-meter-high tower composed of 1,003 video monitors. The outdoor garden features sculptures and installation art by Magdalena Abakanowicz, Tal Streeter and others • **Hours** Mar to Oct: 10 am to 6 pm (weekdays), 10 am to 9 pm (weekends), Nov to Feb: 10 am to 5 pm (weekdays), 10 am to 8 pm (weekends) • **Admission** Free • **Tel** 2188-6000 • **Website** www.moca.go.kr

Seoul Race Course

Korea's only horse racing track is located just outside of town in Gwacheon. Originally built for the 1988 Olympic Games, the facility hosts about a dozen races on Saturdays and Sundays. Bets begin at 100 won and go up to 100,000 won. • **Hours** 9:30 am to 6 pm (Fri), 9 am to 5:30 pm (Sat), 9 am to 6:10 pm (Sun) • **Admission** 800 won • **Tel** 1566-3333

GETTING THERE

Seoul Grand Park, Seoul Land and the National Museum of Contemporary Art can be reached via Exit 2 of Seoul Grand Park Station, Line 4. All three destinations are linked via the so-called "Elephant Train," which you can board in front of Exit 2. Meanwhile, Seoul Race Course is reached via Seoul Racecourse Park Station, Line 4.

PLACES TO EAT: GANGNAM

Apgujeong-dong, Sinsa-dong and Nonhyeon-dong

The Apgujeong-dong, Sinsa-dong and Nonhyeon-dong areas are filled with places to eat, drink and be merry.

Hwassi 167 Degrees Good Korean-style barbecued meat in Nonhyeon-dong. (T. 541-5671) C4, p248

Samwon Garden One of the best meat restaurants in all of Seoul, this place has been around since 1976 and is owned by the father of LPGA golfer Grace Park. In addition to the wonderful food, it has a beautiful Korean-style garden as well. (T. 548-3030) A3, p248

Take Urban Organic coffees and teas. (T. 512-7978) D3, p248

Tasty Boulevard Tasty indeed, if you like Italian food or steak. (T. 6080-3332) B2, p248

Homyeondang They specialize in organically produced noodles. (T. 511-9517) H2, p249

Mercado Wonderful Brazilian barbeque place will fill you up with enough red meat to last you a lifetime. (T. 515-3288) C4, p248

Ongirang Spicy pan-fried octopus is the specialty here. (T. 3446-5538) A2, p254

Jeongyeoun Odeng Jip Japanese sake and *odeng* (Japanese-style fish cakes). (T. 586-5403) A2, p254

Fiorentina Another area Italian restaurant. (T. 544-8831) A2, p254

Sanbong Hwaro Gui Does really high-quality barbecued meats, included Wagyu beef. And as a bonus, it's reasonably priced. (T. 546-2229) C2, p248

Saemaeul Sikdang More grilled Korean meats done right. (T. 6404-9989) C2, p248

Eric's New York Steak House The Yeoksam-dong branch of the Korean New York-style steak house chain. (T. 2155-1636)

Oriental Spoon A cafe-style restaurant specializing in Southeast Asian cuisine, particularly noodles dishes, with some Japanese and Chinese dishes thrown in food good measure. (T. 512-0916) C3, p248

Ganga The Indian restaurant is a bit pricey, but the food is good and the atmosphere refined. (T. 2055-3610) B1, p254

Gorilla in the Kitchen This stylish restaurant specializes in healthy, beautifully prepared dishes. Emphasis on the "healthy": the restaurant menu breaks each dish down by nutrients and kcals. (T. 3442-1688) B4, p248

Lab XXIV Started by Korean celebrity chef Edward Kwon, this trendy eatery in Cheongdam-dong serves high-quality contemporary cuisine at a reasonable cost. (T. 511-4523) C1, p254

Near Gangnam Station p254

Asosan Simple but delicious Japanese cuisine, including Japanese-style pork cutlet and Japanese udon noodles. (T. 566-6659) A3

Café Pasha Turkish kebabs prepared by a Turkish chef. (T. 593-8484) A3

Dos Tacos This California-style Mexican restaurant does tacos, burritos, chimichangas and everything else Mexican. (T. 593-5904) A3, B2

Dineoui Yeowang (Dinner Queen) Fusion cuisine in a cafe setting. Give the cream shrimp salad a try. (T. 514-2707) A3

TomaTillo An outstanding Cali-Mex restaurant with a branch in Gangnam. They also have a branch near Gwanghwamun. (T. 2112-3883) B3

Bongpiyang This place serves up fine Pyongyang-style naenmyeon (cold noodles) and barbeque pork rib. (T. 587-7018) A3

EXCURSIONS AROUND SEOUL

THINGS TO DO AND SEE

- Feel the tension—or the ironic tranquility—at the truce village of Panmunjeom in the DMZ

- Learn about Korea's dramatic first encounters with the West on the island of Ganghwa-do, or just enjoy one of the island's two major Buddhist temples

- Eat Chinese food in Incheon, and take in the colonial-style architecture left over from when the city was an open port.

- Walk along the walls of Hwaseong Fortress, a remarkably modern fortification and the crowning achievement of Korea's 18th century "practical learning" movement

- Play like a kid at Everland amusement park. Or head next door to Ho-Am Art Museum, with its impressive collection of Korean treasures and beautiful traditional garden

- Learn about Korea's independence struggle at the massive Independence Hall in Cheonan

- Purchase some beautiful pottery at Icheon, where artists have been baking some of Korea's best ceramics since the Joseon era

- Wander about Korean War ruins in Cheorwon

- Experience the beauty of Korean landscape architecture at the Joseon royal tombs, a newly registered UNESCO World Heritage site

EXPLORING SEOUL'S HINTERLAND

Seoul itself might have enough to hold your attention for a while, but the area around Seoul also has plenty to do and see, too. Just an hour's drive north of the city is the famed Demilitarized Zone, or DMZ, the world's last Cold War frontier, where North and South Korea face one another in an uneasy peace. If that is not enough, the Korean War ruins of Cheorwon are a somber reminder of the tragedy of war. To the west is the historic island of Ganghwa-do, guarding the mouth of the Hangang River, and the city of Incheon, with Korea's largest Chinatown and old concession areas dotted with exotic European architecture. To the south, meanwhile, are the remarkable walls of Suwon's Hwaseong Fortress, a UNESCO World Heritage Site. Also registered with UNESCO are the Joseon royal tombs, beautiful examples of Korean traditional landscaping.

The young and young at heart might also enjoy Everland, one of the largest amusement parks in the world, while those with more adult tastes won't want to miss Ho-am Museum, one of Korea's best collections of Korean traditional art. History buffs will no doubt appreciate Yongin's Korean Folk Village and Cheonan's massive Independence Hall of Korea. The pottery kilns of Icheon, meanwhile, offer visitors a chance to appreciate the beauty of Korea's proud ceramics tradition.

Best of all, most of these things can be fully enjoyed with just a day trip from Seoul.

Tomb of Emperor Sunjong (r. 1907-1910)
Hongyureung Tomb Complex, Namyangju

Shrine, Freedom Bridge and Imjingang River railway bridge, Imjingak

THE DMZ

It's often said the Korean Demilitarized Zone, or DMZ, is the most dangerous place on Earth. This distinction may be technically true—the mountains and hillsides on both sides of the 4 km strip of land separating the two Koreas bristle with troops, guard posts, tanks, missiles, bunkers, gun emplacements, land mines and other tools of death and destruction. A one-hole golf course at the so-called "truce village" of Panmunjeom warns not to retrieve balls from a fairway lined by land mines—needless to say, it was once designated as the "world's most dangerous golf course."

Yet the DMZ is perhaps the supreme irony in a land of ironies. As you gaze out upon the DMZ from Checkpoint 3 of Panmunjeom's Joint Security Area, your attention is drawn not to the rare opportunity to peek into mysterious North Korea, the North Korean soldiers perched on the watchtower nearby, or your chances of survival in a sudden re-opening of hostilities. Instead, you're captivated by the supreme tranquility—the quiet, the lush green hillsides, the rare birds swooping into untouched marshlands. Here, at the most militarized border on the planet, you feel completely at peace.

Panmunjeom

With the fall of the Berlin Wall, Panmunjeom became the world's last Cold War frontier, where democracy and communism stare at each other in the face of an intense standoff. The men standing guard on Freedom's Frontier, as the DMZ is called, don't take their task lightly. Civilians cannot enter the DMZ without prior permission, and tourists can visit Panmunjeom only as part of organized group tours. Even then, visitors must follow strict dress codes and, above all, closely follow the instructions of official guides, who are usually US soldiers.

The highlight of Panmunjeom is the iconic Joint Security Area, or JSA, where North and South come face-to-face with one another—almost literally. The JSA is split down the middle by the Military Demarcation Line (MDL), the actual "border" between North and South Korea. On the southern side are the impressive Freedom House and Peace House. On the northern side of the MDL is the Panmungak, a gray Stalinist structure which, your guides will point out, is probably smaller than it actually appears. Soldiers from both sides stare down visitors and each other. Between the two borders is the sky-blue Military

Armistice Commission building, where with a guide, you may briefly cross over into North Korean territory (permissible ONLY within the building). Most tours will take you to other Panmunjeom landmarks as well, including the famous Bridge of No Return.

• **Getting There** The most popular way—in fact, the only way—to see Panmunjeom is through a guided tour. The most popular tour is the one run by the USO, an entertainment organization for the US military. The USO tour is also the cheapest at US$77. (T. 795-3028) Several other tour companies take groups to the DMZ, usually for about 77,000 won— inquire with the Korea Tourism Organization for assistance. It should be noted that those hailing from certain nations may be barred from visiting Panmunjeom or must undergo extra security scrutiny—be sure to ask first.

Imjingak

If you're into traveling alone, or want to forgo the Panmunjeom tour, Imjingak is worth a visit. The closest thing most South Koreans can get to the DMZ without special permission from the government, Imjingak is literally a shrine to national division. Major landmarks include an altar where families originally from the North come to perform ancestral rites (usually performed in one's ancestral hometown) on the Korean holidays (Chuseok and Seol), an observatory and Freedom Bridge, the hastily constructed bridge where some 130,000 South Korean and Allied POWs crossed to return home at the end of the Korean War. You may also purchase North Korean goods or eat North Korean food at some of the park's shops and restaurants. • **Getting There** Hourly commuter trains go directly to Imjingang Station from Seoul Station. The trip takes about an hour.

Panmunjeom's Joint Security Area (JSA), where North and South Korea come face-to-face

Korean War & National Reunification

The 1945 division of Korea along the 38th parallel was supposed to be little more than a footnote to the end of World War II. With the Soviets pushing into northern Korea, the Americans proposed a division of the peninsula along the 38th parallel into two zones of occupation. With this, occupational regimes were established in Seoul and Pyongyang. The plan was ultimately to set up an independent Korean government and leave.

Unfortunately, the division of Korea became permanent, with a pro-Soviet communist regime led by former guerrilla fighter Kim Il-sung set up in the North, and a pro-American, anti-communist regime led by independence activist Syngman Rhee in the South. The regimes left behind by the departing Soviets and Americans were locked in bitter enmity. Finally, on June 25, 1950, the communist North—armed with Soviet weaponry and buoyed by returning Korean veterans from the Chinese Civil War—invaded the woefully unprepared South, driving nearly to Busan. With massive international support, particularly from the US, the South both stopped the attack and launched its own invasion of the North, which in turn was driven back following massive Chinese intervention. A bloody stalemate developed and a ceasefire was finally signed in 1953.

But the ceasefire did not signal the end, as the two Koreas began an intense competition to rebuild and strengthen their countries—the North took the early lead, but by the 1980s, the dynamic economy of the South was clearly pulling ahead. With the drying up of Soviet support in the 1990s, the North Korean economy totally collapsed—the result was a famine that may have killed up to 3 million people.

Since the division of Korea, reunification has been an important slogan on both sides of the DMZ. But while talk is cheap, reunification will not be. The differences between the two Koreas could not be more stark—one is democratic and wealthy with a worldly and educated population, while the other barely survives on Chinese aid, extortion payments from its nuclear program and hypernationalism. Dietary differences have even resulted in physical differences, where South Koreans are now considerably taller than their Northern cousins.

The so-called "Sunshine Policy" initiated by late President Kim Dae-jung in 1998 focused on peaceful coexistence and opened up a new era in inter-Korean relations that culminated in summits between South Korean and North Korean leaders in 2000 and 2007. South Korean company Hyundai Asan opened up a tourist resort in North Korea's scenic Mt. Kumgangsan, and an industrial complex wedding South Korean capital and North Korean labor was established in North Korea's Kaesong. The election of an aid-weary conservative government in South Korea in 2008 and a series of grave provocations by North Korea, including a second nuclear test in 2009, and the sinking of South Korean warship and shelling of a South Korean island in 2010, has led to a worsening in relations, but as hard as it may be to believe, things are still much better than they used to be.

The ancient Buddhist temple of Bomunsa, founded in 635, looks out over the West Sea.

GANGHWA ISLAND

About two hours west of Seoul is historic Ganghwa Island, one of Korea's most fascinating travel destinations. A major tourist destination for Seoulites looking to get out of town for a weekend, the island now hosts visitors who come to take in its stunning vistas over the Gyeonggi Bay, appreciate its expansive mudflats teeming with life, and sample its outstanding seafood. Some just come for a nice drive along the island's coastal roads.

But in centuries past, the island played host to visitors of a completely different kind. From 1232 to 1270, the royal court of the kingdom of Goryeo took refuge in the island's fortifications as Korean and Mongolian armies shouted insults at one another across the narrow strait, perhaps right where the bridge linking the mainland with Ganghwa now stretches. In the second half of the 19th century, French, American and Japanese invaders set foot on the island, the "unsinkable battleship" blocking the mouth of the Hangang River, the ancient highway to Seoul. Later, missionaries from Britain and other countries came, leaving behind relics and legacies of an altogether more peaceable nature.

Ganghwa Island is also home to several large temples, an international Zen center and the mountaintop altar atop Mt. Manisan, where the mythical founder of the Korean nation is said to have offered sacrifices to the heavens several millennia ago. All this gives the island a spiritual vibe all its own. Then there are the hearty and friendly locals, many of whom are employed in the island's fishing and agricultural industries, with Ganghwa ginseng being particularly famous throughout Korea.

Cannons at Gwangseongbo Fortress

FRENCH, AMERICAN AND JAPANESE RAIDS ON GANGHWA ISLAND

The 19th century witnessed a good deal of imperialist activity in East Asia by the Western powers. The British—later joined by the French—humiliated China in two Opium Wars, and the US Navy under Commodore Matthew Perry forced open Japan to foreign trade. Russia, meanwhile, was encroaching on Chinese territory and increasing its influence in the region.

Korea would fall victim, too.

In 1866, the ruling prince regent, the arch-conservative Heungseon Daewongun (see p147), launched a brutal crackdown on Korea's growing Catholic community. Nine French priests–who had illegally smuggled themselves into Korea to proselytize—were executed. Three French missionaries, however, managed to escape. One made his way to China, where he told French authorities what had happened. Enraged, Rear Admiral Pierre-Gustave Roze, commander of the French Far East Squadron, decided on a punitive expedition against the Koreans.

A French naval task force carrying about 800 men set sail from China for Korea. French marines landed on Ganghwa Island on Oct 16, taking and looting Ganghwa Town. Limited manpower and determined Korean resistance prompted the French to withdraw by mid-November. They did take with them, however, the very valuable manuscripts of the royal archive on Ganghwa Island. These manuscripts were kept at the National Library of France until 2011, when they were loaned back to Korea on a five-year renewable basis.

Also in 1866, an armed US merchant ship sent at the behest of a British trading company in China entered Korean waters, sailing all the way up the Daedong River to Pyongyang with orders to negotiate a trade treaty. Unwelcome, the ship was told to turn back. What happened next is uncertain, but the result isn't—the ship was burnt and its crew killed. Unpleased, the Americans launched a retaliatory raid of their own in 1871. Led by a Civil War veteran Rear Admiral John Rogers, five warships carrying 100 marines sailed for Korea with a demand the Koreans open up their country to trade. When Korean fortifications on Ganghwa Island fired on the ships, the Americans landed marines on the island. The marines took and dismantled several fortifications—one fortress, Gwangseongbo, was captured only after a brutal 15-minute fight that left three Americans and over 200 Koreans dead. Still, the Korean royal court would not consider a trade treaty, and the Americans went home with little to show for their efforts.

Finally, in 1875, it was Japan's turn. A small Japanese warship, the Unyo, entered the waters off Ganghwa Island—it launched a small boat, ostensibly to look for drinking water. The Korean fortresses opened fire, but they were no match for the Japanese naval guns, which quickly silenced the fortresses. A Japanese naval blockade followed, and Japanese demands for an apology resulted in the signing in 1876 of the Treaty of Ganghwa, which opened Korea to foreign trade.

Things to Do and See

Ganghwa Town

The friendly rural center of Ganghwa has a number of interesting sites of historical and cultural interest, including some old city gates and walls, a popular ginseng market, Ganghwa History Hall, the site of the old Goryeo palace and Ganghwa Anglican Church, which was built in Korean traditional style by British missionaries at the turn of the 20th century.

Jeondeungsa Temple

One of Ganghwa Island's two most famous temples, this beautiful place was first built in 372 and rebuilt several times since then. The temple is home to many treasures and cultural properties. Of particular note is the grotesque carving of a naked woman who seems to hold up the roof of the Main Hall. According to legend, the carpenter who built the temple fell in love with a local barmaid who ultimately absconded with all his money. As revenge, he worked her into his creation to hold up the heavy roof of the temple hall for all eternity. Surrounding the temple is Samnang Fortress, a set of defensive walls that have seen much combat over the centuries. • **Admission** 2,500 won • **Getting There** Local buses to Jeondeungsa depart from Ganghwa Bus Terminal • **Tel** 032-937-0125

Coastal Fortification

Along the eastern coast of the island is a set of Joseon-era gun emplacements and fortifications that used to guard the entrance of the Hangang River—the highway to the royal capital of Seoul—in olden times. The most impressive of these forts are Chojijin and Gwangseongbo Fortress, which was the scene of fierce fighting

Jeondeungsa Temple, one of Korea's most beautiful Buddhist monasteries

between Korean defenders and invading US marines in 1871. • **Getting There** Local buses to Chojijin and Gwangseongbo depart from Ganghwa Bus Terminal.

Mt. Manisan

One of Korea's most sacred mountains, this peak is where Korea's mythical founder Dangun (see p281) is said to have offered sacrifices to Heaven from the top of this peak. The 469-meter-high peak offers outstanding views of the island, and at the summit is an altar where ceremonies are held on Foundation Day. You can use a set of stairs to climb to the top. • **Admission** 1,500 won
• **Getting There** Local buses to Mt. Manisan depart from Ganghwa Bus Terminal.

TIPS

ACCOMMODATION

If you're planning to spend the night, accommodation shouldn't be a concern. Korean motels and inns can be found not only in Ganghwa Town, but throughout the island. You can also try a *minbak* (home-stay) if you'd like. Likewise, you shouldn't worry about food. In some places, you'll be tripping over restaurants.

Bomunsa Temple

Located on the nearby island of Seongmodo, this beautiful temple was founded in 635 and is best known for the beautiful engraving of the Buddha high above the temple precinct.

Bomunsa Temple

[1] Ferry to Seongmodo Island and Bomunsa Temple [2] *Hanok*-style Onsu-ri Anglican Church, near Jeondeungsa Temple [3] Wood carving, Jeondeungsa Temple [4] Korean-style Ganghwa Anglican Church, built by British missionaries at the early 20th century

Ganghwa Dolmen Sites

Thoughout the island of Ganghwa-do can be found simple, stone Bronze Age tombs called dolmen (or in Korean, *goindol*). Table-like structures that consist of two or more stones holding up a large, flat capstone, the tombs can be found in particular abundance in the village of Bugeun-ri in west-central Ganghwa-do. Some of these can be pretty impressive— one *dolmen* capstone (long since fallen) is over seven meters long and five meters wide. In 2000, Korea's dolmen sites—including those in Ganghwa-do—were added to UNESCO's list of World Heritage Sites. • **Getting There** Local buses to Bugeun-ri's dolmen sites depart from Ganghwa Bus Terminal.

Map labels:
- North Korea
- Old Goryeo Palace
- Dolmen Sites
- Ganghwa Town
- Gimpo
- Woepo Ferry
- Ganghwa Anglican Church
- Gwangseongbo Fortress
- Bomunsa Temple
- Onsuri Anglican Church
- Jeondeungsa Temple
- Choijin Fortress
- Mt. Manisan

Prehistoric tombs, Ganghwa's dolmens have been designated a UNESCO World Heritage Site

GETTING TO GANGHWA ISLAND

Traveling to Ganghwa Island from Seoul is a breeze. Buses to Ganghwa Town leave from Shinchon Station, Line 2. The buses leave every 10 minutes between 5:40 am and 10 pm. The trip takes about an hour and a half. Ganghwa Bus Terminal, located a short taxi ride outside of downtown Ganghwa Town, is useful as this is where you'll come to catch a bus to anywhere else on the island. There is also a Tourist Information booth in the terminal where you can score English-language maps and tourist information. Similar booths can be found at several other spots on the island.

KOREA'S FOUNDATION MYTH: DANGUN   *History and Culture*

On October 3, Korea celebrates Gaecheonjeol, or National Foundation Day. This holiday marks the traditionally accepted date of Korea's founding in 2333 BC by the king Dangun Wanggeom. On Ganghwa Island, the holiday is accompanied by ceremonies atop Mt. Manisan, where it's said Hwanung, the son of the Lord of Heaven and Dangun's father, descended from heaven to establish Sinsi, the "City of God."

The Dangun myth is as follows. Hwanin, the Lord of Heaven, had a son by the name of Hwanung, who wished to live among the humans on Earth. With 3,000 followers, he descended from heaven to the peak of Mt. Taebaeksan (several peaks claim this title, including Ganghwa-do's Mt. Manisan), where he founded Sinsi, instituted laws and taught humans such useful skills as agriculture and medicine.

One day, a tiger and a bear prayed to Hwanung that they may become human. Hearing their prayers, Hwanung told them to hole-up in a cave for 100 days. For food, they were given 20 cloves of garlic and some mugwort—they were ordered to eat only this during their stay in the cave. This proved too difficult for the tiger, but the bear toughed it out, and was thus transformed into a woman, who was given the name Ungnyeo ("Bear Woman").

Unfortunately for Ungnyeo, she could not find a husband, and she prayed for a child. The ever attentive Hwanung heard these prayers as well, and took her as a wife. She soon gave birth to a son, Dangun Wanggeom.

Dangun became king, and set up a new capital near Pyongyang. He named the kingdom Joseon—Land of the Morning Calm—although to avoid confusion with the much later Joseon kingdom of 1392-1910, Dangun's kingdom is usually called Gojoseon, or Old Joseon. He is said to have ruled until he became a mountain god at the ripe old age of 1,908.

While the tale itself is widely accepted as myth, it may hint at historical truths, such as the founding of an ancient Korean nation from the tribes living in northern Korea by a powerful chief or king. The myth also shares similarities with the myths of other East Asian and Siberian ethnic groups, indicating the tribes that eventually formed the Korean nation may have migrated from deep within Asia.

Old bank buildings in Incheon's old Japanese concession area

INCHEON

For many—if not most—the bustling city of Incheon is little more than a gateway via either Incheon International Airport or the increasingly busy ferry route with China. Korea's second busiest container port and home to the Incheon Free Economic Zone (IFEZ) and Songdo New City, Incheon is very much a city rushing towards the future.

Underneath the gantry cranes and glass skyscrapers, however, is a city rich in history and exotic charm. A century ago, this was the treaty port of Jemulpo (Chemulpo), the West's portal to Korea and Korea's portal to the West. Like the treaty ports of China, Jemulpo was home to large foreign settlements, where foreigners from China, Japan and the West brought their unique foods, architecture and faiths. The settlements have long since gone, but much remains of Jemulpo's international heritage in Incheon's old waterfront area, making for a relaxing, romantic and educational day trip from Seoul.

Things to Do and See

Chinatown

Incheon's Chinatown was born in 1884 as the Qing settlement. By the 1930s, Chinatown was home to a prosperous community of some 100,000 Chinese, many from nearby Shandong province, but tough times would follow, leading to mass emigration. Today it is home to about 500 Chinese residents. Incheon's Chinatown won't rival San Francisco's by any stretch, but it's nonetheless Korea's oldest and largest such community. Like Chinatowns all over the world, this is a great place to eat—Incheon's Chinatown is the birthplace of *jajangmyeon* (see p391), a dish of noodles with black bean sauce that has become a Korean favorite.

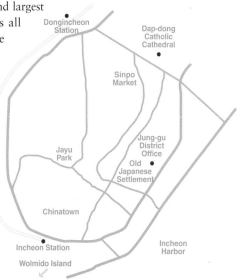

GETTING THERE

Incheon is the last stop of Seoul Subway Line 1. From downtown Seoul, it takes about an hour and a half. The entrance to Chinatown is just across the street from Incheon Station.

Colonial-style Incheon Post Office, built in 1924

Old Japanese Settlement

As you head east, you'll come to a flight of stone steps lined with a row of stone lanterns. This marks the old boundary between the Chinese and Japanese settlements. The old Japanese settlement was centered on the old Incheon City Hall (now the Jung-gu District Hall), which in turn was the site of the former Japanese consulate. Here you'll find some of Incheon's most beautiful examples of early modern architecture—of particular note are the old bank buildings (one of which is now a museum of Incheon's early modern architecture) and the Incheon Post Office.

Jayu Park

Korea's first Western-style park, designed in 1888, Jayu Park was for a time home to lovely European-style summer cottages owned by wealthy expatriate Westerners. It's now home to a statue of General Douglas MacArthur*(see p287), the American war hero who helped turn the tide of the Korean War with the brilliant amphibious landing that made Incheon famous. The park sits atop a breezy hill with fine views of the harbor. Just below the park is the beautiful old Jemulpo Club, formerly a social club for Incheon's foreign community founded in 1901. Recently restored, it is now a museum of the treaty port era.

1 Old Chemulpo Club, founded in 1901 2 *Jajangmyeon*, Incheon's most famous dish 3 Uiseondang, a Chinese-style temple founded in 1893 4 Ornate entrance to office of old Japanese shipping company

Dap-dong Cathedral, built by French missionaries in 1897

St. Michael's Anglican Church and Dap-dong Cathedral

Many of Korea's early Western missionaries first set up shop in Jemulpo. St. Michael's Anglican Cathedral and Dap-dong Cathedral are two reminders of this history. St. Michael's Anglican Cathedral, located near Jayu Park, was founded in 1891 by British missionaries. A short walk from St. Michael's brings you to the massive Dap-dong Cathedral, one of Korea's oldest Catholic churches. Founded by French missionaries in 1897, the cathedral remains virtually unchanged since additions in 1937.

Wolmido Island

Attached to the mainland by a 1 km causeway, Wolmido is a popular weekend destination for Seoulites. Basically one massive concentration of seafood restaurants, cafés, and a small amusement park, it has a Coney Island-esque atmosphere. You can also catch a cruise of the harbor from here. • **Getting There** Take blue buses No. 2, 23, 45 from Incheon Station, Line 1

THE CONTROVERSIAL STATUE

To many Koreans, particularly older ones, Gen. Douglas MacArthur is a hero and savior, the man who rescued South Korea from North Korean invaders. To a small but passionate minority of leftist and nationalist activists, however, he is a war criminal who prevented Korea from being reunified, and his statue in Jayu Park represents a slight to national honor. Accordingly, the statue has been the scene of a couple of clashes between leftist and conservative groups, with the latter trying to protect against attempts by the former to pull the general down.

Even to his fans, Gen. Douglas MacArthur is a controversial figure. A hero of the Pacific War, MacArthur was the commander of the Allied occupation of Japan when the Korean War broke out in 1950. While his role in rebuilding Japan was commendable, his maintenance of the war-fighting capability of the men under his command left much to be desired, something that became painfully obvious in the early disasters suffered by US forces in the Korean War.

Still, as commander of UN forces in Korea, he did manage to turn things around. While at times dangerously arrogant, he could also be exceptionally brilliant. This brilliance was at no time more apparent than on Sept 15, 1950, when he launched — over the objections of other generals who considered the operation too risky, if not impossible — an amphibious landing at Incheon, far behind enemy lines. Timing the notorious Incheon tides right, Allied forces (mostly US Marines) successfully landed on the beaches and took the city; due to a deliberate misinformation campaign, the North Koreans were expecting a landing further south. By the end of the month, allied forces had liberated Seoul, cutting off the supply lines feeding North Korean troops fighting on the Busan Perimeter. About half of the North Korean invaders were killed or captured, while the rest fled back to the North.

Statue of Gen. Douglas Macarthur in Jayu Park

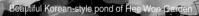
Beautiful Korean-style pond of Hee Won Garden

YONGIN

Everland, Ho-Am Art Museum and Korean Folk Village

For many Seoulites, the suburb of Yongin represents a nice day trip out of the big city. Within the lushly forested hillsides of this conveniently located Seoul suburb are some of Korea's most popular tourist destinations, including the massive Korean Folk Village and, of course, Everland theme park—one of the most visited theme parks in the known universe. If you're looking for somewhere to escape the masses, Yongin might not necessarily fit the bill; on any given weekend, the masses may very well follow you down here.

Everland

The Everland Resort, owned by the Samsung Corporation (which owns a rather large chunk of Yongin itself), is one of the largest amusement parks on the planet. Sitting on some 3,700 acres of prime real estate, the park ranked sixth worldwide in park attendance in 2002 and eventually worked its way to number five, beating out luminaries such as Epcot, Disney MGM and Disney's Animal Kingdom and earning a place on Forbes' list of best amusement parks.

If you've been to Disneyland, you know what to expect. If you're prepubescent, or just really into amusement parks, Everland is a dream come true. Even if you aren't, it's still worth checking out for the sheer scale and surrealness of it all.

Everland is broken up into six zones—American Adventure, Magic Land, Aesop's Village, European Adventure, Zoo-Topia and Global Fair. Leave any hope you have of seeing it all in a single day at the ticket booth—you could spend a month wandering around and not see everything. And that's not even including Caribbean Bay, the Everland Resort's summer water park, and its large zoo. Each section has its own unique rides and attractions. The architecture and atmosphere is very Disney-like—the Disney Castle is missing, but instead you're greeted at the entrance with mock-ups of St. Basil's Cathedral, the Hagia Sophia and what appears to be a giant wall-mural of a Tuscan village.

There's even a well-regarded golf course and a race track where the aspiring Mario Andrettis of the world can earn their racing licenses. Entry to Everland isn't cheap—for adults, it's 31,000 won for a single-entry pass (23,000 won for children). A day pass will run you 38,000 won (29,000 won for children). Throw in Caribbean Bay, and it could add up to a very pricey weekend.

• **Hours** 9:30 am to 10 pm (subject to change) • **Getting There** The shortest way to get to Everland is by bus 5002 from Exit 6 of Gangnam Station, Line 2—in theory, it should get you there in less than an hour. There are also buses from Dongdaemun History & Culture Park Station (Line 2, 4 and 5) and Exit 1 of Sadang Station (Lines 2 and 4), as well as from

Suwon Station (in Gyeonggi-do Province, Line 1). If you're going there from Korean Folk Village, take bus 10-5 from in front of the parking lot. • **Tel** (031) 320-5000

Ho-Am Art Museum and Hee Won Garden

The largest private museum in Korea, this is undoubtedly one of the world's finest collections of Korean art. The museum houses the private collection of the late founder of Samsung, Lee Byung-chul, and includes several pieces that were designated as national treasures by the Korean government.

Its collection aside, the museum is worth visiting for the setting alone. Spread in front is the splendor of the Hee Won, one of the most spectacular examples of Korean traditional garden design anywhere. You can spend hours here contently doing absolutely nothing but relaxing and listening to the sound of the wind and running water. Overlooking the garden, atop stone terraces that blend in with the surroundings, are the museum hall and a pleasant tea house where you can enjoy a cool beverage and gaze out upon the majesty below.

• **Hours** 10 am to 6 pm. Closed Mondays • **Admission** 4,000 won • **Getting There** Free shuttle bus service will take you to the museum from the ticket booth area of Everland, but the last bus returning from the museum leaves at 4 pm. If you miss it (admittance is available only until 5 pm; the museum closes at 6 pm), the front gate will happily assist in calling a cab—the ride back to Everland costs about 5,000 won. • **Tel** (031) 320-1801~2

Korean Folk Village

Korean Folk Village is, natch, a Korean folk village, and a large one at that. You could literally spend an entire day wandering around the place—or two days, if you happen to get lost.

It's been said by some that Korean Folk Village is "artificial." This is true—unlike Andong's Hahoe Village or Suncheon's Nagan Eupseong, Korean Folk Village is not a pre-existing historic village that has been preserved. It was purpose-built in 1974 as an open air folk museum. That being said, Korean Folk Village has been done quite tastefully as folk villages go. The homes and buildings—and there are a lot of them, with some 260 structures sitting on a grand total of 243 acres—have been painstakingly reconstructed as close to period as possible. So good are the reconstructions and atmosphere that the village is frequently used as a film set; the 2003 film *Scandal*, the hit TV miniseries *Daejanggeum* and the Korean blockbuster *The King and Clown* (see p455) were all shot here. The place is very picturesque—a camera is essential.

• **Hours** 9 am to 6:30 pm (closes earlier in winter) • **Admission** 15,000 won • **Getting There** From Exit 6 of Gangnam Station, Line 2, you can take buses No. 5001-1 or 1560 to Korean Folk Village. The trip takes about 40 minutes. • **Tel** (031) 286-2116

1 Wind chime of Korean Folk Village 2 Washing your hair with iris-infused water, Korean Folk Village 3 Peacock, Hee Won Garden 4 Everland, one of the world's most visited amusement parks

長安門

Imposing walls of Suwon Hwaseong Fortress

SUWON HWASEONG FORTRESS

Suwon Hwaseong Fortress is by far Korea's most impressive historical fortress. Constructed as the walls of a planned new royal capital, Hwaseong Fortress was built upon the bitter defeats against the Japanese and Manchus and made use of scientific building methods. Its imposing walls and intimidating guard towers are truly a sight to behold, a sentiment apparently shared by UNESCO, which designated the fortress on its list of World Heritage Sites in 1997.

Silhak: Practical Learning

Hwaseong was built between 1794 and 1796 by King Jeongjo (see p58), one of the greatest kings of the Joseon era. Jeongjo was a reformer, who enjoyed the support of scholars associated with the *silhak* movement, a school of Confucian thought that valued practical learning over metaphysical debate. One of the stars of this movement was the brilliant scholar "Dasan" Jeong Yak-yong whom Jeongjo entrusted with the construction of the defenses of Suwon, where the king hoped to relocate the royal capital. Jeong's use of brick and a complex system of pulleys and cranes would not seem out of place even for architects today.

Walls and Gates

At one time, all of Suwon was contained within the fortress, but urban development in the modern era has caused the city to sprawl out way beyong the old walls. The fortress has four gates, the most impressive of which are the northern gate of Janganmun and southern gate of Paldalmun, which are grand, imposing structures that are themselves protected by crescent-shaped outworks. Also worth seeing are the western gate of Hwaseomun (with its intimidating, three-story brick watchtower) and Hwahongmun Gate, with seven arches that allow the Suwon River to flow through the fortress. A key point of interest is the Ammun Gate, a postern or secret gate that was used to transport food, weapons and men out of view of the enemy.

The best way to appreciate the fortress is to stroll around it—the walls total about 5.7 km in length and can be walked in about two to three hours. Also of interest is the "Bell of Filial Piety," a large Korean-style bell with a log ringer that you, the humble visitor, can ring (for a small donation) to pay respect to your parents. • **Admission** 1,000 won • **Getting There** From Seoul, take Subway Line 1 south to Suwon Station. From Seoul Station, it takes about one hour. • **Website** hs.suwon.ne.kr

TIPS

SUWON GALBI
Suwon is famous for Suwon *galbi*, healthy portions of marinated barbecued ribs. Many restaurants in Suwon do this dish—Yeonpo Galbi near the Hwahongmun Gate is a good place to try (031-245-5900)

Monument to the Nation

CHEONAN INDEPENDENCE HALL

For visitors, the regional center of Cheonan is best known as the home of Independence Hall, a truly awesome memorial to Korean independence and one of Korea's best museums.

Independence Hall opened to the public in 1987 as a museum and research center to preserve the history of Korean opposition to Japanese colonial rule. The complex, built at a time when Korea was ruled by a military dictatorship, is in some respects almost Stalinist in scale—note the intimidating concrete Grand Hall of the Nation, which the museum boasts is the largest tile-roofed structure in the Far East. The hall was built in Korean traditional style to house a social realist tribute to the triumph of Korean nationalism over the forces of Japanese imperialism. The sprawling courtyard has more gargantuan monuments to the Korean nation. It's all very impressive, and on a positive note, at least Korea had the wisdom to wait until after its post-war economic boom was well underway before splurging on this massive project.

After you've taken in the massive outdoor exhibits, step in the Main Exhibition Hall and make your way through the museum's seven exhibitions, most of which are dedicated to various aspects of the anti-Japanese struggle. The countless exhibits and photos on display are fascinating, especially if you have an interest in Korean history. As you can imagine, the nationalism here comes at you fast

Korean flags a'waivin' at Cheonan Independence Hall

and furious. Some of the displays can be quite shocking, and nobody will accuse the museum of presenting the Japanese in a favorable light—one of the more popular exhibits is a series of recreations of Japanese torture of Korean independence activists, with smirking Japanese soldiers inflicting cruel treatment on beaten, bleeding Koreans. Japanese visitors might not necessarily appreciate it all, and the history of the colonial era is probably more complicated than the museum would like to admit, but the bitterness is not without reason—Japanese colonial rule was not a pleasant experience, as Korea's imperial masters systematically attempted to denigrate Korea's unique history and culture and involve the colony in Tokyo's imperial aggression in the region.

• **Hours** 9:30 am to 6 pm (Mar to Oct), 9:30 am to 5 pm (Nov to Feb) Ticket sales stop one hour to closing. Closed Mondays
• **Admission** Free • **Getting There** Take Line 1 to Cheonan Station. The trip takes about two hours. From Cheonan Express Bus Terminal, take a bus (No. 400) to Independence Hall (about 30 minutes); From Cheonan Train Station, take a bus (No. 400) to Independence Hall (about 20 minutes) • **Tel** (041) 560-0114
• **Website** www.i815.or.kr

Plaza of the Nation

"Statue of Indomitable Koreans," a granite monument to Korean nationalism

Stacks of pottery at Incheon Ceramics Village

ICHEON

The Beauty of Joseon Ceramics

To get a real appreciation for Korea's proud ceramics tradition, head to Icheon, a small town just an hour southeast of Seoul. Icheon and the surrounding towns of Yeoju and Gwangju have for centuries served as the heart of Korea's ceramics industry. Icheon is home to countless small kilns, including a number of traditional wood-burning clay kilns that operate in the time-honored fashion.

Icheon Ceramics Village

Today, most of Icheon's ceramic producers are located in the rural hamlet of Sindun-myeon, a short taxi ride from Icheon's express bus terminal. The producers have largely gathered in two "potters' villages," or *doyechon*—one in Sindun-myeon proper and one in a valley called Sagimakgol. Both are similar— dozens of studios and shops where you can spend days going through the beautiful wares, which include both works of art like priceless vases and daily items like cups, plates and spoons. The artisans are often manning the shops, so if you'd like to talk to the artist, there's plenty of opportunity to do so. Both areas have traditional wood-burning kilns for good measure.

TIPS

EXPERIENCING THE ART

The ceramics villages also offer classes and hands-on programs for those who'd like to try their hand at pottery. One such place, in the Sagimakgol *doyechon*, is the Sun and Moon (Hae wa Dal) Gallery and Classroom, where the friendly operators—limited language skills aside—will take you through the entire ceramics process (and mail you your work after it's all baked!). Prices differ depending on what you create— to make an average-sized plate, for instance, will cost 20,000 won.

Haegang Ceramics Museum

The Haegang Ceramics Museum, located not far from the ceramics villages in Sindun-myeon, was founded in 1990 by the late "Haegang" Yoo Kun-hyung, a ceramics master who dedicated his life to rediscovering Korea's proud Goryeo celadon tradition. The museum is a good place to learn about Korea's ceramics tradition, as well as to appreciate the beautiful collection of work. • **Hours** 9:30 am to 5:30 pm. Closed Mondays • **Admission** 2,000 won • **Tel** (031) 634-2266~7 • **Website** www.haegang.org

Icheon Ceramics Festival

The best time of year to come to Icheon is springtime, when the town is in the midst of the month-long Icheon Ceramics Festival. This celebration of the town's proudest artistic tradition, going strong since 1987, brings people from all over to see and purchase the wares, enjoy hands-on experiences and take in the many cultural performances on hand. • **Tel** (031) 644-2944 • **Website** www.ceramic.or.kr

TIPS

ICHEON SSALBAP

Icheon's gift to Korea's culinary landscape is the *ssalbapjip*, a restaurant that specializes in Icheon-style *jeongsik* (table d'hôte). *Jeongsik* will differ slightly from place to place, but in Icheon, it generally consists of rice in a stone pot, steamed meat, crab seasoned with soy sauce, soup and an array of countless side dishes. It's as appealing visually as it is to the taste buds.

The area around Sindun-myeon—indeed, everywhere in Icheon—is full of places to have *ssalbap jeongsik*, and as close to Seoul as the town is, they do good business. The most famous of these restaurants is Imgeumnim Ssalbapjip (T. 031-632-3646) in Sindun-myeon. Locals, however, recommend Taepyeong Seongdae (T. 031-638-8088), a massive place just across from the Sagimakgol *doyechon* that seems to be doing a roaring trade. A very pleasant culinary experience can also be had at Gomijeong (T. 031-634-4811), an exquisitely appointed *hanok*-style restaurant located on a quiet hillside just off the road in Sindun-myeon. Dining areas are private, entered through Korean-style wood and paper doors.

GETTING TO ICHEON

Buses to Icheon depart from Seoul's Gangnam Express Bus Terminal—the trip takes about an hour. Once you're in Icheon, most of the ceramics-related sites are a short taxi ride away from the bus terminal. You may wish to take the taxi driver's name card when you reach your destination—to get to your next destination (or back to the bus terminal, for that matter), you may have to call him again. This is all quite easy to do and makes getting around much easier—especially if you're carrying around a bag of ceramics you've just purchased.

KOREAN CERAMICS

While Korean ceramics date back to prehistory, their golden age was the Joseon era, when ceramics became Korea's most beloved art form. The artisans of the previous dynasty, the Buddhist Goryeo kingdom (918-1392), produced intricate porcelains renowned for their beautiful celadon glaze. With the overthrow of Goryeo by the neo-Confucian founders of the Joseon kingdom (1392-1910), the ornate celadon styles fell out of favor. Taking their place was *baekja*, or Joseon white porcelain. These wares, pure white in color and almost completely unadorned, better reflected the simpler, austere tastes of the times.

The Icheon region, along with the neighboring towns of Yeoju and Gwangju, became the center of the Joseon ceramics industry. This is partly thanks to the area's rich supply of kaolinite, or china clay. It also helped that the region was blessed with a good supply of water and wood, as well as, perhaps most importantly, easy transport access to the royal capital of Seoul.

Toward the end of the Joseon era, a flood of cheaper foreign-produced ceramics and, later, imperial pressure led to a decline in Icheon's ceramics industry. Since Liberation in 1945, however, the kilns have been burning bright again as artisans gather in the region's valleys not only to keep alive the traditions of the past, but also to put their own spin on the ancient craft and share their knowledge with the public.

Life springs from the ruins of war at former Cheorwon Office of the Workers Party of Korea

CHEORWON

Just across the provincial border into the mountainous region of Gangwon-do is the town of Cheorwon, home to some of Korea's most impressive Korean War ruins. Once a large, prosperous railroad and road junction controlling the Geumhwa Valley, a vital north-south passageway to Seoul, the town was virtually wiped off the map in the bitter fighting of the Korean War. After the war, the town was rebuilt several kilometers away. Where the old town once stood, all that remains are shattered ruins in the rice fields.

The most impressive of the ruins is the former Cheorwon Office of the Workers' Party of Korea, a Stalinist concrete edifice that once served as the local headquarters of North Korea's ruling party (located north of the 38th parallel, Cheorwon was under North Korean administration before the war). Ruthlessly shelled during the war, the building was reduced to a burned out, bullet scarred skeleton. And so it remains today, a monument to the horror of war and the pain of national division.

Seungil-gyo Bridge, which according to legend was started by North Korea and finished by South Korea

Nearby are more ruins just across the Civilian Control Line, the furthest point north civilians can freely go. Also in the military zone past the Civilian Control Line is an old train station and an observatory. Visiting these sites is a bit tricky— see "Getting To Cheorwon." Another site worth seeing is the Seungil-gyo Bridge, a concrete arch bridge over the Hantangang River that, according to legend, was started by the North Koreans and finished by the South Koreans. Recent evidence suggests the bridge was begun by the Japanese and finished by the US Army, but it's still a beautiful site—the two halves of the bridge are clearly different, revealing its unusual history.

GETTING TO CHEORWON

To get to the ruins of the Workers Party of Korea, just take Line 1 to Dongducheon, transfer to the Gyeongwon line commuter train and get off at the last stop (and we do mean last—any further and you're in North Korea) of Sintan-ri. From Sintan-ri, there are buses that pass by the ruins. All told, it takes about two hours.

To get to some of the sites across the Civilian Line of Control, you need a car. Access to the area is open four times a day on weekdays (9:30, 10:30 am, 1, 2:30pm, closed Tuesdays)—you need to inform the Iron Triangle Tourism Office (033-450-5558) in the hamlet of Goseokjeong at least 20 minutes beforehand. On weekends, you must take a shuttle bus (8,000 won) from the afore mentioned office. If you don't have a car, you can hire a taxi (about 60,000 won).

To get to the Seungil-gyo Bridge, just take a taxi from Goseokjeong.

Former Cheorwon Office of the Workers Party of Korea

[1] Old Woljeong-ri Station, located in the military zone near the DMZ [2] Ruins of Cheorwon Methodist Church, destroyed during the Korean War [3] If your tank weighs more than 13 tons, please do not drive it over Seungil-gyo Bridge [4] Old Cheorwon Agricultural Inspection Office, built in 1936 and left in ruins after the Korean War

Stone soldier guards the tomb of King Seonjo, Donggureung Tomb Complex

JOSEON ROYAL TOMBS

A Look into Confucian Cosmology

In 2009, UNESCO designated Korea's Joseon dynasty royal tombs as World Heritage Sites. And for good reason—the entire lineage of the Joseon kingdom, from King Taejo (r. 1392-1398) to Emperor Sunjong (r. 1907-1910), can be accounted for. Easily accessible from Seoul, the tombs are exquisite examples of Korean landscaping and provide visitors with insight into the history and worldview of the Confucian-inspired kingdom of Joseon.

Characteristics of Joseon Royal Tombs

The majority of the 40 Joseon royal tombs are located between 10 and 100 *ri* (4 and 40 km) from Gyeongbokgung Palace. The location and arrangement of the tombs are highly informed by Confucianism* (see next page) and *feng shui*. In accordance with Confucian etiquette, each tomb is divided into three spaces, an entrance, usually marked by a simple red gate and a stone bridge; a place to conduct rites, usually a T-shaped Korean-style hall; and the burial spot itself, with the grave and stone monuments. The burial grounds are typically located on hillsides with mountains to their rear for protection and streams nearby to let energy flow. Much care went into the surrounding landscapes, as well—tombs are usually surrounded by splendid verdant forests of pine and oak.

Tomb of King Taejo, the founder of the Joseon Dynasty, Donggureung Tomb Complex

KOREAN CONFUCIANISM

It's often said Korea is the most Confucian nation in the world.

Confucianism originated in China, where it developed from the teachings of its namesake, the social philosopher Confucius (551-479 BC). Whether it is a religion or philosophy is a matter of debate, and not one we intend to go into here. Confucianism is concerned with the development of human morality, social harmony and good governance. Common themes include the importance of rituals and etiquette, knowing one's position in relation to others and filial piety. As a philosophy of government, it placed importance on rule through upstanding moral virtue rather than force or coercive laws.

Along with Buddhism, Confucianism came to Korea from China in the Three Kingdoms Period (57 BC to 668 AD), but Korean Confucianism reached its height during the Joseon Dynasty (1392-1910), when neo-Confucianism—an interpretation of Confucianism attributed largely to the 12th century Chinese Confucian thinker Zhu Xi—became the guiding ideology of Korean government and society. Confucian schools were set up throughout the country to prepare students for the all-important civil service exam, which required a thorough learning of the so-called *Four Books and Five Classics*, the primary texts of Confucian philosophy. Confucianism had a profound influence on the arts such as ceramics, painting and calligraphy as well.

With the fall of the Joseon Dynasty, Confucianism ceased to be Korea's ruling ideology, but it continues to govern many day-to-day interactions between Koreans. See, for instance, the importance Koreans place on age and seniority, a phenomenon even codified in the language in the form of higher and lower forms of speech. Koreans are generally more polite and deferential to their elders than are Westerners, a fact tourists would be wise to remember when dealing with elderly (or just older) Koreans. In personal relationships, the junior-senior relationship is crucial—even a year's difference in age requires the junior to treat the senior with according respect. The Confucian influence is seen in Koreans' enthusiasm for education, a legacy of the Confucian principle that education is the way to moral improvement (and, just as important from a practical standpoint, a good job).

One Confucian rite that is still performed widely in Korea is the *jesa*, or ancestral memorial rite performed annually on the anniversary of an ancestor's death. Similar memorial services, called *charye*, are performed on the autumn Chuseok and winter Lunar New Year's holidays.

Major Tomb Sites

Donggureung Tomb Complex (Guri-si, Gyeonggi-do)

The largest of the Joseon tomb clusters, Donggureung is the final resting place of seven kings and 10 queens, including the founder of the Joseon dynasty, King Taejo (r. 1392-1398). The tomb of King Seonjo (r. 1567-1608) is particularly grand, while King Taejo's tomb is unique as it is covered in rushes from the northern Korean town of Hamhung, Taejo's hometown. • **Hours** 6 am to 6:30 pm (March to Oct), 6:30 am to 5:30 pm (Nov to Feb). Ticket sales stops 1 hour to closing. Closed Mondays • **Admission** 1,000 won • **Getting There** Bus No. 1-1 or 9-2 from Gangbyeon Station (Line 2). Get off at Donggureung. Trip takes about 40 minutes.

Seonjeongneung (Samseong-dong, Seoul)

The burial place of King Seongjong (r. 1469-1494) and King Jungjong (r. 1506-1544), Seonjeongneung is today located in the heart of one of Seoul's busiest commercial districts. The visual contrast of the tombs against their urban backdrop is striking. Despite the location, the site is surrounded by rich forests and is quite tranquil, making it an excellent urban park. • **Hours** 6 am to 9 pm (Mar to Oct), 6:30 am to 9 pm (Nov to Feb) Ticket sales stops 1 hour to closing. Closed Mondays • **Admission** 1,000 won • **Getting There** Exit 8 of Seolleung Station, Line 2

Taereung (Gongneung-dong, Seoul)

Also located in Seoul, this tomb belongs to one of Korean history's most powerful queens, Queen Munjeong, who served as the virtual ruler of Korea throughout much of the mid-16th century as regent to her son, the young King Myeongjong. • **Hours** 9 am to 6:30 pm (Mar to Oct), 9 am to 5:30 pm (Nov to Feb) Ticket sales stops 1 hour to closing. Closed Mondays • **Admission** 1,000 won • **Getting There** Exit 7 of Taereung Station, Line 6 and 7, and take bus No. 1155 or 1156 to Taereung Gangneung (10 minute ride).

Gwangneung (Namyangju-si, Gyeonggi-do)

Located in one of Korea's most beautiful forests (which is also home to the Gwangneung National Arboretum), Gwangneung is the tomb of King Sejo, one of the dynasty's most energetic kings. This is a particularly beautiful place to visit in autumn, when it can be combined with a visit to the arboretum. • **Hours** 9 am to 6:30 pm (Mar to Oct), 9 am to 5:30 pm (Nov to Feb) Ticket sales stops 1 hour to closing. Closed Mondays • **Admission** 1,000 won • **Getting There** Take bus No. 21 from Uijeongbu Station, Line 1 to Gwangneung (trip takes about 40 minutes).

Hongneung and Yureung (Namyangju, Gyeonggi-do)

These two tombs are unique in that they are the burial places of emperors: Emperor Gojong (r. 1863-1907) and Emperor Sunjong (r. 1907-1910) of the Daehan Empire (see p91) and their wives. As imperial rather than royal burial sites, the tombs adopt the layout of imperial Chinese tombs—the stone animals and guardians are located along the path to the rites pavilion, which have been expanded into palatial structures. • **Hours** 6 am to 6:30 pm (Mar to Oct), 6:30 am to 5:30 pm (Nov to Feb) Ticket sales stops 1 hour to closing. Closed Mondays • **Admission** 1,000 won • **Getting There** Take bus No. 30, 65, 165-3, 330-1, 765, 1330 or 3300 from Cheungnyangni Station and get off at the tombs. Trip takes about 40 minutes.

MOUNTAINS

THINGS TO DO AND SEE

- Take in the views of downtown Seoul from Mt. Namsan's N Seoul Tower
- Hike Seoul's old fortress walls on Mt. Bugaksan
- Learn about Korean shamanism at Mt. Inwangsan's Guksadang Shrine
- See southern Seoul—from above—at the peak of Mt. Gwanaksan
- Conquer the rugged peaks of Mt. Bukhansan National Park

MT. BUKHANSAN

This dramatic collection of rocky peaks in northern Seoul has been declared a national park. In addition to being a popular hiking place, it's also home to the granite face of Insubong Peak, one of the most popular rock-climbing locations in Korea. Other major peaks include Baegundae (the highest peak at 836 m) and Mangyeongdae. History buffs will want to check out Bukhan Mountain Fortress, a medieval fortification that protected the royal capital in the Goryeo and Joseon eras. Several Buddhist temples are located here, too, including the major Zen center of Hwagyesa Temple.

MT. INWANGSAN

A sacred mountain in Korean shamanism, Mt. Inwangsan's granite face and bizarre rock formations have captivated Koreans for ages. The peak is not high (338 m) but still offers wonderful views of downtown Seoul. It is home to the Guksadang, Korea's most important shamanist shrine, and Seonbawi, an unusual rock formation that also serves as a site of shamanist rites.

Mt. Bugaksan

Long kept off-limits to the public as a special security zone, this peak just behind the presidential palace of Cheong Wa Dae is now fully hikable, albeit within specific hours—entry is from 9 am to 3 pm (April to Oct), 10 am to 3 pm (Nov to March), and you must leave the area by 5pm. Historical sites include the old city walls, Sukjeongmun Gate and Changuimun Gate.

Mt. Namsan

Mt. Namsan is perhaps Seoul's most famous peak thanks to the landmark N Seoul Tower, which is located on its summit. This low, gentle peak (262 m) can be climbed by just about anyone, and makes for a nice retreat from the urban jungle below.

Mt. Gwanaksan

This relatively gentle massif in southern Seoul offers splendid views of the Gangnam area and Hangang River, especially from the Yeonjudae Pavilion, which is perched dramatically atop the mountain's highest peak, Yeonjubong (629 m).

Downtown seen from Mt. Inwangsan

N Seoul Tower, Seoul's most recognized landmark

Mt. Namsan

Scenic Hike in the Heart of Seoul

At 265 m high, nobody will ever confuse Mt. Namsan with K2. That said, Seoul's "South Mountain," with the landmark N Seoul Tower crowning its peak, makes for a wonderful urban hike that provides some of the best views in Seoul.

History

Mt. Namsan translates as "South Mountain" and was regarded as Seoul's southern "protective spirit." It also marked the southern limit of the old royal capital of Seoul—sections of the old fortress wall can still be found along its slopes.

The mountain has undergone its fair share of ups and downs in recent history. When the Japanese colonized Korea, they forcefully relocated Korea's most important shamanist shrine (see "Guksadang Shrine" on p326) to build a massive Shinto shrine. After Korea's liberation from colonial rule, the shrine was destroyed and replaced with a botanical garden.

In recent years, Seoul has expended a good deal of energy beautifying the mountain and restoring its natural condition. As a result, hiking paths have been upgraded and facilities improved.

View of Seoul from plaza of N Seoul Tower

Hiking

There are a ton of ways up this mountain. Easy paths start from Dongdaemun, Myeong-dong, Itaewon and elsewhere. The National Theater of Korea (see p164) on the north side of the mountain and Hyatt Hotel on the southern side are good places to start. Getting there to N Seoul Tower and the summit takes about 30 minutes.

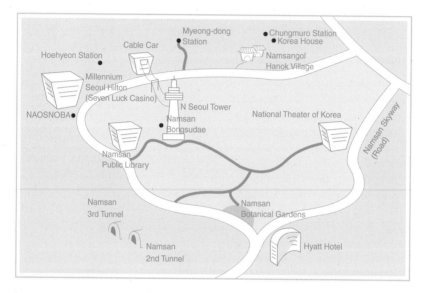

Things to See

N Seoul Tower

One of Seoul's most recognizable landmarks, N Seoul Tower—originally named Namsan Tower or Seoul Tower—was built in 1969 as a communication tower and opened to the public as a park in 1980. In 2005, the tower's new owners—the CJ Corporation—gave the tower a major face lift, renovating the facilities and making it a much nicer place to visit, especially with a date. There are several restaurants, including the upscale N Grill, a revolving restaurant with killer views, and the stationary Korean restaurant Hancook,

Dusk over downtown Seoul, seen from Mt. Namsan

which has just as nice views with a much more affordable menu. There's also an observation deck and one of the most jaw-dropping restrooms you're likely to ever use.

- **Hours** 10 am to 11 pm
- **Admission** 9,000 won • **Tel** 3455-9277 • **Getting There** The tower sits atop a 262-m-high mountain—how you climb it is up to you. There are regular buses to the tower that depart from near Exit 2 of Chungmuro Station, Line 3 or 4 between 8 am and midnight. There's also a cable car—the lower terminal is a 10-minute walk from Myeong-dong Station, Line 4, Exit 3. A round-trip ticket is 7,500 won, while a one-way ticket is 6,000 won. You could also hike it—it's not particularly strenuous, and will take you about 40 minutes to get to the top.

Namsangol Hanok Village

In a small valley on the northern slope of Mt. Namsan is Namsangol Hanok Village, a wonderful collection of historic Korean homes that were moved to the spot and lovingly restored.

In the old days, this area used to be a prime scenic location and summer retreat—aristocrats used to pen poems in praise of it. In order to preserve the traditional character of the valley, the authorities built a pleasure pond and several Korean traditional pavilions and relocated to the area five architecturally and historically important Korean homes. The homes, of various social classes, were restored and adorned with class-appropriate furnishings to give visitors a sense of Joseon-era lifestyles.

In addition to the Korean homes and beautiful Korean-style pond and garden, there's also a time capsule—it'll be opened on the millennial anniversary of the founding of Seoul on Nov. 29, 2394. So please, mark your calendars.

The village hosts various events and programs to give visitors a taste of Korean traditional culture, including art and craft classes. On the Chuseok and Seol (Thanksgiving and Lunar New Year) holidays, the place is overrun with visitors. Those with an interest in Korean traditional music will want to check out the newly opened Namsan Gugakdang (see p426). • **Hours** 9 am to 9 pm (Apr to Oct), 9 am to 8 pm (Nov to March). Closed Tuesdays • **Admission** Free • **Tel** 2264-4412 • **Getting There** Chungmuro Subway Station, Line 3 or 4, Exit 3 or 4

Namsangol Hanok Village

Korea House

Just in front of Namsangol Hanok Village is Korea House, one of Korea's most famous Korean restaurants. Modeled after one of the halls of Gyeongbokgung Palace, the beautiful *hanok* eatery is more than a restaurant—it's a cultural experience. Lunch and dinner is served, with the house specialty being *hanjeongsik* (Korean banquet cuisine, see p426). Folk performances are staged in the evenings as well. The venue is also frequently used to host Korean-style weddings. • **Hours** noon to 2 pm (lunch), 5:30 to 7 pm (dinner I), 7 to 8 pm (performance), 7:20 to 8:50 pm (dinner 2), 8:50 to 9:50 pm (performance) • **Tel** 2266-9101~3 • **Getting There** Chungmuro Subway Station, Line 3 or 4, Exit 3 or 4 • **Website** www.koreahouse.or.kr

Namsan Bongsudae

This beacon fire mound dates from the Joseon era—authorities could determine the national security situation depending on how many fires were lit. For instance, one fire meant peace, while five meant the nation was at war. The Namsan beacon was the central beacon of a nationwide system—signals from anywhere in the country could reach it within 12 hours.

THINGS TO EAT

If you don't want to eat at N Seoul Tower (which can be a bit pricey), a cheaper option are the *donkkaseu* (Japanese-style pork cutlet) restaurants near the cable car terminal—try Namsan Donkkaseu (T. 777-1976) or Namsan Wang Donkkaseu (T. 755-3370).

Namsan Botanical Gardens

Located on the southern side of the mountain just beside the Hyatt Hotel, this area of walking paths, trees and flowers is a pleasant enough place to have an evening stroll.

Patriot Ahn Choong-gun Memorial Hall

This memorial located near Namsan Public Library is dedicated to Korean freedom fighter Ahn Choong-gun, who assassinated former Japanese prime minister and resident-general of Korea Ito Hirobumi in 1909.

GETTING THERE

The most common path, from the National Theater of Korea, can be reached via Exit 6 of Dongguk University Station, Line 3. From the Itaewon side, it's best to take a taxi from Itaewon or Noksapyeong stations, Line 6 to the Hyatt Hotel. There's also a cable car that takes passengers up the mountain—the terminal is a 10-minute walk from Myeong-dong Station, Line 4. Round trip is 7,500 won. Hours: 10 am to 11 pm.

Lastly, you can take a bus to N Seoul Tower. Yellow buses leave from near Exit 3 of Chungmuro Station, lines 3 or 4. Buses leave every 5-6 minutes between 8 am and midnight. The fare is 700 won.

門靖肅

Sukjeongmun Gate, one of old Seoul's four major gates

MT. BUGAKSAN

A Treasure Returned to the People

Just a couple of years ago, Mt. Bugaksan—located just behind the presidential palace of Cheong Wa Dae—was closed off to the general public for security reasons. It is now one of Seoul's best hiking routes, where history and wonderful views come together.

History

Bugaksan was considered one of Seoul's four protecting mountains, along with Mt. Namsan to the south, Mt. Inwangsan to the west and Mt. Naksan to the east. Not surprisingly, it was considered key to the capital's defenses, with long stretches of the city's fortress walls—including Seoul's northern gate—constructed along its slopes.

In 1968, 31 North Korean commandos climbed up and down Mt. Bugaksan on their way to Cheong Wa Dae (see TIPS on p65), the blue-roofed presidential mansion located at the foot of the mountain, on a mission to kill South Korean president Park Chung-hee. Posing as South Korean soldiers, they were discovered just 800 m from their destination. A firefight ensued, and the commandos fled, leading to a massive manhunt that left 29 North Korean commandos, 68 South Koreans and three US soldiers dead. After the incident, Mt. Bugaksan was declared off limits to the general public. In 2006, however, its hiking trails were finally reopened to the public. It's still a sensitive security area, though, with several military bases on the hillside, and hiking restricted to a set path.

Hiking

Most hikers begin from the Malbawi Rest Area near Waryong Park. From there, you begin the trail that takes you past parts of Seoul's old fortress walls and up some wooden flights of stairs that provide nice views of the surrounding city and hills.

You'll eventually get to the Malbawi Entance of the park—here you must sign in (bring your passport and/or ID) to continue your hike. From there it's a fairly straight-forward slog along the fortress wall to the Baegak Peak (342 m), passing along several scenic points, rock formations and the historic Sukjeongmun Gate. From the peak, its another hike down to Changuimun Gate in the charming Buam-dong neighborhood. All in all, the course takes about two hours.

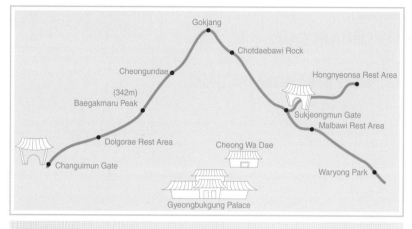

Gokjang

Chotdaebawi Rock

Cheongundae

Hongnyeonsa Rest Area

(342m)
Baegakmaru Peak

Sukjeongmun Gate
Malbawi Rest Area

Dolgorae Rest Area

Cheong Wa Dae

Changuimun Gate

Waryong Park

Gyeongbukgung Palace

IMPORTANT! The Bugaksan trail is open only at certain hours. From April to October, entry onto the trail is 9 am to 3 pm, and from November to March it is 10 am to 3 pm. Hikers must exit the trail by 5 pm.

Things to See

Seoul Fortress Walls

Like many medieval towns around the world, old Seoul was a walled city, ringed by 18 km of 7 m-high stone ramparts. Work on the walls began in 1396, not long after the designation of the city as the capital of the newly founded Joseon kingdom. The walls linked the city's four surrounding peaks: Mt Baegaksan (now Mt. Bukgaksan) to the north, Mt. Naksan to the east, Mt. Namsan to the south and Mt. Inwangsan to the west. To build the walls, some 120,000 laborers were mobilized in the spring of 1395; in the fall, another 80,000 men were raised to replace the earthen sections of the wall with stone fortifications. Passage through the wall was controlled by four large gates in the north, south, east and west and four smaller gates.

Major repairs and upgrades were made on the walls in 1422 and 1704. The modern era, however, did not prove kind to the city walls. Large sections of them were torn down by the Japanese to build roads and make way for a new streetcar system. The Great West Gate, or Seodaemun, was torn down in 1915. Only sections of the walls located on remote mountainsides (including the Great North Gate) were spared; the Great South and East Gates (Namdaemun and Dongdaemun), meanwhile, were turned into traffic islands.

Mt. Bugaksan is home to one of the most impressive stretches of remaining wall. Places of note include Gokjang, a curved buttress that was used to stop would-be attackers from climbing the wall, and Cheongundae, where the names of those who built the wall are engraved, along with the the fortifications' date of completion.

Seoul's fortress walls were first built in 1396, although most of the current ones date from later reconstructions.

Sukjeongmun Gate

Sukjeongmun Gate was one of old Seoul's northern gates, one of the four larger gates that controlled passageway into and out of the royal capital. Unlike the other three gates, however, Sukjeongmun was rarely opened. In fact, its function was primarily metaphysical—according to the philosophy of *yin-yang*, north represents *yin* (negative) and south represents *yang* (positive) nature. As *yin* also represents water, the gate was opened in times of drought, but otherwise kept closed.

The current gate was restored in the 1970s. Nearby is a tree with 15 bullet holes in it, a reminder of the 1968 attack by North Korean commandos.

Changuimun Gate

One of old Seoul's four lesser gates, Changuimun is now the entryway to northwest Seoul. Dating from a 1740 reconstruction, the gate underwent significant restoration in 1958, but is otherwise the only of Seoul's lesser gates to remain in complete condition.

GETTING THERE

The easiest way is to take a green local bus (No. 2) from Exit 2 of Anguk Station, Line 3, and get off at the last stop (the back gate of Sungkyunkwan University). From there it's a 10-minute walk to Waryong Park. Alternatively, it's a short taxi ride from Anguk Station to the park.

Birds sit upon Seon (Zen) Rocks, a mysterious rock formation venerated by shamanists.

MT. INWANGSAN

Seoul's Sacred Peak

Thanks to its many Buddhist temples and shamanist shrines, Mt. Inwangsan has a mystical atmosphere quite unique among Seoul's major peaks. It is also home to a long stretch of Seoul's old fortress walls.

History

Mt. Inwangsan used to mark the western limit of old Seoul. During the Joseon era, its granite peaks were greatly admired and figured prominently in landscape art.

In 1925, the Guksadang Shrine, Korea's most important shamanist shrine, was moved by the Japanese from Mt. Namsan to Mt. Inwangsan. Not long after, shamans began setting up shop in the mountain's deep valleys, transforming the peak into a spiritual center. This transformation was assisted by the mountain's many unusual rock formation, which lent a cosmic air to the peak.

Hiking

The best path begins just behind the Hyundai Apartments near Seodaemun Prison Museum. The trail takes you past several Buddhist temples and hermitages until you reach the Guksadang Shrine. A short hike above the shrine is Seonbawi (Zen Rock), and above that are several other smaller shrines and prayer sites before you reach the peak. Be warned, however—as of the writing of this book, the final section of the path to the peak was closed due to restoration work.

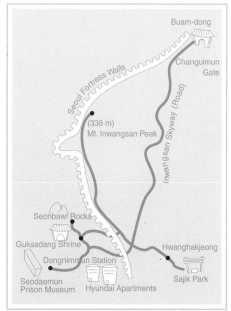

Alternatively, there's also a path—which starts at the same place—that takes you along the old fortress walls to the peak. This path offers outstanding

views of downtown Seoul. You can also follow the path eventually to
Changuimun Gate and Mt. Bugaksan (see p322).

Plan on spending at least two hours on the mountain.

Things to See

Guksadang Shrine

Located on the slopes of Mt. Inwangsan, a
mountain long regarded as holy by shamanists,
the Guksadang is a shamanist prayer hall that
enshrines not only the portraits of shamanist
gods, but also the spirits of King Taejo (r. 1329-
1398)—the founder of the Joseon kingdom—
and the Venerable Muhak Daesa, a high-
ranking Buddhist monk who served as the
king's advisor. Both Taejo and Muhak came to
be considered Buddhist gods.

TIPS

SEE A SHAMANIST RITE

Guksadang hosts about three
to four *gut* (rites) a day. In
March and October, it gets
especially busy. Every two
years, the master of the shrine
hold a particularly large rite,
called a *maji*, in the last month
of the lunar year.

The shrine used to be located atop Mt.
Namsan (near where N Seoul Tower is now), but was moved to Mt. Inwangsan in
1925. The move was sparked by the construction by Japanese colonial authorities
of a massive Shinto shrine on the slopes of Mt. Namsan. The Japanese, it would
appear, believed it inappropriate that the Guksadang should occupy a higher
position than the new imperial Japanese shrine.

Today, the shrine is a colorful but simple structure. Inside the hall, you can find

Guksadang, one of Korea's most important shamanist shrines

the portraits of shamanist gods, along with food offerings given by the faithful, who come here in droves from all over the country, particular in the first lunar month. While many kinds of shamanist ceremonies, or *gut*, are held in the hall, there is no "shaman in residence," so to speak. Instead, the keeper of the shrine rents it out to shamans who ask.

Seonbawi (Zen Rocks)

A short hike from Guksadang is Seonbawi, a large, almost prehistoric-looking rock so called because it resembles a robed Buddhist monk in meditation. Some say the rock bears the likeness of King Taejo and Venerable Muhak. Regardless of whom or what it resembles, the rock was (and still is) a favorite place for women to pray for sons.

Since the Guksadang was moved to the spot below Seonbawi, the rock has been closely linked to Korean shamanism. There is a small shrine in front of the rock where devotees pray and light candles. The rock also provides an outstanding view of downtown Seoul. It's breathtaking.

There is also an interesting story related to Seonbawi. When the city walls to protect the royal capital were being built during the reign of King Taejo, there was a good deal of debate whether or not the rock should be included within the

Shrine in front of Seon Rocks

city walls. Venerable Muhak lobbied for its inclusion within the walls. Another close advisor of the king, the Confucian scholar "Sambong" Jeong Dojeon (1342-1398), lobbied for its exclusion, believing that if it were included within the walls, Buddhism would flourish over Confucianism. Jeong won the day, and the rock was left outside the walls. Accordingly, Buddhism's fortune in the new kingdom began to wane as the religion took a back seat to Confucianism.

At any rate, there can be no denying the mystical power of Mt. Inwangsan with its bizarre, almost surreal rock formations and dramatic granite cliffs. When you climb up here, you really do feel as if you've entered another world far from the hustle and bustle of the city below. It's no wonder why so many shamanists congregate here.

GETTING THERE

Leave Exit 2 of Dongnimmun Station, Line 3, and start walking to Hyundai Apartments. Follow the road behind the apartment complex until you reach the Korean-style gate that marks the entrance to the mountain.

KOREAN SHAMANISM

History and Culture

Before the arrival of Buddhism, Taoism, Confucianism and Christianity, Koreans were shamanists. Even after the arrival of those foreign faiths, in fact, shamans and shamanist practices continued to persist and survive to this day.

Korean shamanism is a legacy of Koreans' Central Asian roots, and is not dissimilar to shamanistic traditions in Siberia, Mongolia and Manchuria. Ultimately, shamanism is about connecting with the spirits that inhabit this world, including the trees, mountains and rivers. It is the role of the *mudang* (shaman) to act as the bridge between the human and spirit worlds. In Korea, *mudang* have traditionally been women.

Throughout most of their history, Koreans have tended towards the eclectic in matters religious. Accordingly, elements of shamanism have found their way into Buddhism and even Christianity. One example of this is the *Sansingak* (Mountain God Hall), a shrine that can be found at most Buddhist temples across Korea. It's a favorite of women praying for sons.

In the immediate post-independence period, the authorities took a very dim view of shamanism, which they regarded as an obsolete and embarrassing superstition. Koreans were encouraged to keep shamanist ceremonies out of the public view and especially out of the view of foreigners. Over the last several decades, however, shamanism has witnessed a comeback as part of a general trend of greater pride and confidence in Korean traditional culture.

Shamanist rite at Guksadang shrine. Photo courtesy of Prof. David Mason.

THE GUT: A shamanist rite is called a *gut*. In a *gut*, a *mudang* seeks to intercede between human and spirit, often for some human aim. Through singing and dancing, the *mudang* enters a trance. The nature of the *gut* differs from region to region. In coastal regions, for example, the fishing season is often commenced with a grand *gut* to pray for a bountiful catch. *Mudangs* are often hired by families who have lost loved ones in a violent death (such as car accidents) to release their spirit.

OTHER SHAMAN RITUALS: Businessmen and families will often perform a *gosa* (an offering to the spirits) at the start of a new business venture, a move to a new home or even the purchase of a new car. You'll recognize a *gosa* from the pig head, often with money stuffed in its mouth, nose and ears. Another popular legacy of shamanism is Korea's tradition of fortune telling. Women in particular seek out fortune tellers to give them advice on difficult life decisions. The Apgujeong-dong area is full of cafés specializing in this form of fortune telling. Fortune telling services include the *saju* ("Four Pillars of Destiny"), a way of telling the future using the year, month, day and hour of one's birth, and the *gunghap*, in which the *saju* of a prospective couple are examined to determine the chances for marital bliss.

LEARNING MORE: To get a fuller understanding of Korean shamanism, you're encouraged to watch two outstanding documentaries on the subject, Park Ki-bok's "Mudang: Reconciliation Between the Living and the Dead" (2003) and Lee Chang-jae's "In Between" (2007). Two good books, meanwhile, are "Folk Art and Magic: Shamanism in Korea," by Alan Carter Covell, and "Spirit of the Mountains," by David A. Mason.

Weather station atop Mt. Gwanaksan

MT. GWANAKSAN

Seoul's Southern Massif

A broad massif that straddles the current boundary between southern Seoul and the Seoul suburb of Gwacheon (see p263), Mt. Gwanaksan provides plenty of fine scenery and a pleasant place to "get away," if you will, from the urban grind.

History

Marking the southern limit of the Seoul basin, Mt. Gwanaksan was long regarded as a strategic peak. It has also long served as a place of refuge for royal figures and retainers seeking sanctuary from the political squabbles below. During the Joseon era, the mountain's peaks were said to resemble a flame, and accordingly, the massif was regarded as a well-spring of fire. Gyeongbokgung Palace's *haetae* statues, in fact, were installed to stop the fire energy from Mt. Gwanaksan from engulfing the wooden palace.

Hiking

On a weekend, there are a great many hikers on Mt. Gwanaksan, and the paths are well-marked, so there's little reason to worry about getting lost. From the

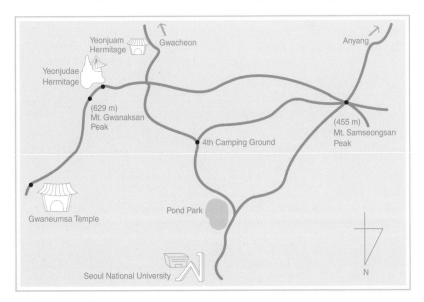

Seoul side of the mountain, the primary path starts just next to the main gate of Seoul National University. It leads past a pretty Korean-style pond and along a cool mountain stream. There are several mineral water springs and camp grounds along the way, too.

When you reach the ridge, you're faced with a choice of continuing along the narrow ridge path past a weather station to the dramatic Buddhist hermitage of Yeonjudae, or beginning your descent to the historic Buddhist temple of Yeonjuam and Gwacheon City. The hike takes about three to four hours.

Things to See

Yeonjudae Hermitage
Perched breathtakingly atop a granite cliff, the small Buddhist hermitage of Yeonjudae has a history that goes back to 677 AD, when it was founded by one of Korea's greatest Buddhist monks, the Ven. Uisang. In 1392, with the Joseon Dynasty replaced the Goryeo Dynasty, Goryeo loyalists fled to this tranquil spot, from which they could gaze out at their lost capital. In the 15th century, Princes Yangnyong and Hyoryeong retreated here upon learning that their father planned to make their younger brother—the eventual King Sejong the Great (see p409)—the king.

Yeonjuam Hermitage
Along with the smaller Yeonjudae Hermitage, Yeonjuam was founded in 677 AD by the Ven. Uisang, although most of its halls are of recent reconstruction. Of historic note is its old three-story stone pagoda from the Goryeo era and its portrait of Prince Hyoryeong. If you're hiking up from the Gwancheon side, the temple has a welcome mineral water spring.

TIPS

THINGS TO EAT
The nearby Sillim-dong neighborhood is famous for its *sundae* (Korean blood sausage). Sillim-dong Sundae Town is a collection of *sundae* restaurants specializing in *sundae bokkeum* (blood sausage pan fried with noodles, vegetables and spices). Ddosuni (T. 884-7565), on the first floor of the Minsok Sundae Town building, is a good place to try.

GETTING THERE
There are local buses to the front gate of Seoul National University from Seoul National University Station, Line 2.

[1] Bodhisattva image, Yeonjuam Hermitage [2] Goryeo-era stone pagoda and newer additions, Yeonjuam Hermitage [3] Dramatic Buddhist hermitage of Yeonjudae [4] Taking in the view of Gwacheon from Mt. Gwanaksan

Clear skies above Seoul, seen from Mt. Bukhansan

MT. BUKHANSAN

Rock Climber's Paradise

Guarding Seoul to the north is Mt. Bukhansan, a ridge of several magnificent rocky peaks, including Baegundae Peak, which at 836 m is Seoul's highest point. This rugged area provides some of Seoul's best (and most challenging) hiking, as well as some of the best rock-climbing in Korea.

History

Guarding the northern passes into Seoul, Mt. Bukhansan has long been of strategic significance. During the Joseon era, the mountain was ringed by impressive fortifications that stand to this day. Due to its thick forests and scenic beauty, the mountain is home to several Buddhist temples, including Hwagyesa Temple, a major Zen center famous for its large contingent of foreign monks.

Hiking

The area of Mt. Bukhansan National Park spans several dozen square kilometers, so not surprisingly, there are a number of paths up the mountain. The direct path to the peak can take as little as two hours (be warned—it's a strenuous two hours),

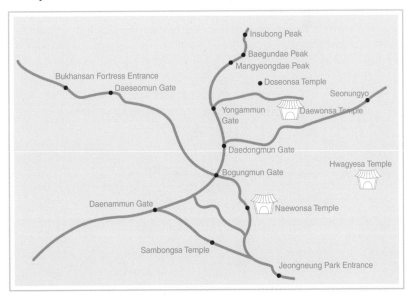

while more scenic routes can take up to four or five. The most popular—and the shortest—route takes you from Doseonsa Temple to the Yongammun Gate of Bukhansan Fortress. From there, it's a slog along the ridgeline until you reach the granite peak of Baegundae—there are ropes and steps to assist you in the task.

A longer hike (one of many) takes you from Jeongneung Park Entrance to the Buddhist temple of Sambongsa, and from there the Daenammun Gate of Bukhansan Fortress. From the gate, you can follow the ridgeline (and the fortress wall) until you reach Baegundae. To reach the peak will take about three and a half hours.

Things to See

Bukhansan Fortress

As a strategically vital peak, Mt. Bukhansan has played host to fortifications of one sort or another for about 1,900 years. In the Middle Ages, for instance, fierce battles were fought here against Mongol and Khitan invaders. Following the Japanese invasions of the late 16th century and Manchurian invasion of the mid-17th century, however, Korea's rulers felt compelled to strengthen and expand the mountain's fortifications. In 1711, work got underway on a 9.7 km ring of fortifications along the ridges of the mountain. With 14 gates, the walls are some of the most extensive Joseon-era fortifications in Korea.

Hwagyesa Temple

Hwagyesa is a relaxing Buddhist temple on the lower slopes of Mt. Bukhansan. While the temple itself goes back to 1523, the current complex dates from an 1866 reconstruction. It is most famous as the home of the Hwagyesa International Zen Center (T. 900-4326), opened in 1994 by Zen Master Seung Sahn (1927-2004). As the founder of the Kwan Um Zen School, Seung Sahn played an active role in promoting Buddhism in the West; accordingly, Hwagyesa is home to a prominent community of Western monks. For foreigners interested in Zen, the Zen Center holds Sunday mediation sessions and Dharma talks beginning at 1pm.

GETTING THERE

- **Doseonsa Course:** Take subway line 4 to Suyu Station. From there, take buses No. 2, 120 or 153 to its final destination
- **Jeongneung Course:** Take buses No. 171, 1114, 1213 or 7211 from Gireum Station, Line 4. Get off at Bongguksa Temple.
- **Hwagyesa Temple:** Take small bus 2 from Exit 5 of Suyu Station, Line 4. Get off at Hanshin University (Hanshin Daehakyo) and walk up the path to the temple.

1	3
2	
	4

[1] Watch your step. Mt. Bukhansan [2] Yonganmun gate of Bukhansan Fortress [3] Rock climbers scale Insubong Peak [4] Ropes along the way help you scale this rocky massif

FACTS FOR VISITORS

INFORMATION FOR VISITORS

BEFORE YOU ARRIVE

Korea Tourism Organization (KTO)

Korea's national tourism agency, the appropriately named Korea Tourism Organization (KTO), does an outstanding job of providing information about tourist sites, accommodation, transportation and just about anything else you'd need to know while traveling in Korea. The KTO headquarters (729-9600) is located on the Cheonggyecheon Stream, a short walk from Exit 2 of Eulji-ro 1-ga Station, Line 2. Perhaps more useful, however, is their outstanding website at http://english.visitkorea.or.kr.

The KTO also has a number of overseas offices that will be all too happy to dispense information to visitors. See the list below for contact info:

North America

Los Angeles	1-323-634-0280	la@kntoamerica.com
New York	1-201-585-0909	ny@kntoamerica.com
Toronto	1-416-348-9056/7	toronto@knto.ca
Hawaii	1-808-521-8066	

Oceania and Southeast Asia

Singapore	65-6533-0441/2	kntosp@pacific.net.sg
Bangok	66-2-354-2080/2082	koreainfo@kto.or.th
Sydney	61-2-9252-4147/8	visitkorea@knto.org.au
Dubai	971-4-331-2288	knto@eim.ae
Kuala Lumpur	60-3-2143-9000	info@knto.com.my
New Dehli	91-11-4609-5707	india@knto.or.kr
Hanoi	84-4-3831-5180	hanoi@knto.or.kr

Japan

Tokyo	81-3-3580-3941	tokyo@visitkorea.or.kr
Osaka	81-6-6266-0847	osaka@visitkorea.or.kr

Fukuoka	81-92-471-7174/75	fukuoka@visitkorea.or.kr
Nagoya	81-52-223-3211/2	nagoya@visitkorea.or.kr

China

Beijing	86-10-6585-8213/4	beijing@visitkorea.or.kr
Shanghai	86-21-5169-7933	ssanghai@mail.knto.or.kr
Guangzhou	86-20-3893-1639	kntogz@126.com
Qindao	86-532-8587-5692	qdknto@yahoo.com.cn
Shenyang	86-24-2281-4155/4255	kto_sy@126.com
Hong Kong	852-2523-8065	general@knto.com.hk
Taipei	886-2-2720-8049/8081	kntotp@ms5.hinet.net

Russia

Moscow	7-495-735-4240	kntomc@col.ru
Vladivostock	7-4232-49-1163/1154	knto_vl@mail.ru

Europe

Frankfurt	49-69-233226/234973	kntoff@euko.de
Paris	33-1-4538-7123	knto@club-internet.fr
London	44-20-7321-2535, 7925-1717	london@mail.knto.or.kr

Seoul Tourism Promotion Division

Seoul Metropolitan Government also provides a wealth of information to tourists visiting the city. Visit http://english.visitseoul.net.

Travel Agents

If you're tired of doing things on your own and would like something a bit more organized, there are plenty of English-speaking tourism agencies happy to assist you. Here are just a couple:

Aju Incentive Tours	786-0028	www.ajutours.co.kr
Bridge Travel	754-2252	www.bridge-tour.com
Grace Travel	332-8946	www.triptokorea.com
DiscoverKorea Jejueco	064-738-7706	www.discoverkorea.co.kr
Cosmojin Tour Consulting	318-0345	www.cosmojin.com
Exodus DMC	031-907-8044	www.koreabound.com
GOnSEE	6243-7071	www.gonseekorea.com
Holiday Planners Co., LTD	336-3532	www.holidayplanners.co.kr
Plaza 21 Plus Travel Inc.	364-4171	www.plaza21travel.com
KOREAHAS & Good Morning Tours	757-1232	www.koreahas.com
Korea Business Travel Co., Ltd.	739-8111	www.kbs-travel.com
Plaza 21 Travel Service, Inc.	364-1670	www.koreatourplaza.com
US Tour and Travel	720-1515	www.ustravel.kr
Xanadu Travel Service Co.,Ltd.	795-7771	www.xanadu.co.kr
TOUR ROAD	031-244-6003	www.tourod.com

IMMIGRATION & CUSTOMS

Visas

All foreign visitors to Korea need a valid passport and a visa obtained prior to arrival. Some 99 countries (including the US, Canada, the UK, Australia and many Western European nations) have visa waiver agreements with Korea or are given visa waiver status for national interest reasons—for citizens of these nations, tourist visas are automatically given upon arrival at the airport. (See http://english.visitkorea.or.kr for further information) Depending on the nation, these visas may last for 30, 60, 90 or—in the case of Canada—180 days.

To extend your visa, you need to visit your local Immigration Office (for location, call the Immigration Contact Center at 1345) at least a day before your visa expires and fill out an application—you'll need a recent passport-sized color photo and the application fee. Visa extensions are usually for 90 days. All visas are single entry only. To get a multiple entry visa, you need to apply at your local Immigration Office. This can also be taken care of at the Immigration Office of Incheon International Airport prior to your outbound flight.

Work Visas

If you'd like to work in Korea—teaching English, for example—you need a work visa. These must be obtained from an embassy or visa outside of Korea (for example, in your home nation). Work visas are usually valid for one year. To get a work visa, you need to have an endorsement from your potential employer in Korea.

Be warned—if you engage in money-making activities without a proper work visa, you can be fined and/or deported. Moreover, work visas are usually good only for your specific place of employment—to change jobs, you need to leave the country and get a new visa.

> * Ministry of Foreign Affairs and Trade   www.mofat.go.kr
>   Korea Immigration Service   www.immigration.go.kr

Driver's License

If you're a short-term visitor to Korea, you can drive on an international driver's license. It's probably best you obtain your international driver's license in your home country. Citizens of several countries, including the United States, Canada and Japan, can exchange their foreign licenses for Korean ones.

If you're staying longer and don't want to turn in your foreign license, you can apply for a local Korean license—you need to pass a rigorous written test (in English), pass a driving test and attend a safety class.

> * Korean Driver's License Agency   www.dla.go.kr/english/index.jsp

Customs

Duty-Free Articles
- Visitor goods you will take with you when you leave Korea (do declare the quantity of the goods, though)
- Goods you declared upon leaving Korea and are bringing back
- One bottle of alcohol (not over a liter) and 200 cigarettes (or 50 cigars or 250 grams of tobacco)
- Two ounces of perfume

Foreign Currency
If you are carrying in foreign or Korean currency worth over US$10,000, you must declare it to a Customs official. If you are departing Korea with over US$10,000 in local or foreign currency, you must obtain permission from a bank or customs (not including the amount you carried in).

Restricted Articles
- Guns, firearms, knives and explosives
- Drugs (narcotics and psychotropic substance)
- Quarantine-required goods (food, animal material, plant material, etc.)
- Articles controlled by CITES convention

Prohibited Articles
- Books, publications, drawings and paintings, films, phonographic materials, video work and other items of similar nature that may either disturb the constitutional order or be harmful to public security or traditional custom
- Goods that may reveal confidential information on the government or that may be used for intelligence activities
- Coins, currency, bank notes, debenture and/or other negotiable instrument counterfeited, forged or imitated

For a full rundown on Korea's customs regulations, visit the website of the Korea Customs Service (see below).

> * Korea Customs Service   http://english.customs.go.kr/

Basic Korean Culture

While Korea has modernized rapidly in the past couple of decades, Confucian ideals remain embedded in society. Koreans place a great deal of emphasis on showing respect based on social and age hierarchies and adhere to many unstated social rules in their daily interactions.

Koreans tend to judge people based on their appearance. People dressed neatly and with greater care are treated with more respect than those dressed sloppily.

Etiquette

• **Greetings**: Bow or nod slightly to show respect when greeting somebody or departing.

• **Shoes**: In private homes, temples, Korean-style restaurants, and guesthouses, take off your shoes and leave them by the entrance.

• **Gifts**: When invited to visit someone's home, always bring a small gift. Gifts can be flowers, fruit, dessert, a bottle of alcohol, tea or a token from your home country. Your host may initially protest the gift to avoid appearing greedy, but you should insist that they accept it. Present and receive gifts using both hands. If you must use one hand, however, be sure to use your right one.

• **Tipping**: There is no tipping in Korea, including taxis and restaurants.

• **Dining**: Never pick up your eating utensils before your elders. After finishing your meal, return your spoon and chopsticks to their original setting. Do not rise from your seat unless your elders have finished their meals. After finishing your meal, be sure to compliment the chef or host.

• **Drinking**: Always pour drinks for your elders using two hands, or with one hand supporting the wrist of the other. When receiving a drink from an elder, use two hands. If drinking with elders, turn your glass and body away from your elders as you drink.

Language

Koreans, of course, speak Korean, a language sometimes placed—somewhat controversially—in the Altaic language family along with Turkish and Mongolian. It is characterized by a subject-object-verb sentence structure, and parts of speech are identified by suffixes. While the language itself is in no way, shape or form related to Chinese, much of its vocabulary—particularly nouns— has been borrowed from Chinese, the result of centuries of cultural influence from Korea's giant neighbor to the West.

English is widely studied in Korea, but relatively few Koreans are proficient in the language. That being said, you may still be able to communicate in basic English if you're in a fix, especially at public places like train stations, etc.

Korean is considered a difficult language to learn for speakers of Western languages like English. Few Koreans expect tourists to be fluent in the language, but a few basic phrases will go along way. See the "Basic Korean" (p408) for help.

Religion

Korea has been, by and large, a fairly tolerant place in terms of religion, with Buddhism (see p81), Christianity (see p234) (including Catholicism and Protestantism), shamanism (see p328) and other smaller faiths existing side-by-side in relative harmony with little in the way of sectarian strife. Roughly half the population identifies itself as religious—that half, in turn, splits about 50-50 between Christians and Buddhists. Over the last several decades, Protestant Christianity has been especially vibrant—Korea is home to several of the world's largest churches. Buddhism, too, has witnessed a revival in recent years with heightened interest and confidence in Korean traditional culture. Few people identify themselves as shamanists, per se, but shamanism and shamanistic practices influence larger Korean faiths, including Buddhism and Christianity.

Ultimately, however, it's Confucianism (see p308) that has provided the philosophical underpinnings of Korean society—it's said, in fact, that Korea is the most Confucian country in the world. Even in Korea's increasingly cosmopolitan and modernized society, Confucian ideals and principles still have a tremendous influence (regardless of the professed faith of the individual), particularly in family and personal relations. Traditional Korean rites and practices such as regular ancestral remembrance rites (*jesa*) are derived from Confucianism as well.

LOCAL INFO

Business Hours

• Banks operate 9 am to 4 pm, Monday to Friday.

• Government offices and organizations are open 9 am to 6 pm, Monday to Friday.

• Post Offices are open 9 am to 6 pm (Monday to Friday) and 9 am to 1 pm (Saturday).

• Business hours for foreign diplomatic missions differ from country to country.

• Department stores, meanwhile, are open 10:30 am to 8 pm. They are usually closed one Monday a month.

Korean Holidays

Koreans might be some of the hardest-working people on the planet, but at least one can't accuse the nation of skimping on public holidays. Major Korean holidays include:

Spring

• **Independence Declaration Day** (March 1): This holiday marks the beginning of the March 1, 1919 Independence Movement (see p78), a nationwide uprising against Japanese colonial rule. Like Liberation Day, it's marked by lots of flying flags and an address by the President.

• **Buddha's Birthday** (8th day of the 4th lunar month): This spring Buddhist holiday is celebrated at Buddhist temples across Korea with beautiful paper lotus lanterns. In Seoul, it is preceded by several days by the Lotus Lantern Festival (see p436), one of the city's best-loved festivals.

• **Children's Day** (May 5): Yep, children get their own day. Needless to say, theme parks are considerably more busy.

• **Memorial Day** (June 6): This holiday celebrates those Koreans who fell in war or fighting for the nation's independence.

Summer

• **Liberation Day** (Aug 15): Marks the end of Japanese colonialism in Korea with Japan's surrender in the Pacific War.

Autumn

• **Chuseok** (15th day of the 8th lunar month): The second of Korea's two major holidays, Chuseok is Korea's autumn harvest celebration. Like Seol, it is accompanied by a long holiday during which Koreans return to their ancestral hometowns. The representative dish for Chuseok is the *songpyeon* (a rice cake steamed on pine needles)—you'll be consuming these until you're sick of them.

• **National Foundation Day** (Oct 3): Known in Korean as *Gaecheonjeol*, this celebrates the mythical foundation of Korea by Dangun (see p281) in 2333 BC. Originally celebrated according to the lunar calendar, it is now celebrated according to the solar calendar.

Winter

• **Christmas** (Dec 25): Yes, Koreans—well, Christian ones, anyway—celebrate Christmas, although it's nowhere near the family holiday it is in the traditionally Christian West. Young people use it as a day to meet friends and go on dates.

• **Seol** (1st day of the 1st lunar month): The Lunar New Year, Seol is one of Korea's two biggest celebrations. It is marked by a long holiday, and city dwellers flock to their ancestral hometowns for family gatherings. Seoul will become eerily quiet, although most tourist sites will remain open. If you're planning a trip to the countryside during the holiday, be sure to book your transportation way in advance, and if you're going by road, prepare for the worst traffic you've ever seen (this applies to the Chuseok holiday, too). It is traditional to eat a bowl of *tteokguk* (rice cake soup) on the morning of the New Year.

History and Culture

VALENTINE'S DAY, WHITE DAY, BLACK DAY, PEPERO DAY

Like much of the rest of the world, Korea celebrates Valentine's Day on Feb 14. However, unlike in other countries, women give chocolate to men. The favor is returned one month later on March 14, or White Day (an importation from Japan), when men give candy (but not chocolate) to women. On April 14, those who received nothing on Feb 14 or March 14—i.e., the unattached—mourn their solitude over a bowl of Chinese black *jajangmyeon* noodles for "Black Day." Finally, there is Pepero Day on Nov 11, when young couples exchange chocolate-dipped cookie sticks known as Pepero (produced by the company Lotte)—Pepero because they look similar to the four "1"s in Nov 11 (11/11).

Legal Matters

It's always best to stay out of trouble, of course. Still, if legal trouble does befall you, you're going to need a lawyer. Your embassy can often provide a list of recommended lawyers.

If you're the victim of a crime, the police are there to help, although language may be an issue. To their credit, police will eventually find a translator, but it can take some time, depending on the station.

*List of English-Speaking Lawyers	http://wiki.galbijim.com/English-speaking_lawyers_throughout_Korea
Ministry of Justice	www.moj.go.kr
Korean National Police Agency	www.police.go.kr

Money and Banking

The Korean currency is the won. Bills come in 50,000 won, 10,000 won, 5,000 won and 1,000 won denominations, while coins come in 500 won, 100 won, 50 won and 10 won denominations. Koreans are not big users of cheques, and you'll find yourself frequently walking around with large wads of cash. For travelers from places such as the United States, this can be uncomfortable.

ATM machines are a ubiquitous presence in Seoul—for instance, they can be found in most major convenience store chains. Nowadays, a larger number accept foreign cards, but many do not. If you have an account with Citibank, however, you can visit a local Citibank branch (www.citibank.co.kr, T. 3704-7100) for ATM or counter services. ATM hours vary, and often depend on your card.

Changing Money

Most banks will change money for you. US dollars are the most commonly converted currency, although you should find no trouble exchanging most common hard currencies. If you're having trouble converting the currency you're carrying, give Korea Exchange Bank (www.keb.co.kr/main/en) a try.

Besides banks, most major hotels and, of course, the airport will change money for you, but the rates might not be as good. The Itaewon area (see p201) has a number of licensed currency exchangers, too.

Wire Transfer

Foreign residents can transfer money overseas at the bank. No restrictions exist for transfers under US$1,000. Fees and transfer restrictions vary depending on the bank. In order to transfer money, you must bring your passport, employment contract, foreigner registration card, and receipts. Money may be remitted freely up to US$10,000; amounts exceeding US$10,000 must be reported to the tax office. Remittances greater than US$50,000 must be reported to the Bank of Korea. However, up to 100% of a foreigner's legally earned annual income may be remitted if individuals provide proof from their employer verifying the amount earned, such as pay stubs.

Credit Cards

International credit cards are widely accepted in Seoul. Still, many places— especially smaller shops and restaurants—operate on a cash-only basis.

Communication

Internet Cafés

Korea is one of the most wired countries in the world, and internet cafés (known locally as PC *bang*, meaning "PC room") are ubiquitous in Seoul. In every neighborhood of the city PC *bangs* abound. Korean internet cafés are open 24 hours a day, and are generally dark rooms filled with lines of glossy-screened modern computers connected to high-speed internet. Patrons can surf the web, and send e-mails at a PC *bang*; most, however, don't have printers, so to print things out, you're better off going to somewhere like Kinkos. Most Koreans frequent these locations to play the latest computer games. Use of a computer at a PC *bang* generally runs you 1,000 to 1,500 won per hour. Headsets with attached microphones are available free of charge.

Pay Phones

Pay phones are available in Seoul but, given the ubiquity of cellphones, are rarely used. Phones are operated by coins or phone cards. On coin-operated phones, only domestic calls are possible. Card-operated phones accept phone cards, credit cards, and IC cards. Phone cards can be purchased in 2,000 won, 3,000 won, 5,000 won and 10,000 won denominations at newsstands and banks. The rate for local land-line calls is 70 won per three minutes, and the cost for calls to mobile phones is 100 won per minute. When making international calls from a pay phone, the number of the service provider must be entered before the country code. Pre-paid phone cards offer the best prices on overseas calls and can be purchased at convenience stores or online shopping malls. For more information, visit www.cardstation.net.

> • To call Korea from abroad, press the international call code + Korea's country code (82) + area code (*sans* the first zero) + phone number.
>
> • To call abroad from Korea, press the international call code* + country code + area code (*sans* the first zero) + phone number.   * 001, 002 or 00700

Cell Phones

Korea's cellphone network operates on a highly specialized CDMA system. Unlocked GSM phones will not function in Korea, and it is not possible to simply replace a phone's SIM card to access service. Three service providers allow cellphone rentals: SK Telecom, KTF and LG Telecom. Cellphones can be rented at the airport or at major hotels.

The most convenient option for short-term visitors is to rent a cell phone at the airport. KTF operates two phone rental booths in Incheon International Airport that allow foreigners to rent a phone for 3,000 won a day. Service on these phones costs 100 won per 10 seconds plus VAT for outgoing domestic calls. The cost of international calls depends on the call destination, and all incoming calls are free.

KTF rental phone booths can be found on both the arrivals (between Gate 10 and 11 on the first floor; open 24 hours) and departures level (third floor, open 6 am to 10 pm) of the airport. Have your passport and a credit card or 800,000 won deposit ready. You can estimate the total cost of your cell phone rental service on the KTF website at www.mobile.olleh.com, or call 2190-0901 for English service.

There are also websites that offer phone rental and service with optional insurance and free shipping. One such company is Mobal Korean Phone (www.mobalrental.com), which offers service for US$7 per day. All incoming calls are free, and all other domestic calls are US$0.99 per minute. Another option is Cellhire, which costs US$19 per week or US$69 per month. Incoming calls are free, and domestic calls are US$0.59 per minute.

Post

Post offices in Korea are recognizable by a red and white sign that says Korea Post with a flying-bird emblem. There is a local post office in every neighborhood of Seoul, as well as mailboxes on the street. Although postal codes are not used frequently in common use, they are required when sending any piece of mail within or outside of Korea.

Domestic postage for standard size letters runs between 220 and 270 won. Non-standard mail is 340 won for the first 50 g and an additional 120 won for every additional 50 g. International postage varies according to the destination. Airmail letters to North America, Europe, the Middle East, Australia and New Zealand cost 580 won. Parcel post to the United States of a 2 kg package costs 27,700 won by airmail and 12,000 won by surface mail. The weight limit for parcel post is 20 kg, which costs 182,500 won by airmail and 48,000 won by surface mail.

Addresses in Korea follow the opposite order of addresses in Western countries and appear as follows:

Country + City + Postal Code District Office (gu) + Ward (dong) + Street + Building/Unit Number + Name of Recipient

However, even if letters are addressed in the Western format, they will generally reach their recipient. Mail is delivered Monday through Saturday in most areas. Most post offices in Seoul remain open from 9 am to 6 pm Monday through Friday. The Seoul Central Post Office and a few other large branches are open 9 am to 8 pm Monday through Saturday.

For more information on rates, fees, zip codes and branch locations, visit www.koreapost.go.kr or call 1588-1300.

Other options for sending post and larger shipments:

DHL Korea	www.dhl.co.kr	**Hanjin Shipping**	www.hanjin.co.kr
FedEx	www.fedex.com/kr_english	**EMS**	www.epost.go.kr
UPS	www.ups.com	**Korea Express**	www.korex.co.kr

Newspapers and Magazines

The primary English-language newspapers distributed in Korea are *The Korea Times* (700 won; www.koreatimes.co.kr) and *The Korea Herald* (1000 won; www.koreaherald.com). These newspapers are issued daily Monday through Saturday, although the Friday Korea Times and the Saturday Korea Herald include a weekend update section with listings and articles on Seoul events, restaurants, and performances.

The other newspaper offerings are translated from Korean into English. Major Korean-language dailies like the *Chosun Ilbo* (http://english.chosun.com), *Donga Ilbo* (http://english.donga.com) and *Hankyoreh* (http://english.hani.co.kr) have online English editions.

The Joongang Daily accompanies *The International Herald Tribune* as its Korean news partner. This is also translated directly from Korean to English. *The Joongang Daily* also includes a comprehensive weekend preview and calendar.

Koreana (www.koreana.or.kr) is a quarterly academic magazine that analyzes a particular theme in depth each issue, with the intent of raising awareness of Korea's cultural heritage overseas. The content of this publication can be read in its entirety online in English, Russian, Arabic, Chinese, French, German, Japanese, Russian and Spanish.

SEOUL, a monthly travel and culture magazine, presents a diverse array of information and resources on the happenings and cultural hotspots of Seoul. This artfully designed magazine presents up-to-date information and recently added a section of valuable tourist maps of the major regions of the city.

10 is another monthly entertainment and culture guide to Korea. It offers an extensive listing of local events, as well as feature articles about different aspects of Korean society.

Television & Radio

Korea has three major television broadcasting companies: KBS, MBC, and SBS. These companies are all Korean-language TV networks, although if American movies are shown dubbed in Korean, most TVs have a button that reverts the sound to the English original. EBS is Korea's educational channel.

AFN Korea is an English-language TV station operated by the US military that offers American programs, sports and films. Arirang is a Korean government-funded channel that broadcasts programming in both Korean and English. This channel is only available with cable or satellite subscriptions. On that note, Seoul offers a vast array of cable and satellite channels with a subscription. Many American shows are available on cable. A cable subscription provides numerous options for foreign news, films, sports, religious programming, documentaries and talk shows. On radio, TBS eFM (101.3MHz) does music and English-language programming almost around the clock.

Blogs

In the age of the Internet, it seems everyone's got a blog, including a good many English-speaking expatriates in Seoul. Good ones to check out for information on things to see and do in the city include:

- **ZenKimchi** (www.zenkimchi.com): Run by long-time Korea hand and foodie Joe McPherson, this blog is one of the best sites on the planet for info on Korean dining. Another great site to check out for food and dining info is **Seoul Eats** (www.seouleats.com).

- **Discovering Korea** (discoveringkorea.com): Travel and culture journalist Matt Kelly of Korean broadcaster KBS introduces destinations across Korea, including many in Seoul. Recommended.

- **The Marmot's Hole** (www.rjkoehler.com): This writer's personal blog deals mostly with political, social and media matters, but it does on occasion feature travel-related photo essays.

- Two non-blog websites worth checking out are **Galbijim** (wiki.galbijim.com), the definitive wiki on everything Korean, and **Korea4expats.com** (www.korea4expats.com), which has a ton of info about visiting, living and working in Korea.

Medical Services

Pharmacies

Pharmacies are ubiquitous in Seoul. Just look for 약국 (*yakguk*—"pharmacy") or 약 (*yak*—"medicine") in the window. Korean pharmacies stock both over-the-counter and prescription medications. Pharmacists in Korea, while not able to distribute prescription medications freely, give excellent recommendations for medications based on the described symptoms. If you have trouble communicating with your pharmacist, it may help to write your symptoms on a piece of paper. Another option is to call the Korean tourist helpline at 1330 for an interpreter.

Foreigner Medical Facilities

Seoul's medical facilities have opened more international clinics to meet the needs of the city's continuously growing expatriate population. The Seoul Global Center (SGC) manages a 24-hour Medical Referral Service (MRS) for the city's foreign residents. The entire English-speaking staff is medically trained and provides foreigners with information and advice on Korea's medical services. The MRS team routinely visits medical facilities serving foreigners and gathers feedback from foreigners who have used the services. The MRS can be reached during regular business hours (8 am to 8 pm) at 010-4769-8212 or 010-8750-8212, or by e-mailing medicalreferral@seoul.go.kr. In the case of emergencies, the MRS can be used during the hours of 8 pm to 8 am at the same contacts.

English is spoken in many medical facilities in Seoul, but it is still recommended that foreigners use the international clinics at Seoul's largest hospitals. These facilities include the Asan Medical Center, Severance Hospital, Samsung Medical Center, and Seoul Medical Center. These four public hospitals offer medical consultations and treatments to foreign residents of Seoul with the assistance of volunteer interpreters.

The international clinics of these four facilities are generally open between the hours of 9 am and 4:30 pm on weekdays, and all require advance appointments. Severance Hospital is also open on Saturdays from 9:30 am to 12 pm.

• Asan Medical Center	T. 1688-7575	www.amc.seoul.kr
• Samsung Medical Center	T. 1599-3114	www.samsunghospital.com
• Seoul Medical Center	T. 2276-7000	www.seoulmc.or.kr
• Severance Hospital (International Health Care Center)		www.yuhs.or.kr/en
Sinchon	T. 2228-5810	
Gangnam	T. 2019-3690	

Emergency Information

• Emergency, Fire, Ambulance: **119**	• Seoul Metropolitan Police Foreign
• Medical Emergency: **1339**	Affairs: **700-6200 (1566-0112)**
• Police: **112**	

If English-speaking staff are not available, call the 24-hour tourist information and help line: **1330**.

Foreign Embassies in Seoul

Country	Tel	Website
	Address	
Australia	2003-0100	www.southkorea.embassy.gov.au
	19th Flr., Kyobo Bldg, Jongno 1-ga, Jongno-gu	
Canada	3783-6000	www.korea.gc.ca
	16-1, Jeong-dong, Jung-gu	
China	738-1038	www.chinaemb.or.kr
	54, Hyoja-dong, Jongno-gu	
France	3149-4300	www.ambafrance-kr.org
	30 Hap-dong, Seodaemun-gu	
Germany	748-4114	www.seoul.diplo.de
	308-5 Dongbinggo-dong, Yongsan-gu	
Ireland	774-6455	www.irelandhouse-korea.com
	13th Flr., Leema Bldg, 146-1, Susong-dong, Jongno-gu	
Japan	2170-5200	www.kr.emb-japan.go.jp
	18-11 Junghak-dong, Jongno-gu	
Netherlands	311-8600	http://southkorea.nlembassy.org
	10th Flr., Jeong-dong Building, 15-5 Jeong-dong, Jung-gu	
New Zealand	3701-7700	www.nzembassy.com/korea
	8th Flr., Jeong-dong Building, Jeong-dong, Jung-gu	
Philippines	796-7387	www.philembassy-seoul.com
	5-1 Itaewon 1-dong, Yongsan-gu	
Russia	318-2116	http://seoul.rusembassy.org
	34-16 Jeong-dong, Jung-gu	
Singapore	744-2464	www.mfa.gov.sg/seoul
	28th Flr., Seoul Finance Center, 84 Taepyeongno 1-ga, Jung-gu	
Taiwan	399-2767	www.taiwanembassy.org/kr
	Visa Office, 6th Flr., Gwanghwamun Bldg, Jongno-gu	
UK	3210-5500	http://ukinrok.fco.gov.uk
	4 Jeong-dong, Jung-gu	
USA	397-4114	http://seoul.usembassy.gov
	32 Sejongno, Jongno-gu	

Travel Hotline 1330

The Korea Tourism Organization operates a free, 24-hour tourism hotline that dispenses all sorts of tourism information. Just dial 1330. If you're on a cellphone, first dial the local area code before dialing 1330 (in Seoul, this means dialing 02-1330).

Dasan Center 120

Seoul Metropolitan City operated a call center that dispenses up-to-date tourism information in English, Japanese and Chinese. To use the service, just dial 120 (or 02-120 from a cell phone) and press "9" for foreign language services. Business hours are 9 am to 6 pm, Monday to Friday.

Organized Tours

Highly recommended are the tours conducted by the Korean branch of the Royal Asiatic Society (RAS). RAS tours are conducted on the weekend—many of them are to destinations outside of Seoul, but some are of the city and its environs, too. Non-members are free to join as well (albeit for a slightly higher price). For information on tours, including the schedule, check out the RAS website at www.raskb.com.

If time is an issue, the Seoul City Bus Tour is not a bad option. It offers two tour options—a Downtown Course and Night Course. Best of all, you can get off the bus and reboard as much as you like for the price of one ticket and tickets get you good discounts at many tourist destinations. For more information, see p367.

Cycling

Seoul is not the most bicycle-friendly city in the world. Between the hills and—more importantly—the aggressive drivers, you're best off leaving the bike at home. The city is trying to improve the situation, opening up bike paths in some neighborhoods and operating free bike rentals similar to the Velib System in Paris—for example, in the scenic Bukchon area. But things are still at a rudimentary stage. One area that IS rather pleasant to bike around is the Hangang River area. Hangang River Citizen's Park (see p237) and Ttukseom Seoul Forest (see p229) have bike paths (in the case of Hangang River Park, 36.9 km of bike paths), with a number of bike rentals along the way. The rental fee is 3,000 won per hour, or 6,000 won for a bike for two.

TIPS

A BRIGHTER FUTURE FOR SEOUL CYCLING?

In late 2008 and early 2009, Seoul's City Transportation Headquarters announced elements of a "Master Plan for Increasing Bicycle Use," involving the establishment of 17 cycle route axes and an inner and outer circle route, amounting to almost 300 km of road space reserved for pedal pushers. A 7.9 km tourist cycle route will run around the central Gyeongbokgung Palace, Cheonggyecheon Stream and Mt. Namsan areas, while routes from downtown Seoul to the existing cycle paths along the Hangang River and its main urban tributaries will also be created.

The new cycle route network will be accompanied by various facilities that, if built, integrated and maintained well, could really put Seoul at the cutting edge of cycle commuting. These include "bicycle centers" at four major subway stations, where bikes can be stored, hired and fixed; locker and shower facilities for cycle commuters at 16 subway stations, such as Jamsil, Siheung and Konkuk University; CCTV surveillance for many other bicycle stands; bicycle lifts at points on routes with sharp changes in elevation; and 12 "bicycle-friendly towns" in urban areas such as Nowon and Yeouido.

The aim of these projects is to make cycle commuting a viable option in the capital so that cyclists account for 4.4% of Seoul's vehicular traffic by 2012, and eventually 10% by 2020.

Until their completion, however, cyclists have to make do with sharing roads with buses, cars, lorries and other vehicles. Cycling on the pavement is against the law, since bicycles are classed as vehicles. Until the new bicycle routes are completed, cycling is not the safest or most convenient way to explore Seoul.

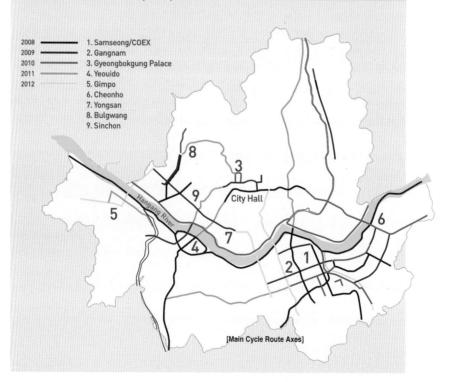

2008	———	1. Samseong/COEX
2009	———	2. Gangnam
2010	———	3. Gyeongbokgung Palace
2011	———	4. Yeouido
2012	———	5. Gimpo
		6. Cheonho
		7. Yongsan
		8. Bulgwang
		9. Sinchon

[Main Cycle Route Axes]

Books on Korea

There are a ton of good books about Korea out there, but for starters you might wish to try:

- **Korea's Place in the Sun:** Although Bruce Cumings is sometimes criticized as a "revisionist scholar," particularly about North Korea and the Korean War, his book *Korea's Place in the Sun* remains one of the best introductions to Korea ever written.

- **The Two Koreas:** Written by former journalist Don Oberdorfer, *The Two Koreas* examines the divergent paths of North and South Korea, with plenty of anecdotes and interesting history.

- **The Koreans: Who They Are, What They Want, Where Their Future Lies:** Long-time Korea resident and journalist Mike Breen introduces the truth about Koreans to a largely ignorant world.

- **Korea Old and New: A History:** Produced by several prominent Korea scholars, including Harvard University Korean history professor Carter Eckert, this is one of the most widely used texts on Korean history.

- **Korea and Her Neighbors:** An 1898 account of Korea by English female traveler and adventurist Isabella Bird, this wonderful—if Orientalist—read looks at pre-modern Korea during one of the most eventful periods in the nation's history.

- **The Dawn of Modern Korea:** While Andrei Lankov is best known as one of the world's most respected experts on North Korea, his *The Dawn of Modern Korea* is a fascinating look at the development of modern South Korea, with tons of fascinating historical tidbits.

- **Korea Film Director Series:** The Korean Film Council's series of 18 books are chock full of interviews, film reviews and essays on some of Korea's greatest film directors.

- **Spirit of Korean Cultural Roots:** With 25 volumes so far, this bilingual series produced by Ewha Womans University Press examines the evolution of Korean culture.

- **Korean Culture Series:** This Korea Foundation series on Korean traditional culture is expertly written and a good resource for those looking for a deeper understanding.

- **Korea Bug:** A collection of fascinating interviews from J. Scott Burgeson's zine *Bug*, this book is full of irreverent observations on both Korean and expat culture.

- **Pop Goes Korea:** Korean pop culture expert Mark Russell examines the rise of Korean film, music and Internet culture.

TIPS

BUYING BOOKS

Most of these books can be found in the English section of Kyobo Bookstore (located in Gwanghwamun and Gangnam, T. 1544-1900) or, at Seoul Selection Bookshop (located in Gwanghwamun, T. 734-9565; online purchases can be made at www.seoulselection.com).

TRANSPORTATION

GETTING TO/FROM KOREA

Airport

Although Korea operates eight international airports, only one services destinations outside of Asia: Incheon International Airport (T. 1577-2600 or www.airport.kr). Located 52 km west of downtown Seoul, Incheon International Airport is seated on reclaimed tidal lands between two islands on the Yellow Sea. Incheon Airport's international airport code is ICN, and it is alternately known as IIA.

Limousine Bus

Limousine buses offer the most efficient, low-cost means of transport to the airport. Airport limousine buses run between the airport and most areas of Seoul. Limousine bus information and ticket stands are located just outside airport exits 2, 4, 9 and 13 on the ground floor (baggage claim level). Each limousine bus has a clearly marked post on the curb, which shows a map of its route. Most buses begin service from Seoul between 4 and 6 am and the last buses to the city depart the airport anywhere between 7 and 11 pm. A detailed schedule of routes and departure times is available on the Incheon Airport website (www.airport.kr/eng). Limousine bus tickets run from 9,000 to 15,000 won to Seoul, 7,000 won to Gimpo Airport and 15,000 to COEX (5:20 am to 10:30 pm).

> * Airport Limousine Company recently opened late-night bus services for those traveling at red-eye hours. These buses offer infrequent service to the main areas of Seoul and can be found at platform 5A. Bus fare is 9,000 won.

Train

Another option is to take the airport express train (A'REX) from Seoul Station or Gimpo International Airport, which can be reached via the Seoul Metro subway. The government linked A'REX to multiple lines of the Seoul Metropolitan subway, including Seoul Station, Gongdeok Station, Hongik University Station and Digital Media City Station, connecting all residents of Korea to the airport via train. The A'REX will take you from Gimpo to Incheon International in 33 minutes, 53 minutes from Seoul Station (43 minutes for the express train) and runs every twelve minutes (six minutes between Seoul Station and Geomam Station). The express train runs every 30 minutes from Seoul Station to Incheon International Airport. Operating hours are 5:20 am to 12:00 am. The fair is 3,700 won from Seoul Station to Incheon International Airport. For more info, visit www.arex.or.kr.

Taxi

Private taxis are the fastest mode of transportation to and from the airport. A private taxi costs approximately 44,000 won from the Seoul City Hall area and takes about one hour to reach the airport. A taxi from Gangnam should cost around 55,000 won and take 75 minutes. In addition to the fare, the passenger is responsible for a 7,500 won toll. The fare increases by 20% between the hours of midnight and 4 am.

Deluxe taxis are also available, offering a more luxurious ride for approximately double the price. A taxi to or from Seoul City Hall costs about 80,000 won, while a taxi to or from Gangnam runs about 90,000 won. For those departing from the airport, taxi stands are located on the arrivals level (1F) between platforms 5C and 8C.

Ferries

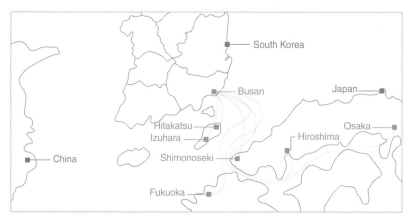

An alternate mode of transport to Korea from Japan, China or Russia is via sea. Korea's two major sea ports are Busan and Incheon. Busan, Korea's largest port, offers maritime access to Japan, including high-speed hydrofoils. Ferries to various locales in China depart from Incheon, and service to Russia departs from Sokcho. Special tickets are available for joint Korea-China travel or Korea-Japan travel that provide the bearer with discounts on train services in both countries of travel and ferry transport between the two. These tickets are valid for between one week and 20 days from the first date of travel.

For more information, visit http://english.visitkorea.or.kr and see Getting To Korea section.

GETTING AROUND KOREA

Domestic Flights

Korea's not that big, but for those so inclined, you can travel by air. Korea's domestic flight network is operated by Korean Air and Asiana Airlines, linking 15 major cities. Although domestic flight fares fluctuate depending on the season, prices generally range from 58,000 to 85,000 won. An airport tax of 5,000 won (4,000 won from Gimpo Airport) is included in all fares. Reserve tickets by calling Hanjin Travel Service (T. 726-5541,5) or contacting the airlines directly.

- **Korean Air:** T. 1588-2001 or www.koreanair.com
- **Asiana Airlines:** T. 1588-8000 or http://flyasiana.com

Trains

The Korean National Railroad provides access to all areas of Korea with an extensive, fast and reliable railway system. There are three major railway line

Travel Times

	TO BUSAN	TO MOKPO
KTX	2 hours, 40 minutes	2 hours, 58 minutes
Saemaeul	4 hours, 10 minutes	4 hours, 42 minutes
Mugunghwa	5 hours, 20 minutes	Over 5 hours

Fares (Seoul—Busan)

KTX	Saemaeul	Mugunghwa
55,500 won	41,100 won	27,700 won

TIPS

KR PASS

Overseas visitors can buy a special KR Pass, which must be purchased overseas at a ticket office, through a travel agent, or on the Korean National Railroad website (www.korail.com). The KR Pass can be used an unlimited number of times during its period of validity to obtain a registered ticket, regardless of travel class. KR Passes are valid for 3 to 10 days and come in normal adult and children passes, saver passes, and youth passes.

categories in Korea. First, the KTX, or Korea Train Express, is a bullet train that runs from Seoul to Busan, Gwangju and Mokpo. This high-speed train runs at 300 km/h, cutting the time to Busan just under three hours (two and a half hours to Gwangju and two hours and 58 minutes to Mokpo). The second fastest service is the Saemaeul, which only stops in major cities. Next, there is the Mugunghwa, which offers comfortable and relatively fast service with more frequent stops. Finally, the Tongil Express stops at every station and offers the cheapest fares.

Train tickets can be purchased up to one month in advance at a train station or with a travel agent. Trains tend to be full on weekends and holidays, and it is advisable to reserve tickets in advance. This is particularly the case on the Chuseok and Lunar New Year holidays (see "Korean Holidays" on p346), when tickets can sell out weeks or even months in advance. Information about train timetables and ticket prices is available at the Korea Railroad Corporation(T. 1544-7788 or www.korail.com).

Express Buses

Buses offer an alternate means of cross-country transport that service virtually every town in Korea. Unlike with trains, it is not necessary to

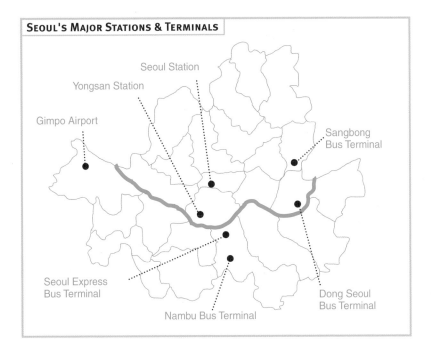

SEOUL'S MAJOR STATIONS & TERMINALS

Seoul Station

Yongsan Station

Gimpo Airport

Sangbong
Bus Terminal

Seoul Express
Bus Terminal

Dong Seoul
Bus Terminal

Nambu Bus Terminal

purchase tickets in advance, unless traveling during a major holiday or weekend. Deluxe express buses are pricier than the regular option, but offer spacious seating and attractive facilities such as mobile phones and on-board films. Buses depart Seoul from four major terminals: the Seoul Express Bus Terminal (Gangnam Gosok Terminal), Dong Seoul Bus Terminal, Sangbong Bus Terminal and Nambu Bus Terminal.

Seoul Express Bus Terminal
This two-building terminal is the main departure point for travel between Seoul and other major cities. For ticket and logistical information, call 536-6460~2 or visit www.kobus.co.kr. To reach the terminal, take subway Line 3 or 7 or 9 to Express Bus Terminal Station, Exit 1 or 7.

Dong Seoul Bus Terminal
Serves similar destinations as the Seoul Express Bus Terminal, but with fewer options and less frequent service. For ticket information, call 1688-5979. The terminal is adjacent to Gangbyeon Station, Line 2, Exit 3.

Sangbong Bus Terminal

Operates routes to Cheongju, Daejeon, Jeonju and Gwangju. For ticket information call 323-5885. Take Line 7 to Sangbong Station, Exit 2.

Nambu Bus Terminal

Operates to southern destinations like Pyeongtaek, Yongin, Anseong and Osan. For ticket information, call 521-8550. Take Line 3 to Nambu Terminal Station, Exit 5.

Car Rental

Due to a high traffic density and loose adherence to standard driving practice, driving in Seoul can be a challenge. In addition, given the high number of public transport options, driving is unnecessary and not advised. However, if the following criteria are met, a rental car can be secured for approximately 62,000 won to 460,000 won per day:

• Over one year of driving experience
• Possess an international driver's license
• Over 21 years of age
• Possess a valid passport
• Will pay by credit card

Kumho Rental Cars: T. 1588-1230 or 797-8000
Avis Rental Cars: T. 862-2847

Both are available at the airport; numerous other options are available in the city.

City Bus System

Seoul has a comprehensive bus system that provides easy access to and from all parts of the city. The bus system is made up of three different types of buses: *ilban* buses, *jwaseok* buses and *maeul* buses. Bus numbers begin with digits indicating the areas of departure and arrival and end with a single or double digit for bus route identification purposes. For example, Bus #7011 starts in area 7 (Mapo-gu), ends in Area 0 (Jongno) and follows route 11.

A comprehensive, searchable map of Seoul's bus routes in English is available online at http://bus.seoul.go.kr. Bus service begins around 4:30 am and the buses make their last rounds around 1 am. Over 8,500 city buses and 400 express buses transport Seoulites every day.

Ilban buses

Ilban buses are commonly known as city buses, traversing and connecting all regions of the city. They come in three different colors: blue, green, and yellow.

Blue buses connect the suburban areas of Seoul to downtown Seoul. Green buses are privately operated. They connect residential areas, subway lines and bus terminals, circulating within a particular district. Yellow buses circulate downtown Seoul, connecting the major tourist, shopping and business areas of the city.

Jwaseok buses

Jwaseok buses, or city express coaches, are red buses that provide comfortable and speedy transport for inter-city commuters. These buses seat every passenger and provide commuters with easy access to neighboring cities, such as Ilsan, Bundang, Suwon and Incheon.

Maeul buses

Finally, *maeul* buses are significantly smaller buses with shorter routes, often connecting residential areas.

Bus fares can be paid on board with cash or a transportation card (see Tips for more). *Ilban* bus fares for 10 km or less are 1,000 won when paid in cash, and 900 won when paid with transportation card. Each additional 5 km increases the fare by 100 won.

TIPS

T-MONEY/ TRANSPORTATION CARDS

The most cost-efficient means of using the public transportation system is to use a T-Money or transportation card. A T-Money card is more convenient and offers discounted fares on all public transportation. Fares are 100 won less when you use the T-Money card rather than cash, and discounts are offered on transfers. When you transfer within 30 minutes of exiting the bus, the base fare remains the same for rides up to 10 km, and 100 won is added for each additional 5 km traveled. Also, when you transfer from bus to subway, 50 won is deducted from the fare. To register a transfer, the T-Money card must be swiped when you exit the bus, too. A T-Money card costs approximately 2,500 won and can be purchased at automated machines in every subway station or in local convenience stores (Family Mart, GS25, Buy the Way and 7-Eleven). These cards can be recharged easily at an automated machine in the subway station. Another option is a credit-based transportation card, including debit cards, credit cards and e-cards. These cards tabulate the amount spent each month and deduct the total fare in one charge.

Subway

The Seoul Metro is extremely easy to navigate: each line is color-coded, and each station is labeled with a three digit code that indicates the subway line number with the first digit and the station number with the last two digits. In addition, subway maps generally indicate whether the platform is on the right or left hand side of the train with a square or circle around the station number in order to facilitate easy departure on crowded rush-hour trains. Subway service begins around 5 am and ends around midnight. Travel time between stations is generally just over 2 minutes. All subway maps are labeled in both Korean and English, and announcements of the station arrival on the train are also delivered in English as well.

Subway fares, similarly to bus fares, can be paid in cash or with a transportation card. Tickets (which take the form of plastic cards) can be purchased from automated ticket-dispensing machines located at all stations—instructions are given in Korean and English. Fares vary depending on the distance, so it is important to purchase the appropriate ticket for your destination. A subway fare of 1,000 won (900 won with a transportation card) takes you up to 10 km, and each additional 5 km tacks on an additional 100 won. The average ride within Seoul costs between 900 and 1,500 won. Please note that if you purchase a one-trip ticket, your fare will also include a 500 won deposit fee, which you can retrieve when you turn in your used ticket at a deposit machine upon reaching your destination. See the end of the book for a subway map.

Taxis

Taxis in Seoul are relatively affordable, offering a speedy and comfortable means of transport around the city. There are two types of taxis: *ilban* and *mobeom*.

Ilban taxis are regular taxis and come in silver or white. Those with white caps are privately owned taxis, while those with blue caps are company-owned vehicles. Standard fare for *ilban* taxis is 2,400 won for the first 2 km and 100 won for every additional 144 m. In heavy traffic, 100 won is added every 35 seconds. Fares are increased by 20% between the hours of midnight and 4 am.

TIPS

Many taxis offer a free interpretation service via phone, but it is a good idea to have your destination written down in Korean to show your driver (For basic Korean expressions, see p410). Tipping is not expected.

Mobeom taxis are luxury taxis, identifiable as black cars with yellow caps. These taxis offer a more comfortable ride at an inflated price. Basic fare in a *mobeom* taxi is 4,500 won for the first 3 km, and increases by 200 won every 164 m.

Another taxi option is the call taxi, which are sometimes useful when you're out late or in an area not frequented by taxis. You can get an English-speaking "international taxi" at (02) 1644-2255, but these are 20% more expensive than ordinary cabs. If you're out and would like to call a taxi, the place you're at will most likely know a number to call. Taxis (but not international taxis) charge an extra 1,000 won when they are called.

Hangang River Water Taxi

In an attempt to lessen daily commuter traffic and frustration, Seoul Metropolitan City now offers the "Express Shuttle," an express water taxi service from Ttukseom to Yeouido and from Jamsil to Yeouido. Travel time from Ttukseom to Yeouido on the water taxi is 14 minutes. Morning commute water taxis run every 20 minutes between the hours of 7:10 am and 8:30 am, and evening commute water taxis run every 20 minutes from 6:30 pm to 8 pm. The last evening taxi departs from the station at 7:30 pm. Water taxi fare is 5,000 won each way, and each taxi holds seven passengers. Reservations can be made by calling the reservation hotline between the hours of 9 am to 10 pm at 1588-3960. Reservations can also be made online, although the site is only available in Korean. Please see www.pleasantseoul.com for more information.

Tourist Transportation

Seoul City Tour Bus

The Seoul City Tour Bus offers tourists a comfortable and convenient means of transport between Seoul's most notable tourist attractions. You can choose from four tours: a daytime downtown tour, Cheonggyecheon and palace tour (double decker bus), and two night tours, one in a single decker bus and the other in a double decker. The downtown tour costs 10,000 won, while the night tour costs 5,000 won. The double-decker Cheonggyecheon and palace tour costs 12,000 won, while the double-decker night tour costs 10,000 won. The best part of the single-decker tours is that you can get on and off as much as you like for the price of one ticket (the Cheonggyecheon/Palace tour allows you to get off only at the palaces, while the double-decker night tour is non-stop). Tourists with a Seoul City Tour Bus ticket receive considerable discounts on admissions to the sites along the route. Also, each bus offers information about the sites visited in Korean, English, French, Japanese and Chinese. No tours on Monday. Buses depart from in front of the Donghwa Duty Free Shop near Exit 6 of Gwanghwamun Station, Line 5. For more information, call 777-6090 or visit www.seoulcitybus.com.

- **Downtown Tour:** 9 am to 9 pm (last departure, 7 pm). Buses depart every 30 minutes
- **Night Tour:** Bus departs at 8 pm • **Cheonggyecheon/Palace Tour:** Every hour from 10 am to 5 pm • **Night Tour (double decker):** 8 pm

ACCOMMODATIONS

Seoul offers a wide range of accommodations for travellers of all styles, purposes and budgets. Whether you prefer customary Western-style beds, a Korean-style *ondol* (heated floor) room, a luxury suite with all the latest amenities or a cheap bunk in a revolving-door hostel, there is a room that meets your needs in Seoul. In terms of location, while Gwanghwamun, Insa-dong and Myeong-dong are the most central locations, the sites of Seoul are scattered about and all accessible by public transportation.

Hotels

For business and leisure travelers with a bulge in their wallets and an interest in being pampered, Seoul is home to some of Asia's most luxurious hotels. In the 90s, as Korea's business and IT sectors rapidly advanced and Korea became one of Asia's most active financial centers, the hospitality industry adjusted to meet the needs of this growing clientèle base. Seoul offers a wide range of posh accommodations that should meet, if not exceed, the expectations of travelers with even the deepest pockets.

Downtown Seoul and the Gangnam area near the financial district offer the most expensive accommodations.

Imperial Palace

Hanok Stay—Bukchon Hanok

All visitors to Korea should spend at least one night in a *hanok*, for a taste of traditional Korean living. *Hanoks* are traditional Korean houses that give foreign visitors a taste of traditional Korean culture. They are an increasingly rare find in Seoul's modernized landscape. With *ondol* rooms arranged around a central courtyard, decorated with wooden beams and *hanji* (traditional Korean paper) windows, *hanoks* offer an authentic traditional Korean experience. Seoul's *hanok* guesthouses are all located in the Bukchon area, a preserved neighborhood in the heart of Seoul between Gyeongbokgung and Changdeokgung Palaces.

Budget Hotels / Inns

There are thousands of budget-range lodging choices scattered throughout the city. Motels in Korea—called *yeogwan*—are basic but meet the needs of the overnight guest. The *yeogwan* category of accommodation includes love motels, which can be rented by the hour—although you may wish to approach this option with caution.

Backpacker Guest Houses & Youth Hostels

While only three youth hostels in Seoul are members of the Korean Youth Hostel Association, there are many other budget options also available in the city.

Homestay—Minbak: Accommodations Outside of Seoul

For an opportunity to experience authentic Korean culture directly, opt for a homestay—known in Korean as *minbak*. *Minbak* are more of an option for those traveling in the Korean countryside than in the city. Although less private than a hotel, *minbak* allow you to indulge in Korean food and observe Korean customs and family relations firsthand. Another advantage of *minbak* is the relatively low cost.

Apartment Rental

Serviced apartments are an increasingly common option as the numbers of foreign businesspeople increase. These apartments are extremely modern and include all the amenities of a high-class hotel, but with the comfort of a home. Long-term visitors may choose to rent an apartment, although this may be difficult given the Korean rental system.

ACCOMMODATION LIST

H1 Luxury Hotel

H2 Mid-Range Hotel

K Hanok Guesthouse

G Guesthouse or Hostels

S Service Residence

GWANGHWAMUN AREA

Seoul Plaza Hotel **H1**

Central location near City Hall makes this an ideal location for businessmen. Also within easy reach of most central tourist attractions.
- **Price range** KRW 280,000–5,000,000
- **Address** 23 Taepyeongno 2-ga, Jung-gu • **Tel** 771-2200 • **Website** www.hoteltheplaza.com/eng

Westin Chosun **H1**

Korea's oldest international hotel, established in 1914, but recently refurbished with state-of-the-art facilities and Western-style services. Has the beautiful historical Wongudan altar in its back yard. Ideal central location.
- **Price range** KRW 220,000–1,500,000
- **Address** 87 Sogong-dong, Jung-gu
- **Tel** 771-0500 • **Website** http://twc.echosunhotel.com

Koreana Hotel **H1**

A prime central location just across the road from City Hall, Seoul Plaza and Korea Press Center and within easy walking distance of many more key institutions. 10 minutes by taxi from Seoul Station, and right next to the Deoksugung Palace.
- **Price range** KRW 172,000–900,000
- **Address** 61-1 Taepyeong-ro 1-ga, Jung-gu • **Tel** 2171-7000 • **Website** www.koreanahotel.com

Best Western-New Seoul Hotel **H2**

Another centrally-located hotel, boasting excellent business facilities such as a dedicated business center and high-speed Internet service in each room.
- **Price range** KRW 126,000–261,000
- **Address** 29-1 Taepyeongno 1(il)-ga, Jung-gu • **Tel** 735-8800 • **Website** www.bestwesternnewseoul.co.kr

Holiday Inn Seongbuk Seoul **H2**

Dedicated to providing "peace both in body and mind" to all customers. Recently expanded and re-opened as a five-star business hotel, with diverse facilities for all-round comfort.
- **Price range** US$ 160–330
- **Address** 3-1343 Jongam-dong, Seongbuk-gu • **Tel** 929-2000
- **Website** www.holiday.co.kr/eng/index.htm

Somerset Palace, Seoul

Doulos Hotel H2

Provides efficient English and Japanese language service, plus free breakfast for business guests and a wide range of 24-hour facilities. Also operates a dedicated theater for guests. Discounts available for on-line reservations.

- **Price range** KRW 100,000–120,000
- **Address** 112 Gwansu-dong, Jongno-gu
- **Tel** 2266-2244
- **Website** www.douloshotel.com

Biwon Hotel H2

Located just 10 minutes away from Changdeokgung Palace, Changgyeonggung Palace and Chongmyo shrine, this is a good hotel for sightseeing. It's also just up the road from Seoul's bustling Daehangno theater district. 20% discount for Internet bookings.

- **Price range** KRW 100,000–160,000
- **Address** 36 Wonnam-dong, Jongno-gu
- **Tel** 763-5555
- **Website** www.biwonhotel.com

Hotel SunBee H2

Ideal for both tourists and business travelers thanks to its location in Insa-dong, this hotel also prides itself on the best service. Brand new facilities include whirlpool baths and computers with Internet in every room.

- **Price range** KRW 77,000–110,000
- **Address** 198-11 Gwanhun-dong, Jongno-gu • **Tel** 730-3451
- **Website** www.hotelsunbee.com

New Kukjae Hotel H2

Another centrally located first-class hotel within easy reach of many major attractions. Located behind Seoul City Hall, close to Cheonggyecheon Stream.

- **Price range** KRW 80,000–200,000
- **Address** 29-2 Taepyeongno 1(il)-ga, Jung-gu • **Tel** 732-0161• **Website** www. newkukjehotel.com

Seoul Rex Hotel H2

Ideal location close to Lotte Department Store, Namdaemun Market and Dongdaemun Market. Visit the website for a 10-30% discount service.

- **Price range** KRW 113,000–305,000
- **Address** 65 Hoehyeon-dong 1(il)-ga, Jung-gu • **Tel** 752-3191• **Website** www. hotelrex.co.kr

YMCA Tourist Hotel H2

Convenient location on Jongno, one of central Seoul's busiest streets. Close to historic Tapgol Park. Four types of rooms available at reasonable prices, plus a 10% discount for YMCA members. Opened in 1967.

- **Price range** KRW 55,000–110,000 (triple) • **Address** 9 Jongno 2(i)-ga, Jongno-gu • **Tel** 734-6884 • **Website** www.ymca.or.kr/hotel

Anguk Guesthouse K

Provides traditional Korean-style rooms and hotel-standard comfort. Nearby parks and forest offer exercise and relaxation in a natural environment. Located in a beautiful neighborhood between the Gyeongbokgung and Changdeokgung palaces. Built under the supervision of the Korean Tradition Preservation Center of Seoul.

- **Price range** KRW 50,000–80,000
- **Address** 72-3 Anguk-Dong, Jongno-gu
- **Tel** 736-8304
- **Website** www.anguk-house.com/lodging.htm

Bukchon 72 Guest House K

Experience the unique feel of a totally remodeled Korean traditional-style house at reasonable rates. Featuring Korean environmentally-friendly yellow earth walls and *ondol* (under-floor) heating, this guest house is located in a key cultural neighborhood and prides itself on its friendly staff. A great place to stay for a Korean sojourn with some character.

- **Price range** KRW 40,000 (single)–90,000 (triple) • **Address** 72 Gye-dong, Jongno-gu • **Tel** 010-6711-6717 • **Website** www.bukchon72.com

Rak-Ko-Jae ⓚ

Meticulously renovated by a Korean master carpenter according to traditional principles, Rak-Ko-Jae is not simply a traditional guesthouse. It's a cultural space where guests can experience the elegance of Korean traditional food, music, dance, art, poetry and the dignity of past scholars—as well as lodging. The ultimate cultural guesthouse experience within Seoul.

- **Price range** KRW 180,000–450,000
- **Address** 98 Gye-dong, Jongno-gu
- **Tel** 742-3410 / 010-8555-1407 (En)
- **Website** www.rkj.co.kr

Seoul Guesthouse ⓚ

Traditional Korean guesthouse located in a historic, protected neighborhood between two palaces. Within 15 minutes' walk of Insa-dong. A chance to stay in an atmospheric area at reasonable prices.

- **Price range** KRW 40,000–220,000
- **Address** 135-1 Gye-dong, Jongno-gu
- **Tel** 745-0057
- **Website** www.seoul110.com

Sophia Guest House ⓚ

A rare surviving example of a detached royal palace, Sophia Guest House makes use of buildings dating back more than 150 years. Staying here is a wonderful opportunity to experience the sense of time and Korean aesthetics offered by such traditional hanok architecture. Lying in the beautiful and tranquil cultural quarter of Bukchon, the guest house offers both a relaxing atmosphere and easy access to some of Seoul's most attractive tourist spots. Suitable for both tourists and business travelers.

- **Price range** KRW 35,000–70,000
- **Address** 157-1 Sogyeok-dong, Jongno-gu • **Tel** 720-5467
- **Website** www.sophiagh.com

Tea Guest House ⓚ

Built carefully over a long period by skilled carpenters, Tea Guest House is another traditional-style establishment, opened in 2006. All rooms are in buildings made from old pine, bamboo and loess, which, together with the *ondol* heating system in winter, make for a healthy and relaxing night's sleep. The guest house also boasts an attractive Korean-style courtyard and garden, and guests can sample the delights of Korean tea. This guest house is also situated in the attractive Bukchon cultural quarter.

- **Price range** KRW 60,000 (single)–160,000 (special room)
- **Address** 15-6 Gye-dong, Jongno-gu
- **Tel** 3675-9877
- **Website** www.teaguesthouse.com

Yim's House ⓖ

Another reasonably-priced hotel very close to Changdeokgung Palace, Jongmyo Shrine and Insa-dong.

- **Price range** KRW 35,000–45,000
- **Address** 33 Waryong-dong, Jongno-gu
- **Tel** 747-3332
- **Website** www.seoulbusinesshotel.com

Holiday in Korea Hostel ⓖ

H.I.K. aims to provide guests with freedom, enjoyment and safety. Located just a teapot's throw from Insa-dong, it offers easy walking access to the best of Seoul's old palaces and traditional neighborhoods. Children enjoy discounted accommodation rates.

- **Price range** KRW 17,000–44,000
- **Address** 53 Ikseon-dong, Jongno-gu
- **Tel** 3672-3113
- **Website** www.holidayinkorea.com

Banana Backpackers ⓖ

Formerly named Seoul Backpackers, this establishment has now been colorfully rebranded and named after a popular yellow fruit. A good range of facilities includes free laundry, free luggage storage, free (wireless) Internet access and more (see website).

Located just off Insa-dong's main thoroughfare, the hostel offers a great location at a reasonable cost. Rates are slightly higher during peak season (July and August).

- **Price range** KRW 20,000 (dorm bed, off-peak)–65,000 (family room, off-peak)
- **Address** 30-1 Ikseon-dong, Jongno-gu
- **Tel** 3672-1973
- **Website** www.bananabackpackers.com

Beewon Guest House ⑥

Located next to Changdeokgung Palace. Facilities include dormitory rooms, private rooms, a family room, an *ondol* room with a heated floor, a kitchen, computers with Internet and a washing machine. Breakfast is provided.

- **Price range** KRW 19,000 (dorm)–KRW 65,000 (room for three)
- **Address** 28-2 Unni-dong Jongno-gu
- **Tel** 765-0670 • **Website** www. beewonguesthouse.com/en/

Guesthouse Korea ⑥

Boasts a typical full portfolio of guest house facilities, as well as employing young Korean volunteers who enjoy sharing Korean culture and society with guests. Learn about Korean Culture through various activities such as kimchi-making parties, samgyeopsal parties, beer parties, and the preparation of other Korean foods.

- **Price range** KRW 18,000 (dorm)–40,000 (double)
- **Address** 155-1, Kwonnong-dong, Jongno-gu • **Tel** 3675-2205
- **Website** www.guesthouseinkorea.com

Hostel Korea ⑥

As well as being within five to 20 minutes' travel from most major Seoul tourist attractions, this guest house's proximity to the huge shopping area in Dongdaemun means it is ideal for those whose number one priority in Seoul is picking up bargain clothes and shoes.

- **Price range** KRW 25,000 (dorm)–65,000 (triple ensuite) • **Address** 178-65 Sungin-dong, Jongno-gu • **Tel** 762-7406
- **Website** www.hostelkorea.com

Songwontel ⑥

Clean and convenient facilities at satisfactory rates. Traveler's information and tips provided.

- **Price range** KRW 30,000 (single)–35,000 (double)
- **Address** 103-62 Donui-dong, Jongno-gu • **Tel** 742-4469 • **Website** http://serdle. cafe24.com

Fraser Suites Serviced Residences ⑤

The first choice for ex-pats with large budgets, these fully-serviced luxury apartments are ideally located in Insadong. Suitable for both temporary and long-term stays.

- **Price range** KRW 300,000–800,000
- **Address** 272 Nagwon-dong, Jongno-gu
- **Tel** 6262-8282 • **Website** http://seoul. frasershospitality.com/

Somerset Palace, Seoul ⑤

The other luxury-serviced residence suite near Insadong, offering a similarly rounded portfolio of services and facilities at similar prices. Mid- to long-term stays are also the norm here.

- **Price range** KRW 140,000–260,000
- **Address** 85 Susong-dong, Jongno-gu
- **Tel** 6730-8888
- **Website** www.somersetpalaceseoul.com

Vabien ⑤

Serviced luxury residence suite in northwestern Seoul. Special services include a golf range and barbecue. Shuttle bus service to major areas.

- **Price range** 9,000,000–13,200,000 (monthlly)
- **Address** 32-2 Uijuro, Jung-gu
- **Tel** 2076-9000
- **Website** www.vabiensuite.com/eng

MYEONG-DONG AREA

Astoria Hotel

Lotte Hotel Seoul 🏨

One of the five branches of Lotte Hotel throughout Korea, this super-deluxe hotel hosts major international events. Renowned for its top-notch duty free shop.

- **Price range** KRW 350,000–12,000,000
- **Address** 1 Sogong-dong, Jung-gu • **Tel** 771-1000 • **Website** www.lottehotel.com

Millennium Seoul Hilton Hotel 🏨

Located at the foot of Mt. Namsan, offering splendid views of this island of green in central Seoul. A health club and golf driving range allow you to recover or hit balls while enjoying the view, respectively.

- **Price range** KRW 230,000–360,000
- **Address** 395 Namdaemunno 5(o)-ga
- **Tel** 753-7788 • **Website** www.hilton.co.kr

Astoria Hotel 🏨

Chungmuro's Astoria Hotel opened in 1959, making it one of Seoul's oldest hotels. Recent renovations have given the Astoria's five categories of room attractive, contemporary interiors. The hotel's distinctive New York-style Italian restaurant, Bella Coolla 63, is a great place to enjoy genuine Western food, while the Astoria's location makes it a great base for shopping and enjoying the bustling heart of Seoul. Staff at the front desk speak English and Japanese.

- **Price range** KRW 90,000–144,000
- **Address** 13-2 Namhak-dong, Jung-gu
- **Tel** 2268-7111

Hotel PJ 🏨

A great hotel for those on a shopping trip, the PJ is within easy reach of Myeong-dong, Namdaemun and Dongdaemun shopping areas. It also offers easy access to Lines 2, 3, 4 and 5 of the Seoul Metro, making it highly convenient for transport to further-flung areas of the city as well.

- **Price range** KRW 160,000–336,000
- **Address** 73-1 Inhyeon-dong 2-ga, Jung-gu • **Tel** 2280-7000
- **Website** http://eng.hotelpj.co.kr

Metro Hotel 🏨

Convenient location near Lotte Department Store and CGV Cinema. Dating from the 1960s, the Metro reopened in 2005 as a business hotel.

- **Price range** KRW 90,000–190,000
- **Address** 199-33 Eulji-ro 2-ga, Jung-gu
- **Tel** 752-1112
- **Website** http://metrohotel.co.kr

Pacific Hotel 🏨

Located close to Mt. Namsan, offering great opportunities for hiking and jogging.

- **Price range** KRW 160,000–250,000
- **Address** 31-1 Namsan-dong 2(i)-ga, Jung-gu • **Tel** 777-7811
- **Website** www.thepacifichotel.co.kr

Prince Hotel 🏨

Located just next to Myeong-dong subway station. Japanese and English are spoken, and a free bus service runs to Seoul Station and Incheon International Airport.

- **Price range** KRW 130,000–260,000
- **Address** 1-1 Namsan-dong 2(i)-ga, Jung-gu • **Tel** 752-7111 • **Website** www. hotelprinceseoul.co.kr

Savoy Hotel 🏨

Motto: "A hotel just like home and with such friendly service, you're sure to return."

Established in 1957, but recently refurbished.
- **Price range** KRW 99,000–216,000
- **Address** 23-1 Chungmuro 1(il)-ga, Jung-gu • **Tel** 776-2641 • **Website** www.savoyhotel.co.kr

Sejong Hotel ⒣

This hotel was named after the great Joseon dynasty king whose virtue and spirit it strives to emulate. It is situated in Myeong-dong, making transport and shopping convenient.
- **Price range** KRW 140,000–280,000
- **Address** 61-3 Chungmuro 2-ga Jung-gu • **Tel** 773-6000 • **Website** www.sejong.co.kr

Myeong-dong Guest House ⒢

A guest house boasting the usual convenient points associated with a Myeong-dong location, this establishment claims to offer clean and modern facilities and cheaper prices than anywhere else in the area. The owner is proficient in both English and Japanese, and Chinese language assistance is also available.
- **Price range** KRW 35,000–45,000

- **Address** 17 Namsan-dong 3-ga Jung-gu
- **Tel** 755-5437
- **Website** www.mdguesthouse.com

Namsan Guest House ⒢

Located on Mt. Namsan, where you can breathe the fresh air and take in the hill's famous sites. Also close to Myeong-dong. The mountain's hiking path is just nearby. Provides information and even translation services for guests.
- **Price range** KRW 110,000 (room for six) • **Address** 50-1 Namsan-dong 2-ga, Jung-gu • **Tel** 752-6363 • **Website** www.namsanguesthouse.com

Seoul Backpackers ⒢

A newly-opened hostel located conveniently close to Seoul Station and Namdaemun Market–an area with few hostels. Mt. Namsan is also just a few minutes' walk away, offering great walks and views of the city for those who get tire of shopping and traffic.
- **Price range** KRW 45,000–60,000
- **Address** 205-125 Namchang-Dong, Jung-gu • **Tel** 3672-1972
- **Website** www.seoulbackpackers.com

DONGDAEMUN AREA

The Shilla Seoul ⒣

Listed among the top hotels in the world, the Shilla is a good place to head if you want

The Shilla Seoul

no-expenses-spared comfort and refined cultural performances. You might not even get round to going out and looking around Seoul.
- **Price range** KRW 230,000–7,200,000
- **Address** 202 Jangchung-dong 2 ga, Jung-gu • **Tel** 2233-3131
- **Website** www.shilla.net/en/seoul

Grand Ambassador Seoul ⒣

Boasts a full hand of services and facilities following a recent 50-year anniversary renovation.
- **Price range** KRW 167,000–413,000

• **Address** 186-54 Jangchung-dong 2(i)-ga, Jung-gu • **Tel** 2275-1101~9 • **Website** https://grand.ambatel.com

Dongdaemun Hotel (H2)

A cozy yet practical and elegant second-class hotel. Offers traditional Korean rooms, buffet and even a sauna. Ideally located for Dongdaemun shopping sprees.

• **Price range** KRW 70,000 (single), 80,000 (double) • **Address** 444-14 Changshin-dong, Jongno-gu • **Tel** 741-7811

Wind Road Guesthouse (G)

The guesthouse for theater-loving backpackers, Windroad is just one block from the gates of Sungkyunkwan University and close to culturally vibrant quarter of Daehangno. Proximity to the university means plenty of good, cheap restaurants. Run by a seasoned traveler by the name of Park.

• **Price range** KRW 11,000 (dorm)–60,000 (room for four) • **Address** 85-5 Myeongnyun-dong 3-ga, Jongno-gu • **Tel** 6407-2013 • **Website** www.backpackerkorea.net

Travelers A Hostel (G)

Located just around the corner from Cheonggyecheon Stream, this hostel is within easy reach of all locations in the Dongdaemun area and offers pleasant walks along the stream in either direction.

• **Price range** KRW 40,000–100,000 • **Address** 106-2 Jugyo-dong, Jung-gu • **Tel** 2285-5511, 2265-2156 • **Website** www.travelersa.com

Ulji-ro CO-OP Residence

Young Home Guest House & Home Stay (G)

This hostel is very close to Korea University, one of Korea's leading higher education institutions. The university's eponymous subway station on Line 6 offers easy access to central Seoul, while nearby Cheongnyangni Station is the terminus for the line leading east and into Gangwon province–a route famous for romantic train journeys.

• **Price range** KRW 900,000 (one month) • **Address** 122-513 Jegi-dong, Dongdaemun-gu • **Tel** 927-5546

Ulji-ro CO-OP Residence (S)

A residential block of studios and suites, aimed at mid- to long-term residents. The Ulji-ro CO-OP is one of several CO-OP residences across Seoul: other locations include two more in the Dongdaemun area, one in Omokgyo and one in Samseong (near COEX). Prices and nature of accommodation vary between each residence. The Ulji-ro CO-OP residence's main selling point is its location near the attractions of Dongdaemun. It also boasts kitchen and bathroom facilities.

• **Price range** from KRW 80,000 (single) per night, with discounts according to season. Better rates available for periods of 15 days and above. • **Address** 32 Eulji-ro 6-ga, Jung-gu • **Tel** 2269-8411 • **Website** http://residences.co-op.co.kr

Western CO-OP Residence (S)

Another CO-OP residence in the Dongdaemun area. Ideal for long term stays of several months and for those with generous budgets. More luxurious and expensive than the Ulji-ro CO-OP residence.

• **Price range** KRW 2,472,250 per month–4,364,500 per month • **Address** 77-2 Eulji-ro 5-ga. Jung-gu • **Tel** 2279-4500 • **Website** http://rent.co-op.co.kr

SEODAEMUN AREA

Grand Hilton Seoul

Grand Hilton Seoul ⓗ

Seoul's closest Super Deluxe Hotel to Incheon International Airport. Located outside the city center by a mountain offering fresher air, and connected to downtown areas by a shuttle bus service.
- **Price range** KRW 300,000–3,000,000
- **Address** 201-1 Hongeun-dong, Seodaemun-gu • **Tel** 3216-5656 • **Website** www.grandhiltonseoul.com

Hotel Seokyo ⓗ

Offers rapid access to both Gimpo and Incheon airports. Close to Hongik, Yonsei and Ewha Womans universities, as well as a branch of Hyundai Department Store. Boasts Chinese and Japanese restaurants.
- **Price range** KRW 200,000–245,000
- **Address** 354-5 Seogyo-dong, Mapo-gu
- **Tel** 330-7777
- **Website** www.hotelseokyo.co.kr

Carpe Diem ⓖ

This is a guest house for women only. Its location is ideal for those who want to enjoy the fashionable Hongdae (Hongik University) area in western Seoul, and also is closer to Incheon International Airport than other parts of Seoul. Situated in a modern building, this is a clean hostel with a cozy living room. No credit card payments accepted.

- **Price range** KRW 20,000 (all dorm beds) • **Address** 26 Hansolgil, Mapo-gu
- **Tel** 6497-6648
- **Website** www.carpediemkorea.com

Hongdae (guesthouse) ⓖ

Another guest house in the Hongdae area, just next to Hongik University subway station (Line 2). Opened in 2007, it is on the third floor of a modern building just across the road from the throbbing Hongdae nightlife. Ideal for travelers that want to experience the young and (even more) vibrant side of Seoul.
- **Price range** KRW 21,000 (dorm)– 120,000 (family room) • **Address** 159-6 Donggyo-dong, Mapo-gu • **Tel** 336-0003
- **Website** www.hongdaeguesthouse.com

Kims' Guest House ⓖ

This hostel is located near the Hangang River, as well as being just one subway stop away from the nightlife of Hongdae. Not far away is the unique Seonyu-do Park, a beautiful recreational space on an island in the Hangang that used to be a water treatment plant.
- **Price range** KRW 18,000–80,000
- **Address** 443-16 Hapjeong-dong, Mapo-gu • **Tel** 337-9894
- **Website** www.kimsguesthouse.com

Stay Korea ⓖ

Conveniently situated near the university areas of Hongdae and Sinchon, this hostel is run by a young couple that speaks French, English and Japanese. Free facilities include bicycles.
- **Price range** KRW 19,000 (dorm bed)– 80,000 (four-person room)
- **Address** 566-4 Yeonnam-dong, Mapo-gu • **Tel** 336-9026
- **Website** www.staykorea.co.kr

Yongsan Area

Hotel Capital 🔴

Located in the Itaewon area, this hotel is in a practical location for those needing access to both the north and south of the Hangang River. It also boasts a ginseng spa and indoor swimming pool.

- **Price range** KRW 180,000–500,000
- **Address** 22-76 Itaewon-dong, Yongsan-gu • **Tel** 6399-2000
- **Website** www.hotelcapital.co.kr

Crown Hotel 🔴

Since opening in Itaewon Special Tourism Zone in 1990, the hotel has striven to become a home away from home to all its guests. "Once a guest, always a guest..."

- **Price range** KRW 146,410–360,000
- **Address** 34-69 Itaewon-dong, Yongsan-gu • **Tel** 3676-8000
- **Website** www.hotelcrown.com

Hamilton Hotel 🔴

Plant yourself in the middle of pulsing Itaewon for the most cosmopolitan atmosphere available in Korea. The Hamilton Hotel takes safety particularly seriously and is equipped with CCTV.

- **Price range** KRW 90,000–213,000
- **Address** 119-25 Itaewon-dong, Yongsan-gu • **Tel** 794-0171
- **Website** www.hamilton.co.kr

Hamilton Hotel

Gangnam Area

COEX InterContinental Hotel 🔴

Situated within the Korea World Trade Center complex, offers great access to the various conference centers and exhibition halls nearby.

- **Price range** KRW 310,000–2,800,000
- **Address** 524 Bongeunsaro, Gangnam-gu • **Tel** 3452-2500 • **Website** www.seoul.intercontinental.com

Grand InterContinental Seoul 🔴

Conveniently located near COEX and the Korea City Air Terminal, where luggage can be checked in before taking a limousine bus out to Incheon International Airport.

- **Price range** KRW 260,000–3,340,000
- **Address** 521 Teheran-ro, Gangnam-gu
- **Tel** 555-5656 • **Website** www.seoul.intercontinental.com/

Imperial Palace Hotel 🔴

Aims to provide a unique European ambiance and artistic interior at the heart of Gangnam. It is also home to Imperial Palace Medical Square, with a skincare clinic and dentistry that lets guests go home rested and healthier.

- **Price range** KRW 300,000–4,000,000
- **Address** 313 Eunju-ro, Nonhyeon-dong, Gangnam-gu • **Tel** 3440-8000 • **Website** www.imperialpalace.co.kr

JW Marriot Seoul 🔴

Famed for being home to Asia's biggest spa and fitness club, the hotel is well furnished with Japanese, Chinese, buffet, and grill restaurants to restore the calories you burn off there.

- **Price range** KRW 328,000–3,600,000
- **Address** 19-3 Banpo-dong, Seocho-gu
- **Tel** 6282-6262
- **Website** www.jw-marriott.co.kr

Park Hyatt Hotel

Park Hyatt Hotel 🄷

Opened only on April 15, 2005, the hotel is located near Samseong subway station in one of Seoul's key business districts. Regular deluxe rooms are spacious, boasting natural rock bathroom walls. The 24th-floor lobby offers breathtaking views of Seoul.

- **Price range** KRW 280,000–545,000
- **Address** 995-14 Daechi 3(sam)-dong, Gangnam-gu
- **Tel** 2016-1234
- **Website** http://seoul.park.hyatt.com

Lotte Hotel World 🄷

Located slightly outside the center of Seoul, Lotte Hotel World is adjacent to the huge indoor theme park of Lotte World. If you manage to escape Lotte World, you can regain your sanity in the nearby Olympic Park.

- **Price range** KRW 310,000–2,000,000
- **Address** 40-1 Jamsil-dong, Songpa-gu
- **Tel** 419-7000
- **Website** www.lottehotelworld.com

The Ritz-Carlton, Seoul 🄷

A hotel priding itself on outstanding service and the usual collection of nice dining and fitness facilities. A chance to enjoy marble baths and Frette cotton linens from Italy.

- **Price range** KRW 210,000–4,000,000
- **Address** 602 Yeoksam-dong, Gangnam-gu • **Tel** 3451-8000 • **Website** www.ritzcarltonseoul.com

Novotel Ambassador Doksan, Seoul 🄷

Describing itself as a business hotel, this place has the usual business facilities plus banquet halls, a wedding hall and three meeting rooms. And a bakery and lots of other things.

- **Price range** Available on request; varies according to date and nationality
- **Address** 1030-1 Doksan 4(sa)-dong, Geumcheon-gu • **Tel** 838-1101
- **Website** www.ambatel.com/doksan

Renaissance Seoul Hotel 🄷

Selected by English language daily The Korean Times as Korea's best city hotel in 2000 and best food service in 2001. It is located in Gangnam and includes no less than 10 eating and drinking establishments.

- **Price range** KRW 312,000–4,700,000
- **Address** 676 Yeoksam-dong, Gangnam-gu • **Tel** 555-0501, 556-0601
- **Website** www.renaissanceseoul.com

Hotel Prima 🄷

Situated in the well-heeled Gangnam neighborhood of Cheongdam-dong, this hotel has a museum boasting Korean celadon items and paintings, in addition to the usual range of restaurants and saunas.

- **Price range** KRW 156,000–1,200,000
- **Address** 52-3 Cheongdam-dong, Gangnam-gu • **Tel** 6006-9114
- **Website** www.prima.co.kr

Hotel Riviera 🄷

This establishment sits on top of the popular night club, Club I. The blueberry cheesecake from its bakery is delicious. The hotel is close to COEX and other key Gangnam locations.

- **Price range** KRW 192,000–800,000
- **Address** 53-7 Cheongdam-dong, Gangnam-gu • **Tel** 541-3111
- **Website** www.hotelriviera.co.kr

Ellui Hotel (H1)

Having recently undergone a thorough remodeling, this hotel now boasts brand new facilities for businesspeople and other guests. Its location, on the southern end of Yeongdong Bridge in Gangnam, also offers guests both charming, natural surroundings and easy access to COEX and other key Gangnam venues.

- **Price range:** KRW 160,000–640,000
- **Address:** 129 Cheongdam-dong, Gangnam-gu • **Tel.** 514-3535
- **Website** www.ellui.com

Seoul Palace Hotel (H2)

A hotel that prides itself on offering "personalized" service to suit every guest. Its arcade includes an art gallery, a skin management and a foot health center. Worth viewing are its statues of prancing horses elsewhere on the grounds.

- **Price range** KRW 140,000–330,000
- **Address** 63-1 Banpo-dong, Seocho-gu
- **Tel** 532-5000
- **Website** www.seoulpalace.co.kr

Dynasty Hotel (H2)

A hotel claiming to focus on ensuring convenience for business guests, offering at lower prices a number of business facilities found in larger hotels.

- **Price range** KRW 84,700 • **Address** 202-7 Nonhyeon-dong, Gangnman-gu • **Tel** 540-3373

Hotel Hawaii (H2)

Just reopened after redecoration, this hotel is close to the COEX complex and the usual major Gangnam destinations. Its rooms are reasonably priced, especially for this area of Gangnam.

- **Price range** KRW 70,000–80,000
- **Address** 77-9 Samseong-dong, Gangnam-gu • **Tel** 547-9663~4
- **Website** www.hotelhawaii.co.kr

Hotel Popgreen (H2)

This hotel is located in Gangnam on (or rather just next to) the Apgujeong subway station (Line 3) crossroads, making transport convenient to places both north and south of the Hangang River. It has a café-bakery called Eros & Psyche, which should be enough to tempt anyone.

- **Price range** KRW 126,000–193,600
- **Address** 614-1 Sinsa-dong, Gangnam-gu • **Tel** 544-6623~7
- **Website** www.popgreenhotel.com

Hotel Sunshine (H2)

Located in the Apgujeong/Sinsa-dong area, this business hotel boasts a nightclub, plus sports massage and video arcade facilities. The nearby Rodeo Street area of Apgujeong is crammed with various boutiques, restaurants, cafés and beauty clinics.

- **Price range** KRW 100,000–210,000
- **Address** 587-1 Sinsa-dong, Gangnam-gu • **Tel** 541-1818
- **Website** www.hotelsunshine.co.kr/

Tiffany Tourist Hotel (H2)

This hotel is also located in Gangnam, only minutes away from the World Trade Center, Korea Exhibition Center, ASEM Tower, department stores and fashion shops. Note that room rates increase slightly on days when the hotel is almost full.

- **Price range** KRW 78,000–84,000
- **Address** 132-17 Cheongdam-dong, Gangnam-gu • **Tel** 545-0015
- **Website** www.tiffanyhotel.com

New Olympiana Tourist Hotel (H2)

Boasts a sky lounge and views of the Olympic Park and Peace Gate. Within 15 minutes of both COEX and Lotte Department Store.

- **Price range** KRW 113,000–302,500
- **Address** 44-5 Bangi-Dong, Songpa-Gu
- **Tel** 421-2131~5

The Ritz-Carlton, Seoul Hotel

Samjung Hotel ⒣
A modern hotel located in the heart of Gangnam, with the usual range of restaurants and other facilities.
- **Price range** KRW 170,000–330,000
- **Address** 604-11 Yeoksam-dong, Gangnam-gu • **Tel** 557-1221 • **Website** www.samjunghotel.co.kr

Bali Tourist Hotel ⒣
Recently renovated. 15-minute walk from Seoul's Olympic Park and located in a quiet residential area. Five-minute walk from Dunchon-dong Station (Line 5). Some rooms have computers and Internet access.
- **Price range** KRW 66,000–77,000
- **Address** 417-5 Seongnae-dong, Gangdong-gu • **Tel** 488-5911

Human Starville ⒮
Complexes of studios exclusively for foreigners, available for rent or lease for either long-or short-term stays. With branches in both Yeoksam-dong and Cheongdam-dong. Fully equipped for expatriates with large budgets living south of the Hangang River.
- **Price range** KRW120,000–160,000
- **Address** 5-25 Cheongdam-dong, Gangnam-gu / 606-18 Yeoksam-dong, Gangnam-gu • **Tel** 553-0050 (Yeoksam); 556-0070 (Cheongdam) • **Website** www.humanstarville.com

Oakwood Premier COEX Center ⒮
Another set of serviced residences offering accommodation for periods of one night to several years. Provides a shuttle bus service to key shopping and business locations. Situated near the COEX and World Trade Center complex.
- **Price range** KRW 255,300–
- **Address** 159 Samseong-dong, Gangnam-gu • **Tel** 3466-7000
- **Fax** 3466-7700
- **Website** www.oakwoodpremier.co.kr

Seoul Residence ⒮
This hotel in the Gangnam area is ideally located for access to the COEX complex, the City Air Terminal, Bongeun-sa Temple, LG Arts Center and much more. Stays of just one or two nights are possible, but several weeks or months is the norm. Accordingly, each room is equipped with laundry and cooking facilities.
- **Price range** KRW 110,000–150,000 KRW 3,600,000–4,200,000 (per month)
- **Address** 708-16 Yeoksam-dong, Gangnam-gu • **Tel** 6202-3100 • **Website** www.seoulresidence.co.kr

HANGANG RIVERSIDE + NEAR INTERNATIONAL AIRPORT

Hyatt Regency Incheon H1

This the only super-deluxe hotel in the immediate vicinity of Incheon Airport and is a nice place to eat Sunday brunch. Only three minutes by free shuttle bus from the airport, this is the perfect hotel for people who tend to miss flights.
- **Price range** Available upon request; depends on date of stay • **Address** 2850-1 Unseo-dong, Jung-gu, Incheon Hyatt
- **Tel** 032-745-1234
- **Website** http://hyattregencyincheon.com

Sheraton Grande Walkerhill H1

Offering outstanding views of Mt. Achasan and the Hangang River. First established in 1963, after which continuous renovation has created a truly classy hotel. Two free shuttle buses convey guests to and from central Seoul.
- **Price range** from KRW 200,000
- **Address** 21 Gwangjang-dong, Gwangjin-gu • **Tel** 455-5000
- **Website** www.sheratonwalkerhill.co.kr

W Seoul - Walkerhill H1

Only 15 minutes from the financial heart of Seoul, the W is nonetheless situated in 180 acres of parkland on a mountain overlooking the Hangang River. The hotel's super-elegant design puts it head and shoulders above many other Seoul hotels and makes it unquestionably the place to stay for aesthetes.
- **Price range** KRW 375,000–5,850,000
- **Address** 21 Gwangjang-dong, Gwangjin-gu • **Tel** 465-2222
- **Website** www.wseoul.com

Mayfield Hotel H1

5 minutes from Gimpo Airport and 30 from Incheon International Airport. The ideal hotel for plane spotters, who can observe aircraft from the hotel's European-style garden. The swimming pool has clean artificial sea water.
- **Price range** KRW 300,000–1,300,000
- **Address** 426 Oebalsandong, Gangseo-gu • **Tel** 2660-9000

Best Western Premier Incheon Airport H2

Located close to Incheon International Airport, making it ideal for businessmen.
- **Price range** KRW 120,000–300,000
- **Address** 2850-4 Unseo-dong, Jung-gu, Incheon • **Tel** 032-743-1000
- **Website** www.airporthotel.co.kr

Hotel Dongseoul H2

This is a hotel where the customer becomes a VIP as soon as he or she steps into the lobby.
- **Price range** KRW 100,000–180,000
- **Address** 595 Guui-dong, Gwangjin-gu
- **Tel** 455-1100 (#0)
- **Website** www.idshotel.co.kr

River Park Hotel H2

10 minutes from the Sangam World Cup Stadium and 30 minutes from both Gimpo Airport and Seoul City Hall. Equipped with a sauna and a jacuzzi.
- **Price range** KRW 90,000–162,000
- **Address** 261-4 Yeomchang-dong, Gangseo-gu • **Tel** 3665-3000
- **Website** www.riverpark.co.kr/

Seoul Youth Hostel H2

Located in Yeondeungpo, an industrial area just on the south side of the Hangang River, this city-run hostel provides clean rooms.
- **Price range** KRW 115,000–200,000
- **Address** 10-3 Yeouido-dong, Yeongdeungpo-gu
- **Tel** 782-0121~9
- **Website** www.yoidohotel.co.kr

KOREAN FOOD

Korean food is one of the country's greatest draws. Korean cuisine is made from all-natural ingredients and covers a wide range of tastes and styles. The origins of most Korean foods date back thousands of years, and most dishes are recognized for carrying tangible health benefits.

The foundation for creating delicious Korean dishes is in the use of spices and seasonings, as well as fermentation. The staple Korean ingredients are *gochu*, or red hot peppers, used as a crushed powder and also a fermented red pepper paste called *gochujang*; *doenjang*, a fermented soybean paste with evidence of cancer-preventing properties; *ganjang*, or soy sauce, made through a similar soybean fermentation process with *doenjang*; as well as onions, garlic, scallions, ginger and sesame oil.

Korean restaurants are plentiful throughout the city and generally reasonably priced. There is no tipping at Korean restaurants.

KIMCHI

Kimchi, fermented cabbage seasoned with plentiful garlic and crushed red pepper, is considered the most representative food of the Korean peninsula. It is generally consumed with every meal. There are over 200 types of *kimchi*, depending on the fermentation process and weather. *Kimchi* is considered one of the world's healthiest foods, full of vitamins A, B and C, but most importantly, plentiful in healthy bacteria called lactobacilli, which are found in fermented foods like yogurt. Lactobacilli aid in digestion and prevent yeast infections; the compounds found in the fermented cabbage are even reported to inhibit the growth of cancer.

Korean Banquet Cuisine

Hanjeongsik

Hanjeongsik—often referred to as Korean Table d'hote—is the most lavish of Korean meals, consisting of rice, soup and a dizzying array of tasty side dishes, brought out in stages. How many side dishes—and which side dishes—varies widely (there are currently about 1,500 side dishes in use throughout the country), depending on region, season, restaurant, and price. Traditionally speaking, however, side dishes have varied from three to twelve, depending on social class. The dishes are prepared and arranged by taste and color, which reflect the Asian philosophies of ying and yang and the five primary elements. The Bukchon area and Seoul have a number of restaurants specializing in *hanjeongsik*, but be warned—meals can cost up to 100,000 won per person.

Royal Cuisine

The *surasang* was the dining setting for the king and queen and included only unique ingredients of the finest quality, imported from every province of the country as tribute to the king. Ingredients used in the *surasang* had to pass a quality control test by the royal chefs, and the recipes and cooking methods in the palace were known only to the exclusive palace chefs.

Luckily for modern citizens, anyone can enjoy the tastes of royal cuisine in a restaurant. Unlike a standard Korean meal, where all side dishes are served simultaneously with the main meal, a royal cuisine meal is supposed to come out in different courses and include a set of 12 side dishes.

Temple Cuisine

Korean temple cuisine, a creation of the Buddhist monastics, is very simple and excludes any foods thought to be potentially harmful to monks' health or mental discipline. Temple food avoids tastes that are too spicy or salty, as it is believed that these strong flavors carry with them the threat of overexciting emotions and thus interfering with Buddhist discipline. Temple food does not include meats or fish out of compassion for living beings, and necessary proteins and fats are therefore obtained from grains, beans and soy, nuts, and vegetable proteins. Ideal for vegetarians.

STEWS

- **Kimchi Jjigae:** A tasty *kimchi* stew made with older *kimchi* and slices of pork. This extremely spicy dish is loved by Koreans but can be a bit of a shock for foreign visitors unaccustomed to the sharp, spicy flavor of this stew. Eating it with rice will soften the intensity of the spiciness and make it a bit easier to consume.

- **Doenjang Jjigae:** Another fermented favorite, *doenjang jjigae* is a fermented soybean-paste stew that is considered one of Korea's representative dishes. It often contains dried anchovies and clams, and the special ingredient of *doenjang* is widely touted as having anti-cancer properties.

- **Cheonggukjang:** Somewhat similar to *doenjang jjigae*, but the soybeans are fermented for only two or three days rather than three months. The result is a rich, nutritious stew that's absolutely delicious if you can get past the smell, which has sometimes been likened to a rotting corpse.

- **Budae Jjigae:** Literally, "Army Base Stew," this spicy dish is made from sausages, Spam, beans, instant noodles and rice cakes, among other variations. It dates back to the era after the Korean War, when the ingredients entered Korea via US military bases.

TIPS

DRIVERS' RESTAURANTS

It's said that taxi drivers know where to eat quality food on the cheap. The result are so called *gisa sikdang* (Drivers' Restaurants), establishments that target taxi drivers in particular. These are wonderful places for budget travelers—you get large portions of good food at decent prices. Moreover, unlike most Korean restaurants, nobody will look at you strange for eating alone. The Seongbuk-dong area (see p150) has a number of good *gisa sikdangs*.

- **Sundubu Jjigae:** Handmade soft tofu, stewed in a spicy soup of vegetables and red pepper. A raw egg is often placed in the boiling stew. It's a filling and nutritious dish that has been catching on overseas as well.

- **Gamjatang:** An extremely popular stew, *gamjatang* is a spicy dish created by boiling a pork spine with potatoes and other vegetables. It is most popular during the cold winter months.

- **Samgyetang:** Made by boiling a whole chicken with ginseng, jujubes and garlic, this soup is believed to restore people's energy on hot summer days. It is chockful of quality, healthy ingredients with noted health benefits.

Kimchi Jjigae · Doenjang Jjigae · Samgyetang

- **Seolleongtang:** If spicy dishes aren't your thing, this might do the trick. Seasoned only with salt and spring onions, this soup is made from ox bones that have boiled for an entire day.

- **Kkori Gomtang:** Another hearty stew, this one is made from ox tail bones boiled for hours and beef brisket. If you'd like a break from the spicy dishes, give this dish a try.

- **Jeongol**
  Jeongol differs from *jjigae* primarily in that while the latter is prepared primarily from one ingredient, the former is made from a variety of ingredients. Historically, *jeongol* was eaten by the upper classes, while *jjigae* was eaten by the lower cases. Common *jeongol* dishes include:

  * **Sinseollo:** A rich meat, mushroom and vegetable stew, served in a large silver bowl with a hole in the center where hot embers were placed to heat the dish. The dish is a staple of Korean palace cuisine.
  * **Beoseot Jeongol:** Mushroom stew
  * **Soegogi Jeongol:** Beef stew
  * **Nakji Jeongol:** Octopus stew

- **Haejangguk:** This rich stew is commonly referred to as a "hangover stew," as it is commonly eaten in the wee morning hours after a night of hardcore drinking. The broth is prepared by boiling ox bones over

a long period of time, while the soup itself contains bean sprouts, radish, scallions and cabbage. There are several varieties of *haejangguk*, including *Kongnamulguk* (heavy on the bean sprouts), Ugeojiguk (made with dried Chinese cabbage leaves) and *Seonjiguk*.

  * **Seonji Haejangguk:** A soup made from cabbage, beef broth and other vegetables, it is particularly good to chase a hangover. Some might be turned off by the big globs of coagulated ox blood, though.

- **Chueotang:** This spicy dish—a specialty of southern Korea—is prepared by boiling a mudfish whole—bones and entrails included. The result is a rich stew that is both filing and nutritious.

NOODLES

- **Kalguksu:** The name of this soup literally means "knife-cut noodles." *Kalguksu* consists of handmade knife-cut wheat noodles served in a broth made with anchovies, shellfish and kelp. This dish is most popular during the summertime.

- **Sujebi:** This dish is similar to *Kalguksu*, with the primary difference being that while the latter is made with thick wheat

| Seolleongtang | Haejangguk | Kalguksu |

noodles, the former is prepared with big wheat flakes. It is a dish particularly enjoyed on rainy days.

- **Janchi Guksu:** The noodle dish is literally translated as "Banquet Noodles," as it was traditionally eaten at weddings, birthdays and other festivities (the noodle represents longevity). The thin wheat noodles are prepared in a light broth with green onions and a sauce of soy, sesame oil and chili powder.

- **Mul Naengmyeon:** This icy noodle soup is a refreshing favorite, with thin buckwheat noodles in a sweet and sour meat broth. Served with sliced vegetables, sesame seeds and a boiled egg.

- **Bibim Naengmyeon:** Like its cousin above, this dish consists of iced buckwheat noodles, but served with a spicy red pepper sauce.

- **Kong Guksu:** One of Korea's most unique dishes, this summer specialty consists of wheat noodles in a cold, thick broth made from soybeans.

- **Makguksu:** Another cold noodle dish, this specialty of the mountain town of Chuncheon is similar to *naengmyeon*, but the noodles use more buckwheat, while the dish itself makes more plentiful use of cold vegetables.

- **Ramyeon:** Better known in the West as ramen, instant noodles are ubiquitous in Korea—you'll find stacks of them in just about any shop. Korea's *ramyeon* dishes, however, tend to be a good deal spicier than its Japanese (and Western) counterparts. The spicy Sin Ramyeon is a particularly popular brand.

GRILLED MEATS

- **Galbi:** One of the most popular Korean foods among foreigners, *galbi* is a dish of barbecued, marinated beef ribs. Each restaurant's methods of marinating their *galbi* ribs differs, but this is a dependably delicious dish. Served either on the bone or deboned (*galbi sal*), the meat is cooked on a fire in front of the diner and eaten wrapped in a lettuce leaf. You can usually get either beef or pork ribs, although the former is considerably more expensive.

- **Bulgogi:** Another popular dish among the foreign population, *bulgogi* is another type of barbecued and marinated meat, though thinly sliced in this dish. Generally garnished with sesame seeds and green onions.

- **Dak Galbi:** A specialty of the city of Chuncheon, this popular dish consists of chunks of chicken pan fried in red pepper paste with vegetables, sweet potato and

Janchi Guksu Makguksu Bulgogi

rice cakes. If you like spicy food, you'll love this. After the chicken is consumed, rice is fried up in the remaining sauce.

• **Jjim Dak:** A specialty of the Andong region in southeastern Korea, *jjim dak* ("steamed chicken") is, as the name would suggest, pieces of steamed chicken, served in a sweet sauce with vegetables and cellophane noodles.

• **Samgyeopsal:** Made from unmarinated and unseasoned grilled pork belly, these slices of meat are grilled directly on the diners' table, then dipped in a mixed sauce of sesame oil, ground pepper and salt, and wrapped in a fresh lettuce leaf or sesame leaf with a slice of garlic and mixed *gochujang* (red pepper) and *doenjang* (fermented soy bean) paste.

• **Jokbal:** Marinated pigs feet, deboned and sliced into thin strips and served on a platter. Usually eaten wrapped in a lettuce leaf, often with a condiment of fermented shrimp. Try washing it down with a shot of *soju*. The Jangchung-dong neighborhood is famous for its many *jokbal* restaurants. (see p170)

• **Bossam:** Steamed pork, wrapped in a leaf of lettuce and topped with sweet *kimchi* and a thick paste of fermented soybean and red pepper.

SEAFOOD

• **Maeuntang:** Literally "spicy stew," *maeuntang* is a fish—which fish depends on the restaurant—boiled in a soup prepared with red pepper paste, chili powder and vegetables. This is often served after a dish of sashimi, with the unused parts of the fish boiled up in the soup. Makes a great accompaniment to *soju*.

• **Haemultang:** As the Korean name (meaning "seafood stew") would suggest, *haemultang* is a spicy stew made from various seafood products, including but not limited to crab, shrimp and shellfish.

• **Heamuljjim:** Steamed seafood, including squid, shrimp, clams and mussels.

• **Agujjim:** A spicy dish of bean sprouts and steamed anglerfish, this specialty of southeastern Korea is actually quite nice, even if the fish itself has to be the ugliest sea creature on God's green earth.

• **Nakji Bokkeum:** Commonly known as one of Korea's spiciest dishes, *nakji bokkeum* is prepared from tiny octopuses, chopped up and pan fried with a red pepper paste sauce. After consuming, the leftovers are used to prepare a spicy fried rice.

Jjim Dak　　　　Samgyeopsal　　　　Nakji Bokkeum

• **Sannakji:** Tiny octopuses, sliced up and eaten while the parts are still wiggling about. Be sure to chew well — the octopus parts will fight back, and this can present a choking hazard.

• **Hoe:** Known better in the West by its Japanese name of sashimi, *hoe* is slices of raw fish, served with a dipping sauce of soy sauce and wasabi paste. Red pepper paste mixed with vinegar is often used as a dipping sauce, too. Best enjoyed with a shot of *cheongha*, a rice wine similar to Japanese sake.

• **Chobap:** Referred to as sushi in Japan and the United States, *chobap* is vinegar rice usually topped with a slice of raw fish. A cheaper, non-fish variant is *yubu chobap*: vinegar rice in a pouch of fried tofu.

• **Saengseon Gui:** Grilled fish. Popular fishes to grill include mackerel and cutlass fish.

• **Jangeo Gui:** Grilled marinated eel. This dish is eaten primarily in summer, when it is believed to provide the extra energy boost needed to overcome heat exhaustion.

• **Hongeohoe:** Slices of raw, fermented skate. No, we're not making it up — it's particularly popular in southwestern Korea, and you can find it at seafood restaurants in Seoul. High in ammonia, the meat will clean out your sinuses quick — it's sort of like eating sashimi in a latrine.

RICE DISHES

• **Bibimbap:** This simple yet healthy concoction is another representative Korean dish. It is a mixture that includes rice, an assortment of vegetables, meat, an egg, and red pepper paste. Varients include the *sanchae bibimbap*, prepared with wild mountain vegetables; the *dolsot bibimbap*, which comes in a stone hotpot; and *yangpun bibimbap*, a *bibimbap* for two served in a large bowl.

• **Sotbap:** *Sotbap* is a stone hotpot of rice, usually served with steamed chestnut, jujube, ginkgo nuts and mushrooms. The rice is eaten with soy sauce. After eating the rice, you pour hot water into the hotpot, which turns the leftover rice stuck to the pot into a soup called *nurungji*.

• **Ssambap:** Steamed rice, meat and side dishes, served in a wrap of lettuce and leaf vegetables.

• **Boribap:** A throwback to Korea's less prosperous days, rice and barley are mixed together with vegetables for a hardy meal.

Saengseon Gui   Hongeohoe   Bibimbap

- **Juk:** Rice porridge, *juk* comes in many varieties, including *jeonbokjuk* (abalone porridge), *jatjuk* (pine nut porridge), *hobakjuk* (pumkin porridge), *patjuk* (red bean porridge), *saeujuk* (shrimp porridge) and *yachaejuk* (vegetable porridge).

OTHERS

- **Japchae:** Cellophane noodles, stir fried in sesame oil and served with a variety of vegetables, including sliced carrots, onions and peppers. This dish is commonly found at parties and tends to be popular with foreigners. Chinese restaurants often serve it on a bed of rice as a dish called *japchae-bap*.

- **Gejang:** Fresh, raw crab, marinated in soy sauce or red pepper sauce. This is something of an acquired taste, mostly thanks to the consistency, but is quite nice once you've gotten used to it.

- **Tteokguk:** This rich soup of boiled slices of rice cake is a New Year's Day treat, when it is believed to bring good fortune in the coming year. A popular variant is *tteok manduguk*, in which large *mandu* (Korean meat dumplings) are added.

- **Mandu:** *Mandu*, or Korean dumplings, are a popular cheap meal. Variants include *jjin mandu* (steamed dumplings) and *gun mandu* (fried dumplings). Several different fillings are used, including *kimchi* and meat.

- **Bindae Tteok:** A savory Korean pancake made from ground mung beans. A good place to score these is at Gwangjang Market (see p160).

- **Pajeon:** Another form of Korean pancake, *pajeon* is made from egg, flour and green onions. A variant is *haemul pajeon*, in which seafood like sliced squid is added to the recipe.

- **Dubu Kimchi:** As the name would indicate, this dish consists of slices of *dubu* (tofu) and *kimchi*. It is a popular side dish when drinking.

Patjuk   Gejang   Tteokguk

KOREAN CHINESE FOOD

Just as Chinese food transformed itself when it was brought to the United States to suit American tastes, so it changed to suit Korean tastes when it was brought here. Chinese food in Korea is based primarily on the cuisine of China's Shandong region, the place of origin of the bulk of Korea's ethnic Chinese population.

TIPS

CHINATOWN FOOD

Some of the best Chinese restaurants in Seoul can be found in the small Chinatown in Myeong-dong (see p123). If you're in Incheon, of course, you can score outstanding Chinese fare in the city's famous Chinatown (see p283).

• **Jajangmyeon:** The most popular of Chinese dishes in Korea, *jajangmyeon* is noodles covered in a sweet black bean sauce. Based on the Northern Chinese dish of *zha jiang mian*, this dish was reportedly invented by Incheon's Chinese population.

• **Jjamppong:** A spicy seafood and noodle soup, this dish is based on *champon*, a Chinese dish invented in Meiji-era Nagasaki, Japan, for Chinese students.

• **Bokkeumbap:** Fried rice, often topped with a fried egg.

• **Tangsuyuk:** Sweet and sour pork, not all together different from what you'd get in Chinese restaurants in the West.

STREET FOODS

Seoul is a haven of delicious street foods, purchased from street snack stalls called *pojang macha*. Street food, all selections under 3,000 won each, is conveniently found in virtually any location of Seoul that has a great deal of foot traffic.

• **Gimbap:** *Gimbap* is a favorite fast food of Korean schoolchildren and probably one of Korea's most popular dishes. It can be likened to a vegetarian sushi roll—a seaweed roll filled with rice and slices of fried egg, ham, cucumber, picked radish and other varieties as desired. You can find it everywhere—at convenience stores, Korean "fast food" shops and often streetside stalls. It's served at almost every Korean picnic.

• **Tteokbokki:** *Tteokbokki* is a *pojang macha* staple—a bright red, spicy rice cake dish broiled in a *gochujang* (red pepper) seasoning with vegetables and *odeng* (Japanese-style fish cakes).

• **Odeng:** Japanese fish cakes, usually served on a stick. Great tummy warmer in the winter.

Pajeon · Dubu Kimchi · Jajangmyeon

TIPS

GIMBAP CHEONGUK

Literally, "Gimbap Paradise," this popular chain of restaurants serves up several kinds of *gimbap* along with other simple Korean fare. Great for a cheap meal.

GIM-TTEOK-SOON

Some food stalls sell a set of *gimbap*, *tteokbokki* and *sundae*. This is a good way to sample the three pillars of Korean street cuisine.

• **Sundae:** This Korean-style sausage is stuffed with a mix of viscid rice, ox or pig's blood and potato noodles. This is really quite good, although the additional slices of pork liver and kidneys might put some off. The neighborhood of Sillim-dong (in front of Seoul National University) is famous for its many *sundae* restaurants (see p332).

• **Twigim:** *Twigim* are assorted fried foods, including hard-boiled eggs, sliced vegetables, squid, potato slices, shrimp and more. These delicious items are difficult to resist, especially when the vendor serves them piping hot out of the fryer.

• **Gunmandu:** Fried dumplings are another popular selection off the *pojang macha*.

They come in a range of meat-filled and vegetarian options.

• **Dak-kkochi:** Chicken kebabs, served with a hot sauce.

• **Hotteok:** Sino-Korean pancakes filled with a honey sauce. The good ones are baked without oil.

• **Bungeo-bbang:** Carp-shaped fried bread filled with sweet red bean paste, *bungeo-bbang* is a quick, sweet street snack.

• **Toast:** Yes, the standard piece of toast, although this one is pan fried in butter and served with a fried egg. The Seokbong Toast franchise can be found throughout the city.

• **Bbeongtwigi:** These popped rice disks are a popular snack among those watching their calorie intake. A Korean equivalent to low-fat popcorn.

• **Beondegi:** These are boiled, seasoned silkworm pupae, often served in a paper cup and consumed as a snack. Definitely an acquired taste. This is often cited as Korea's most "bizarre" food, mostly because it is in full public view at streetside food vendors everywhere.

Gimbap · Tteokbokki · Twigim

DESSERTS

- **Hangwa:** Korean confections that come in all shapes, sizes and colors. A popular kind is *yakgwa*, a small fried honey cake. *Hangwa* are commonly served with Korean traditional teas.

- **Yaksik:** Translated as "medicinal food," *yaksik* is steamed steaming glutinous rice mixed with chestnuts, jujubes and pine nuts and sweetened with honey.

- **Tteok:** Made from steamed rice flour, *tteok*—Korean rice cakes—are a staple of Korean dessert cuisine. There are hundreds of kinds of *tteok*, some of which are consumed on holidays and special days. Some of the more popular forms of *tteok* include:
  * **Injeolmi:** Soft clumps of pounded rice cake covered in mugwort or red bean powder.
  * **Sirutteok:** Steamed rice cakes that also come in a wide variety of shapes and colors. A common form is the rainbow-colored *mujigae tteok*, usually served at a baby's first birthday.
  * **Jeolpyeon:** Made from steamed rice powder that has been pounded and cut into shape, *jeolpyeon* are pressed with intricate designs.
  * **Kkultteok:** Rice cakes with honey inside.
  * **Songpyeon:** These half-moon shaped rice cakes filled with nuts or honey are steamed on a bed of pine needles. You'll eat a ton of'em on the Chuseok holiday.

DRINKS

- **Soju:** *Soju* is the most popular alcoholic beverage in Korea. A clear liquor, *soju* is made by distilling fermented rice or sweet potatoes. It is extremely cheap, and therefore ubiquitous in the restaurants and grocery stores of Korea.

- **Makgeolli:** *Makgeolli* has the longest history of all Korea's liquors and is frequently referred to as the "liquor of the common people" because of its popularity among farmers. This liquor, made from fermented sweet rice, has the appearance of milk and a very low alcohol content.

- **Insamju:** A liquor made with *insam* (Korean ginseng), *insamju* is believed to have special medicinal properties. Sometimes sold with a ginseng root visible through the glass bottle, this alcohol makes a popular souvenir.

- **Maesilju:** This liquor is created from plums and is available in grocery stores, although it is commonly made at home. *Maesilju* has a very low alcohol content.

| Yaksik | Songpyeon | Makgeolli |

TIPS

LOCAL FOLK LIQUORS AND SPIRITS

While *soju, makgeolli* and beer might be the potent potables of choice for the masses, Korea does produce a wide range of higher-quality folk liquors and spirits. While most are regional in character, they can often be found outside their home province, too, especially in Seoul.

- **Gyeongju Gyodong Beopju:** Brewed for generations by the Choi family of Gyeongju, this clear, slightly yellow firewater is about 16% alcohol. It has a sweet taste with a full aroma. Price: 32,000 to 35,000 won.

- **Jeonju Leegangju:** Made from pear, ginger, cinnamon, honey and rice, this liquor has an alcohol content of around 22 to 25%. Price: 16,000 to 220,000 won.

- **Andong Soju:** Brewed forever by the Cho family of Andong, this is one of Korea's most famous traditional alcohols. With an alcohol content of 45%, it's got a bit of a kick, and indeed, has been used as a folk medicine. Price: 20,000 to 50,000 won.

- **Munbaeju:** If it was good enough for the South-North Korean Summit of 2000, it's good enough for you. Be careful, though—it has an alcohol content of 40%. Price: 30,000 to 100,000 won.

- **Hansan Sogokju:** Once enjoyed by the Baekje royal family, this specialty of Chungcheongnam-do is famous for its taste and medicinal properties. It's also rather mild with an alcohol content of 18%. Price: 10,000 to 140,000 won.

- **Gochang Bokbunjaju:** A sweet liquor made from raspberries, this drink is said to have anti-aging and anti-cancer effects. Price: 20,000 to 50,000 won.

- **Sikhye:** *Sikhye* is a unique Korean dessert drink created from malt and rice. This sweet drink is said to aid with digestion.

TRADITIONAL TEA

- **Boricha:** Barley tea
- **Oksusucha:** Corn tea
- **Gyeolmyeongjacha:** Senna tora tea
- **Dunggeullecha:** Solomon's Seal tea
- **Hyeonmi Nokcha:** Green tea blended with roasted rice
- **Saenggangcha:** Ginger tea
- **Daechucha:** Jujube tea
- **Yujacha:** Yuja (yuzu) tea
- **Ssanghwacha:** Herbal medicine tea
- **Omijacha:** "Five flavor" tea
- **Sujeonggwa:** Spicy persimmon punch

Sujeonggwa   Omija Punch   Ssanghwacha

DOG MEAT AND BOYANGSIK

As you've no doubt heard—either from late-night talk show comedians or concerned friends and family—Koreans eat dog meat. Well, *some* Koreans eat dog meat—many others see it as a national embarrassment. Since the 1988 Olympics, when dog meat restaurants were banned from using the term *bosintang* (the common name for dog meat soup) out of fear it would make Korea look bad in the eyes of foreigners, dog meat has been a source of heated controversy. Even foreigners have jumped into the fray—French actress and animal rights activist Brigitte Bardot, for instance, attempted to use Korea's hosting of the 2002 World Cup to launch a campaign against dog meat, generating a fierce nationalist counterattack by Korean defenders of the delicacy.

Dog meat—procured from dogs specially raised for human consumption—is most often consumed in a soup called *bosintang* and a heavier stew called *bosinjeongol*. Consumers—usually but not exclusively men—cite its energizing effect in summer and its supposed effect on the male libido. Both the soup and stew make for a rich, hardy meal—the meat is stewed with a generous amount of sesame leaves, onions, garlic and pepper. If you're able to get past the cultural taboo you may or may not have against eating dog, it's really quite delicious.

Interestingly enough, dog meat represents something of an odd legal gray area—it's not legally recognized, but it's not expressly forbidden, either. Supportive politicians have for some time tried to correct this situation by officially legalizing it, but this has run into resistance from animal rights activists and politicians afraid of creating a national embarrassment. Interestingly enough, the ownership of dogs as pets has skyrocketed in recent years, too—nowadays, it seems like everyone has one.

A funny byproduct of the 1988 ban on the use of the term *bosintang* was the proliferation of new names for the dish. Some of these are still in use, including *sacheoltang* ("All Season Soup") and *yeongyangtang* ("Nutritious Soup").

Dog meat is only one of many foods Koreans consume in summer to boost one's stamina during the—sorry for this—dog days of summer. Other energy-boosting dishes include *samgyetang* (chicken and ginseng soup), *otdak* (chicken and lacquer sap stew), *jangeogui* (broiled eel) and *chueotang* (mudfish soup). All these are quite delicious and worth trying, although a word of caution is warranted about the *otdak*—the lacquer sap causes allergic skin rashes and itching in some people. These high-protein dishes are referred to in Korean as *boyangsik*, or "Vitalizing Food."

RECOMMENDED DOG MEAT RESTAURANT

If you're really in the mood for the meat of the dog, Ssarijip near Buam-dong (see p145) is one of Seoul's best places to try *bosintang*. Located in a Korean-style *hanok* home with a wonderful courtyard, the restaurant is packed in the summer, but is still a relaxing place to have a meal. A bowl of *bosintang* will cost you 15,000 won, but a heavier stew, or *jeongol*, is worth the money at 28,000 won. Hours: 11 am to 9:30 pm. (T. 379-9911)

SHOPPING

Seoul is a shopping paradise. From flea markets to designer boutiques, from ancient Oriental medicine stalls to a nine-story mecca of the latest electronic goods, any and every visitor can find what they are looking for in some nook of Seoul.

Some areas of Seoul have housed markets for thousands of years, while others are modern high-rise complexes with vendors bumping elbows selling similar wares. Depending on your price range and the type of goods you seek, a different region of Seoul is appropriate. But whatever you seek, you are sure to find it somewhere—whether it be a marble-tiled department store or a rutted alleyway where goods are sold off a cart.

THINGS TO BUY

- **Clothing:** For quality clothing at budget prices, few places beat Korea. In particular, the sprawling Dongdaemun Market (see p157) is a budget fashion shopper's paradise, home to countless young designers and manufacturers hawking their wares at bargain prices.

- **Shoes:** Shoes—all leather goods—tend to be cheaper in Korea than they are elsewhere. Give Myeong-dong (see p117) a try.

- **Fabrics:** If you're a clothing producer, or just like fabric, Dongdaemun (see p157) is the place to go.

- **Ginseng and Herbal Medicines:** Korea is one of the world's largest exporters of ginseng, the magic root sought after in much of Asia for its rejuvenatory effects. The Gyeongdong Market (see p161) is a great place to pick up ginseng and other herbal medicines.

- **Traditional Liquor:** Korea produces a number of fine traditional firewaters, including *soju, baekseju, yakju* and more.

- **Antiques:** If you've got the money and means to bring it home, you can purchase very nice antique furniture and art. Insa-dong (see p75) and Itaewon (see p201) have a number of good antique shops.

- **Pottery:** Korea has been producing high-quality ceramics for centuries. When Queen Elizabeth II visited Korea in 1999, she purchased pottery in Insa-dong.

- **Cosmetics:** Cosmetics are everywhere in Korea. Faceshop is a popular Korean cosmetics shop. Myeong-dong is a good place to go (see p117).

- **Tea:** Health fanatics will want to buy Korean green tea, produced on plantations in the southern part of the country and on Jeju Island. Korea also produces a number of other traditional teas, including ginseng tea.

Insa-dong is probably the place you want to go, though any supermarket will do.

- **Seaweed:** A favorite of Japanese travelers, you can buy *gim* (dried seaweed) or , which you buy cheaper in Korea than in most other places. Namdaemun Market (see p125) is a good place to purchase *gim*, although you can find it in just about any supermarket.

- **Electronics:** Koreans love their gadgets, and Korea produces some of the world's highest quality consumer electronics. The places to pick up gadgets are the better structured but pricier Techno Mart, and the bustling and cheaper Yongsan Electronics Market (see p211).

MARKETS

Namdaemun Market p126

Namdaemun Market (see p125), named after the famed southern gate, is one of the most famous markets in Seoul. Running all hours of the day, Namdaemun is a traditional market bustling with vendors and goods. The action of Namdaemun begins late, around 11 pm; retailers from all over Korea come to the market during the late night and early morning hours to stock their businesses. The offerings of this market are diverse—a hodge-podge of items including socks, glasses, camera lenses, food, beauty products, shoes and bags. It's a traditional market, so prices are not always listed, and haggling is in order. However, items can generally be bought at very low prices.

> **TIPS**
>
> **SHOPPING ETIQUETTE**
>
> Many markets and street vendor stalls in Seoul do not have displayed prices. It's a good idea to get an idea of price ranges before you venture into the markets, so that you have a general idea of appropriate prices. Shopkeepers vary between quoting a severely inflated price and a lightly inflated one. While you can generally expect to bargain down approximately 10 to 20% from the stated price, the best way of determining the lowest price is simply walking away. Away from the markets, however, most other shops—including department stores—operate on a fixed-price basis. Bargaining will get you nothing but, at best, funny stares.

Though it offers an abundance of goods, this market is manageable in size and can easily be navigated in a reasonable amount of time. It is generally organized into different districts that feature a certain type of product. The largest section of the market is devoted to women's clothing, and many of the complexes in Namdaemun have been seen as standing at the forefront of women's fashion for 30 years.

Other regions of Namdaemun feature glasses, cameras, watches, restaurant wholesale items and accessories.

• **Hours** While Namdaemun is a 24-hour market, some sections of the market close earlier, and others are closed on Sundays. • **Getting There** Hoehyeon Station, Line 4, Exit 7

Dongdaemun Market p158

Dongdaemun Market (see p157) is an overwhelming expanse of retail options. Named after the great east gate, Dongdaemun is one of the largest markets in the world. Approximately 30 shopping centers and 30,000 stores make up this market. While the shopping complexes may look like department stores, inside is a labyrinth of booths and stalls reminiscent of an old bazaar. Many adjacent stalls, if not the entire complex, sell extremely similar goods, which makes comparison shopping and bargaining very easy.

Dongdaemun Market at night

Another appeal of Dongdaemun Market is that it is the site from which approximately 10,000 budding Korean designers strive to make their start. As a result, many unique and innovative pieces by young, unknown designers can be found here, with creations that rival elite design labels.

Dongdaemun also offers the unique Korean experience of the Night Market. The Night Market runs from 8 pm to 5 am, during which time the goods of the market are available at a heavily discounted price for wholesale. Items are generally in the range of 1,000 to 50,000 won, but visitors should not expect attentive service or dressing rooms.

• **Getting There** Dongdaemun Stadium Station, Lines 2, 4 and 5, Exit 1; Dongdaemun Station, Lines 1 and 4, Exits 6 and 7 • **Hours** 24-hour market

Janganpyeong Antiques Market

Organized around 1983, this well-established antique market sells a unique assortment of antique goods, most of which date back from the Joseon era to the time of Japanese colonial rule. The wide range of goods sells for a wide range of prices, from 5,000 won to millions of won. This is a fascinating place to stroll around, and can be a literal treasure hunt—for example, Goryeo-era Buddhist paintings and Joseon era pottery sometimes get found here. If you're in the market for a stone pagoda for your garden, too, you've come to the right place.

• **Getting There** Dapsimni Station, Line 5, Exit 2

Gyeongdong Market D2, p158

Gyeongdong is Seoul's finest and largest traditional herbal market. The market carries the strong aromas of natural herbal remedies. From roots and barks to flowers and fungi, all items possess medicinal properties. (see p161) • **Hours** 9 am to 7 pm, Partially closed on the 1st and 3rd Sundays of each month. • **Getting There** Jegi-dong Station, Line 1, Exit 2

Noryangjin Market p223

This massive covered market is the largest marine market in Korea. In operation for over 80 years, this one-of-a-kind market displays its wares live in aquariums or chilled on beds of ice. From king crabs and shellfish to all types of fish and rays, anything you see you can buy and eat. Sea cucumbers and sea worms are some of the more unusual choices available here. The down-to-earth shopkeepers at Noryangjin are very friendly to foreigners and often offer samples of more unconventional items. • **Hours** Open 24 hours a day • **Getting There** Noryangjin Station, Line 1, Exit 1

Hwanghak-dong Flea Market D3, p158

If you can't find it here, you won't find it anywhere. The 500 shops that make up this sprawling complex sell just about anything used, including antiques, home appliances, clothings, stamps, Buddhas statues or anything else you can imagine. It's not a bad place to pick up old books and videos, too—if you still use videos. The market is usually open 9am to 7pm, although the electronics stores tend to be open until 10pm. (see p162) • **Getting There** Sindang Station, Lines 2 and 6, Exit 2

SHOPPING AREAS

Myeong-dong p118

The Myeong-dong area (see p117) is famous for relatively cheap clothing for women and youth. The streets of Myeong-dong are almost always filled with young crowds of shoppers looking for the latest clothes, shoes, bags, accessories and cosmetics. The area is always bubbling with energy, with street vendors and small shops filling the area. There are also a few shopping complexes in the area specializing in certain types of products.

Migliore, attached to Myeong-dong Station (Line 4), is a high-rise mall filled with hundreds of small fashion stalls. The goods of Migliore are organized by type, with a floor for accessories, a floor for women's sportswear, a floor for shoes, a floor for men's clothing, and so on.

ABC Mart is a shoe superstore with thousands of options, enough to overwhelm the biggest shoe fanatic.

The Myeong-dong branch and flagship store of Lotte Department Store is probably the most famous of Korea's largest department store chain. It's got everything you'd expect in a high-end department store. For real luxury, however, you've got to check out Avenuel, Lotte's luxury goods shop located just next door. Lotte Young Plaza, meanwhile, specializes in fashions for younger shoppers.

At the entrance of Myeong-dong is the grand old edifice of the Shinsegae Department Store, with a massive new wing just behind it. Like the Lotte Department Store, this is upscale shopping at its downtown finest.

• **Lotte Department Store** D2: One of Korea's biggest department store chains, Lotte's flagship store in Myeong-dong is a chock-full of major international brands If you'd like to go even more upscale, Lotte's luxury brand shop, Avenuel, is just next door. Younger shoppers can also check out the nearby Lotte Young Plaza.
  • **Hours** 10:30 am to 8 pm • **Tel** 771-2500

• **Shinsegae Department Store** C4: The historic Shinsegae Department Store has just about everything you'd expect in an upscale department store, including major international labels and luxury brands. • **Hours** 10:30 am to 8 pm • **Tel** 1588-1234

• **Noon Square** D3: Formerly the Avatar mall, Noon Square is full of fashion distributors like Mango, Steve Madden, UGG, Foot Locker and Zara. • **Hours** 11 am to 9:30 pm • **Tel** 3783-5005

• **New Balance** F3: Clothing for the active lifestyle, including sports and exercise apparel and sneakers.
  • **Hours** 10 am to 10 pm • **Tel** 775-6727

• **ABC Mart** F2: The Myeong-dong branch of this major Japanese shoe distributor carries all the major international brands
  • **Hours** 10 am to 10 pm • **Tel** 778-4877

• **Uniqlo** E4: This Tokyo-based casual fashion brand targets younger shoppers. About two-thirds of their customers are teenagers. • **Hours** 11:30 am to 9:30 pm • **Tel** 771-0720

• **Daiso** B4: The Japanese home accessory and living ware giant opened its largest shop in Korea in mid-2009. • **Hours** 10:00 am to 9 pm • **Tel** 752-5776

• **Gap** F4: The Myeong-dong branch of the popular US purveyor of casual fashion.
  • **Hours** 11 am to 10 pm • **Tel** 778-3600

Yongsan Electronics Market p211

The electronics market at Yongsan offers the best deals on electronics items in Seoul. The lowest prices on electronics can generally be found here, but bargaining is essential, and consumers must be cautious because prices are generally not marked. The market is partially closed on the 1st and 3rd Sunday of each month. • **Getting There** Yongsan Station, Line 1, Exit 3

• **Wonhyo Electronics Arcade:** Located in the heart of the market, this arcade is home to some 700 shops specializing in all things electronic, including computers, computer parts and accessories, consumer electronics, lighting and more.
• **Hours** 9 am to 8 pm. Closed Sundays •
Tel 701-6767

• **Seonin Electronics Arcade:** This arcade specializes in computers, laptops and peripheries.
• **Hours** 9 am to 8 pm (weekdays), 9 am to 6 pm (weekends). Closed first and third

Sundays • **Tel** 718-7113

• **Etland (Electronics Land):** The massive Etland is essentially a department store for electronics, including computers, accessories and telecommunication goodies. There's a good DVD shop on the first floor, too, and a cinema.
• **Hours** 10 am to 7:30 pm. Closed every first and third Tuesday • **Tel** 707-4700

• **Dokkaebi Market:** Computer and console gamers will enjoy the two underground markets where they can find the latest in computer and console games. Be sure you're buying games with the correct region code, though.
• **Hours** 10 am to 8 pm. Closed first and third Sunday

• **Space 9:** Technically not part of the Electronics Market but attached by skyway over Yongsan Station, Space 9 is one of Seoul's biggest shopping malls. It's got a great food court and one of the city's best movie theaters.
• **Hours** 10 am to 8 pm. Closed every first and third Tuesday

Technomart

This enormous high-rise just outside Gangbyeon Station (Line 2), built in 1998, is chock-filled with electronics goods. Seven floors of the complex are devoted to electronics, with each floor specializing in a particular type of item, such as camera lenses, computers, stereo equipment, and so forth. The subterranean levels of Technomart offer a food court, a general shopping mall, and a Lotte Mart. The Hangang River Observation Platform at Sky Garden on the 9th floor offers romantic panoramic views of southern Seoul and the Hangang River. The 10th floor houses a CGV theater. • **Hours** Closed the 2nd and 4th Tuesday of each month. • **Getting There** Gangbyeon Station, Line 2, Exits 1 and 2

Apgujeong p248

The Apgujeong area, one of the trendiest neighborhoods in Seoul, has a number of notable shopping districts.

Just outside the Apgujeong subway station is the Hyundai Department Store, with its offering of fine designer items.

Rodeo Street, a few blocks east of the Apgujeong subway station, is across the street from the luxury department store Galleria. Rodeo Street is noted for its collection of small stores featuring mostly imported goods and some Korean designers. It is a generally high priced area, with a very fashionable clientèle.

The Cheongdam area of Apgujeong is the designer shopping district. Displaying the goods of Gucci, Louis Vuitton, Prada and Boss, this shopping area is for those fashion-conscious individuals with deep pockets and expensive tastes.

Garosu-gil is a unique shopping area to the west of Apgujeong Station. This quiet tree-lined street offers many boutique clothing and art stores, as well as an array of unique cafés. A European-style street with a charming atmosphere, it's a wonderful place to spend a Sunday afternoon.

• **Galleria Department Store** E1: This Apgujeong landmark—the West Wing of which is noted for its unique electronic façade—is widely regarded as Seoul's most exclusive department store. If you're looking for the world's top brands, this is a good place to start. The West Wing targets younger shoppers, while the East Wing is for older shoppers looking for more traditional luxury brands. • **Hours** 10:30 am to 8 pm • **Tel** 3449-4114

• **Boon The Shop** E3: This beautifully designed department store sells about 80 high-end brands. It's a good place to view your luxury brands in a refined atmosphere.
• **Hours** 11 am to 8 pm • **Tel** 542-8006

• **Jimmy Choo** E2: One of the biggest names in women's shoes, this is where you get to express your inner "Sex and the City." • **Hours** 11 am to 8 pm. Closed Sundays • **Tel** 3443-4570

• **Maki** D3: This fairy tale-like shop is the proud Korean purveyor of illustrated home items by the Lang Companies of the United States. • **Hours** 10 am to 10 pm. Closed Sundays • **Tel** 541-5972

Ewha Womans University p178

The streets around Ewha Womans University are bursting with small shops specializing in the latest fashions, accessories, and shoes, as well as hair and beauty care, catering to the university's fashion-conscious student body and other fashionistas. Items and beauty services in this area are reasonably priced and at the forefront of current fashion trends.

• **Getting There** Ewha University Station, Line 2, Exit 2

• **Yes apM** D3: Basically one big shopping mall for fashion, with eight floors of shops, restaurants and a lounge area.
 • **Tel** 6373-7000 • **Hours** 10:30 am to 9:30 pm. Closed Tuesdays

• **Nylon** D3: Used, vintage, imported clothing, including brands like Levi's, Patagonia, Dickies, Wrangler and the like.
 • **Hours** 10:30 am to 9:30 pm • **Tel** 364-5477

• **Judy's** D2: This fashion accessory specialty shop is a good place to pick up trendy earrings, necklaces, bracelets, hairpins and other jewelry items.
 • **Hours** 10:30 am to 9:30 pm • **Tel** 364-9885

• **Indonara** D3: This unique shop specializes in piercings, Indian-clothing, bags, henna and other more exotic accessories. • **Hours** 10:30 am to 10:30 pm
 • **Tel** 365-3665

TIPS

LOCAL BRAND SHOPS

It's always good to know some of the local brands—some are purely indigenous, while others are international chains.
• **Convenience Stores:** Family Mart, GS25, By the Way, Mini Stop, 7-Eleven
• **Drugstores:** Olive Young, GS Watsons
• **Cosmetics:** Faceshop, Missha, Skinfood, Etude House, Innisfree, Bodyshop, Nature Republic

Hongik University p184

The area surrounding the arts university offers a wide array of fashion and arts stores. Most notably, the small park just outside the main entrance of Hongik University hosts the unique Hope and Free Markets (see p183). Every Saturday afternoon from about 1 pm to 6 pm, local artists come to sell their one-of-a-kind items in a fun, artsy environment. • **Getting There** Hongik University Station, Line 2, Exit 9

Insa-dong p76

Insa-dong (see p75) offers a special atmosphere absent from other areas of Seoul. With its small stores specializing in traditional Korean arts, visitors get a taste of old Korea. The stone-paved street of Insa-dong is lined with small art galleries exhibiting and selling pieces from some of Seoul's top artists, as well as many small stores vending Korean pottery, antique items, calligraphy brushes, handmade paper called *hanji*, embroidery and myriad tourist trinkets. Insa-dong also offers many unique tea shops and street vendors selling traditional Korean candies. Insa-dong Road is cleared of traffic Saturdays from 2 pm to 10 pm and Sundays from 10 am to 10 pm. • **Getting There** Anguk Station, Line 3, Exit 6

Itaewon p202

Itaewon, adjacent to the Yongsan US military base, caters specifically to Seoul's foreign community. The 1 km shopping strip running through the heart of the region houses a plethora of small specialty stores, offering goods difficult to find in other areas of the city. Custom-tailored shirts and suits, as well as custom-tailored shoes and custom embroidery, are particularly popular offerings of the area, especially for foreign residents who find Korean sizes an awkward fit for their frames. Itaewon (see p207) is also popular for its leather goods, antique furniture, and second-hand items.

Besides these offerings, visitors looking for cheap souvenir goods and T-shirts will likely find what they are looking for in this area. Itaewon is often an especially comfortable shopping district for foreigners because the majority of store owners speak English. However, on the flip side, Itaewon is a favorite foreigner haunt, and so visitors must be wary of highly inflated prices that take advantage of the relative unfamiliarity of non-Koreans with the value of Korean goods. • **Getting There** Itaewon Station, Line 6, Exit 1

• **Hilton** E3: If this custom suit tailor is good enough for Steven Seagal, it's certainly good enough for you. • **Hours** 9 am to 9 pm • **Tel** 792-1196

• **Peter Choi** D3: High-quality handmade leather bags and wallets. If you can wait 10 days, you can have things specially made, too. • **Hours** 9:30 am to 9 pm • **Tel** 798-8734

- **Itaewon Underground Market** C3: Looking to pick up a Dallas Cowboys jersey? Maybe the latest in hip-hop fashion? Stroll around here long enough, and you're likely to find what you're looking for. • **Hours** 8:30 am to 9:30 pm. Closed fourth Tuesday • **Tel** 794-5682

- **Daeboo Antiques** H2: Korean and Asian antique furniture.
- **Hours** 9:30 am to 6:30 pm • **Tel** 797-6787

- **Chosun Antiques** F3: One of the oldest and most reputable antique dealers in the Itaewon area. • **Hours** 9:30 am to 7 pm. Closed Sundays • **Tel** 749-6954

- **Royal Antique** G3: Another venerable Itaewon antique dealer with more Korean furniture than you can shake a stick at, as well as chests from China, Tibet and Mongolia.
- **Hours** 10 am to 6 pm. Closed Mondays • **Tel** 797-8637

- **Morning Calm** F3: This shop has a wide range of Korean, Asian and Western antiques.
- **Tel** 790-2420 • **Hours** 9 am to 7 pm. Closed Mondays

COEX p254

An enormous underground mall, COEX is a maze of shopping options including many Western brands—from electronics to clothing, accessories, sports equipment and apparel. COEX has a fantastic Bandi and Lundi's bookstore, as well as an impressive record store. Also, whenever visitors feel weary from shopping, they can choose from hundreds of dining options to reenergize their weary bodies.

- **Hours** 10 am to 10 pm. • **Getting There** Samseong Station, Line 2, Exit 6 • **Website** www.coexmall.com

- **Bandi & Luni's** C4: The COEX branch of this bookshop chain has a large foreign-language book section and is a pleasant place to browse.
- **Hours** 9:30 am to 10:30 pm • **Tel** 6002-6002

Filipino Market A1, p158

Each Sunday, Seoul's thriving Filipino community gathers at the Hyehwa Roundabout to socialize and buy Filipino CDs and DVDs, phone cards and second-hand cell phones. Visitors should come to the market to feel the energy and pulse of one of Seoul's largest immigrant populations, as well as to sample delicious authentic Filipino dishes such as longaniza sausage, banana spring rolls, cassava cakes, adobo chicken and pancit noodles.

- **Hours** 9 am to 5 pm • **Getting There** Hyehwa Station, Line 4, Exit 1

BASIC KOREAN

As in any foreign country, any and all efforts to speak the local language—Korean, in this case—are highly appreciated and may sometimes be necessary.

Hangeul* is a phonetic writing system created in 1446 by the revered King Sejong the Great* (see next page). The alphabet is comprised of 14 consonants and 10 vowels, and each consonant mimics the placement of the tongue and lips when the sound is created.

The Romanization of *hangeul* varies depending on which system is used, although the Korean government released the Revised Romanization system in 2000 as the official Korean language Romanization system. Revised Romanization does not include any non-alphabetic symbols, which simplifies and standardizes Romanization of Korean.

Koreans place a great deal of emphasis on respect and social hierarchy, and the Korean language reflects this. Korean includes different levels of speech, depending on the relationship between the speaker and listener, their level of familiarity with one another, the setting, and the age difference. The phrases listed on the following pages use the honorific from of speech.

Statue of King Sejong the Great, Deoksugung Palace

KING SEJONG THE GREAT AND THE HANGEUL ALPHABET

Ask a Korean who Korea's greatest king was, and he or she is almost certain to answer "King Sejong the Great." This remarkable 15th century monarch—one of only two Korean kings to earn the appellation "the Great"—was one of the most enlightened rulers of his age, a scholar-king whose interests extended far beyond politics into science and culture.

King Sejong, who ruled from 1418 to 1450, was the fourth king of the Joseon era. The third son of the energetic King Taejong, he proved an excellent student and managed to win his father's favor. He was fortunate enough, too, to have elder brothers who, far from feeling threatened, actually conspired to have him put on the throne—both got themselves banished from the court, with one becoming a wandering traveler while the other became a Buddhist monk.

Upon assuming the throne, Sejong put his leadership skills to immediate work, launching military campaigns against Japanese pirates to the south and Manchurian raiders to the north. A tremendous patron of the sciences, he oversaw the development of a number of key publications and technologies, including agricultural handbooks, weather instruments (including the world's first rain gauge) and a water clock.

King Sejong's greatest accomplishment, however, was overseeing the creation of Korea's ingenious indigenous writing system, the *hangeul* alphabet. Prior to the creation of the alphabet, Chinese characters were used for written communication, which limited literacy to only a small, educated elite. Since Korean is completely different from Chinese in terms of its grammar, this also posed difficulties in properly putting the language to paper. To rectify this, the king put together a committee to create a scientific but easy-to-learn alphabet that could better express the sounds of the Korean language. The result, promulgated in 1446, was a 28-letter alphabet— consonants were designed to reflect the position of the lips, tongue and throat during pronunciation, while the vowels reflected Korea's traditional yin-yang cosmology. Originally called the Hunminjeongeum ("Proper Sounds for the Instruction of the People"), the alphabet is today known—at least in South Korea—as *hangeul*, or "Korean letters."

Conservative aristocrats were not immediately impressed. Yet as time passed, the use of the alphabet flourished, and in 1894, it was adopted for use in official documents. In 1896, the first *hangeul* newspaper was published. The current alphabet and spelling rules were largely finalized in 1933, although North and South Korea would carry out separate smaller reforms: the latest South Korean spelling reform was promulgated in 1988.

Today's *hangeul* alphabet has 24 letters—14 consonants and 10 vowels. When it was first promulgated in 1446, the accompanying explanatory guide said a smart man could learn it in a morning, while even a dumb man could pick it up in 10 days. This is probably about right—the alphabet is so simple, you can pick it up with relatively little effort. And for travelers, it IS worth putting in the time to learn—you'll be able to recognize place names, menu items and other pieces of helpful information.

USEFUL EXPRESSIONS

Greetings

Hello.	Annyeong hasimnikka / Annyeong haseyo. 안녕하십니까? / 안녕하세요.	
Goodbye.	Annyeonghi gaseyo (if the listener is leaving) / Annyeonghi gyeseyo (if the listener is staying). 안녕히 가세요 / 안녕히 계세요.	
What's your name?	Ireumi moeyo? 이름이 뭐에요?	
My name is...	Je ireumeun ...imnida. 제 이름은 ...입니다.	
Where are you from?	Eodieseo osheosseumnikka? 어디에서 오셨습니까?	
I'm from...	Jeoneun _____-eseo wasseoyo. 저는 ____에서 왔어요.	
Nice to meet you.	Mannaseo bangap seumnida. 만나서 반갑습니다.	

Basic Terms

Yes.	Ne/Ye.	네/예.
No.	Ahniyo.	아니요.
Please... (always attached to the end of a request)	...Haejuseyo.	...해주세요.
Thank you.	Gamsa hamnida.	감사합니다.
You're welcome.	Cheonmaneyo.	천만에요.
Excuse me.	Sillye hamnida.	실례합니다.
Sorry.	Jwoesong hamnida.	죄송합니다.

How to Ask for Direction

Excuse me.	Sillye hamnida.	실례합니다.
Where is...?	...eodie isseoyo?	...어디에 있어요?
I'm looking for a...	...reul/eul chatgo isseoyo.	...를/을 찾고있어요.

Question Words

Who?	Nugu seyo?	누구세요?
What is this?	Igeo moyeyo?	이게 뭐예요?
When?	Eonjeyo?	언제요?
Where?	Eodieyo?	어디에요?
How?	Eotteokeyo?	어떻게요?

How much is this?
Igeo eolma eyo?
이거 얼마에요?

Please lower the price.
Jogeum kkakka juseyo.
조금 깎아주세요.

That's too expensive.
Neomu bissayo.
너무 비싸요.

Please give me one.
Hana juseyo.
하나주세요.

Please give me a different one.
Dareun geo hana juseyo.
다른 거 하나 주세요.

Do you have any other colors?
Dareun saekkal iseu saeyo?
다른 색깔 있으세요?

Please give me a larger size.
Deo keun saijeu juseyo.
더 큰 사이즈 주세요.

Please give me a smaller size.
Deo jageun saijeu juseyo.
더 작은 사이즈 주세요.

Please give me a receipt.
Yeongsujung juseyo.
영수증 주세요.

Numbers and Shopping

Two numerical systems are used in Korea—Sino-Korean, or numbers based on Chinese characters, and native Korean. The two number systems are used in different situations. For example, Sino-Korean numerals are used when counting money, while native Korean numbers are used for telling a person's age.

	Sino-Korean		Native Korean	
0	영/공	young / gong	–	–
1	일	il	하나	hana
2	이	i	둘	dul
3	삼	sam	셋	set
4	사	sa	넷	net
5	오	oh	다섯	daseot
6	육	yuk	여섯	yeoseot
7	칠	chil	일곱	ilgop
8	팔	pal	여덟	yeodeol
9	구	gu	아홉	ahop
10	십	ship	열	yeol
11	십일	shib-il	열 하나	yeol hana
12	십이	shib-i	열 둘	yeol dul
13	십삼	ship-sam	열 셋	yeol set
14	십사	ship-sa	열 넷	yeol net
15	십오	shib-oh	열 다섯	yeol daseot
16	십육	shimnyuk	열 여섯	yeol yeoseot
17	십칠	ship-chil	열 일곱	yeol ilgop
18	십팔	ship-pal	열 여덟	yeol yeodeol
19	십구	ship-gu	열 아홉	yeol ahop
20	이십	i-ship	스물	seumul
30	삼십	sam-ship	서른	seoreun
40	사십	sa-ship	마흔	maheun
50	오십	oh-ship	쉰	swin
60	육십	yuk-ship	예순	yesun
70	칠십	chil-ship	일흔	ilheun
80	팔십	pal-ship	여든	yeodeun
90	구십	gu-ship	아흔	aheun
100	백	baek	온	on
1,000	천	cheon	즈믄	jeumeun
10,000	만	man	드먼	deumeon
100,000,000	억	eok	잘	jal

Accommodations

I'm looking for a ....

... chatgo isseoyo. ... 찾고 있어요.

- guesthouse / yeogwan 여관
- hotel / hotel 호텔
- youth hostel / yuseu hoseutel 유스호스텔

Do you have any rooms available?

jigeum bang isseoyo? 지금 방 있어요?

I'd like a...

...juseyo. ... 주세요.

- bed / chimdae 침대
- shared room / gachi sseuneun bang 같이 쓰는 방
- Western-style room / chimdae bang 침대 방
- Korean-style room / ondol bang 온돌 방
- room with a bathroom / yoksil itneun bang 욕실 있는 방

How much is it...?

... eolmayeyo? ... 얼마예요?

- per night / harut bam 하룻밤
- per person / han saram 한 사람

Days of the Week

- Sunday   iryoil   일요일
- Tuesday   hwayoil   화요일
- Thursday   mogyoil   목요일
- Saturday   toyoil   토요일
- Monday   weoryoil   월요일
- Wednesday   suyoil   수요일
- Friday   geumyoil   금요일

Directions

- North   bukjjok   북쪽
- East   dongjjok   동쪽
- Left   woenjjok   왼쪽
- South   namjjok   남쪽
- West   seojjok   서쪽
- Right   oreunjjok 오른쪽

When Driving Or Giving Directions, Use These Terms

- Go straight   jikjin   직진
- Turn left   jwahoejeon   좌회전
- Turn right   uhoejeon   우회전

Transportation

Please take me to...

... gajuseyo.   ... 가주세요.

How can I get to...?

...e eotteoge gayo?   ...에 어떻게 가요?

What time does the ... leave/arrive?

... eonjae tteonayo/dochakhaeyo?

... 언제 떠나요/도착해요?

- airport bus   gonghang beoseu 공항 버스
- ferry boat   yeogaekseon   여객선
- bus   beoseu   버스
- city bus   sinae beoseu   시내 버스
- train   gicha   기차
- subway   jihacheol   지하철

I want to go to...

...e gago sipseumnida.   ...에 가고 싶습니다.

- the first / cheot 첫
- the last / majimak 마지막
- bus station / beoseu jeongnyujang 버스정류장
- subway station / jihacheol yeok 지하철역
- train station / gicha yeok 기차역
- ticket vending machine / pyo japangi 표 자판기
- timetable / siganpyo 시간표

Food

- breakfast   achim   아침
- dinner   jeonyeok   저녁
- eat   meogeoyo   먹어요

- lunch   jeomsim   점심
- snack   gansik   간식
- drink   masyeoyo   마셔요

Can you recommend a...?

..chucheon hae jusillaeyo?   ...추천 해 주실래요?

- bar/pub   sul jip   술 집
- café   kkapae/keopisyop   까페/커피숍
- restaurant   sikdang   식당

Ordering Food

I would like ___, please.

____ juseyo.   ____ 주세요.

Please give me more water.

Mul deo juseyo.   물 더 주세요.

Please ring up the bill.

Gyesan hae juseyo.   계산 해주세요.

Emergencies

Help!   Dowa juseyo!   도와주세요!

I'm lost.   Gireul ireoss eoyo.   길을 잃었어요.

Leave me alone!   Jom naebeoryeo duseyo!   좀 내버려 두세요!

Call...!   ...bulleo juseyo!   ...불러 주세요!

- a doctor / uisa 의사
- the police / gyeongchal 경찰
- an ambulance / gugeupcha 구급차

LANGUAGE PROGRAMS

Opportunities for learning Korean are numerous in the country. The most rigorous programs are offered by the universities, which have 5-day-a-week programs with a policy requiring attendance in order to advance to the next level. Programs of varying intensities exist, however, including evening classes and weekend classes.

University Classes

University classes are the most intensive and usually the most effective, but are also the most rigorous and time-consuming. Sogang University is recognized for its strong emphasis on spoken Korean. The Yonsei, Seoul National University, and Ewha University programs are well-known and extremely popular. They tend to emphasize written Korean, but build a strong base for learning the Korean language.

- **Sogang University:** Korean Language Education Center
- Tel 705-8088 • Website http://klec.sogang.ac.kr
- **Yonsei University:** Korea Language Institute
- Tel 2123-8550 • Website www.yskli.com
- **Seoul National University:** Korean Language Education Center
- Tel 880-5483 • Website http://lei.snu.ac.kr
- **Ewha Womans University:** Ewha Language Center
- Tel 3277-3682~3 • Website http://elc.ewha.ac.kr

Private Language Academies

Private academies are also available for learning Korean. Language academies are significantly cheaper than university programs, and tend to be much more flexible. However, the quality of instruction varies widely between academies, so be sure to observe a class before enrolling.

Free Language Programs

Free Korean language classes are available from a few civic organizations and volunteer groups, particularly for people in the migrant worker population.

- **Korean Foundation Cultural Center:** Classes are offered once a week on either Monday, Wednesday or Friday from 4 to 6 pm or 7 to 9 pm.
- Tel 2046-8500 • Website www.kfcenter.or.kr
- **Seoul Global Center:** Classes meet twice a week.
- Tel 2075-4130 • Website http://global.seoul.go.kr

PERFORMING ARTS

KOREAN PERFORMING ARTS

Music

Like most societies, Korea has a long musical tradition, best represented by so-called *gugak* ("national music"). In recent years, however, it's popular music of Western forms such as rock, pop and hip-hop that is dominating the airways. And not just Korea's airways, mind you—Korean pop music is gaining followers in China, Taiwan, Japan and other Asian markets.

Gugak

Gugak ("National Music"), or Korean traditional music, is quite diverse and includes both vocal and instrumental music. Some forms of *gugak* are derived from Chinese musical forms, while others are native Korean forms.

Broadly speaking, Korean traditional music can be divided into court music, chamber music and folk music. *Aak* (court music) was the music that accompanied the important royal rites of the Joseon era. This is rarely performed today except by specialized organs such as the National Center for the Korean Traditional Performing Arts or at rare events like the Jongmyo Jerye. *Jeongak* (chamber music) was the music that accompanied aristocratic banquets and parties. Folk music, meanwhile, were folk songs and other musical forms for the masses.

With the introduction of Western musical forms, Korean traditional music has suffered from general lack of interest, but it has nevertheless survived. Korean traditional musicians have also been experimenting, breaking from set musical forms to create new works. Some musicians, meanwhile, are merging Korean and Western form to create "fusion" music (see p426 for *gugak* and *pansori* venues).

KOREAN TRADITIONAL MUSICAL INSTRUMENTS

- **Gayageum**: A 12-string zither, frequently used as both a solo instrument and as accompaniment for vocal pieces.
- **Geomungo**: A 6-string zither.
- **Daegeum**: A bamboo transverse flute with a beautiful, breathy tone.
- **Piri**: A double-reed wind instrument that sounds similar to an oboe.
- **Haegeum**: A Korean fiddle with silk strings.

Pansori

Thanks in large part to director Im Kwon-taek's 1993 classic film "Sopyonje," the Korean art of lyrical storytelling known as *pansori* has become one of Korea's best known traditional performing arts.

Often compared to the blues tradition of the United States, *pansori* is an extremely soulful way of singing. It involves a single vocalist accompanied by a drummer. The singer carries a folding fan to punctuate movements and announce scene changes. The *pansori* repertoire initially consisted of 12 tales, but only five remain today. The five include some of Korea's best loved folk tales, including the beautiful love story of Chunhyang and the moving tale of filial piety, Simcheong.

It's said that to be a real *pansori* master, you need to first embody the feeling of *han*, a sense of bitterness and loss that many Koreans will tell you is a uniquely Korean emotion. By all means, watch "Sopyonje" to get a better understanding of both *pansori* and *han*.

Pop Music

Korean pop music's history goes back to the 1930s, when Korean singers began performing Japanese musical forms—so-called "trot" music, similar to Japanese *enka* music, has its roots in this period. After independence, US pop music began infiltrating the country through the many US military bases around the country. Some of the early names in Korean pop, for instance, learned their craft in the clubs in front of US bases.

Since the 1990s, the most popular forms of music in Korea have included rap, pop, R&B, hip-hop and rock. In recent years, boy and girl bands have grown popular. A couple of big names are:

- **Rain:** Born Jeong Ji-hoon, Rain has been dazzling crowds with his smooth dancing and R&B tunes. He's also moved into acting, appearing in Hollywood films such as "Speed Racer" and "Ninja Assassin."

- **BoA:** This female singer, influenced by American hip hop and R&B, is actually even more popular in Japan than she is in Korea. Trained for stardom from a young age, she has used her language skills—she speaks Korean, Japanese, English and some Chinese—to good use in winning fans throughout Asia. She has recently attempted to break into the US music industry by her debut English album, BoA.

Dance

Koreans are a dancing people. Dance was traditionally used in both palace ceremonies and by the common people as a way of satirizing the nation's social elites. It also featured prominently in shaman ceremonies. Nowadays, it's mostly done for fun, although Korea has also produced a number of noted ballerinas, choreographers and modern dancers. Most notably, Korean crews have featured prominently in the world of B-boying, better known to those who grew up in the 1980s as breakdancing.

Traditional Dance

- **Court Dance:** Korean court dances, traditionally performed at state functions in the Joseon era, were divided into two forms, Chinese-derived dances and natively developed ones. These dances were often performed by large numbers of specially trained dancers. Since the end of the monarchy, these dances are rarely performed, although specialized organs like the National Center for the Korean Traditional Performing Arts keep the tradition alive.

- **Folk Dances:** Korean folk dances, traditionally performed by farmers, Buddhist monks, shamans and other non-royal types, were performed for various social and religious functions. Some, like the *talchum* ("mask dance"), also served as a means of expression, a way for the masses to criticize the corruption and absurdities of the Joseon kingdom's political and social elites. Some popular folk dances include:

KOREAN TRADITIONAL DANCES

Seungmu: ("Monk Dance"): Reportedly developed by Buddhist monks, this dance was further developed by Korea's *gisaeng*, or female entertainers. Performed in long, flowing robes, it is considered one of the most beautiful of Korean dances.

Taepyeongmu ("Great Peace Dance"): The origin of this dance for peace is unknown, but it was developed into a folk dance in the early 20th century. It is performed by dancers wearing attire similar to that of Korea's kings and queens.

Talchum ("Mask Dance"): As the name would suggest, this dance was performed while wearing masks. The masks represent different social figures—corrupt aristocrats, lecherous monks, etc. These dances were performed by commoners to lampoon Korea's high-handed aristocracy. The Andong International Mask Dance Festival, held in the southeastern city of Andong every autumn, is probably the best time to see this form of dance.

Ganggangsullae: Traditionally performed by a circle of *hanbok*-clad women for the Chuseok holiday, this dance was offered as a prayer for a good harvest.

Buchaechum: ("Fan Dance"): Despite being a relatively modern creation, this dance—a development on earlier shaman and court dances—is one of the more commonly performed dances at traditional folk dance shows. The dancers use their fans to create images of flowers, butterflies and more.

* Places to see Korean traditional dance include the National Gugak Center (see p426) and Chongdong Theater (see p426).

Modern Dance

Western dance forms first came to Korea during the colonial period. Today, modern dance and ballet have healthy followings in Korea, while Korean dancers like Stuttgart Ballet principal dancer Kang Sue Jin bring their talents to a global audience.

• **B-Boy:** While its roots may be found in the streets and clubs of the South Bronx of the 1970s, B-boying a.k.a. Breakdancing has developed a huge following in Korea. Performed by small groups, or crews, this acrobatic form of dancing can be quite exhilarating to watch. In recent years, Korean B-boy crews have done

exceptionally well in international competitions. B-boy is an important element in a number of Korean non-verbal performances, too, including "B-boy Korea," "Sachoom," "Battle B-boy," "Ballerina who loves B-boy" and more.

VENUES

Seoul is home to countless venues of the performing arts, both large and small.
Major venues like the Sejong Center for the Performing Arts and Seoul Arts
Center often host big-name international artists as well as top Korean ones, while
smaller venues like those in the Daehangno theater district are good places to see
emerging talent. The National Center for the Korean Traditional Performing Arts
and Namsan Gugakdang, meanwhile, are some of Korea's top venues for Korean
traditional music and dance. A number of non-verbal performances have opened
their own theaters as well.

Large Performing Arts Complexes

Sejong Center for the Performing Arts B3, p38
One of the iconic buildings lining the central boulevard of Sejong-no opposite
Gwanghwamun Square, the Sejong Center is one of Seoul's key performing arts
venues. See p105. • **Getting There** Gwanghwamun Station, Line 5, Exit 1, City Hall station,
Line 1, Exit 3 and Gyeongbokgung station, Line 3, Exit 6 & 7 • **Tel** 399-1111 • **Website** www.
sejongpac.or.kr/english

Seoul Arts Center A4, p254
A huge arts complex in the south
of Seoul, regularly attracting the
very best artists from Korea and
abroad. See p255. • **Getting There**
Nambu Bus Terminal Station, Line 3,
Exit 5 • **Tel** 580-1300 • **Website**
www.sac.or.kr

LG Arts Center B3, p254
This modern performance venue
is equipped with state-of-the-art
acoustics and located in
Gangnam, one of Seoul's most
thriving business districts. See
p257.
• **Getting There** Yeoksam Station,
Line 2, Exit 7 • **Tel** 2005-0114
• **Website** www.lgart.com

National Theater of Korea B4, p158

The home of Korean theater occupies a beautiful site on the flank of Mt. Namsan. See p164. • **Getting There** Dongguk University, Line 3, Exit 6 • **Tel** 2280-4114 • **Website** www.ntok.go.kr

Seongnam Arts Center

Located in the Seoul suburb of Seongnam, this complex is one of the country's most important venues of the performing arts, complete with an opera house, concert hall and ensemble theater. It hosts regular performances by top Korean and international artists. • **Getting There** Imae Station, Bundang Line, Exit 1 • **Tel** 031-783-8000 • **Website** www.snart.or.kr

Uijeongbu Arts Center

Located just north of Seoul in the satellite city of Uijeongbu, this performing arts venue has a main theater with over 1,000 seats. In Spring, it is home to the Uijeongbu International Music Theater Festival, which draws both local and international acts. • **Getting There** Uijeongbu Station, Line 1. Walk in the direction of City Hall. • **Tel** 031 828-5841 • **Website** www.uac.or.kr

Goyang Aram Nuri Arts Complex

Located in the Seoul suburb of Goyang, this massive arts complex is one of Korea's most modern. Houses within its confines are an opera house, concert hall, digital theater and outdoor theater. Like Korea's other major art centers, it hosts performances by many renowned Korean and overseas artists. • **Getting There** Jeongbalsan Station, Line 3, Exit 3 • **Tel** 031-960-0180 • **Website** www.artgy.or.kr

Concert Halls

Hoam Art Hall B4, p38

Opened in 1985, the Hoam Art Hall has been one of the top performing arts venues north of the Hangang River. It hosts a variety of different performances, but with a special emphasis on classical music. • **Getting There** City Hall Station, Line 1 and 2, Exit 9 • **Tel** 751-9607~10 • **Website** www.hoamarthall.org

Kumho Art Hall B3, p38

The Kumho Art Hall near Gwanghwamun is the performing arts venue of the Kumho Asiana Cultural Foundation, one of Korea's most generous benefactors of the arts. In addition to classical performances of all kinds, it is also home to the prestigious Kumho Art Hall Chamber Music Society. • **Getting There** Gwanghwamun Station, Line 5, Exit 7 • **Tel** 6303-7700 • **Website** www.kumhoarthall.com

KEPCO Art Center

This performing arts complex in the Seocho-gu neighborhood south of the river has been hosting high-quality performances since 2001, particularly musicals and classical music. • **Getting There** Yangjae Station, Line 3, Exit 1 • **Tel** 2105-8133 • **Website** cyber.kepco.co.kr/artcenter/main/main.jsp

Olleh Square C3, p38

The Olleh Square in Gwanghwamun is all about jazz. Performances are held every evening. And tickets are insanely inexpensive at only 1,000 won (with proceeds going to charity). There's a gallery and cafe, too. • **Getting There** Gwanghwamun Station, Line 5, Exit 2 • **Tel** 1577-5599 • **Website** www.ollehsquare.kt.com

Doosan Art Center A2, p158

Located in Jongno, the Doosan Art Center—which opened in 2007—has a musical stage, a gallery and a space for arts development that can host anything from film to theater and dance. Performances here are free of charge. • **Getting There** Jongno 5-ga, Line 1 • **Tel** 708-5003 • **Website** www.doosanartcenter.com

AX-Korea

Located in Gwangjin-gu in eastern Seoul, the oddly named AX-Korea is Korea's first performing arts venue dedicated to pop music, and has the lighting and stage effects appropriate for the job. • **Getting There** Gwangnaru Station, Line 5, Exit 2 • **Tel** 457-5114 • **Website** www.ax-korea.com

KT&G Sangsang Madang F3, p185

Operated by KT&G, the eye-catching Sangsang Madang is an arts venue and incubation space in the indie Hongdae neighborhood. It is home to an independent film theater, stage, studio, art square, arts academy, art market and more. • **Getting There** Exit 5 of Hongik Univ. Station, Line 2 • **Tel** 330-6200 • **Website** www.SangsangMadang.com

Theaters

Daehangno Theaters A1, p158

The Daehangno area is home to about 40 small theaters, where visitors can find both veteran and emerging actors playing their trade. The Hakjeon Blue Theater,

Dongsoong Art Center, Batangol Art Center, Comedy Art Hall and Madang Sesil Theater are just a few of the names. The area is particularly alive in summer during the Seoul Performing Arts Festival (www.spaf21.com). Since most of the performances are in Korean and translations are rarely provided, you may wish to bring someone who can translate for you. • **Getting There** Hyehwa Station, Line 4

Arko Arts Theater A1, p158

Part of the Arko arts complex run by the Arts Council Korea in Daehangno, this prominent theater, which opened in 1981, has both large and small theaters that host a variety of theater, music and dance events. And it's at the heart of Daehangno's theater district, home to countless small theaters. Outdoor performances can often be enjoyed nearby, too. See p167.
• **Getting There** Hyehwa Station, Line 4, Exit 2 • **Tel** 760-4877 • **Website** http://artstheater.arko.or.kr/eng

63 Art Hall p224

Housed in the landmark 63 Building in Seoul's "Manhattan" of Yeouido, the 63 Art Hall is probably best known for its IMAX Theater, but it also hosts other performing arts events as well, including an open run of the non-verbal performance, "Fanta-Stick" Tickets for the IMAX theater cost 8,000 won, "Fanta-Stick" costs 50,000 won. • **Getting There** Yeouinaru Station, Line 5, Exit 4 • **Tel** 789-5663 • **Website** www.63.co.kr

Korean Traditional Performing Arts

National Gugak Center A4, p254
This is the mother of all venues when it comes to Korean's traditional genres, including theater, folk music, classical music and much more. See p257.

Seoul Namsan Traditional Theater p316
Located in Namsangol Hanok Village on Mt. Namsan, Namsan Gugakdang is one of Korea's newer performing arts venues, having opened in 2008. This beautiful Korean traditional *hanok* complex, operated by the Sejong Center of Performing Arts, hosts regular performances of Korean traditional dance and music. See p318.

Korea House p316
Operated by the Korea Cultural Heritage Foundation, this beautiful complex of Korean traditional structures at the foot of Mt. Namsan serves as a cultural center and restaurant. See p319.

Chongdong Theater B4, p38
This theater enjoys a prime position in the historical neighborhood of Jeong-dong and is devoted to traditional performing genres. See p98.

Gwanghwamun Art Hall A3, p38
This new performance venue in Gwanghwamun hosts PAN, the creation of Samulnori developer Kim Duk-soo. PAN includes a number of folk performances associated with village festivities, including Korean traditional drumming, *samulnori* (see p99), *pansori*, mask dance and more. Definitely not to be missed. Performances are at 8pm (Wed to Fri) and 2 pm (weekends & holidays). Tickets range from 30,000 to 50,000 won. • **Getting There** Gyeongbokgung Station, Line 3, Exit 1 • **Tel** 722-3416 • **Website** www.ghmarthall.co.kr

Gyeonggi Arts Center
Right next to Korean Folk Village in Yongin, the Gyeonggi Korean Traditional Music Center is one of Korea's largest venues for Korean traditional music. It hosts both regular and special performances. • **Getting There** Bus No. 37 from in front of Suwon Station, Line 1 • **Tel** 031-289-6400 • **Website** www.ggad.or.kr

Non-Verbal Performances

Nanta Theater B4, p38 / E3, p119 / D3, p248

Only the strongest of structures could withstand the constant vibrations of hyperactive, vegecidal percussion show Nanta. See p98. • **Website** http://nanta.i-pmc. co.kr • **Tel** 739-8288

IBK Jump Theater D4, p76

Another venue dedicated to a single show: the spectacular martial arts comedy Jump. See p84. • **Getting There** Jonggak Station, Line 1, Exit 4 • **Tel** 722-3995 • **Website** www.hijump.co.kr

The B-Boy Theater C2, p184

This theater presents an open run of the wildly popular nonverbal performance "Battle B-Boy." This unique performance combines street B-boy dancing with Korean traditional dance and hip hop music with East Asian music, for an engaging nonverbal performance that appeals to audience members of all ages. This performance's transport of street dancing to the stage has been an enormous success, in large part because of its open audience-engaging style that energizes all who watch it. Tickets are 50,000 won each. See p186. • **Getting There** Hongik University Station, Line 2, Exit 9 • **Tel** 323-5233 • **Website** www.sjbboys.com

Sachoom Theater D3, p76

"Sachoom," which premiered in 2004, is another non-verbal performance, this one expressing itself in the medium of dance. A coming-of-age story of three friends, it incorporates a variety of different dance styles, including modern, traditional, tango and jazz. It was a big hit at the 2008 Edinburgh Festival Fringe. Since 2008, it has made its home at its own theater near Insa-dong. Tickets range from 25,000 to 50,000 won. See p83.• **Getting There** Jongno 3-ga Station, Line 1, 3 and 5, Exit 5 • **Tel** 3676-7616 • **Website** www.sachoom.com

Myungbo Art Hall D4, p38

This performing arts venue in the Eulji-ro neighborhood plays host to many exciting performances such as the all-female percussion theme performance "Drum Cat" and the family performance "Bubble World." • **Getting There** A one minute walk from Exit 8 of Eulji-ro 3-ga Station, Lines 2 and 3 • **Tel** 2274-2121 • **Website** www.myungbo.com

MUSEUMS & GALLERIES

Seoul has a bewildering variety of museums large and small, public and private. They range from the mammoth National Museum of Korea, probably the largest museum in Asia, to smaller, quirkier gems tucked away in unexpected places. Galleries, meanwhile, are also to be found in abundance, exhibiting all forms of art in buildings that are often architectural specimens themselves. Here are just a few of the city's many museums and galleries.

HISTORY MUSEUMS

If there's one thing that Korea has a lot of, it's history. From the arrival of the nation's earliest mythical progenitor in 2333 BC to the kaleidoscopic sequence of upheavals in the late 19th and 20th centuries, at least one museum in Seoul will have events covered.

National Museum of Korea p211

The largest storehouse of artifacts representing Korean history and culture, the National Museum of Korea recently relocated to a new facility in 2005. This new site makes the National Museum the sixth largest museum in the world and the largest in Asia. The museum's collection includes approximately 150,000 artifacts, 5,000 pieces of which comprise the permanent exhibit. There are six permanent exhibition galleries: an Archaeological Gallery, a Historical Gallery, two Fine Arts Galleries, an Asian Arts Gallery, and a Donation Gallery. There is also a Children's Museum, which is a hands-on archaeological museum where children can see and touch replicas of cultural relics housed in the National Museum. Guided tours of the museum are available multiple times daily in

Korean, English, Chinese, Japanese and sign language. See p209.

• **Hours** 9 am to 6 pm (Tue, Thur, Fri), 9 am to 9 pm (Wed, Sat), 9 am to 7 pm (Sun, holidays) • **Admission** Free; special exhibitions ticketed separately. • **Getting There** Ichon Station, Line 4 or Jungang Line, Exit 2 • **Tel** 2077-9045~7 • **Website** www.museum.go.kr

National Palace Museum of Korea B3, p38

Occupying the buildings on the grounds of the Gyeongbokgung Palace that formerly held the National Museum of Korea, this museum's large collection of royal artifacts from the Joseon era offers a fascinating glimpse into the lives of the country's monarchs and their courts. See p44.

• **Hours** 9 am to 6 pm (weekdays), 9 am to 7 pm (weekends) Ticket sales stop one hour to closing. Closed Mondays • **Admission** As of the writing of this book, free. However, the museum plans to introduce ticketing at a yet-to-be-decided date. • **Getting There** Gyeongbokgung Station, Line 3, Exit 5; Gwanghwamun Station, Line 5, Exit 1 • **Tel** 3701-7500 • **Website** www.gogung.go.kr

National Folk Museum of Korea C2, p38

The place to go for those interested in the evolution of the lives of Korean people since prehistoric times. You can often catch folk performances here, too. See p44.

• **Hours** 9 am to 6 pm (Mar to Oct), 9 am to 5 pm (Nov to Feb), 9 am to 7 pm (Sat, Sun, holidays). Ticket sales stop one hour to closing. Closed Tuesdays • **Admission** As of the writing of this book, free. However, the museum plans to introduce ticketing at a yet-to-be-decided date. • **Getting There** Gyeongbokgung Station, Line 3, Exit 5; Anguk Station, Line 3, Exit 1 • **Tel** 3074-3114 • **Website** www.nfm.go.kr

The War Memorial of Korea p211

A huge complex of indoor and outdoor exhibition halls, offering a better understanding of the conflict that left such huge scars on the Korean peninsula in the early 1950s. See p210.

• **Hours** 9 am to 6 pm. Ticket sales stop one hour to closing. Closed Mondays • **Admission** Free • **Getting There** Samgakji Station, Line 4 or 6, Exit 12 • **Tel** 709-3139 • **Website** www.warmemo.or.kr

Seoul Museum of History B3, p38

The place to go for those who want to know the stories that lie behind and beneath today's metropolis. See p105.

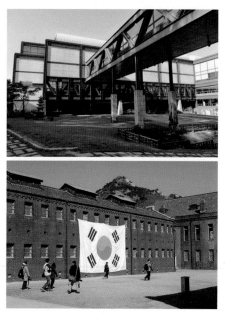

• **Hours** Weekdays 9 am to 9 pm; Weekends & holidays 9 am to 7 pm (Mar to Oct), 9 am to 6 pm (Nov to Feb) • **Admission** Free • **Getting There** Gwanghwamun Station, Line 5, Exit 7 • **Tel** 724-0274 • **Website** http://museum.seoul.kr

Seodaemun Prison History Hall A3, p38

Constructed during the Japanese occupation of Korea, Seodaemun Prison was used to imprison, torture and execute Korean nationalist patriots. The prison is generally well preserved and is a moving monument documenting the history of the Korean independence movement and the exemplary individuals who made incredible sacrifices in the name of Korean nationalism. See p189.

• **Hours** 9:30 am to 6 pm (Mar to Oct), 9:30 am to 5 pm (Nov to Feb). Closed Mondays • **Admission** Adults 1,500 won, Children 500 won • **Getting There** Dongnimmun Station, Line 3, Exits 4 & 5 • **Tel** 360-8582

Independence Hall of Korea

Located about an hour outside of town in the city of Cheonan, Independence Hall aims to educate visitors about the history of the Korean independence movement during the Japanese colonial period. The exhibit focuses on enriching understanding of the patriotism of Koreans throughout history, particularly during the Japanese occupation. Independence Hall also includes a Reunification Monument, a Patriots Memorial and a Circle Vision Theater with a 360-degree screen. See p295.

• **Hours** 9:30 am to 6 pm (Mar to Oct), 9:30 am to 5 pm (Nov to Feb). Ticket sales stop one hour to closing. Closed Mondays • **Admission** Free • **Getting There** From Cheonan Express Bus Terminal, take a bus (No. 400) to Independence Hall (about 30 minutes); From Cheonan Train Station, take a bus (No. 400) to Independence Hall (about 20 minutes). • **Tel** (041) 560-0114 • **Website** www.independence.or.kr

ART MUSEUMS & GALLERIES

Seoul is a city with a vibrant arts culture. Besides a number of nationally sponsored museums, the city is replete with boutique galleries and art collections.

Seoul Museum of Art B4, p38

Housed in the former Korean Supreme Court Building, SeMA is a contemporary art museum that functions as an important cultural space in the city of Seoul. This museum makes a concerted effort to combine pieces that exemplify current trends in Korean contemporary art with the work of foreign artists who represent the work of modern art abroad. See p93.

• **Hours** Weekdays 10 am to 8 pm; Weekends and holidays 10 am to 7 pm (Mar to Oct), 10 am to 6 pm (Nov to Feb). Closed Mondays
• **Admission** Free • **Getting There** City Hall Station, Line 1, Exit 1 or Line 2, Exit 11 or 12
• **Tel** 2124-8800 • **Website** http://seoulmoa.seoul.go.kr

National Museum of Contemporary Art, Korea

The National Museum of Contemporary Art showcases both Korean and international contemporary modern art, with the aim of educating citizens and cultivating a culturally rich atmosphere in Seoul. Established in 1969, the museum rapidly expanded to accommodate increasing interest and moved to its present location in 1986. Visitors can trace the development of modern Korean art, particularly in the genres of painting, sculpture and crafts. See p263.

• **Hours** Weekdays 10 am to 6 pm (Mar to Oct), 10 am to 5 pm (Nov to Feb); Weekends 10 am to 9 pm (Mar to Oct), 10 am to 8 pm (Nov to Feb). Closed Mondays • **Admission** Permanent Exhibition Free; Special Exhibitions 3,000 won. 4th Saturday of each month free.
• **Getting There** Seoul Grand Park Station, Line 4, Exit 4. Take shuttle bus (arrives every 20-30 min). • **Tel** 2188-6000 • **Website** www.moca.go.kr

National Museum of Contemporary Art—Deoksugung B4, p38

The National Museum of Contemporary Art was once housed in this space at Deoksugung before the collection expanded and was relocated to its present location. After the move, this space was transformed into the National Museum of Art, serving as an annex space. Many special exhibitions are hosted here. • **Hours** 10 am to 9 pm. Closed Mondays • **Admission** Depends on exhibition • **Getting There** City Hall Station, Line 1, Exit 2 or Line 2, Exit 12, or a 20-minute walk from Exit 1, 2 or 3 • **Tel** 2022-0600

Seoul Calligraphy Art Museum—Seoul Arts Center A1, p254

The world's only museum dedicated to calligraphy alone, offering education in calligraphy and traditional paintings, as well as exhibitions. See p255. • **Hours** 11 am to 8 pm (Mar to Oct), 11 am to 7 pm (Nov to Feb) • **Admission** Depends on exhibition • **Getting There** Nambu Bus Terminal Station, Line 3, Exit 5. Walk for 5-10 minutes. • **Tel** 580-1651 • **Website** www.sac.or.kr

CALLIGRAPHY

Like in other parts of Confucian East Asia, calligraphy has been a highly respected art form in Korea. Using nothing more than a brush, paper, ink and an inkstone, the calligrapher—who must train for decades— seeks balance and beauty in his work. Calligraphers have traditionally used only Chinese characters for their work, although recently, some Korean calligraphers and designers are experimenting with Korean *hangeul* letters as a basis of calligraphy.

Gana Art Center p148

An architectural gem of a gallery situated in the beautiful mountainside neighborhood of Pyeongchang-dong. See p148. • **Hours** 10 am to 7 pm • **Admission** 3,000 won • **Getting There** Take green bus 1020 or 1711 from Exit 3, Gyeongbokgung Station, Line 3 • **Tel** 720-1020 • **Website** www.ganaart.com

Insa-dong

Insa-dong, the traditional arts and crafts center of Seoul, is home to many small art galleries. Art galleries began to settle in the area in the 1970s and now number around 70. Galleries display the work of both professional traditional artists, whose creations are considered intangible cultural assets, and amateur artists. All works can be purchased for personal collections. See the list of galleries in Insa-dong chapter. See p80 for the list of Insa-dong galleries.

CERAMICS

Koreans have been producing cermaics since the neolithic age. The Golden Age of Korean ceramics, however, was the Goryeo (918-1392) and Joseon (1392-1910) eras, when Korean pottery grew famous throughout Asia. Goryeo artisans were particularly renowned for their jade-colored celadon (*cheongja*) masterpieces, while Joseon potters were known for their white porcelain (*baekja*). So well-respected were Korean ceramic artisans that they were highly valued war booty—during the Japanese invasions of the late 16th century, Korean potters were often dragged away to Japan, where they contributed significantly to Japan's ceramics industry—so much so, in fact, that in Japan, the invasions are sometimes referred to as the "Pottery War."

Korean pottery, naturally enough, has been influenced by religious and cultural trends within society—Joseon ceramics, for instance, are white and simply adorned, a reflection of the rustic simplicity favored by the era's Confucian elites. Even today, Korean potters favor a simple, naturalistic aesthetic you can see at the many pottery shops of Insa-dong.

Korean traditional wood-burning kilns can still be found aplenty in countryside towns just outside of Seoul like Icheon (see p299), Gwangju and Yeoju. The pottery villages of Icheon, in particular, are good places to pick up quality ceramics at reasonable prices.

KOREAN PAINTING

Traditionally, Korean painting has been influenced greatly by Chinese artistic forms and Buddhism. In a country as scenically beautiful as Korea, perhaps it's no surprise that landscape paintings were a particular favorite of Korean painters, especially so-called *sansuhwa*, or "Mountains and Water Paintings." Buddhist temples, meanwhile, are home to countless treasures of Buddhist iconography, including brilliantly colored hanging screens and wall murals. In the 18th century, great painters like Kim Hong-do and Sin Yun-bok focused their brushes on depicting the daily lives of Koreans, both aristocrats and commoners, often to great comedic effect. Separate from the highly rarefied paintings preferred by the upper class, the common folk have traditionally enjoyed so-called folk paintings. Folk paintings were typically produced by unknown artists for practical purposes, including simple decoration and to ward off evil spirits. These paintings often use animals such as the tiger, mountain spirits or Confucian

A folk painting from Gahoe Museum (see p70)

symbols as popular motifs. In the modern era, Korean painters have by and large moved away from Eastern painting styles and adopted Western styles, although some continue to plug away at Korean styles or combine Korean and Western styles.

Bukchon

The Bukchon area, a neighborhood of traditional Korean residential homes, has a culturally rich and authentic aura, which makes it an ideal site for art galleries. This unique area is home to a number of traditional and contemporary art galleries, most of them art boutiques. See p69 for the list of Bukchon galleries.

Hakgojae Gallery A3, p64

A gallery by the western wall of the Gyeongbokgung Palace that works on the principle of creating the new by understanding the old. The building itself is divided between traditional and modern styles. See p73. • **Hours** Weekdays 9:30 am to 7 pm, Weekends 10 am to 6pm (Mar to Nov); Mon to Sat 10 am to 6 pm (Dec to Feb). Closed Mondays • **Admission** Free • **Getting There** Anguk Station, Line 3, Exit 1 • **Tel** 720-1524 • **Website** www.hakgojae.com

Museum of Korean Embroidery B2, p254

This small museum provides a glimpse into the world of the feminine craft of traditional Korean embroidery. On display are approximately 3,000 items, from patchwork wrapping cloths and boxes to screens, shoes and thimbles. While there are no English descriptions posted within the exhibit, illustrated books on Korean embroidery are available for purchase. • **Hours** 10 am to 4 pm. Closed Weekends & public holidays • **Admission** Free • **Getting There** Hakdong Station, Line 7, Exit 10 • **Tel** 515-5114 • **Website** www.bojagii.com

FESTIVALS

SEOUL

In recent years, Seoul has grown increasingly keen on hosting festivals, both as a means of building community spirit and, of course, to bring in the tourists. Two highlights of the year are the Hi Seoul Festival, when the entire downtown area becomes one big street party, and the Lotus Lantern Festival, a popular Buddhist celebration and parade most famous for its beautiful floats and lanterns. The regions around Seoul, too, have their own interesting festivals that may interest the visitor.

Hi Seoul Festival Spring
The Hi Seoul Festival, held annually in spring, is one of the biggest bashes of Seoul's social calendar. First convened in 2003, the week-long festival—organized by the Seoul Foundation for Arts and Culture—aims to bring Seoul's residents together to celebrate the city's culture and history and build a stronger sense of community. The festival program includes cultural performances, parades, charity events, international food festivals and more, although the specifics depend on the festival theme, which changes annually. Most of the festival events are held in the old downtown area, particular at Seoul Plaza in front of Seoul City Hall. • **Admission** Free • **Tel** 3290-7000 • **Website** www.hiseoulfest.org

Unhyeongung Festival April, October
On the third or fourth Saturdays of April and October, the wedding ceremony between King Gojong (see p91) and Queen Myeongseong (see p45) is reenacted in this festival, held twice each year on the spot where the marriage actually took place.
• **Place** Unhyeongung Palace • **Getting There**: Anguk Station, Line 3, Exit 4 • **Tel**: 766-9090 • **Website** www.unhyeongung.or.kr

Lotus Lantern Festival May

One of the most highly anticipated celebrations of the year because of its cultural authenticity, this annual celebration takes place around the time of Buddha's

birthday, which falls on the 8th day of the 4th lunar month. At the festival, visitors can create their own lotus lanterns, watch Buddhist performances, experience Buddhist culture and view exhibits of traditional lanterns. The culminating event of the festival occurs on the Sunday evening before Buddha's birthday, when a massive lotus lantern parade of over 100,000 lanterns takes place on Jongno Street running from Dongdaemun Stadium to Jogyesa Temple. The beautiful sight of thousands of paper lanterns winding down the street to Jogyesa Temple is not to be missed. • **Time** Week of Buddha's Birthday (8th day of 4th lunar month) • **Admission** Free • **Getting There** Jonggak Station, Line 1, Exit 2; Anguk Station, Line 3, Exit 6 • **Tel** 2011-1744

Insa Korean Art and Culture Festival May or June

Going strong for two decades, the Insa Korean Art and Culture Festival celebrates Insa-dong's heritage as a center of the Korean traditional arts and crafts. There are street performances, historical reenactments, singing, dancing and more.
• **Place** Insa-dong • **Getting There** Jonggak Station, Line 1, Exit 3

Dano Festival Late May or Early June

In traditional Korea, Dano—held on the fifth day of the fifth lunar month—was one of Korea's most important holidays. In the modern era, its importance has waned, but nobody's told Namsangol Hanok Village this. Participants can try Korean traditional wrestling, wash their hair with water infused with iris, swing on a Korean traditional swing and experience other Dano traditions. • **Place** Namsangol Hanok Village • **Getting There** Chungmuro Subway Station, Line 3 or 4, Exit 3 or 4

Seoul Fringe Festival August

Like its progenitor, the Edinburgh Fringe Festival, the Seoul Fringe Festival is a celebration of non-mainstream and mostly youth-oriented arts, including theater, painting, music and street performances. Not surprisingly, it's held in the Hongik University area, the heart of Seoul's indie culture. Artistic troupes from all over Asia attend. • Place Hongik University Area • Getting There Hongik University Station, Line 2, Exit 9 • Tel 325-8150 • Website www.seoulfringe.net

Chungmuro Film Festival August to September

An outdoor international film festival, the Chungmuro Film Festival features classic works and current trends in the modern film industry. The festival, which draws about 700,000 visitors a year, includes outdoor film screenings, a domestic film competition, a master class, and seminars and workshops. • Place: Film theaters in the Chungmu-ro area. • Tel 2236-6231-4 • Website www.chiffs.kr

Seoul Drum Festival September

This highly anticipated percussion festival features a series of performances by Korean and international drum artists. Visitors are introduced to traditional Korean percussion music as well as the percussion ensembles of various international artists. • Place Ttukseom Seoul Forest • Tel 757-2122 • Website www.seouldrum.go.kr

Seoul International Dance Festival October

The Seoul International Dance Festival, also known as SIDance, began in 1998 with the purpose of promoting Korean dance in the international arena. This notable festival features Korea's leading contemporary dance performers, as well as an array of invited international modern dance groups and collaborative performances. • **Place**: Performing art venues throughout Seoul • **Tel:** 3216-1185 • **Website:** www.sidance.org

Seoul Herbal Medicine Festival October

Held at the sprawling Jegi-dong Herbal Medicine Market, this is a great opportunity for visitors to learn about Korea's herbal medicine heritage. Herbalists perform free medical examines, and expensive herbal medicines can often be had at affordable prices. • **Place** Jegi-dong Herbal Medicine Market • **Getting There** Jegi-dong Station, Line 1

Seoul Performing Arts Festival October to November

This annual performing arts festival showcases the latest theater, dance and fusion pieces in the contemporary performing arts world. Performers hail from all over the world, and the festival includes some collaborative pieces between Korean artists and international artists. This festival, the largest performing arts festival in Korea, always proves itself to be at the cutting edge of modern performing arts. • **Place** Daehangno Theater District • **Tel** 3673-2561 • **Website** www.spaf.or.kr

OUTSIDE SEOUL

Boryeong Mud Festival July

An annual event since 1997, the Boryeong Mud Festival is an enormously popular gathering that draws about two million visitors each year. For ten days, visitors come to Daecheon Beach to enjoy about 200 tons of mud. Activities include a giant mud pool, a mud photography contest, mud body painting, mud *ssireum* (Korean wrestling), mud soccer, and the Super Mud Slide—a 44-m-long, 12-m-high inflatable slide. Additionally, visitors can enjoy street parades and performances and meet celebrity guests. The event is sponsored by a cosmetics company that creates its products out of Boryeong mud, which contains a healthy level of infrared rays that revitalize the skin. • **Place** Daecheon Beach, Chungcheongbuk-do • **Getting There** Trains for Boryeong Station leave from Yongsan Station. Trip takes about 2 hours, 40 minutes • **Tel** (041) 930-3882 • **Website** www.mudfestival.or.kr

Puchon International Fantastic Film Festival July

This unique independent film festival distinguishes itself from traditional film festivals by focusing on works of a more imaginative and futuristic bent. Films featured in this festival come from the genres of fantasy, science fiction, horror, thriller and adventure, as well as animations. • **Place** Bucheon • **Getting There** Songnae Station, Line 1. Exit the station in the North Square direction, from where you can take a shuttle bus or embark on a 15-minute walk to Boksagol Cultural Center • **Tel** (032) 327-6313 • **Website** www.pifan.com

Pentaport Rock Festival Last Weekend of July

The Pentaport Rock Festival is one of the largest live music events in Korea. It features many genres of music, but particularly focuses on rock and electronic styles. The festival aims to cultivate an open environment for collective music appreciation and environmental consciousness. • **Place** Songdo, Incheon • **Admission** 88,000/132,000/165,000 won for 1-, 2-, 3-day tickets • **Getting There** Dongmak Station, Incheon Subway. Take a shuttle bus to venue. • **Website** www.pentaportrock.com

Korean Traditional Performing Arts Festival September

The Korean Traditional Performing Arts Festival showcases Korea's numerous traditional performing arts in different genres, including *madanggeuk* (outdoor theater), shadow theater, dance musicals, *minyo* (traditional Korean folk song) musicals, percussion music and mime. Many of Korea's greatest cultural figures, considered intangible cultural assets, participate in this festival. • **Place** National Museum of Korea • **Getting There** Ichon Station, Line 4 and Jungang Line, Exit 2 • **Tel** 580-3265 • **Website** www.openpan.com

Chungju World Martial Arts Festival Late September or Early October

Hosted by the city of Chungju, newly declared home of the ancient Korean martial art of *taekkyeon*, this festival celebrates martial arts. It includes demonstrations of different martial arts from around the world, boasting participation from over 30 international martial arts groups annually. • **Place** Chungju, Chungcheongbuk-do • **Getting There** Buses leave for Chungju from Seoul's Dong Seoul Terminal. Trip takes about 1 hour, 40 minutes. • **Tel** (043) 850-7981 • **Website** www. martialarts.or.kr

Busan International Film Festival October

One of the most influential film festivals in all of Asia, the Busan Film Festival focuses primarily on Asian films. However, works are screened from all over the world, allowing visitors to gain a comprehensive understanding of international trends in the film industry. Films are screened simultaneously in multiple theaters, as well as on a giant outdoor screen in Suyeongman Bay. • **Getting There** It takes three hours to get from Seoul to Busan by KTX express train. Frequent trains to Busan depart from Seoul Station. • **Tel** (051) 747-3010 • **Website** www.biff.kr

NIGHTLIFE &
ENTERTAINMENT

Like big cities all over the world, Seoul has plenty of places to express your nocturnal you. Drinking is something of a national pastime, so if you're looking to get blotto, you'll find no shortage of establishments in which to do so. If you want to give your liver a break, however, there are plenty of other places to go and things to do, too, including Korean traditional teashops, dance clubs and discos, spas and saunas, movie theaters, karaoke clubs and all-night PC cafes.

TRADITIONAL TEASHOPS

One place you really must try during your visit to Seoul is a Korean traditional teashop. The artsy Insa-dong area (see p111) is home to several good ones, although one of the most charming—the old hanok home of Suyeon Sanbang—is located in Seongbuk-dong (see p150). Traditional teashops usually serve a range of green teas, as well as a colorful assortment of herbal and medicinal teas.
See p394 for a list of commonly served Korean traditional teas.

Insa-dong's Dawon teashop

Recommended Teashops

INSA-DONG p76

Sin Yetchatjip A2: This wonderfully atmospheric *hanok* teashop, hidden away in an Insa-dong back alley, serves all sorts of wonderful teas. Extremely cozy. Just don't be surprised by the parrot that greets you at the entrance. • **Hours** 10 am to 10pm • **Tel** 732-5257

Yetchatjip C2: Also located in an Insa-dong back alley, this two-story teahouse is an Insa-dong institution. You'll love the small bird flying about the second floor and the fish bowls used as tables. • **Hours** 10 am to 10 pm • **Tel** 722-5332

Insa-dong Teahouse B2: Situated on Insa-dong's main road, the relaxing garden area of this teahouse is hidden by an unassuming entrance. A lovely spot to have a cup of tea. • **Hours** 10 am to 10 pm • **Tel** 723-4909

Dawon C2: In the garden of Kyungin Museum of Fine Art, you'll find Dawon, a *hanok* teahouse with a large outdoor courtyard. Very colorful in spring, when the cherry blossoms bloom. • **Hours** 10:30 am to 10:30 pm • **Tel** (02) 730-6305

Gwicheon B2: Run by the wife of late poet Cheon Sang-byeong, Gwicheon is a favorite stop of Seoul's literary crowd. Oh yeah, and they serve high-quality tea, too.
• **Hours** noon to 10 pm • **Tel** 3210-2288

Dalsaeneun Dalman Saenggak Handa B2: Owned and operated by renowned poet Ryu Si-hwa, this Insa-dong teahouse—whose name means "The Moon Bird Thinks Only of the Moon"—serves fine tea in an absolutely charming atmosphere. • **Hours** 10 am to 11 pm • **Tel** 720-6229

SAMCHEONG-DONG/ BUKCHON p64

Cha Masineun Tteul C2: With a pleasant location on a hill behind Jeongdok Public Library, Cha Masineun Tteul —literally, "A Garden Where People Drink Tea"—is a picturesque *hanok* teahouse with plate glass windows that provide relaxing views of the surrounding neighborhood. • **Hours** 11 am to 10:30 pm • **Tel** 722-7006

SEONGBUK-DONG p138

Suyeon Sanbang C2: Suyeon Sanbang is a lovingly preserved *hanok* teahouse that was once the home of novelist Yi Tae-jun, one of the fathers of modern Korean literature. Yi defected to North Korea in 1946, but his descendants still run the shop. Surrounded by a Korean clay and tile wall, the teahouse is a remarkably beautiful and soothing place, complete with a Korean-style garden. The *daechucha* (Korean jujube tea) is the house specialty, but any of the teas on the menu is well worth the money.
• **Hours** 11:30 to 10:30 pm (10 pm on weekends) • **Tel** 764-1736

Suyeon Sanbang

CAFÉS

Coffee was first brought to Korean shores in the late 19th century by European diplomats. It made an immediate impression with Emperor Gojong, who liked the beverage so much he had a Western-style gazebo built in Deoksugung Palace where he could enjoy a cup of java in serenity.

A little over a century later, coffee is all over the place, from streetside vending machines to posh Apgujeong-dong cafés. In fact, you can't walk five minutes in Seoul without encountering a coffee shop or café of some sort. At last check, there were 194 branches of the popular US coffeehouse chain Starbucks in Seoul, and fellow US competitor The Coffee Bean and Tea Leaf has a strong presence, too. Not to be outdone, Koreans have established their own Starbucks-like coffeehouse chains, including Hollys Coffee, Tom N Toms Coffee and Angel-in-us Coffee. Mindeulle Yeongto, a more culturally-oriented coffeehouse chain, is particularly popular with university students.

Of course, if you'd like to avoid the chains, there are plenty of cafés and non-chain coffee houses to patronize, especially in the Apgujeong-dong, Garosu-gil, Samcheong-dong and Buam-dong areas.

If you speak Korean, or have a Korean-speaking friend who can assist you, one fun thing to try might be a saju café, where you can have your fortune taken as you sip your java. There are many such places in the Apgujeong-dong area.

A Café in Garosu-gil

Coffee and scone, Club Expresso

Recommended Cafés

Hakrim Dabang A1, p158: *Dabang* are Korean-style coffee/teahouses that were popular for much of Korea's 20th century history (and are still popular in the countryside). These cafés served as places where elderly men could socialize with friends over a game of *baduk* (Japanese: *go*), university students could discuss politics, families could meet to discuss a potential wedding and more. Daehangno's Hakrim Dabang, which first opened in 1956, is one of the few remaining old-style *dabang* left in Seoul. In addition to its classic décor, it is famous for its impressive collection of classical music LPs. • **Hours** 10 am to midnight • **Tel** 742-2877

Club Espresso p148: Located just past Changuimun Gate in Buam-dong (see p151), this café is known for its house-roasted coffees. It's an atmospheric little place that is well-known among Seoul's coffee aficionados. • **Hours** 9 am to 11 pm • **Tel** 764-8719

Sanmotungi p148: This Buam-dong coffeehouse, easily recognized as the stone house with a yellow Volkswagen Beetle in front of it, offers pleasant views of the surrounding mountains. It grew popular after appearing in a popular Korean drama. • **Hours** 11 am to 10 pm • **Tel** 391-4737

Coffee Smith A2, p254: This big, well-designed café on Garosu-gil serves a mean cup of coffee with a generous helping of Garosu-gil atmosphere. Its open design makes it a great place to people-watch, too. • **Hours** 9 am to 3 am • **Tel** 3445-3372

Yeon C2, p64: Hidden in an alley that climbs the hill off Samcheong-dong's main drag, Yeon is a very traveler-friendly café housed in a renovated Korean *hanok* home. Its attic room is particularly charming. If you're looking for something a bit stronger than tea or coffee, you can get alcohol, too. • **Hours** 1 pm to 11 pm • **Tel** 734-3009

PUBS & WINE BARS

According to 2005 OECD statistics, Korea's per capita consumption of alcohol by population over 15 was 9.3 liters a year. This does not tell the whole story, however, as drinking—well, hard drinking, anyway—tends to be a predominantly male sport in Korea. Alcohol is a ubiquitous presence at Korean social functions, be it an office gathering, wedding, funeral or even Confucian ancestral rite ceremony.

Finding a place to enjoy a drink or ten is not particularly difficult. In fact, most hole-in-the-wall shops or convenience stores sell cheap booze, and some even have chairs set up outside where you can enjoy a beer with a snack or two. Assuming you're not completely destitute, however, you can make use of a wide range of drinking establishments, including beer halls, Western-style pubs, wine bars and even Korean traditional pubs.

While you'll probably have an easy time finding a bar in Seoul, there are some neighborhoods that are particularly known as entertainment areas. These include the following areas:

Itaewon

As close to a foreigner ghetto as it gets in Seoul, Itaewon is home to a gazillion expat-oriented drinking establishments, ranging from sophisticated lounge bars to seedy dives where the drinks are overpriced and the company of dubious character. Don't worry—as a foreign traveler in Seoul, you'll find yourself in Itaewon eventually. Enjoy its unique charms, but be sure to move on to other parts of the city. See p201 for more information.

Sinchon/Hongdae

With their plethora of universities, the Sinchon and Hongik University areas (see p176) have a very youthful nightlife scene. The latter, in particular, is the center of Korea's indie club culture. Since many of the denizens are students, most of the bars here cater to younger, less affluent drinkers, so if you're on a budget, this isn't a bad neighborhood in which to party. In recent years, the Hongik University club district has grown increasingly popular with foreign residents, especially on the monthly Club Day (see p186).

Myeong-dong

Seoul's bustling commercial district, Myeong-dong (see p116) is home to countless pubs and bars, so if you like to mix your alcohol with neon lights and thronging crowds, this is the place to come.

Apgujeong-dong/Cheongdam-dong/Garosu-gil

If you're looking for something a little more upscale—or very upscale, for that matter—head south of the Hangang River to the Apgujeong-dong and Cheongdam-dong neighborhoods (see p246), where the wine bars are posh and the clubs exclusive. Dress accordingly. Garosu-gil, too, is lined with quaint little wine and cocktail bars that make for a pleasant evening.

Gangnam Station A3, p254

Located not far from a major IT business district, the area around Gangnam Station, Line 2 is overgrown with beer halls, late-night meat restaurants (where soju is consumed in mass quantities), karaoke clubs, pubs and bars of various sorts and assorted other entertainment facilities. This area tends to be quite popular with young people, including students and young professionals.

Bukchang-dong

Located in the heart of Seoul's old downtown, right behind the Seoul Plaza Hotel, the Bukchang-dong area (see p101) is lined with meat restaurants, bars, karaoke clubs and room salons (high-end karaoke clubs with female hostesses frequented by wealthy corporate executive types).

NOTE See p393 and 394 for a list and descriptions of some common Korean traditional alcoholic beverages.

TIPS

KOREAN BEER

Koreans have taken enthusiastically to beer—in Korean, maekju—since it was first introduced to the country in the early 20th century. The Korean beer market is dominated by three major producers: Cass, Hite and OB. All three produce primarily lagers, and at least one will be on tap at whatever watering hole you find yourself in. Korean beer producers have been experimenting in dark beers and stouts, but it's still very much a work in progress.

Foreign beers like Heineken and Guinness are widely available, too, especially in the bars of Itaewon, but you're going to pay more for it—a 500cc mug of Guinness might run you 8,000–10,000 won, whereas a local draft will cost only 3,000 won.

On a positive note, beer halls brewing their own house beers have grown greater in number. One such place is Castle Praha, a Czech-themed beer hall with locations in Gangnam and Hongdae. A one-meter sampler of all their brews will set you back 35,000 won.

Oh, and you'll probably find the following phrase useful: Maekju juseyo ("Please bring me a beer.").

Recommended Bars and Pubs

Apgujeong-dong

Monkey Beach D2, p248: Popular with the expat crowd, Monkey Beach is a crowded basement hip-hop club. The bucket drinks of Monkey Beach are a strong drawing point—for only 12,000 won, these potent treats are sure to kickstart your night. The combination of pumping American hip hop and bucket drinks tends to draw the dancers up on the tabletops for a Spring Break-esque atmosphere. • **Hours** 7 pm to 5 am • **Tel** 548-7930

Club Answer C1, p254: Widely considered one of Seoul's hottest dance clubs, Club Answer in Cheongdam-dong plays host to big-name DJs from both Korea and overseas. Specializing in house music, Answer ventures into other genres of electronic music, too. State-of-the-art sound system and lighting make it the perfect place to dance the night away.
• **Hours** 9 pm to 5 am (Sunday to Thursday), 9 pm to 6 am (Friday, Saturday) • **Admission** 30,000 won • **Tel** 548-7115

Once in a Blue Moon E3, p248: One of Seoul's premier live jazz clubs, this place draws a multicultural crowd of jazz enthusiasts. Its extensive wine list and dinner menu can be expensive, but the atmosphere makes it all worth it. Private rooms available, too.
• **Hours** 6 pm to 2 am • **Tel** 549-5490

Abbey Road C2, p248: Nestled down a small alleyway away from the main drag of Rodeo Street, Abbey Road is a cool spot for a drink. With outdoor tables surrounded by greenery and a wooden, European-esque interior seating area, a drink in Abbey Road feels like a brief trip to the British Isles. • **Hours** 5 pm to 3 am • **Tel** 546-9505

Gangnam Station Area

Baekseju Maeul A3, p254: Operated by major Korean traditional liquor brewer Kooksoondang, Baekseju Maeul (Baekseju Village)—named for the company's famous herbal wine—serves a wide variety of Korean traditional rice wines, rice beers and spirits, best consumed with Korean traditional side dishes. In addition to the *baekseju*, give the high-quality *makkeolli* (milky Korean rice beer) a try. • **Hours** 6 pm to 2 am • **Tel** 595-1003

SkyBar Chang B3, p254: This luxurious bar/lounge offers splendid views of the Gangnam area from its 8th/9th floor location. Dark lighting makes for a romantic mood—great date place. Drinks are reasonably priced, too—a mojito will cost you about 13,000 won. • **Hours** 6 pm to 3 am • **Tel** 538-7554

Rainbow Lounge A3, p254: Rainbow is a fun, funky hookah bar in the heart of Gangnam. With an extensive list of hookah flavors, as well as cocktails and beers, Rainbow is a popular night spot. • **Hours** 6 pm to 3 am • **Tel** 3481-1869

Other Areas

For information on bars in Itaewon, Sinchon and Hongdae, see pages 202, 178 and 184.

Dugahun

Luxury Wine Bars

If you've got money to burn on fine wines, here's a list of some places to try:

• **Dugahun** A3, p64**:** This wonderful wine bar/restaurant behind the Gallery Hyundai (next to Gyeongbokgung Palace) is housed in a century-old Korean *hanok* home. It's not cheap, but the French-Italian cuisine is great, the wine cellar is well-stocked with about 320 Old and New World wines, and you can top off your night with a Cuban cigar from the bar humidor. If the weather permits, sit in the outdoor courtyard—the atmosphere cannot be beat. (T. 3210-2100)

• **Tribeca** E3, p249**:** 170 cocktail choices and 120 types of liquor make this high-profile bar the perfect joint for brand launching parties and showcases. (T. 3448-4550)

• **Verrazzano** E3, p248**:** Like a breeze with your wine? Verrazzano offers both 300 types of wine and a rare green terrace to enjoy them on. (T. 517-3274)

• **CASA del VINO** G2, p249**:** Relax in the calm and easy atmosphere of this expert wine sommelier, which keeps upwards of 500 varieties of wine. (T. 542-8003)

• **The Restaurant** A2, p64**:** Wine lovers will be thrilled by the 300 wines arranged around all four walls of Kukje Gallery's The Restaurant—certainly the perfect follow-up to your gallery visit. (T. 735-8441)

• **Margaux** G3, p185**:** Margaux's 300 wines include several mid-priced selections, and all are organized by country, region and brand. (T.333-3554)

• **Pinot** A3, p254**:** Jazz, blues, hard rock and old pop are just some of the genres of live music that Pinot croons, proving that wine isn't all this venue offers. (T. 3477-7622)

• **Tourduvin Seoul** A3, p254**:** Run by wine education institution Bordeaux Wine Academy, Tourduvin holds 400 brands of wine from all over the world. (T. 533-1846)

• **NAOSNOBA** p316**:** Five years of architectural planning and three years of design produced NAOSNOBA, situated atop Namsan. Over 50 brands of superb champagnes complement exquisite French dishes, as well as stunning views of all Seoul. (T. 754-2202)

SPAS & SAUNAS

In Korea, saunas are a popular nighttime destination. In fact, Korean-style saunas are growing increasingly popular outside of Korea, too, especially in the United States, where Koreatown saunas are gaining the attention of neighboring communities.

Like bathhouses everywhere, Korean saunas have shower facilities, hot and cold baths, and saunas (very often several types of saunas). Major sauna/spa facilities—called *jjimjilbang* in Korean—have much more, including unisex lounge facilities, TV rooms, restaurants and massage services. Most have a sleeping room, too—in fact, if you're looking for a place to bed down for the night on the cheap, saunas are a good option.

The Jjimjilbang Experience

All *jjimjilbang* complexes contain a bath section where guests get thoroughly soaked and scrubbed. The Korean concept of getting thoroughly washed goes beyond cleaning the surface of the skin—it involves taking off the surface of the skin. This is usually accomplished with the use of small, rough cloths that rub away the outer layers of dead skin cells, leaving the victim glowing red for a while. These cloths usually come in bright green, yellow or red colors and can be bought very cheaply at the entrance to most bathhouses and steam rooms. Ask for an "*itaeri tawol*" if you can't already see them. Scrubbing each other's backs is considered a good way of expressing friendship between friends or between fathers and sons.

There are plenty of showers around the baths themselves. The unbreakable rule is that bathers wash themselves thoroughly in the shower, from head to foot, before getting into the baths.

Washing in the baths is just the beginning of a proper *jjimjilbang* experience. From here onwards, customers don the comfortable, loose-fitting cotton clothes they were issued at the entrance and settle down for any number of hours in rooms of varying degrees of heat and humidity. Sexual segregation ends at the exit of the baths, allowing whole families, couples or groups of friends to enjoy each other's company. Warm lounges, steamy saunas, massage rooms, PC rooms and sometimes DVD rooms are just some of the elements that make up a typical *jjimjilbang* complex. But it is the opportunity for socializing in a self-contained, comfortable space, free from outside concerns, that gives *jjimjilbang* their enduring appeal.

Dragon Hill Spa

Recommended Spas

Dragon Hill Spa p211: Seven floors of spa goodness await you at this massive complex next to Yongsan Station. The main hall sports a Chinese design motif, but the rest of the place is an assortment of different saunas (including a charcoal sauna), baths, whirlpools, lounge facilities, pools and more. Check out the heated outdoor pool while you're here. The spa tends to be quite popular with foreigners. • **Admission** 10,000 won (5 am to 8 pm), 12,000 won (8 pm to 5 am) • **Tel** 797-0002

Itaewonland F3, p203: Located in the heart of foreigner-friendly Itaewon, this five-story spa has six kinds of steam rooms and kiln saunas (including an ice room), bathing rooms, DVD rooms, massage rooms, a karaoke room and sleeping facilities. • **Admission** 6,000 won (day), 8,000 won (night) • **Tel** 749-4122~3

Central Spa A3, p254: Located in Central City (near Express Bus Terminal), this sauna has all the facilities you'd expect in a spa—including a charcoal sauna—with the added bonus of being located in a big shopping mall. • **Admission** 10,000 won (5 am to 9 pm), 13,000 won (9 pm to 5 am) • **Getting There** Exit 7 of Express Bus Terminal Station, Line 3 or Exit 4 of Line 7 • **Tel** 6282-3400

Spa in Garden 5 p259: This smartly designed spa in the Songpa-gu district of Seoul (near Lotte World) is big and very well-appointed with state-of-the-art facilities. If you like your spas with a big helping of style, this is the place to go. • **Admission** 8,000 won (day), 10,000 won (night), 10,000 won (weekends) • **Getting There** Leave Exit 3 of Jangji Station, Line 8 and walk 700 m • **Tel** 404-2700

Sports Club Seoul Leisure p259: Also located in Songpa-gu, this is a massive complex with a health club, screen golf range, swimming pool and squash court...in addition to a well-equipped sauna and bathhouse and several kinds of Korean-style steam rooms. • **Admission** 8,000 won (day), 10,000 won (night) • **Getting There** Exit 1 of Bangi Station, Line 5 • **Tel** 404-7000

Oh Happyday Sports Center D1, p254: Seven above-ground floors (eight all together) of splish-splashy fun in the district of Gwangjin-gu in eastern Seoul. Make use of the wide variety of Korean kiln saunas, Western-style saunas, hot and cool pools and other facilities. Golf fans will love the rooftop screen golf simulator. • **Admission** 8,000 won (day), 10,000 won (night). 1,000 won deposit for robe rental • **Tel** 452-5656

KARAOKE

Karaoke is a popular nocturnal pastime in Korea, where karaoke clubs are called *noraebang* ("singing rooms"). Unlike karaoke clubs in the West, however, Korean *noraebang* consist mostly of private rooms where friends gather to sing, dance and drink till the wee hours. If you go out for a night on the town with Korean friends, chances are high you will end up in such an establishment before morning's light. Most *noraebang* play both Korean and Western standards; those in Seoul's developing ethnic neighborhoods like Dongdaemun have music in other languages as well.

Be advised that in addition to *noraebang*, there are more upscale forms of karaoke clubs, too. *Dallanjujeom*, for instance, employ hostesses who sing, dance and chat with customers. Really, really upscale *dallanjujeom* are called room salons—if you're independently wealthy or playing with a corporate expense account, these places can be great fun, but an evening can easily cost in the thousands of US dollars.

Noraebang can be found a'plenty in all entertainment areas. Costs differ, but a basic *noraebang* usually costs about 12,000 to 20,000 won an hour.

Recommended Noraebang

Su Noraebang F3, p185/ A3, p254: As the name Su suggests, this *noraebang* has excellent facilities. A dazzling silver vision, this establishment looks more like a posh club than a *noraebang*. For the finest *noraebang* experience, head to Su for a luxurious setting in which to belt out your tunes. Su also has another venue in Apgujeong. • **Hours** Open 24 hours • **Tel** 3481-3990

INTERNET CAFÉS

You'd think in a country where almost every household has a computer and broadband Internet access that there wouldn't be much of a need for Internet cafés.

But you'd be wrong. Seoul is home to countless *PC bang*, or Korean-style Internet cafés. Like their counterparts in the West, the *PC bang* will have rows of computers for costumers to use. Most *PC bang* have vending machines or refrigerators from which you can purchases cans of coffee or soft drinks (or simple snacks like instant noodles). *PC bang* usually have cards at the front desk with an ID number to imput to start up your computer. Hours rates are cheap: usually 1,000 won an hour.

Where the *PC bang* differs from the Western Internet café is its raison d'être— whereas the Internet café is used primarily to check email and surf the web, the

PC bang is dedicated to one thing—gaming. Walk into a *PC bang*, and you'll find dozens of people absorbed in online games. Younger Koreans tend to enjoy RTS (real-time simulation) games like Starcraft and World of Warcraft or first-person shooters like Counter-Strike, while older Koreans tend towards online games of *baduk* (Japanese: *go*) and Go Stop (a card game using Japanese *hanafuda* cards, called *hwatu* in Korean). Many gamers spend hours at a *PC bang*, while some even spend the entire day or, on rare occasions, even more—in 2005, a 28-year-old Korean man made headlines after he dropped dead following a 50-hour gaming marathon.

Korean gaming culture is strongly influenced by Confucian norms, which is to say, they game as a group. The *PC bang* plays an important role in this regard—it allows groups of friends to gather in one spot to enjoy gaming together, barking out commands, jeering and encouraging one another as they go. This contrasts with the Western gamer, who tends toward the "lone wolf" approach to gaming.

TIPS

POPULAR GAMES

- **Starcraft:** The birth of the *PC bang* industry begins with the 1998 release of the sci-fi RTS game Starcraft by US game designer Blizzard Entertainment. Of the 9.5 million of copies of Starcraft sold in the decade since its release, 4.5 million were sold in Korea. At one point, the game probably could have been fairly called Korea's national pastime: there were even TV channels dedicated to it. It's still quite popular, although newer games like Blizzard's World of Warcraft have overtaken it.
- **Counter-Strike:** The Vivendi classic first-person shooter Counter-Strike inspired a number of locally-produced Counter-Strike/Battlefield 2 clones.
- **EA FIFA** In every *PC bang* there's always at least a few people playing EA Sports' popular football game.

Of course, if all you want to do is check your email or chat with your friends back home, you can do that at a *PC bang*, too. Video chatting is quite popular in Korea, and most *PC bang* have computers set up for it.

KOREA'S "BANG" CULTURE

History and Culture

The term *bang* means "room" in Korean, and you'll see it used for a lot of establishments about town. Besides the *noraebang*, PC *bang* and *jjimjilbang*, other bang include:

- **Bidiobang:** "Video Rooms," where you can watch videos.
- **DVD bang:** Like a *bidiobang*, with DVDs.
- **Manhwabang:** "Comic Room," where you can read comic books.

CINEMAS

Koreans love their movies, and you'll find large cinemas throughout Seoul. Cinemas play both Hollywood films and, of course, the latest Korean films. Foreign films—including Hollywood films—are usually screened in their original language with Korean subtitles. Most cinemas do not include English subtitles for Korean films, although a couple do—see below.

A number of cultural centers also screen Korean and foreign films with English and Korean subtitles, respectively.

Korean Film Archive p237

The Korean Film Archive screens Korean and international films multiple times each week. Additionally, the Korean Film Archive has a large collection of films, including unreleased Korean classics and resources about the Korean film industry. Anyone can access the library free of charge, but visitors must be 15 years of age or more. • **Hours** Mon to Fri 10 am to 7 pm Sat, Sun 10 am to 5 pm • **Admission** Free • **Getting There** Take bus No. 7711 at Digital Media City Station, Line 6, Exit 2 and get off at Nuriggun Square • **Tel** 3153-2051 • **Website** www.koreafilm.org

Korea Foundation Cultural Center—DVD Screenings B4, p38

The Korea Foundation Cultural Center screens Korean and foreign films three times weekly, free of charge. Series of screened films follow a particular theme, such as "Smiling at the Prejudices of the World." Korean films are shown with English subtitles, and foreign films are shown with Korean subtitles. • **Hours** Mondays and Wednesdays at 7 pm, Saturdays at 3 pm • **Admission** Free • **Getting There** City Hall Station, Line 1 & 2, Exit 9 • **Tel** 2151-6515 • **Website** www.kfcenter.or.kr/english

The Korea Foundation Cultural Center B4, p38

The library of the Korea Foundation Cultural Center includes Korean films with English subtitles—both in VHS and DVD format. Films can be rented by all members, but can only be watched on site. Membership is free, but patrons must be staying in Korea for at least one month. • **Hours** Mon to Sat 10 am to 6 pm • **Admission** Free with membership • **Getting There** City Hall Station, Line 2, Exit 9 • **Tel** 2151-6506 • **Website** http://library.kf.or.kr

Cine-Café p126

Sponsored by the Europe-Korea Foundation, Cine-Café aims to promote awareness of Korean culture within the foreign population of Seoul by hosting monthly screenings of Korean films with English subtitles. A light snack and beverage are included in the price of admission. Screenings are followed by a film discussion, to which the Cine-Café generally invites film specialists. All proceeds are donated to Motungii Shwimteo, a shelter for young women in Bucheon. This event is held at the French Cultural Center. • **Admission** 8,000 won • **Getting There** Seoul Station, Line 1 or 4, Exit 3 • **Tel** 317-8564 • **Website** http://cinecafé.ekf. or.kr

Yongsan CGV p211

Yongsan CGV, one of the largest movie theaters in Seoul, offers screenings of new Korean film releases with English subtitles. This theater also has an IMAX screen. Call ahead of time to see which screenings offer English subtitles. • **Getting There** Yongsan Station, Line 1 - Directly connected to the station • **Tel** 1544-1122 • **Website** www. cgv.co.kr

COEX Megabox C4, p254

The Megabox Cinema at COEX Mall is one of Seoul's largest theaters. Megabox is always running multiple showing of all the latest films, and offers screenings of current Korean new releases with English subtitles. Check with the theater to see which times offer English subtitles. • **Admission** 8,000 won • **Getting There** Samseong Station, Line 2, Exit 6 • **Tel** 1544-0600 • **Website** www.megabox.co.kr

Seoul Art Cinema D3, p76

Modestly occupying the fourth floor of the aging Nakwon Arcade, a collection of music shops near Insa-dong, Seoul Arts Cinema runs programs of old and new classics from around the world. In its own words, it hopes that "the act of watching a film is not one of consumption, but a conversation between those that love cinema." Just the place for people experiencing blockbuster-induced fatigue. • **Admission** 6,000 won • **Getting There** Jongno 3-ga Station, Lines 1, 3 & 5, Exit 5, 4th flr., Nakwon Arcade • **Tel** 741-9782 • **Website** www.cinematheque.seoul.kr

Korean Film

Korea's film history goes back all the way to the late 19th century, soon after which Korea's first cinema opened in 1903. The 1920s and 1930s witnessed the release of many good silent films, but for much of the pre-Independence era, Korean directors were subject to severe censorship from colonial Japanese authorities.

This would play out in the post-colonial era, too. The relatively free political and social atmosphere between the 1950s and 1970s saw an outpouring of good films, including some of Korea's finest films ever. With the enactment of the dictatorial *yusin* constitution in 1972, however, political and social controls were strengthened, nearly killing Korea's film industry in the process.

In the 1980s, censorship of films was gradually eased, and as a result, the quality of Korean film improved. Unfortunately for the film industry, this also coincided with the opening of the Korean film market to Hollywood and Hong Kong films, and the market share of Korean films dropped precipitously.

From the 1990s on, however, Korean cinema has experienced a renaissance. Granted, this is at least partially thanks to a protective screen quota, but it is also in large part due to a blossoming of new cinematic talent that includes the rise of directors Park Chan-wook, Bong Joon-ho and Kim Ki-duk. Internationally, Korean films began making waves in international film festivals—Park Chan-wook's "Oldboy," for instance, won the Grand Prix at the 2004 Cannes Film Festival. Even Hollywood began taking notice, with the rights to several Korean films being purchased for Hollywood remakes.

Recommended Korean Films

- **Sopyonje (1993):** Directed by master filmmaker Im Kwon-taek, this was one of Korea's most critically received films ever, both domestically and overseas. The tale of a family of traveling pansori singers, the film sparked a wave of renewed interest in Korea's traditional culture.

- **Taekukgi (2004):** Sure, this film feels a lot like *Saving Private Ryan,* but it's probably the best Korean War film ever made, and does a good job of portraying the brutality of a conflict whose impact is still felt today.

- **Oldboy (2003):** Director Park Chan-wook's masterpiece, this dark, brutal drama and thriller depicts a man seeking vengeance after being imprisoned for 15 years for reasons he does not know. Quentin Tarantino wanted to give it the top prize in the 2004 Cannes Film Festival.

- **Anything by director Hong Sangsoo:** Hong is one of Korea's most lauded directors; his films are noted for their frank depiction of human relations. *The Power of Kangwon Province* (1998), *Virgin Stripped Bare by Her Bachelors* (2000) are good ones to try.

- **JSA (2000):** Also directed by Park Chan-wook, this film focuses on a tragic friendship between North and South Korean soldiers at the DMZ. The film was widely praised for its depiction of Korea's national division.

- **Secret Sunshine (2007):** Directed by Lee Chang-dong, one of Korea's most respected filmmakers, this tragic drama—controversial for its criticism of Korean Christianity—won actress Jeon Do-yeon the Best Actress Award at the 2007 Cannes Film Festival.

- **Spring, Summer, Fall, Winter... and Spring (2003):** A beautiful film by notorious Korean art-house director Kim Ki-duk, this depicts the life of a Buddhist monk through the various seasons of his life.

- **The Host (2006):** A slick monster flick by director Bong Joon-ho, this film not only spooks, but also critically examines a number of aspects of Korean society, including the Korea-US relationship and ineffective bureaucracy.

- **My Sassy Girl (2001):** One of the most popular Korean films of all time, this romantic comedy launched the career of one of Korea's most recognized actresses, Gianna Jun.

- **The King and the Clown (2005):** Based on a stage play, this film follows two traveling entertainers who are invited into the tyrannical court of Yeonsangun, one of the Joseon era's most notorious kings. It has beautiful depictions of the Korean traditional arts, and its theme of homosexuality at the court proved quite controversial.

- **The President's Last Bang (2005):** Directed by Im Sang-soo, this sinfully funny black comedy about the assassination of late President Park Chung-hee looks at one of the most pivotal events in modern Korean history.

TIPS

BUYING DVDs

You can purchase many of these films on DVD—with English subtitles—at Seoul Selection Bookshop. Stop by the shop or visit its online shopping mall at www.seoulselection.com.

ACTIVITIES

ZEN PRACTICE

Seoul International Zen Center p335
90-Day Intensive Meditation Retreat Program

Affiliated with Hwagyesa, a Buddhist temple located on a ridge of Bukhansan Mountain, the Seoul International Zen Center offers a 90-day intensive meditation retreat program each summer and winter. Participants examine Buddha's teachings and the concept of enlightenment in this intensive study. Interested individuals can also opt for a shorter program, with a minimum stay of one week. The Seoul Zen Center also offers free Sunday meditation classes.
• **Hours** Sat noon to Sun 10 am • **Admission** 40,000 won (day); 350,000-450,000 (month)
• **Getting There** Suyu Station, Line 4. Take taxi to Hwagyesa • **Tel** 900-4326
• **Website** http://seoulzen.org

Most other Buddhist temples offer one- to two-day temple experience programs, including Jogyesa (the headquarters of the Jogye Buddhist order), Naksan Myogaksa (a temple embedded in a natural environment and the headquarters of the Kwan-Um Order of Korean Buddhism) and Bongeunsa (an expansive temple located next to COEX Mall).

Ahnkook Zen Center D2, p64
Located in Seoul's beautiful Bukchon neighborhood, Ahnkook Zen Center offers foreigners classes (in English) every Saturday from 2:30 to 4 pm. The classes are taught by foreign lecturers who majored in Korean Buddhism, with a focus on the scriptures of Korean Buddhism and Korean Buddhism culture. • **Admission** Free
• **Getting There** Anguk Station, Line 3, Exit 2. From there, walk north toward the Gahoe Museum. • **Tel** 732-0772 • **Website** www.ahnkookzen.org

Jogyesa A2, p76

Jogyesa offers a variety of programs. The basic program includes a tea ceremony, meditation and a guided tour of the temple. The experience program offers a meal at the temple and a program explaining the traditional dishes and dining etiquette of Korean monks. The participation program teaches Buddhist painting and lotus-lantern-making. • **Admission** 10,000 won per program. Reservations should be made one week in advance. • **Getting There** Jonggak Station, Line 1, Exit 2; Anguk Station, Line 3, Exit 6. • **Tel** 732-5115 • **Website** www.jogyesa.kr

Naksan Myogaksa D2, p158

Myogaksa's program includes striking *beomjong* (the temple bell), singing Buddhist songs, dining in the traditional Buddhist manner with traditional Buddhist dishes, constructing lotus lanterns and conversing with monks.

• **Admission** One-day program: 20,000 won, two-day program: 30,000 won; Temple experience participants must bring their own toiletries and personal items. Temple experience uniforms are provided. • **Getting There** Dongmyo Station, Line 1 or 6, Exit 2 • **Tel** 763-3109 • **Website** www.myogaksa.net

Lotus Lantern International Meditation Center

Located not far from Jeondeungsa Temple on the island of Ganghwa Island, this international meditation center is home to foreign monks and nuns and open to lay people who wish to experience Korean Buddhism. It conducts two night and three night programs every weekend (except the last weekend of the month). Instruction is in Engllish. • **Admission** 50,000-70,000 won • **Getting There** Take the bus to Onsu-ri from Sinchon Bus Terminal (Exit 7, Sinchon Station, Line 2). When you get off at Onsu-ri, take a taxi to the Lotus Lantern International Meditation Center (Yeondeung Gukje Seonwon). • **Tel** (032) 937-7032~3 • **Website** www.lotuslantern.net

Seoul International Zen Center

KOREAN TRADITIONAL MEDICINE

Korea has a long and time honored medical tradition with a history as long as that of the Korean people itself—the Korean foundation myth, after all, involves a she-bear eating the medicinal herb of mugwort. Korean traditional medicine shares many of the same practices as Chinese traditional medicine although many

of Korea's medicinal herbs are unique to Korea. Korean medicine is holistic, which is to say, it sees body and mind as an interconnected whole. While acute illnesses and injuries might be better off treated by a modern (i.e. Western) physician, chronic disorders such as arthritis, obesity and fatigue often respond well to Korean medicine. Its holistic approach also promotes wellness and prevents the onset of illness.

Korean Traditional Medical Practices

Korean traditional medicine doctors, or *hanuisa*, proscribe treatment after diagnosing the patient. Diagnosis are given following a patient physical and analysis of his or her lifestyle. Korean medicine also makes use of *sasang uihak*, a medical typology in which individuals are characterized by four body types based on *yin-yang* theory; certain body types are more susceptible to certain illnesses than others. Common treatments include:

Herbal Medicine

Korean medicine makes use of a wide variety of medicinal herbs (the Korea Pharmacopoeia lists 395 medicinal herbs in current use), often used in combination with one another for heightened medical effect. Herb preparation varies widely, too: some herbs are dried, for instance, while others are boiled to create liquid remedies. Most are taken orally, although creams and oils are also made.

Acupuncture

According to Korean traditional medical theory, there are 365 acupuncture points on the human body. When stimulated (using acupuncture needles made of gold, silver or platinum), these point can enhance the flow of energy throughout the body, promoting organ function and curing illnesses. Which points are stimulated depends on the disorder the doctor is attempting to treat.

Moxibustion

In this technique, a stick of burning mugwort is placed on the skin, usually above an ill or injured part, to warm the area and promote blood and energy flow.

Cupping

Similarly, the use of heated glass cups that stick to the skin of the back stimulates energy flow points, promotes circulation and has a detoxifying effect. This technique leaves you with telltale red circles on your back (these go away in a few days, though).

Recommended Korean Medicine Centers

Jaseng Hospital of Oriental Medicine

A2, p248: This well-known hospital specializes in non-surgical treatments for spinal disorders, blending Korean and Western treatment methods. Its international clinic has specialists who speak English, German, Japanese and Chinese. • **Hours** 9 am to 6 pm. Closed Tuesdays • **Getting There** There is hospital shuttle bus service from Exit 2 of Apgujeong Station, Line 3 • **Tel** 3218-2105 • **Website** www.jaseng.net

Oriental Medical Hospital, Kyung Hee University: Founded in 1971, Kyung Hee University's Oriental Medicine Hospital is one of the largest East Asian medical centers in the world, with 300 beds and 99 doctors in eight departments. • **Hours** 9 am to 5 pm (weekdays), 9 am to noon (Sat). Closed Sundays • **Getting There** Hoegi Station, Line 1. Walk 10 minutes or take a local (green) bus from the station to Kyung Hee University • **Tel** 958-8114 • **Website** www.khuoh.or.kr

Amicare A2, p254: Located in Apgujeong-dong, this small Korean traditional medicine hospital is run by Kim So-hyung, a former Miss Korea. It is particularly known for its healthy diet treatments. • **Hours** 10 am to 9 pm (Mon), 10 am to 10 pm (Tue, Thu), 10 am to 7 pm (Fri), 10 am to 4 pm (Sat). Closed Wednesdays and Sundays • **Getting There** Exit 3, Apgujeong Station, Line 3. Walk 400 meters and it's on the left. • **Tel** 544-6500 • **Website** www.n-clinic.com

Jahayun Clinic C4, p248: Located in Sinsa-dong, not far from Apgujeong-dong, Jahayun Clinic specializes in treatments for nervous disorders using herbal medicines. It also provides Korean traditional medicine treatments for dieting, skin care, gynecological health and infertility. • **Hours** 9:30 am to 6:30 pm (Mon, Fri) 9:30 am to 8 pm (Tue, Thu) 2 pm to 6:30 pm (Wed) 9:30 am to 4 pm (Sat) • **Getting There** Exit 3 of Gangnam-gu Office Station, Line 7. Walk 10 minutes to Hakdong Junction. You will see the Cine City building diagonally opposite. Jahayun is on the second floor of the KMD Building, just next door to Cine City. • **Tel** 3448-7575 • **Website** www.jahayun.com

Choonwondang D3, p38: First founded in 1847, this Korean traditional medicine practitioner's has a Korean traditional medicine museum and conducts exhibits and educational programs. • **Hours** 9 am to 6 pm (Mon to Fri), 9 am to 12:30 pm (Sat). Closed Sundays • **Getting There** Leave Exit 5 of Jongno 3-ga Station, Line 5 and walk 100m in the direction of Tapgol Park. Swing a left at Mr. Choi's Suit Shop and walk about 90m. • **Tel** 766-0000 • **Website** www.choonwondang.co.kr

COOKING

There are many programs in which foreigners can learn to cook Korean dishes. Prices at each institute differ, but they generally range from about 40,000 won to 100,000 won.

Institute of Traditional Korean Food D3, p38
At this institute, participants learn to make traditional Korean drinks, rice cakes, and a few dishes of royal cuisine. • **Fee** 50,000 to 70,000 won, depending on class
• **Getting There** Jongno 3-ga, Lines 1, 3 and 5, Exit 6 • **Tel** 741-5411 • **Website** www.kfr.or.kr

Son's Home B3, p254
The Son family hosts guests to learn about Korean cooking in the comfort of their home, where many generations of Sons have lived. Visitors learn to make *kimchi*, set up a traditional tea table, and play traditional Korean instruments. • **Fee** 60,000 to 70,000 won, depending on the class • **Getting There** Yeoksam Station, Line 2, Exit 3 • **Tel** 562-6829 • **Website** www.sons-home.com

Yoo's Family D3, p38
This cultural program, hosted by the Yoo family, teaches visitors how to make *kimchi*, *jeon* and *tteokbokki*. • **Fee** 20,000 to 60,000 won, depending on the class
• **Getting There** Anguk Station, Line 3, Exit 4 • **Tel** 3673-0323 • **Website** www.yoosfamily.com

VOLUNTEERING

In a city of this size, there are plenty of organizations to which visitors can donate their time and talents. Most volunteer organizations use native English speakers for proof-reading, editing and/or teaching English.

Willing Workers on Organic Farms (WWOOF) D3, p64

Since 1996, WWOOF Korea has been connecting foreign visitors with organic farms in Korea, where volunteers can work four to six hours a day in exchange for room and board and the opportunity to experience rural Korea culture. WWOOF experiences usually last between one week and several months, although individual arrangements must be made with the owners of the particular farm. WWOOF Korea is a member of WWOOF International. • Tel 723-4510 • Website www.wwoofkorea.co.kr

Korea International Volunteer Organization D2, p64

Although this organization primarily works on providing aid to populations in need in developing countries, KVO volunteers also support facilities for local homeless elderly persons and orphans. The organization also runs an environmental protection program, which includes leading environmental education field trips for students. • Tel 471-1004 • Website www.kvo.or.kr

HOPE (Helping Others Prosper through English)

A relatively new nonprofit organization started by a group of Canadian teachers, this group's objective is to provide free, accessible English education to those underprivileged students in Korea who do not have the resources to enroll in expensive academies like their wealthier classmates. Because English language skills have become an essential part of enjoying a bright future in Korea, HOPE helps less privileged students stay on par with their peers. Currently, HOPE volunteers at a couple of community centers and an orphanage. • Tel 010-2414-5683 (volunteer director) • Website www.alwayshope.or.kr

While not actually a volunteer opportunity, per se, Planting Love—a Catholic charity group run by the Sisters of Charity of Seton Hall—operates a rehabilitation center in the southwestern city of Gwangju and a school for the visually impaired in Chungju. They can always use a donation—see www.plantinglove.com for more information.

SEOUL SUBWAY MAP

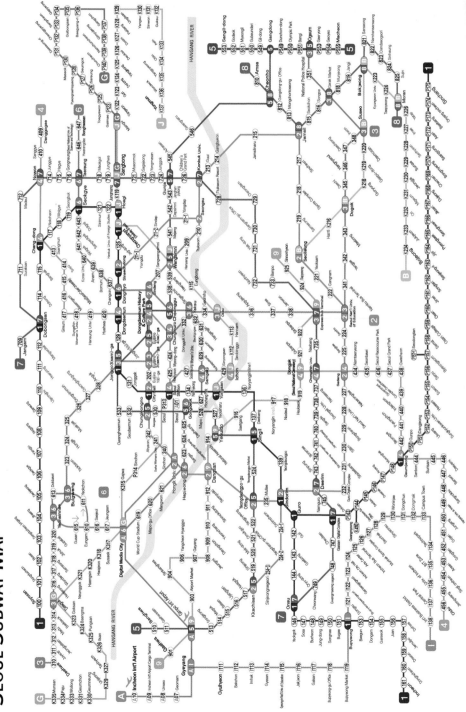

Central Seoul Subway Map

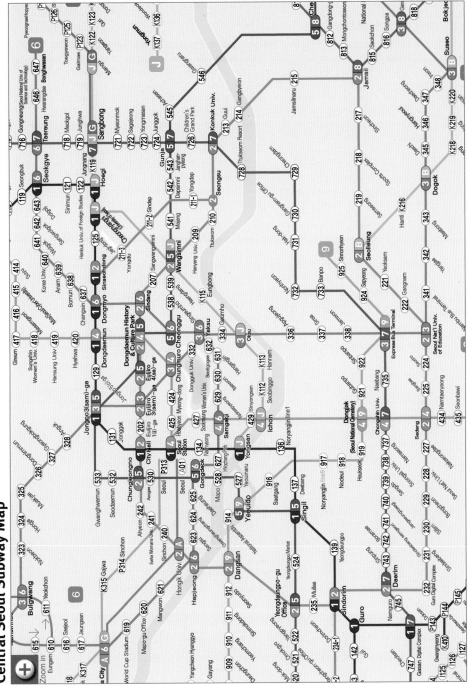

ACKNOWLEDGEMENT

This guidebook could not have been made without the support of a good many individuals. Thanks go to Greg Curley, Joe McPherson, Prof. David Mason, Jinny Kang and Prof. Yoon Sook-ja, who provided some of the photographs that appear in this book. And while it goes against accepted practice to thank individuals who appear in the credits, editor Lee Jin-hyuk and designer Jung Hyun-young have earned my everlasting gratitude for going above and beyond the call of duty, putting in many a late, late night at the office to complete this book.

Thanks go out to Mark Russell for taking a look at the maps and, just as importantly, being an invaluable drinking buddy.

Of course, I'd be seriously remiss if I didn't express appreciation to my publisher and boss Kim Hyung-geun (Hank), who not only provides me with gainful employment as a magazine editor, but also gave me the opportunity to make this guidebook a reality.

Most importantly, however, I'd like to thank my wife Solongo, whose love and encouragement made the long hours huddled over a keyboard bearable.

HISTORY DISCLAIMER

History is a subject that lends itself easy to controversy and disputes, and Korean history is no different. In doing the research for this book, I spent more hours wading through books, magazines, brochures, homepages, blogs, online encyclopedias and wikis—in English and Korean—than I care to count. I tried to be balanced and, more to the point, non-controversial in the historical accounts given in this book, which is, after all, a tourist guidebook, not a university history text. Still, accounts differ, so don't take what you read here as the final word. If you really want to expand your knowledge of Korean history, some English-language resources you may wish to consider are:

Books
- *New History of Korea* by Lee Hyun-hee, et. al. (Jimoondang)
- *Korea Old and New: A History* by Carter Eckert, Ki-baik Lee et. al. (Harvard University Press)
- *Korea's Place in the Sun: A Modern History* by Bruce Cumings (W. W. Norton & Company)

Websites
- Korea.net (www.korea.net)
- Korean History Project (www.koreanhistoryproject.org)

CREDITS

Publisher	Kim Hyung-geun
Writer	Robert Koehler
Assisting Writers	Jacqueline Kim, Ben Jackson
Editor	Lee Jin-hyuk
Assisting Editors	Ko Yeon-kyung, Park Shin-hyung
Proofreaders	Chung Kyung-a, Colin A. Mouat, Helen Lee
Designer	Jung Hyun-young
Cartographers	Jung Hyun-young, Lee Bok-hyun
Photographers	Ryu Seung-hoo & Robert Koehler

* All images are copyright of Seoul Selection unless otherwise indicated.